A Special Gift

Presented to:

From:

Date:

The eyes of the Lord are upon the righteous,
and his ears are open unto their cry.
—Psalm 34:15

BEAUTIFUL IN GOD'S EYES

The Women's Devotional Series

Among Friends

The Listening Heart

A Gift of Love

A Moment of Peace

Close to Home

From the Heart

This Quiet Place

In God's Garden

Fabric of Faith

Alone With God

Bouquets of Hope

Colors of Grace

Beautiful in God's Eyes

ARDIS STENBAKKEN, EDITOR

BEAUTIFUL IN GOD'S EYES

A DAILY DEVOTIONAL FOR WOMEN BY WOMEN

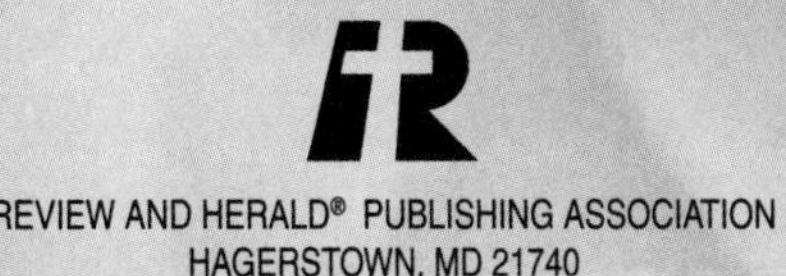

REVIEW AND HERALD® PUBLISHING ASSOCIATION
HAGERSTOWN, MD 21740

The author assumes full responsibility for the accuracy of all facts and quotations as cited in this book.

This book was
Edited by Jeannette R. Johnson
Copyedited by Lori Peckham and James Cavil
Cover design by FreshCut Designs
Cover photo by Getty Images/Stone/Amy Nuensinger
Electronic makeup by Shirley M. Bolivar
Typeset: Minion 11/13.5

PRINTED IN U.S.A.

08 07 06 05 04 5 4 3 2 1

R&H Cataloging Service
Stenbakken, Ardis Dick, 1939- ed.
Beautiful in God's eyes, edited by Ardis Dick Stenbakken.

1. Devotional calendars—SDA. 2. Devotional calendars—women.
3. Women—religious life. 4. Devotional literature—SDA. I. Title.

242.643

ISBN 0-8280-1842-1

A Simple Desire

Suffer little children, and forbid them not, to come unto me: for of such is the kingdom of heaven. Matt. 19:14.

THIS MUST BE THE YEAR of the calendar!" I exclaimed as we received yet another. You know how sometimes there seems to be a run on something? Well, this year it was calendars. Business associates, ministries, and Realtors sent calendars. And, of course, charities hoping that if they remember us, we'll not forget them.

I'd oohed and aahed over them as they came. It seemed that they were more beautiful than usual. We got all kinds: large and small, magnetic-backed, wallet-sized, many with magnificent pictures. My favorite? A creative monthly reminder of special moments with our grandchildren, made especially for us by our daughter.

One calendar in particular attracted my attention. It was a collection of beautiful paintings by Lars Justinen on the life and ministry of Jesus. My husband claimed that one for his study, but I said, "Wait until I've had a chance to share it with Max and Juliet."

When our grandchildren came over the next Sabbath, Juliet and I cozied up on the sofa as we looked at each beautiful picture in the calendar. We talked about them all, and when we came to the one of Jesus' baptism, her eyes lingered on the scene. She noted, "Jesus' hair is wet." I explained that He'd just been baptized in the Jordan River and that the dove was God's way of telling Jesus that He was pleased with His decision. After a few thoughtful moments she said, "I want to be baptized with Jesus." I felt my heart leap.

That evening when I tucked her into bed I said, "Juliet, think of the happy things of today." She named a couple things we had done and then said, "Jesus' baptism."

It took a 3-year-old for me to realize that this is what Jesus wants for me for this year—a simple childlike desire to be close to Him and to be a part of who He is. This is what He was talking about when He told the disciples, "Don't prevent them [the children] from coming to me. God's kingdom is made up of people like these" (Matt. 19:14, Message).

My soul-searching question is this: *Is it a "happy" thought—a simple desire—for me to be close to Jesus? Will God's kingdom be made up of people like me?*

Bernadine Delafield

God's Providence

For he shall give his angels charge over thee, to keep thee in all thy ways. Ps. 91:11.

THE NEW YEAR'S SUN SHONE brightly, and the day was clear. We didn't expect it, as New Year's Eve had been foggy, misty, and cold. Our family of four went to church for a special worship to give thanks to the Lord for keeping all of us safe and sound throughout the past year, and for providing many added blessings that we, as sinners, didn't deserve.

My husband had to leave for New Delhi early that afternoon for an urgent appointment. After a quick lunch and asking God's blessings for the journey, we sped along to the railway station. Within 15 minutes we were at the platform, and the train was ready to leave for New Delhi. A fellow worker, Mr. Lall, who was to travel with my husband, waited near the coach. After my husband settled his things and both men had settled into their seats, we waved goodbye as the train departed.

About four hours later I received a phone call. I was shocked to hear my husband's voice, as I didn't expect to hear from him so soon. He informed me that the train had met with an accident, and the first five coaches had derailed. He assured me that he and Mr. Lall were just fine and that there was nothing to be afraid of. They had been in the sixth coach, and by God's providence were without a bruise or a scratch on their bodies. As I read about the accident in the newspaper and thought about them being in the very next coach, I thanked the Lord again for His loving care. There were few casualties, and a major tragedy was averted because the train was moving at a slow speed at the time.

This incident has made our family realize that our God is great, and that every day is another opportunity for all of us to get to know Him better, to come closer to Him, to grow in His love and grace. Our faith is strengthened by trusting completely in our Lord and Savior, Jesus Christ.

Thank You, Lord, for being our loving Father. TARAMANI NOREEN SINGH

New Year's Resolutions

Jesus replied: "'Love the Lord your God with all your heart and with all your soul and with all your mind.' This is the first and greatest commandment." Matt. 22:37, 38, NIV.

SOME YEARS AGO I gave up making New Year's resolutions. What was the use? It didn't matter how hard I tried; they were shattered within a few weeks. However, this year I am going to make a resolution—only one, but if I can keep it, that one is all I need.

When Jesus was on earth, a Pharisee tested Him with this question: "Teacher, which is the greatest commandment in the Law?" Jesus replied, "Love the Lord your God with all your heart and with all your soul and with all your mind.' This is the first and greatest commandment. And the second is like it: 'Love your neighbor as yourself.' All the Law and the Prophets hang on these two commandments" (Matt. 22:36-40, NIV).

So I hereby resolve that with the guidance of the Holy Spirit I will keep that two-in-one commandment.

Can you imagine how perfect this world would be if we all did that? We wouldn't even need the original Ten Commandments. If we loved God with all our heart, there would be no danger of our loving any other god or of worshipping the likeness of anything else, animate or inanimate. We would not blaspheme His holy name or desecrate His holy day. If we loved our neighbor as much as we love ourselves, we would certainly honor our parents and any other respected figure.

If we loved our neighbors as ourselves, we would not kill them, not even accidentally (we'd drive more carefully), nor run off with their partners. We would not steal from our neighbors (not even their roses that grow over our side of the fence) nor lie to them—not even one little fib.

If we loved our neighbors as much as we love ourselves, we would not covet anything of theirs (neither their Cadillac nor their naturally curly hair). We would rejoice that those dear people owned such delightful possessions.

Keeping the Ten Commandments is not so hard to do, but keeping them with love might prove more difficult. Nevertheless, Paul says, "I can do all things through Christ which strengtheneth me" (Phil. 4:13).

It's a good resolution, and I'm aiming high. GOLDIE DOWN

The Desire of Your Heart

May he give you the desire of your heart and make all your plans succeed. We will shout for joy when you are victorious and will lift up our banners in the name of our God. May the Lord grant all your requests. Ps. 20:4, 5, NIV.

HAVE YOU EVER TRIED personalizing Scripture, applying it directly to yourself and your needs—making it speak just to you? The Bible is, of course, God's way of speaking directly to us, so we do need to take it personally. If you have never tried personalizing Scripture, our text for today is a good place to start. And if you have done it before, enjoy the experience again today.

Begin with verse 4. Write, or say, "May he give [put in your name] the desires of her heart." Then tell God the desires of your heart, those deep-down desires that you hardly dare to admit to yourself, never mind say aloud.

Then move on to verse 5. It says: "We will shout for joy." But neither we nor others can shout and wave banners unless we let them know what we are praying for. Which means we may have to share our desires with others—in our family, our women's group, our church. It may be that when they know of our desires, they will be able to help make them come to pass. God usually uses other people in some way to answer prayers. They probably will want to join you in prayer, too. There is wonderful power in intercessory prayer.

Our verse says nothing about praying according to God's will, but it is something you will want to do. I read something the other day from one of Janet Page's prayer seminars that really struck me: "If God really wanted to punish us, He would answer all our prayers with 'Yes.'" If we are asking God for the desires of our hearts, asking Him to make our plans succeed, we need to be sure that these are according to His will, things He will be glad to grant.

When we do receive the desires of our heart, we need to remember to give God the thanks. The beginning of the year is a good time to enumerate all the blessings we have received in the past. This is a good way to build our faith. We need to share our granted wishes with others, too, so they can rejoice with us. It can help build up their faith as well. They may be struggling with the desires of their hearts and needing to know that God is a personal God who loves to grant the requests of His daughters.

ARDIS DICK STENBAKKEN

Are You There?

And it shall come to pass, that before they call, I will answer; and while they are yet speaking, I will hear. Isa. 65:24.

LORAINE! LORAINE, ARE YOU there? Are you awake?" It was 2:30 a.m., and if I wasn't awake before, I certainly was now.

It was my mother-in-law, who is almost 98 years old, calling to me. Since she is legally blind but still has some peripheral vision, I leave the night-light on in her room. But this night I had forgotten to turn it on. I groggily scurried to her room to fix the problem before she woke the three dogs.

It is amusing now, but it wasn't then, to be awakened so early. I knew I would have little sleep for the rest of the night. As I lay awake, trying to get comfortable once more, I thought about Samuel and how the Lord had called him in the middle of the night. He thought it was Eli and ran to him, only to find that Eli had been sound asleep. When Eli realized it was the Lord calling Samuel, he told him how to reply.

I wonder how many times the Lord has tried to "talk" to us, only for us to ignore His call. We want to know He hears us when we call on Him, but we may not be tuned to His voice. He may not speak to us directly, but He uses various ways to communicate. Sometimes it may be through His Word; other times it may be through a devotional or a sermon. If we listen for His voice, He will find a way to "speak" with us, and He is always there when we call on Him.

With cooking, cleaning, and washing, it is easy to forget to listen to that still small voice that comes to me. It is a challenge to find time to read my Bible daily. My mother-in-law has short-term memory problems and needs care. She has poor judgment because of her Alzheimer's-like dementia. I need God's wisdom more than ever.

I try to listen each day to what God has in mind for me. I know He cares about me, just as He cares for each one of you. My prayer for you today is to listen to what God has for you personally. As you go about your daily living, look for the signs that God has put in your pathway. Know that before you call, He will answer.

LORAINE F. SWEETLAND

Un-Disposable Love

Yes, I have loved you with an everlasting love; therefore with lovingkindness I have drawn you. Jer. 31:3, NKJV.

I AM A COLLECTOR OF "stuff." Actually, a file cabinet full of "stuff." Most of it would be considered trash by anyone else. Even my husband has suggested I throw some (well, most) of it away. He says it's bad for his health, because every time we move the file cabinet, it gives him a hernia! Yet I cling to the precious things in my filing cabinet, refusing to ever let them go.

What could be so important that I would risk my husband's health? There are no artifacts of great historical value, no pictures by well-known artists, and no letters from people of renown in the file cabinet. Just the same, it is filled with letters, art, photographs, and other priceless articles that can never be replaced.

How can I throw away the picture of my 2-year-old (now 26), grinning from ear to ear, with Jell-O smeared all over her face, her hands, and her hair? How can I discard the faded paper Santa with crooked arms that move and a cotton-ball beard? Then there's the little note printed unevenly in a first grader's scrawl: "To Mommy: I love you so much. On Mother's Day I love you more then ane wan lus." The lines are crooked, the spelling is terrible, but that doesn't matter to me, because the best of her ability and her whole heart went into writing that note. More than that, I love her with my whole being.

One day while I was talking to God (complaining, actually) about my inadequacies, I asked how He could accept my puny gifts when I was so full of imperfections. Immediately a picture of my overstuffed files came to mind. He reminded me that just as the letters and childish art are precious to me, imperfect as they are, I am precious to Him, imperfect as I am. He loves me despite my faults, despite my imperfections. He accepts me just as I am. Just as I would never discard the items in my files, He will never discard me, because He loves me. He sees me as I will be, not as I am. He knows my inabilities and inadequacies. I am still His precious child, and He looks at me through His fatherly eyes of love.

JUDY NEAL

A Light at the End of All Tunnels

Leave all your worries with him, because he cares for you. 1 Peter 5:7, TEV.

THE MOVE HAD GONE well, and the aches and pains had to be expected if you did your own moving. But now my pains had become more worrisome. I had rarely visited my previous doctor's office except for the usual checkups, but now I seemed to be visiting my new doctor's practice every week. Why did the soles of my feet burn? Why couldn't I lift my right arm? Then it was my left shoulder. I felt as though I was falling to pieces.

It took my new doctor only six weeks to diagnose the trouble, and another four weeks to get me to a specialist. On Christmas Eve 1996 it was confirmed that I was suffering from rheumatoid arthritis. By the time January arrived, I was bedridden. With the help of my loving husband, David, and a friend, I got through each long day.

In the depths of such awful pain the thought of prayer and talking to God daily got put on the back burner. I had to deal with one thing at a time, and at that moment I was concentrating on trying to breathe.

It all seems so long ago now, but I remember that on the deepest and blackest day of my life I whispered to God, "It's all Yours, Lord. Take my mind and keep it sane; take my hopes and fears and keep them next to Your heart. I'll put up with the pain and the medication each day; You will just have to sort everything else out."

It was a long, slow process, a little more than three months, before I was able to leave my bed to try walking with the aid of David or any piece of nearby furniture.

With the help of a dedicated doctor, a superb specialist, and the best Physician in the world looking after me, how could I not recover? I now have to walk with the aid of a stick. When necessary I use my wheelchair, and, if all else fails, I take to my bed for a few days.

Talking to God is part of everyday life again. If the air goes quiet and He doesn't hear my voice, He knows I'm in trouble and puts His arms around me until I recover. I thank the Lord for always being there for me, even on those days when I don't talk to Him. He always hears me. He hears you, too, when you tell Him all the things that hurt and pain you. What a loving and beautiful God we serve, one who thinks only of the well-being of His children.

WENDY BRADLEY

Rose Parade

Everyone who runs in the Olympics gives it all he has, but only one person wins the laurel wreath. That's how you should run the gospel race, giving it everything you've got. In the gospel race, everyone who . . . finishes is a winner. . . . The prize we receive is the crown of eternal life which will last forever. 1 Cor. 9:24, 25, Clear Word.

FOR MORE THAN 100 YEARS the Tournament of Roses parade has marched in Pasadena, California. On New Year's Day 2002 hundreds of thousands watched 53 floats, 25 marching bands, and 27 groups of horses parade for five and a half miles. Thousands of spectators had camped along the route all night to get a choice spot.

This floral extravaganza displayed larger-than-life chipmunks, birds, flowers, gorillas, giraffes, lions, the Statue of Liberty, a 20-foot-tall robot, a rocket, and even a baby in a bathtub. Real fire burst from a volcano, an acrobat swung on a trapeze, dinosaurs chewed on orchids.

Most floats are designed by organizations, but we were touched by one created by Vietnamese people as a gift of love. They wanted to thank America and the world for helping them after they became refugees from Communism some 25 years ago. They raised the thousands of dollars needed to build their float. One woman was so committed to show her appreciation that she sold her house to help raise the money.

The art is all of natural materials. Hundreds of volunteers work many days to cover the designs with thousands of roses, carnations, daisies, orchids, irises, leaves, dried flowers, grasses, mushrooms, seeds, grains, bark, roots, branches, husks, spices, and vegetables.

Thousands crowded around the floats after the parade. As we walked about, our senses were almost overwhelmed with the dazzling colors and intense fragrance. I thought of the millions of hours that so many had invested in these marvels, and of how soon they would be faded. Twenty-three of the floats won trophies, but many spectacular floats did not. As I walked, I often thought of Paul's comparison of two races: one to win a laurel wreath, and one to win a crown of eternal life, which never fades. If people will devote such dedication to building a spectacular float that will last only a few days, how much more dedication should we invest in building for eternity?

RUTH WATSON

Goodbye Has Different Faces

And God shall wipe away all tears from their eyes; and there shall be no more death, neither sorrow nor crying, neither shall there be any more pain: for the former things are passed away. Rev. 21:4.

THE LONG-AWAITED CHRISTMAS HOLIDAY came in with a flourish, only to disappear with the melting snow. I found myself saying hello to a new year and goodbye to my twin daughters. The girls were returning to Andrews University after the winter break. Despite three weeks of talking and sharing, we didn't seem to lose our momentum, even as we drove to the airport.

While the girls checked in their luggage, I checked out the people in the airport. I noticed that those who were meeting and greeting seemed to be enjoying themselves more than the rest of us whose time with family and friends grew shorter by the minute.

Driving home alone, I thought of instances when people face various kinds of separations. For me they seem to fall into four categories:

We say goodbye to *things,* as when a child outgrows his tricycle.

Some say goodbye to *harmful habits,* such as smoking.

We say goodbye to *people.* Often it's on a short-term basis. This happens at schools. Teachers send students home at the end of the day, expecting to see them again. Other times mean a longer separation. Military members and their families know how difficult that can be.

Then there are life-changing goodbyes, such as losing a job, going through a divorce, or facing the death of a loved one. At such times you have to reassemble your life, knowing that some of the pieces are missing.

God understands firsthand the pain of separation. He went through it with His Son when Jesus left heaven to take our place on a cross.

I've heard it said that Christians never need to say goodbye for the last time because of Jesus. Those who accept Him as their Savior and Lord can say goodbye to eternal death and hello to eternal life. When Jesus comes again we can say goodbye to heartaches and trials and hello to happiness; goodbye to pain and disease and hello to vibrant health; goodbye to loneliness and hello to fellowship; goodbye to tears and hello to laughter.

What a wonderful future! What a wonderful God!

MARCIA MOLLENKOPF

Scheduled Meetings

He shall see of the travail of his soul, and shall be satisfied. Isa. 53:11.

MY HUSBAND AND I had participated in a program and were leaving. My husband went to get the car while I waited at the door of the auditorium. Suddenly three young people came up to me. They introduced themselves, saying that they were from a different religious denomination than mine. I asked them if they were enjoying the program, and we began a friendly chat.

I learned that they were listeners of the Radio Tempo and had heard an advertisement of the event on the radio. They had decided to accept the invitation to be with us on that morning. They also told me that they really liked the station programming and wanted to meet me personally because they always listened to the programs that I presented.

As they said goodbye, each one of them kissed my blushing cheek and then stated, "Dear sister, you are very precious to God. Your programs are a blessing and have helped not only the three of us, but many people. We love you very much."

With these words they disappeared into the crowd. I stood there, not knowing what to say or think. I was taken by surprise. After the emotion of the unexpected meeting had passed, I began to reflect on my joy and desire also to draw near, embrace, and kiss Christ on that day when I can finally meet Him personally. Today I can hear Him only through the Bible, but then I will see Him personally.

I imagine that like those young teens, we will seek to break through the crowd to draw near to Jesus to thank Him for all that He has done so that we can inherit salvation. I picture how we will feel if we can take others to heaven. As they draw near to us these people will say, "Dear sister, you are very precious to God. Your life, your words, your efforts, and your kindness were a blessing to me and contributed so that I could be here today."

I want to experience these two scenes, and I hope that this is also your greatest ambition: to prepare yourself for your meeting with Jesus, and to prepare others, also, for this meeting in eternity!

Use me, Lord, to be Your feet, Your lips, Your eyes, and Your ears for whoever may need me today!

Sônia Rigoli Santos

The Green Coat

You will know them by their fruits. Matt. 7:16, NKJV.

I DON'T KNOW WHEN I bought it, but I do know I ordered it through a catalog order house, because the label is still inside. At any rate, it is my favorite cold-weather coat. It has big pockets to hold my warm knit gloves, my house keys, and some tissues. I even keep a $5 bill in one pocket just in case I need some money, and that really did come in handy one time.

So it is no wonder that when my teacher-principal daughter invited me to accompany her and her pupils on a field trip to the beach, I grabbed my green coat before heading out the door. The children had a good time on the sand and in the water while I chatted with the other teachers, the parents, and some of the youngsters who had come to know me through the years. As the day turned into afternoon, we ate supper. Then one of the parents brought out his guitar, and we started singing. Soon the weather began to cool down, and I reached for my familiar green coat. How cozy it felt against the evening breeze.

A few minutes later I heard a voice behind me say, "Well, hello, Mrs. Williams! I was walking over there on the sidewalk and happened to look over here, and I thought, *That looks like Mrs. Williams' green coat. I believe I'll walk over and see.* And sure enough—it is you!"

I looked into her smiling face and tried to remember who she was. Soon she saw my daughter and began to recall memories of grade school days 25 years before. Then I really began pulling mental files. (Later my daughter admitted that she was trying to recall also.) Finally, when the woman mentioned how my daughter had been the "big fifth grader" who had tutored the first graders, it all came together. It was so good to see this little girl, all grown up, married, and a mother herself now.

Being recognized because of my old but still good green coat was both interesting and amusing. I appreciate the way God has preserved it. But as I thought it over, I realized it is far more important for us to be recognized by the heavenly robe of Christ's righteousness than by our earthly clothes.

Dear Lord, please help us wear Your robe always and forever.

Mildred C. Williams

Good News

He that overcometh, the same shall be clothed in white raiment; and I will not blot out his name out of the book of life, but I will confess his name before my Father, and before his angels. Rev. 3:5.

GOOD NEWS! WHEN DID you last receive some? We all wish to have good news given to us every day.

Several years ago I wrote some devotionals to submit to this book series and sent them off. Some time later I received a letter neither confirming nor disclaiming acceptance. I quickly pushed the experience behind me and forgot all about it.

Some time later I traveled from Ibadan to Akure, a distance of about 150 miles (250 kilometers), for an important church meeting. It was a joy for me to be a part of this historic occasion, the first of its kind in Nigeria. The first few hours were spent greeting old friends. Then—joy, oh, joy—my husband, who had been at the meeting several days already, told me that he had a beautiful surprise for me. I was all ears.

He brought out a copy of *This Quiet Place: A Daily Devotional for Women by Women* and opened it to page 375. And there, in black and white, was my name among the list of contributors.

I was so elated! My heart was so full that it almost burst. That was really good news for me, especially after I assumed that the articles had not been worth publishing. As I moved among my friends and other pilgrims, I shared the good news of being a contributor to the devotional book.

But there is still better news: Jesus Christ is my Savior and Lord. He came down from His throne to save me from my sins. Yes, that is the good news of the century, and it is the news I should share with others.

There is another piece of good news: my name is written in the book of life. If seeing my name in black and white in an international book gave me joy, how great will be my joy when I see my name in the book of life!

BECKY DADA

Unanswered Prayers

Before they call I will answer, while they are yet speaking I will hear. Isa. 65:24, NRSV.

DO YOU SOMETIMES FEEL that some of your prayers go unanswered? A close friend and I share our prayer experiences, especially those for our children. We often tease each other that God must be tired of hearing from us. We've even thought of prefacing our prayers by saying, "God, it's me again!" We usually end our conversations on a more serious note, concluding that God loves and cares for us too much ever to get tired of hearing from us.

Some prayers seem to bring immediate response. When Gabriel was dispatched from heaven to give Daniel the interpretation of his dream, Daniel was still praying (Dan. 9:21). Sarah's prayer for a child was not answered until she was an old woman (Gen. 21:7), yet it was magnificently answered—Sarah became the mother of a whole nation. God does indeed work in mysterious ways. Repeatedly God has proved that He has many ways of answering prayer, ways that we often cannot comprehend. Our duty as His children is to present our petitions to God as often as we feel the desire to do so, and trust Him to do what is best for us. The answer to our prayer might not be what we hope for. It might not come when we want it to, either, but one thing is certain: God does hear and answer prayers.

We live in an age of instant gratification. We have come to expect instant results from all we do. So when we pray, we expect our prayers to be answered instantly also. Otherwise, they are filed away as unanswered prayers. God is all-wise, all-loving, all-kind. He withholds from us those things that in our human frailty we seek, but that if they were granted would bring us only pain and heartache. Sometimes when we look back over the years, we can see clearly where our prayers were lovingly answered, but we were too busy complaining to notice. I know I have thanked God many times for "unanswered" prayers.

Some prayers must be left at the foot of the cross. These include intercessory prayers for our loved ones. It seems that only in eternity will we know the answer to those prayers. Today, however, we can claim the promise found in Philippians 1:6: "I am confident of this, that the one who began a good work among you will bring it to completion" (NRSV).

Avis Mae Rodney

I'm a Child of the King

Wherefore thou art no more a servant, but a [daughter]; and if a [daughter], then an heir of God through Christ. Gal. 4:7.

I REMEMBER THE FIRST TIME I started the new year by beginning to read my Bible through. All went well until I got to the First Book of Chronicles—the begat section of the Bible. The listing isn't only one page or one chapter—it covers eight chapters! Not only are the names difficult to pronounce; I didn't know any interesting stories about most of them. I must confess that this section of the Bible got skimmed over that year.

When my father retired from farming, he spent 10 years delving into our Fitch ancestry. He wrote dozens of letters and spent hundreds of dollars tracing our heritage back to the 1400s in England. As one would with any other family history, he found many illustrious men and women who graced our family tree. There were those of high class, as well as humble folk who were dutiful to their families and communities. There were professional people and godly men and women in all walks of life. Somehow those of ignoble character didn't make the headlines.

He compiled his findings into a book. We read the volume with interest and became proud of our heritage. It was my dad's research that sparked my interest in genealogy. Only when you know your roots, and the struggles, challenges, and triumphs—and even failures—faced by your predecessors, does reading family histories have meaning and purpose.

As I read the genealogy in Matthew 1, I was reminded that each of us can trace our ancestry back to Adam, who was the son of God, which makes Jesus our elder brother. It is good to be interested in one's family history, but it's more important to be devoted to being a member of God's family. My dad didn't find that we were related to royalty, but each one of us can claim that we belong to the family of the King of the universe. There is no greater relationship one can desire. By studying God's History Book, we can gain knowledge and instruction on how to become heirs of His kingdom.

David wrote in Psalm 127:3 that "children are an heritage of the Lord." How wonderful! Let us go about our duties today determined to uphold and honor our Father's name as a child of the King. EDITH FITCH

To Give or Not to Give

With the measure you use, it will be measured to you—and even more. *Mark 4:24, NIV.*

A FRIEND CALLED ONE DAY, justly irritated at something that had happened. She wanted to get it off her chest, so I listened as she related the story to me.

Someone had come to her door asking for money. His car had some emergency need, and he had made the rounds of the mobile home park where she lived collecting money from her neighbors. She is a single mother of two, and it takes all she can earn to keep her children in church school and the university. It was not easy to hand over $20 to a stranger, and she wanted proof that what he asked for was a legitimate cause. How could she verify his statements? He said he was willing to work for the money at that time, or he would come back at a later date to pay off the debt. There were things she could have him do for her, so she asked him to return the following Sunday. She also asked for his cell phone number so she could verify that he was who and what he said he was. He didn't have the phone with him but gladly gave her the number, and she cautiously gave him the last $20 bill in her wallet. She told him that the only reason she was doing this was that she was a Christian.

Well, Sunday morning came—and he did not call her. She tried calling the number he had given her, and guess what? Not only was it not his but no one had heard of him at that number. She was fit to be tied. How could he do that to her? She had worked hard for her money and had very little to spare. She was angry! She had tried to do the right thing, and this was the thanks she got: no money, no work, just a pack of lies.

After I'd listened to her tale of woe, a thought crossed my mind. She did witness to him by doing what Jesus would do. It's important to give, and it doesn't come naturally to us, especially when we ourselves are needy. Giving—not getting—is the way. Generosity begets generosity. Stinginess impoverishes. We'll never know if this man's story was true or just a scam, and it doesn't matter. From our Father who gave us His only Son we have the perfect example of giving. My friend gave because she lives to please God.

May that also be my goal for this day, Father—to glorify You.

Suzanne French

Communication

As soon as you started praying, God asked me to come and help you. Dan. 9:23, Clear Word.

MY CELL PHONE IS A marvelous invention. Since I am by nature a gregarious person (much to my husband's dismay), I feel the need to keep in touch with my relatives, my neighbors, and my friends, far and near. This means a lot of telephoning. I am interested in their welfare and especially their spiritual well-being.

Recently my phone has been giving me connection problems. I reach the intended number all right, but after only a minute of conversation I hear three beeps; then my connection is gone. Once I dialed back five times to get my message across. Of course, I've complained to the telephone company and have taken the phone to be "updated" and have done all the things they advised. But it is still unfaithful. Now they tell me that more towers are needed in my area.

When I'm tempted to be really exasperated, I think, *In spite of the problems, what a wonderful miracle to be able to talk not only to my friends in the continental United States but also to my friend in Hawaii and my friend in Alaska! How many, many miles is that? And here I am complaining.*

And what about talking to God? What kind of communication can we have with Him? Does it take much faith to believe that He hears my prayer? Our text says that back in Daniel's day the towers were all intact, and sometimes God's answers were instantaneous.

When I read of Abraham's discussion with the Lord about Sodom and Gomorrah, it sounds to my finite mind like presumption on Abraham's part. And yet God listened and heeded his request. Genesis 18:33 says, "And the Lord went his way, as soon as he had left communing with Abraham."

When I remember Moses' experience of 40 years in the wilderness, preparing him for leadership of the children of Israel, I marvel at the Lord's patience with him as he argues and offers excuses about his inability to do the job God is asking him to do (Ex. 3:11; 4:10-12).

It's difficult for my imagination to grasp that we can have instantaneous communication with the omnipotent, omniscient, omnipresent God of the universe. He is ever faithful; I trust that others will see me responding to His faithfulness toward me.

RUBYE SUE

The Elastic Time Miracle

But from everlasting to everlasting the Lord's love is with those who fear him, and his righteousness with their children's children. Ps. 103:17, NIV.

MY HUSBAND AND I WORK together in family ministries. It's quite a challenge sometimes, because we have three children still at home. We don't want their needs to go unmet while we are helping other families.

One weekend we were asked to fly to Geneva to lead a marriage retreat. As a treat, we paid for our three children to come along and visit relatives nearby. A month before we were to leave, Bethany discovered that she had major national exams at school on the day we were to fly back to London. It would take a miracle to get her there on time, as we'd have only 75 minutes from the estimated landing time to the start of school! All we could do was pray.

On the morning of the exam we had to get up at 4:30. The flight was bumpy, and we all felt ill. Then there was fog, and the landing was delayed a little. Our luggage was the last off the plane, and we lost one of the children in the airport. When we finally got to our car, the battery was dead. So we all pushed the car down a slope to jump-start it. Once in the car, we discovered we'd lost our parking ticket. Then we hit traffic jams.

At first Bethany prayed that she wouldn't be in time for the exams. There were a lot of things working against us getting to school on time, and she felt tired and sick. Then she prayed that if we did make it to school on time, it would be a sign that God would be with her and help her do her best.

When we finally arrived at the school, we were earlier than we often were on a regular school day. By a miracle God seemed to have stretched time for us! Bethany went in to take the exams while we prayed that everything would work out for her.

She arrived home that evening very tired but excited that the exams had gone well, and she was glad that she'd taken them after all.

Thank You, God, for blessing our children and showing them how much You love them and meeting their needs in miraculous ways, even in the crazy busyness of our ministry.

KAREN HOLFORD

There Is a Way That Seemeth Right

There is a way which seemeth right unto a man, but the end thereof are the ways of death. Prov. 14:12.

In all thy ways acknowledge him, and he shall direct thy paths. Prov. 3:6.

I WAS INVITED TO SHARE lunch with my sister as she tended to her duties as nanny to four small children. She asked if I knew how to get to the house. "I've been there before, remember?" I assured her. I pride myself on being a quick learner.

The next afternoon, up the winding road I went. So far, so good. But when I reached the top of the hill, the road to the left did not say "Fifth Street." And there was no house number 60. After retracing my steps and getting lost for nearly a half hour, I had to admit I was lost.

Deciding to admit defeat, I went to find a phone book (only to look up the address, mind you). I was not ready to hear my sister say, "You should have listened more carefully to my instructions," so I spent another 10 minutes or so wracking my brain, trying to remember what the name of her street was, and scanning the phone book.

When my sister inquired about my late arrival, I had to admit my error. I found out that there were two similar roads about a mile apart. Both roads led off to the hillside, both had paved, upward-winding turns and then dirt roads to the left—but that was where the similarity ended. At the end of the first winding road the houses all had different numbers.

At times we may be perfectly confident in our decisions—and yet be perfectly wrong. The road God chooses may not be to our liking, but it is for our own good. If we could see the end from the beginning, we would not want to be led any other way. If we get on the wrong track because of our own piloting, we can come back to God's highway and use His prayer lines and start over again with Him at the wheel. At the end of the road we will be able to reach our home with a sign on the gate that reads: "Welcome; come on in. I have been waiting for you."

Take me home, Lord. I'm ready and willing to be led.

VIDELLA MCCLELLAN

Daddy's Girl

For he hath said, I will never leave thee, nor forsake thee. So that we may boldly say, The Lord is my helper, and I will not fear what man shall do unto me. Heb. 13:5, 6.

I AM THE THIRD OF SEVEN children, five boys and two girls. When I was growing up in Trinidad, my father referred to me as his "eyeball." That would translate as "the apple of his eye." My father was six feet five inches tall, and very loud. To me he was a giant, and I was proud to be his little girl. I always felt safe because I knew my daddy was big and strong and would protect me. To a child of 8, my daddy was a hero. People in the community looked up to him; some even feared him, and nobody messed with him.

Unknown to me, my parents were experiencing marital difficulties, and my mother eventually left my father. When I was about 9, I was separated from my father. My mother immigrated to Canada, and I was sent to live with my grandparents. I was Daddy's girl, and it was not fair that I had to be apart from him. I didn't fully understand what had happened, but I had to accept it because my parents were both gone.

Sometimes children are torn away from those they love because of things they cannot understand and have no control over. Feelings of loss, confusion, guilt, and emptiness flood their souls. Some young people even contemplate, attempt, or commit suicide because of a sense of hopelessness. That is not the answer—Jesus is. As I grew older, I came to realize that it was not my fault that my parents separated. I realized that I could not blame myself for things I had no control over.

Sometimes life has a way of going contrary to our plans, and we feel as though we have messed up. No matter what your circumstances may be, know that God loves you and that you are special to Him. I find comfort in knowing that God has a plan for my life and for my children and grandchildren. I know that I must trust God no matter what. That is exercising faith. When things don't seem to be going the way you want them to, turn it all over to Jesus.

I may no longer have my earthly father, but to my heavenly Father I will always be Daddy's girl. He has promised never to leave me nor forsake me. I know He keeps His word.

SHARON LONG (BROWN)

Miracles Then and Miracles Now

Because he has set his love upon Me, therefore I will deliver him; I will set him on high, because he has known My name. He shall call upon Me, and I will answer him; I will be with him in trouble; I will deliver him and honor him. Ps. 91:14, 15, NKJV.

DO MIRACLES REALLY HAPPEN in this day and age? I know that Jesus performed many miracles when He lived on this earth—they've been recorded in the Holy Scriptures for our benefit. But how about today? Does He still perform miracles? Definitely! I know He does, because miracles have happened in my life again and again.

Some time ago when my husband I were still living in Toronto, Ontario, Canada, a friend and I went shopping in Chinatown. Knowing it was difficult to find parking, we decided to go by public transportation, first by bus and then by subway. When we arrived at Chinatown, we took time looking for the items we wanted. We found some fresh lychee, longan, and very fresh tropical vegetables. And to our delight we found chestnuts for only 99 cents a pound. We were loaded with bags of goodies when we thought we'd better quit buying things or it would be hard to carry our treasures home on the subway.

We didn't wait long for our train. My friend got on first, and I was following her when the train suddenly started moving. My right foot was in, but my body was out. I tried to get in, but I was caught between the doors. Quick as a flash, I pushed the doors with all my might and jumped in. There was no time to panic.

I was not the one who opened those doors. Someone bigger than I was helped me get on that train. Without a doubt it must have been either my guardian angel or Jesus Christ Himself who opened those doors for me to get in.

Miracle? Most certainly! I was sure of impending death, but God in His mercy saved me from fatal disaster.

Father God, You are so wonderfully good and gracious to me. I could have died because of my carelessness, but You saw fit that I survive to proclaim Your eternal goodness so rich toward me.

Ofelia A. Pangan

The Lost Dogs

What woman, having ten silver coins, if she loses one coin, does not light a lamp, sweep the house, and search carefully until she finds it? Luke 15:8, NKJV.

I CHUCKLED AS I LOOKED down from my loft window on the playful dogs. Jack, a white Pyrenees puppy, was larger than our own white malamute, Ivy. Jack lived a few blocks to the east, and Ollie, a light tan puppy, lived a few blocks west of us. The three dogs were romping in our snowy yard, where Ivy was chained.

We really should let Ivy run free with the others, I thought. But in my heart I feared it wasn't safe, as vehicles moving swiftly on the icy country roads could hit wandering dogs. We did let her go, however. For several days the threesome ran free in the neighborhood. Then Ivy got sick, and we tied her back up to keep her close. Jack was tied as well at his home.

The next day we took Ivy for her usual walk on the leash. It seemed strange that Ollie wasn't waiting for us, and when we walked past Jack's nose, he didn't come running either. I was concerned. Where could they be? Jack's owner set out in the car to search. But he came back empty-handed. Wherever they'd gone, they had gone together. It seemed that Ollie had come over that morning and chewed Jack free.

Later in the day we found out that the dogs had wandered to a hunting camp some distance away. The caretaker had phoned all around before finding someone who knew the dogs. Both owners headed out to fetch their wayward animals.

A very sad Ollie and frustrated Jack were now tied in their respective yards. The lost had been found and the freedom romps curtailed.

Of course, the puppies' owners could have just left them at the hunting camp. They each had two other dogs. But Ollie and Jack were their pets. The dogs didn't know they were lost. Had the owners not come, they would have played until hunger sent them on a difficult and dangerous search for home.

We tie up Ivy because we love her. Christ sought me out when I was lost and didn't know it. He fenced me in with His guidelines for my own protection, and I'm grateful to a God who cares for me more than I could ever care for my precious dog.

Dawna Beausoleil

Feeling, Faith, and Fact

And so, after he had patiently endured, he obtained the promise. Heb. 6:15, NKJV.

CLUTCHING THE TINY BOOK about George Müller, I boarded a plane on a cold January day. It would take me to my new assignment in northeastern Mexico. I was soon informed that the area had just suffered an infrequent freeze that had ruined their crops. Money would be tight.

My temporary quarters were warm, and I soon set about to read the little book of great faith that I had carried along. Yes, George Müller's favorite verse would be mine, I decided—Hebrews 6:15: "And so, after he had patiently endured, he obtained the promise." I needed that kind of faith.

I smiled as I was introduced to my staff and shown around. Later, shivering in my cold office, I wondered how I should tackle this missionary position as director of a university library. The library needed to be enlarged so badly. In my room each night I read the little book while God and I spent time together, building my faith.

Besides my daily lessons in Spanish, I felt impressed that what I found in my desk drawers would be a good start to my job. In the drawer I found the neglected plans for doubling the size of the library, drawn up more than two years before! With them was a colorful brochure from Maranatha Volunteers International, a group of volunteer mission builders, with their mission statement and address.

Bravely I typed a letter to the Maranatha group, carefully wording the most convincing reasons I had learned for university library standards, and mailed it. I was so fearful I did not even ask my secretary to type the letter. Then I waited and prayed.

Clinging to my faith, I pushed my feelings of fear and vulnerability aside and hung on to the fact of need as I learned the language. Weeks passed. Then a letter came! Even though I had acted without counsel from my superiors, the acceptance letter from Maranatha was excitedly read at the administration meeting, and everyone agreed to my idea.

Soon the plans fell into place, and the enlarged library became a reality. I thanked the Lord many times as I continued my work in that beautiful new library building.

Lord, I pray today that I will use again that kind of faith for my new daily needs.

Bessie Siemens Lobsien

Elijah's Cloak or My Father's Shirt

My soul rejoices in my God. For he has clothed me with garments of salvation and arrayed me in a robe of righteousness. Isa. 61:10, NIV.

WHEN MY FATHER DIED, I flew to Sweden to be close to my mother. There were so many matters to be taken care of. We went to the nursing home where he had lived the last years of his life to pick up his personal belongings. While packing his things, I found a lovely soft flannel shirt he had often worn.

"I'll take this along," I said to my mother.

I love to wear this shirt at home. I feel safe and cozy. I have often wondered why I feel so good when I'm wearing the shirt. I think it has something to do with the heritage of my father. He served the Lord with all his might. His faith in God was not to be shaken. And he passed on this devotion and dedication to us, his children. I always wanted to serve the Lord as he did; there was never a doubt about that.

And so the shirt has become a symbol of my heritage, as Elijah's cloak was a symbol of the spirit and mission that Elisha inherited from his master. My mission is different from my father's, but his dedication to the Lord is what made the most indelible impression on me.

My father could have joined Paul in what he wrote to Timothy: "I have fought a good fight, I have finished my course, I have kept the faith: Henceforth there is laid up for me a crown of righteousness" (2 Tim. 4:7, 8).

Now it is my turn to run my race and keep the faith. But I need the soft, warm cloak that is hanging in God's wardrobe, waiting for me. All I have to do is to ask for it and put it on, leaving my old filthy clothes at the foot of the cross. We need these garments of salvation and the robe of righteousness. Without them we'll never make it.

My father showed me the way. When I wear his shirt I'm reminded of his example. Do you want to wear a soft, warm cloak? Come with me to God's storehouse. There's a robe and a crown waiting for me "and not only [for] me, but also [for] all who have longed for his appearing" (2 Tim. 4:8, NIV).

HANNELE OTTSCHOFSKI

January 24

Prayer in the Sanctuary

You are awesome, O God, in your sanctuary. . . . Praise be to God! Ps. 68:35, NIV.

LIKE THE PSALM WRITERS of the Bible, I sometimes have problems understanding God's ways. Asaph, the author of Psalm 73, explains that when he struggled with understanding why God didn't deal more directly with the wicked, he found the answer when he entered the sanctuary. As he contemplated the work of the priests, he began to understand more clearly God's plan to rid this world of sin.

I too have wondered about such things—but on a more personal basis. Ten years ago I swirled in grief for days, weeks, and months when I met estrangement with a loved one. Why, why, why? My prayers seemed to bounce off the ceiling back into my face. And then, like Asaph, I too found meaning through the sanctuary.

A young Jewish Christian suggested that the steps the priests took daily in their sanctuary work is a wonderful guide for personal prayer. I had no working illustration of the sanctuary services to observe, as Asaph did, but Scripture gives us word pictures. From the moment I began sanctuary prayer, I sensed God's presence and was able to trust His plan for my life.

Here are the steps to personal prayer I found in the sanctuary illustration: praise to God as you enter the gates of prayer; repentance and confession at the altar of sacrifice—the cross, where Jesus died; daily cleansing, emptying of self and sin, and rebaptism at the laver; and daily asking for the fullness of the Holy Spirit at the lampstand. I also learned growth: obedience and action as I eat at the table of His Word; joining Jesus in intercession for others at the altar of incense; and judgment, investigation, discipline, and instruction in the Most Holy Place—learning to listen for God's voice in my daily life.

Praying through the sanctuary has changed my prayers. I've lost my panic. My wandering thoughts are contained, and I easily move on to the next part of my prayer. Confession at the altar gives me the confidence that I am forgiven. I remember to pray daily for the Holy Spirit. Each morning my prayer is different as I find new ways to praise God, new scriptures to feast on at the table, new people to intercede for, new lessons to learn in the Most Holy Place.

Praise God for the daily ministry of Jesus in the heavenly sanctuary!

CARROL JOHNSON SHEWMAKE

Heavenly Revelations

That the God of our Lord Jesus Christ, the Father of glory, may give to you the spirit of wisdom and revelation in the knowledge of Him. Eph. 1:17, NKJV.

A LARGE WINDOW IN THE downstairs den of my house looks out onto a wooded area. It is a beautiful view of undisturbed nature. One morning I could see deer peacefully foraging for food just beyond the old stone fence that runs down one side of the yard. I could see squirrels scurrying about and birds hopping and playing. It was a serene scene.

However, when I went upstairs to my office, which is directly above the den, and looked out the windows that face the same direction, it was an entirely different scene. Dozens of birds of varying kinds were flying frantically to and fro. They flitted from tree to tree, from tree to ground, from limb to limb. The once-grounded squirrels now became airborne as they fearlessly leaped to distant branches. They chased each other relentlessly as they climbed higher and higher. The view from upstairs was more chaotic than serene. It was a totally different perspective, and one I hadn't really noticed before.

I could say that I never noticed the contrast until then because the weather had never been just as it was on that day—it was snowing beautifully. Or I could assume it was the particular time of day I happened to look out that made me so keenly aware. But in reality I know what opened my heart and eyes to this heavenly happening.

Earlier that morning I had experienced a special time with God. I had sought His face in a way I hadn't done before. I didn't rush through my study and prayer. I lingered and shared the desires of my heart. This time I really meant it when I gave Him my feeble plans and said, "Your will be done." This time I reached out and took hold of His promise, trusting Him to finish the work that He had begun in me. And with that surrender came a tiny revelation of His workings.

Sometimes from my earthly vantage point it looks as though nothing too exciting is going on. Things can look relatively calm and consistent. God knows that from down here I can't see the whole picture in regard to my life. But I am convinced that there is quite a lot of activity going on "upstairs." From my window on the world I have learned that He is repositioning, redirecting, and refocusing events in my life every day—even if I can't see it happening.

EMILY FELTS JONES

Superhuman Strength

I will never leave thee, nor forsake thee. Heb. 13:5.

THE DAY HAD A DISAPPOINTING START. My job entails personal calls to homes, and this day's agenda required many such calls. The very first visit was out in the country, where there were few neighboring houses and many fields. As I turned into the driveway I checked the name on my list, got out of the car, and knocked on the door. There was no response. No one was home. It was indeed a great disappointment, and my day had only begun.

I made my way back to the car, jotted a few explanatory notes on the pad of paper, shifted, and backed out, not paying particular attention. Suddenly the car's tires slipped off the driveway, and the axle came to rest on the culvert that ran under the driveway. The car couldn't move one way or the other. I was stranded.

My God and I have a partnership, and it was a time to pray. I bowed my head and laid my petition upon the One who is always ready to hear and help. I needed help, and soon, if I was going to get anything done this day. There was no house close enough to go to for help, and there was no way I could move the car myself.

Moments later a postal truck rounded the bend in the road and stopped by the driveway. The driver stepped out and said, "You need help!" It was not a question but a statement of fact. "You stay in the car and steer, and I'll have you back on the road in no time," he instructed.

So saying, he lifted the car with superhuman strength and set it back on the road. I was still seated in the driver's seat and was so overwhelmed with what had happened that my appreciation was much too feeble. I drove up and down the road looking for the postal truck to thank the driver properly, but I never saw him or his vehicle again, not even on adjoining roads.

A miracle? An answer to prayer? An angel?

As I made the rest of my calls that day, I was filled with the realization that we are never alone. His helpers are everywhere, just waiting to be sent on a special mission. That mission might even be for a postal worker with superhuman strength to be sent to rescue a woman in distress. He will always be near when we need Him. He is true to His promises!

LAURIE DIXON-MCCLANAHAN

Book Sale

I will never forget you. See, upon the palms of my hands I have written your name. Isa. 49:15, 16, NAB.

I LOVE BOOKS, AND I love reading, so I look forward to the yearly book sale at the public library, when I can buy discarded library books for a fraction of their cost. The library also accepts donations of personal books, so I can clear out our packed bookshelves, getting rid of books we don't plan to read again.

One year we packed up two cartons of books. Our son, Garrick, brought a pile of picture books he'd outgrown; my husband, Larry, added some volumes we had purchased years before, when we lived in the Philippines; and I contributed a stack of craft books that I never had time to use. I dropped the cartons at the library and noted the date of the big sale.

When the day arrived, I put an empty box in the car and vowed not to buy more books than it would hold. I first looked at the children's books, discovering the next volumes of a series that Garrick enjoyed, and books I had enjoyed as a child. The box was more than half full, so I left the children's section to find some books for myself.

I walked past the cookbooks and stacks of worn romance and Western paperbacks to the tables piled high with general reading. I found two books by my favorite author, and picked up several Canadian classics. The box was almost full, but I wanted to find something for Larry.

And then the cover of a book caught my eye. I had heard of the title. I read the blurb on the back cover and decided that it sounded like something my husband would enjoy. I drove home, anticipating his smile.

"Here's a book for you," I said, handing the book to Larry.

"But we already have this book," he responded. "I read it several years ago."

Surprised, I looked more carefully at my 25-cent treasure. I opened the front cover, and on the title page was written a price—in Philippine pesos. No wonder I had recognized the cover and title. The book had been sitting on our shelves for years! I had donated it to the library just a few weeks earlier. And now I had bought it back.

I had forgotten our own book.

How glad I am that our heavenly Father does not forget His own.

Denise Dick Herr

January 28

Collections

I have hidden your word in my heart that I might not sin against you. Ps. 119:11, NIV.

PEOPLE COLLECT EVERYTHING imaginable these days. Precious Moments figurines, art, jewelry, teapots, hostas, coins, stamps, picture albums, spoons—you name it! Many of these items need to be insured; others collect a lot of dust sitting on a shelf; and all consume the thoughts, time, and money of the owner.

When I was younger, I collected napkins. I had napkins from everywhere imaginable—restaurants, weddings, church, and school. They were every color of the rainbow, and then some. I always treasured the ones from vacations and special events. They sat around in a big box until eventually all were thrown away.

As an adult, I don't think much about collecting things. However, as I was paging through my Bible I noticed all the verses I have collected over the years. They are the ones highlighted and underlined along with dates etched in the margin. Many of these verses I had committed to memory. There was the verse God gave me when I decided to birth my second child at home. Or the verse when our real estate agent got papers mixed up and we were buying a house we had never seen. And there is the verse from the time my brother was in the hospital having seizures. And also a verse when our business contracts were so few that we didn't think we were going to make it financially. I could go on and on.

Jesus was a collector of verses too! With verses He resisted temptation from Satan, rebuked the Pharisees, and instructed the disciples. Jesus knew the power in Scripture—not only in reading it, but in memorizing it and applying it.

He wants us to be collectors of His Word too, for He knows it will last for eternity. He wants us not only to read and mark verses but to apply them to our lives, just as He did. And the beauty is that they don't have to be insured—they are insurance. They do not have to be dusted, although it's good to look at them frequently. They don't cost money or take much time. But they do fill our minds with useful strength. What a worthwhile collection!

Karen Phillips

Patience

Here is the patience of the saints. Rev. 14:12.

OCCASIONALLY MY HUSBAND (although not a critical person) reminds me that I am a little short on one of the virtues God requires of His people: patience! And I respond jokingly, "That's the reason the Lord gave me you!"

Our neighbor tells of spending hours on the bank of a lake waiting to catch a fish. That is not my idea of a way to develop patience. Too much patience is required. And what would I do with the fish if I caught it? Someone has written a prayer for the likes of me: *Dear Lord, give me patience; and give it to me right now!*

Since the Lord created each of us as a unique individual, it's not surprising that different trials are required to develop our characters. My friend Anita Martin, who worked in an office with me years ago, used to say, "Job never owned a typewriter!" Her patience was tried by using the typewriter, but it was my delight to type (and still is).

In one of His parables Jesus told about the good seed in the good soil. He said, "They are those who, hearing the word, hold it fast in an honest and good heart, and bring forth fruit with patience" (Luke 8:15, RSV).

Paul had a lot to say about patience. In Romans 9:22 he reminds us that God has had a lot of patience with us. In his list of traits that we need he tells us we need patience (Col. 3:12). In Romans 12:12 he tells us to be patient in tribulation.

When James speaks of the prophets being an example to us of patience (James 5:10), my thoughts turn to Moses and the 40 years he spent in the wilderness. And what about Job? Someone in our Bible class pointed out that losing your wealth is one thing, but losing all your children is something else!

James also reminds us to be patient, for the coming of the Lord is at hand (James 5:8). That is more true today than when this text was first written. And, of course, Revelation describes those who are in heaven at last as having patient endurance (Rev. 2:2-19).

So my prayer is that God will give me whatever trials I need to teach me the patience to be what He wants me to be—in this world, and in the better world He is preparing for me. RUBYE SUE

January 30

Lessons From a Philodendron

And he shall be like a tree planted by the rivers of water, that bringeth forth his fruit in his season; his leaf also shall not wither; and whatsoever he doeth shall prosper. Ps. 1:3.

WE RENTED AN OLDER HOME while our new home was being built. I purchased a philodendron plant and put it by the bathtub. The skylight in the ceiling let in sunny rays that shone on its lovely green foliage. It thrived, sitting there on the tub's edge.

When we moved into our new home, I placed the philodendron in a wrought-iron plant stand in the den, next to the sliding-glass door. In the warm afternoon sun it flourished, and soon its tendrils reached the floor. My sister wrapped the vines in a circle around the pot and plant stand. This worked very well for quite some time. It was truly a beautiful sight to behold, and I was quite proud of my only living plant.

The plant did well for a couple years; then it reached the floor again—and even climbed up the leg of a nearby end table. One day my gardener sister suggested that it needed a haircut. She suggested I have my husband, also a garden enthusiast, help me do the job.

One afternoon, while my husband was at work, I decided it was time and felt confident I could do it alone. So, scissors in hand, I began to carefully cut. My biggest problem was determining which end was attached to the plant. I began to unwrap and snip, until soon I had a trash bag nearly full of clippings. When I surveyed my handiwork, I realized that the plant was no longer lush and green. Instead, it now appeared thin and scraggly. I tried to even up the vines, until the philodendron ended up with a very short bob.

My husband was aghast at its much-altered appearance. He requested that in the future I not undertake such a task without his assistance. I was chagrined at the damage I had inflicted on my once-luxuriant plant. I decided to give it some Miracle-Gro and see what would happen. Within a few months many green shoots and leaves began to appear. I was delighted.

Today the philodendron is once again a joy to behold. Its full green tendrils once more touch the floor. Whenever I look at it I am reminded of the difficult times in my life when I have been tempted to give up. But with the sunshine of God's love, the warmth of His arms, and the watering of the Holy Spirit, I find courage to face my problems, knowing He is always with me!

ROSE NEFF SIKORA

The Empty Cup

But my God shall supply all your need according to his riches in glory by Christ Jesus. Phil. 4:19.

A GLANCE AT THE SCHOOLROOM clock on the wall reminded me that recess time was near. The children in my class had been working hard on their lessons and would welcome a break. So would I.

Just then the cook from the cafeteria came into the room carrying a tray filled with little cups of peanuts. The children were delighted.

One of the students asked if the class could eat their treats outside, just like having a picnic. Everybody liked that suggestion. The sunshine outside seemed to validate the idea. I told the boys and girls they could carry their own snacks while walking to the playground. We talked about the importance of being careful so that nothing would spill; then we were out the door and down the hall.

In a single file the class members made their way down two flights of stairs, carefully holding their little containers of peanuts. Outside the building, as we made a turn, the line came to a standstill. All eyes were focused on Tina. The look on her face reflected a combination of surprise and horror as she looked at the peanuts scattered on the ground and the empty cup in her hands.

I waited to see if someone would offer to share their snack with Tina. Nobody said a word. Finally I asked the class, "How many of you would be willing to give Tina just one of your peanuts?" Every hand went up.

I told Tina to walk down the line of classmates and collect one promised peanut from each volunteer. She started at the back of the line. As she held out her little cup, each child dropped in one peanut. Before Tina could get down the whole row of children, she stopped. She looked up at me and smiled. Her cup was full, and so was her heart.

We all have "empty cup" days, days when a little bump we didn't see causes our expectations to spill on the ground. When we need it most, God seems to send people with bits of help and encouragement our way. Then, with full cups and grateful hearts, we, in turn, can let God use us to bless others.

Marcia Mollenkopf

Without Power

Wealth and honor come from you; you are the ruler of all things. In your hands are strength and power to exalt and give strength to all. 1 Chron. 29:12, NIV.

I RARELY PROCRASTINATE EXCEPT when it comes to preparing a newsletter. But I finally buckled down as the deadline stared me in the face. When I was three hours into the project the electricity went out for a few seconds, then came back on. Within a few minutes, however, it went off again and did not come back on. I continued working until the battery gave out on my laptop.

Curiosity led me to discover the source of the trouble. A power pole down the street had caught on fire. Fire trucks were pouring fire retardant on the pole, and power lines dangled precariously from trees.

By now it was noon and time for lunch. So we ate a cold lunch in a relatively dark house. After lunch I tried to work by candlelight in my office, but I simply couldn't see well enough to complete any task. So my husband and I headed for the mall. By suppertime power still had not been restored. One cold meal we could tolerate, but two, back to back, wouldn't do. So we ate out. After supper the power still wasn't restored, so we looked for friends who would take us under their wing for a few hours.

By 9:00 we felt obligated to return home, where we still had no power. As we entered our very dark, cold home, we recognized how little we could do without power: we couldn't read, watch TV, or even listen to music. Our electric blanket would do us no good. I lit several candles, and we settled in front of our cozy fireplace for a much-needed heart-to-heart talk.

The power was out for almost 14 hours. We made it through those 14 hours, but with difficulty. Living without electric power might be likened to trying to live without being connected to heavenly power. We sometimes think we can go for days, even weeks, without being hooked up to the heavenly Source. We have a million excuses—I'm too busy, my kids are sick, we took a trip, I had to work extra hours. But the only way to live a vibrant Christian life is to stay connected to the Power Source—minute by minute, day by day. You may not have fewer problems, but you'll have increased wisdom and power to deal with the problems you do have. And once you try it you won't want to live life any other way!

NANCY L. VAN PELT

A Hug of Life: Barbara Thomas's Story

Immediately the boy's father exclaimed, "I do believe; help me overcome my unbelief!" Mark 9:24, NIV.

BARBARA WAS IN THE intensive-care unit for six weeks in a coma. As her condition got progressively worse, the doctors saw no more medical support that they could offer her—or hope that they could offer her family. This young woman was going to die. They spoke to her family members, who resigned themselves to what they heard and what they also saw. The respirators and drugs could no longer help or heal.

Barbara's brother, Michael, was distraught. This was another great disappointment. Just seven years before, their 18-year-old nephew, a good boy, a child of great possibility, had died. He had been riding a bicycle and had turned into traffic. When the nephew had died, Michael, in his grief, vowed he would never again believe there was a God. How could there be a gracious God if He allowed such tragedy? And now Michael was faced with another loved one's death.

Michael was returning to England. Since he didn't have return fare, the family sold all Barbara's furniture and bought him a plane ticket. Her house was returned to the manager. Barbara wouldn't be coming home.

The day before his flight to Liverpool, Michael went to see his dying sister. He picked her up in his arms, the respirator and myriad lines dangling from her body, and announced, "Dear God, if You are really there, please give me back my sister. I can't bear to lose her." Immediately Barbara's eyes opened, and tears streamed down her face. The very next day she was off the respirator, and the lines were pulled. And Michael believed!

I work in the hospital, where I met Barbara. Although she is no longer in ICU, she still has aches and pains and has a way to go to complete recovery. At one point she was even discharged to the returned rental house but had to come back for further medical intervention. Yes, she has to get furniture all over again, but everyone is helping.

Barbara said it was her brother's hug, his quest for God, that saved her. And it was God's hug that brought him back to faith. WANDA DAVIS

Sons of Mischief

He will send His angels to protect you as you walk in His ways. They will lift you up in their arms so you won't stub your toe on a rock. Ps. 91:11, 12, Clear Word.

MY HUSBAND WAS REMODELING our main bathroom and painting the walls. He thought it was safe to put his tools and paints in the bathtub since we were using the other bathroom.

And it was safe until the day of mischief. My son Malachi, who was about 3½, called, "Mommy, I have to potty!"

Not thinking, I said, "OK; I'll be right in to help you." I was busy working and didn't notice that Matthan, my 2-year-old, had followed him.

I noticed that the house was suddenly quiet, and Malachi hadn't emerged from the bathroom. I went to investigate. I didn't find him in the spare bathroom, so I immediately checked the main bathroom. It was locked. I panicked. "Malachi, open the door, please."

When he replied, "Don't spank me," my suspicion rose to an all-time high. When I asked what he had done that I should spank him for, an excited little voice responded, "Me painting!"

I heard myself demanding, " Malachi, open this door right now!"

His next words really shook me: "Me painting Matthan."

Then I heard crying. No, it sounded more like giggles. It was giggles. Matthan's giggles. I was relieved somewhat, but I had to get that door open. I resorted to threats, to which Malachi replied, "You not spank me, Mommy?" I had no choice but to promise.

The door opened, and there was Matthan, on his hands and knees, proudly displaying his brand-new color. He was mauve from his blond hair to his tiny toes. And not only Matthan had been painted—so had the tub, walls, and floor. I grabbed Matthan, ran to the second bathroom, and proceeded to give him a bath. Well, it took at least three baths. When I was finished, I turned to Malachi. I must have given him a rather stern look, because he felt it necessary to remind me about my no-spank promise.

Our bathroom is no longer mauve, except for a tiny mauve handprint on the back of the door. It serves as a constant reminder that God watches over even the smallest of us. Whenever I think of that day, I thank God for His watch care. Then I sit back and laugh with the angels as mauve scenes replay in my mind.

Tammy Barnes Taylor

Abandoned Luggage

Is any one of you in trouble? He should pray. James 5:13, NIV.

IN FEBRUARY OF 2001 a high school classmate was coming to visit me in Florida. Unfortunately, Lucille had had a stroke at the young age of 60, so she was not getting around as well as she had in the past. Her outlook on life, however, is very upbeat in spite of her difficulties, and she is a joy to have around. It was nearly midnight when her plane arrived, and both of us were tired.

After meeting her at the gate, I led her to the parking garage where my vehicle was parked. As we walked out of the elevator I volunteered to get my pickup and drive it close to the elevator so she would not have so far to walk.

There was a sport utility vehicle parked in front of the elevator, blocking the regular access. Lucille walked in front of the SUV, set her suitcase down in front of it, and walked around to where I would be driving up. I helped her into the vehicle, and down the road we started. About 25 miles later I said to Lucille, "I don't remember putting your suitcase into the back of the truck." She couldn't remember it either. I pulled off to the shoulder of the road and took a look. No suitcase! We were approaching a tollbooth, so I told the attendant our problem. She told me where I could turn around immediately without having to go to the next exit

We did a lot of praying that the luggage would still be there. Visions of it having been taken by someone or by airport security were very present in our minds. I drove up several levels in the parking garage to the place we had left about an hour before. There was the luggage in front of the SUV, which was still parked there. Were we ever thankful our prayers had been answered! Should we have been surprised that the luggage was still there? In our human frailty I am sorry to admit that we actually were.

Thank You, Lord, for guarding that luggage and for taking care of us in our excitement over getting together. And most of all, thank You for answering our prayers. It did increase our faith that night and helped us realize that You do watch over Your own.

MARGE MCNEILUS

She Chose to Be a Christian

Your people will be my people and your God my God. Ruth 1:16, NIV.

RAJAMMA CAME TO OUR home at a time when I needed a helper. My pastor-husband had to be away most of the day, and I had recently undergone surgery and could not take care of my son. But now Rajamma had come to stay with us, and I felt at ease. I could relax and rest and do my reading and writing, which had been neglected for a long time.

Rajamma came from a Hindu background. She was very poor, owning nothing. But she was happy with us. I taught her to sew, clean, cook, and do a little knitting. She was treated as one of the family. We didn't force anything upon her, but she was a keen observer. She watched us having family worship every morning and evening. She watched our lifestyle. After a few months she began to attend church with us. I opened a savings account in her name, depositing her salary into the bank, and she began to pay tithe.

I asked my husband to give her some Bible studies, and soon we both were teaching her the Scriptures. She was learning our songs and liked our lifestyle and seemed very happy. Eventually she was baptized as a Christian.

About the time Rajamma turned 18 we started looking for a husband for her. We found a young man who also was poor, and almost like an orphan. Rajamma had a brother and two sisters who were very prejudiced against Christianity and for whom we used to pray often. They (especially her brother) didn't like the idea of her becoming a Christian and having a Christian wedding.

But God was so good, and the wedding went well. We were happy and thankful because both her sisters and her brother came to the wedding.

After the wedding we set up a home for the couple and furnished it with necessary things. Rajamma and her husband, Paulraj, have taken upon themselves the responsibility of cleaning the church and arranging the chairs for vespers and the church service. They are paid for their service and, in turn, pay tithe and offerings from that money. They are happy, and we thank the Lord.

Lord, there are so many who are waiting to see the evidence of Christ in our lives. Help us to be faithful in our daily witness. WINIFRED DEVARAJ

Powerlessness

"Not by might nor by power, but by My Spirit," says the Lord of hosts. Zech. 4:6, NKJV.

IT WAS A DREARY, rainy Sabbath morning in early February. As everyone else tried to squeeze in a few more minutes of sleep, I finished my devotions and mentally checked off what needed to be done before Sabbath school. A family breakfast of oatmeal and toast would be first; then the casserole for lunch would need to be placed in the oven and the timer preset. Next Steve would need to "motivate" our boys to look presentable, while I got my shower and blow-dried my hair.

As I reviewed my mental to-do list, I got up and headed into the kitchen. Suddenly there was an incredible flash of lightning with an almost simultaneous earsplitting crack of thunder, and all our lights went out. All was suddenly very quiet. Checking the fuse box revealed no blown fuses, and the nice man on the Florida Power recording said our electricity would be back on in two or three hours. Now what? I stood in the kitchen, holding the pot that was supposed to cook the oatmeal, and glared at the rain. I couldn't cook breakfast, we wouldn't have any prepared food for lunch, my hair wouldn't be presentable. I needed the electricity back on now!

As our boys started to stir in their rooms, I became aware of the sound of the rain. The trees around our house were gently swaying, and raindrops were dancing on our little pond. The world seemed to have slowed down, and I realized that whether I wanted it or not, I had a bit of free time. As I stood looking out the window, I was overwhelmed with the verse "Be still, and know that I am God" (Ps. 46:10). It was Sabbath, and all I had been concerned with were mundane, temporary things, while God had so much more He wanted to share with me.

We ate cold cereal for breakfast and talked about God's incredible love. We all managed to make it through Sabbath school and church without our hair frightening anybody, and nobody starved at lunch. God was in the "quiet," not the "whirlwind," and I had almost missed His voice. I determined to stick closer to Him, where there is real power, never-failing power.

SUSAN WOOLEY

Sing a Song of Joy!

How shall we sing the Lord's song in a strange land? Ps. 137:4.

WHEN MY FAMILY AND I came to the United States in August 2001, we knew that life would be different from life in the islands. We came from the twin islands of Trinidad and Tobago, expecting there would be changes. What we did not expect was September 11 and the adjustment of having to live with terrorists' threats as a part of daily life.

Suddenly life changed, and we neither liked nor welcomed the change. We wanted what we had had before. We longed for those days back home when we only heard about such events happening in some other country, never where we lived. Our lives had been turned upside down. My children wanted to return home, and, secretly, my husband and I felt the same way.

Yet in the midst of all this uncertainty, fear, and feeling of impending doom, we had to keep on living. And not only living, but as Christians we had to live the joyful life. Now I knew how the Israelites felt while sitting by the banks of the river in Babylonian captivity. Their captors must have been crazy to ask them to sing the songs of their homeland. How could they sing these songs of joy and praise in this foreign land of despair and hopelessness?

Each day as you face your struggles and trials, I know that you must ask yourself a similar question. *How can I sing the song of joy and praise to God when life is filled with despair and sadness? How can I sing when my heart is heavy with the sadness of failed dreams and past hurts, and there seems to be no hope for the future?*

But that's where you are wrong. One thing we do have is hope for the future. Peter reminds us that God has "begotten us again to a living hope through the resurrection of Jesus Christ from the dead" (1 Peter 1:3, NKJV). Now, that is something to sing about! God reminds us through these wonderful words of hope that even though life on this earth may be filled with uncertainty and fear, there is always hope for the future. Hope that we will survive these trying times. Hope that we can have the assurance of salvation. Hope that eternal life is assured for all who know Jesus as their Savior. And hope that one day life on this earth will end and new life will be ours—a life with no sadness, no sickness, no pain, no sorrow. That's hope.

So don't despair; you have hope. Living hope. Now, that's something to sing about!

HEATHER-DAWN SMALL

God's Little Promises

And so, Lord, where do I put my hope? My only hope is in you. Ps. 39:7, NLT.

WE HAD BEEN HAVING A lot of fun in the women's ministries tent during the seminar I was presenting on how to deal with anger. Each woman had been given an envelope that contained a balloon. I explained that the balloon represented the person, and that we were going to have a party. We all had a bit of a giggle as we looked at the beautiful bright colors of our personalities. But a balloon does not reach its full potential until it is inflated, and we were going to blow up our balloons.

First, however, there were very tiny pieces of paper in each envelope. These nine little papers had a variety of words written on them: "hope," "hurt," "love," "joy," "anger," etc. The women were instructed to insert these papers into their balloon, because this would more closely represent them as people. Then we would all inflate our balloons and tie them off.

The happy chatter turned to sounds of profound blowing as the balloons were inflated. As we waved our balloons in the air, there was a real party atmosphere. I spoiled all this by announcing that our team leaders were going to hand out dressmaking pins and, on the count of three, we would all pretend to be very angry and burst the balloons with our pins.

The laughter became a bit hysterical as the bursting took place. We held up what was left of our balloons; they didn't look very beautiful in their ragged, deflated state. We reflected that this is what we are like when we burst with anger, sending feelings flying all over the place.

After the seminar one dear person came to me and said that something had happened to her. I knew that she was facing a traumatic situation because we had discussed it previously. She told me that after her balloon had burst and she sat listening to me talk, she noticed a little piece of paper on her lap. When she picked it up and turned it over, she read the word "hope." She was quite sure that this was God's message to her. I was in awe as we hugged.

About 15 minutes later another woman came to talk with me and breathlessly recounted how she had found two little pieces of paper on her lap. She said that as she turned them over, "joy" and "peace" seemed to be God's words to her for her special encouragement. Ah, what an amazing God we serve, whose plans are far greater than ours! URSULA M. HEDGES

Lost!

They should always pray and not give up. Luke 18:1, NIV.

I DROVE HOME, WENT TO my office, curled up in the chair, and put my head in my hands. My friends had trusted me. I had let them down.

They were on vacation, and I had volunteered to feed Prince, their Shetland sheepdog. I remembered locking the gate behind me when I walked out of their backyard the evening before. Now it was open, and Prince was gone. In one week they'd be home. I had to tell them their elegant little dog with the collie face would not be there. Prince was lost.

Where do I go from here? I wondered. I pasted "Dog Lost" signs on the telephone poles and put an ad in the newspaper's lost-and-found column. I trudged the neighborhood, knocking on door after door. No one had seen the golden-and-white dog. In desperation I prayed each night that he'd come home, that God would take care of him.

One evening the telephone rang. A man who lived a half mile away had discovered a collar in his front yard. I drove over. It was Prince's collar. This wasn't good news.

My friends came home. I relived the unhappy experience. Again, we knocked on doors and walked the streets.

Suddenly I had an idea. In the newspaper I had said, "Lost sheltie." *Perhaps,* I thought, *most people wouldn't know what a sheltie is.* I ran the ad again, this time saying "Lost little Lassie-like collie." Most people know about the movie dog Lassie. Many have read the children's book *Lassie Come Home,* which tells the story of the collie that traveled hundreds of miles to return home to her young master.

The next day the phone rang. "I think I have your dog," the woman said. "He sure looks like a little collie." Yes, it was Prince! The same day he got out of the yard he had wandered two miles to her home near a busy street. She had found him sitting on the front porch. He was so happy to see us that he wagged all over and lifted an elegant paw to shake hands.

God had answered my prayer the same day I prayed it, but I hadn't known the answer was there. God hears every prayer, but we may not know the answer until later—a lifetime later, or even in heaven.

EDNA MAYE GALLINGTON

Cleaning Agent

Purge me with hyssop, and I shall be clean; wash me, and I shall be whiter than snow. Ps. 51:7, NKJV.

I'VE BEEN DELAYING SURGERY on my right shoulder for months now. Sometimes it seems as though my rotator cuff is healing, and at other times I experience excruciating pain. The idea of surgery is scary. Who wants to have a disability? As a result of my injury, only the bare, minimal cleaning has been done in my home.

Scrubbing left me with such wrenching pain that I was forced to give up my independence and solicit the help of Nicolosa. When I first saw Nicolosa, for a brief moment I wondered about her choice of attire. She was immaculately dressed in a white sweater and pants. After she understood the instructions, however, Nicolosa changed into her cleaning garb. When she was through cleaning and scrubbing the bathrooms and kitchen, they sparkled as if they had just been installed. I was thoroughly satisfied with her service.

While evaluating Nicolosa's work, I started thinking about the spiritual aspects of my life and the cleaning that goes on there. I know there are times I try to do the cleaning myself, but my feeble attempts are useless. There isn't much change. How I hate giving up my independence! But lately I realize that when I submit myself to God, He cleanses me and makes me sparkle even more brightly than my bathroom and kitchen—He makes me brand-new. Like Nicolosa, He doesn't work on every dirty area at the same time, because He knows I would soon become discouraged and give up. Instead, He slowly and painstakingly removes the stains of doubt and fear, the mildew of past hurts and unforgiveness, and the dust of despair. He gives me hope and a future. Sometimes He uses the cleaning agents of disappointment and sorrow to purify me. I must admit that the scrubbing hurts, and sometimes I wish I could avoid it, because at times He has to dig deep to remove those stubborn, sinful habits. I've also learned that complaining doesn't help, but praise and thanksgiving make it easier for me to cope.

I am amazed at what I have become through the entire process, and today I pray for grace to endure the next cleaning. I'm glad He keeps at it until He can see His reflection in me, because I now like what I am becoming.

ANDREA A. BUSSUE

Smiley Faces I Need

Always be joyful. Keep on praying. No matter what happens, always be thankful, for this is God's will for you who belong to Christ Jesus. 1 Thess. 5:16-18, NLT.

TO BE HONEST, I just don't think I'm that smart, and in no way was I prepared for my burden—the responsibility of caring for my severely mentally challenged son. The Lord must be in control of our lives, because I just say, "Jesus, please help me!" I believe He does send His special angels to be with me. He has promised: "For he orders his angels to protect you wherever you go" (Ps. 91:11, NKJV). And again the Lord says, "I will rescue those who love me. I will protect those who trust in my name" (verse 14, NKJV).

What is the good of wisdom if it's not shared? I know what it feels like to be discouraged, so I pray for others who are struggling. In return, I believe that the prayers of others have kept me sane, and that's something to be joyful about. I like to give credit where credit is due.

I believe that my guardian angels select my friends and nurture my relationships. They also provide me with inspirational material to share in the hope of helping others to trust in the Lord. I can't see my guardian angels, but I feel their presence wherever I go. I'm pretty sure that most of the time they're smiling, because Sonny is—and so am I. It delights me to share what I've learned by being Sonny's mommy these 16-plus years. I like to share things with these friends, but my sharing habit requires funding. The Lord provides in various ways, but this one way is very special. More than 10 years ago my husband and I made a decision. We chose to drive small, fuel-efficient cars, and the savings by doing this has greatly supported my sharing habit, which involves *Dimensions of Love,* a journal I love to share. We've owned four Toyotas, and we consider many of the staff at the dealership to be friends. Recently I noticed my Easter sharing letter on the coffee table in the service waiting area, available to the public for reading. My heart almost burst with joy! I've been blessed to share whatever my guardian angels help me to prepare.

As I have shared through my writing, I have also felt the blessing of others praying for me and for my family. I share a blessing, and a blessing is shared with me. I need those smiley faces, and so do you. *Thank You, Lord.*

DEBORAH SANDERS

Lord, Help Me to Remember!

I can do all things through Christ who strengthens me. Phil. 4:13, NKJV.

AS I LOOKED THROUGH the most recent issue of a Christian supply catalog one evening, my eyes fell on a number of little plaques that were very reasonably priced. I thought they might make lovely gifts. One especially attracted my attention with the saying "Lord, help me to remember that nothing is going to happen to me today that You and I together can't handle." It was the greeting of an unnamed preacher to each new day. The longer I looked at it, the more meaningful it seemed, and I decided that I would order a plaque for each graduating senior from the Christian high school where I worked. When I placed the order, I decided also to order one for my home and one for my office at school. It became a great conversation piece, not only for the students and staff but for parents as well, who often mentioned that the message was just what they needed to make it through that day.

The thank-you notes I received from those students caused me to continue to give that same gift each year for the next several years, until the company discontinued making the plaques. Each one met with the same appreciation, but I never had any idea just how meaningful that gift would become to a parent until several years after the graduation of a young man named Dale.

Dale was a scuba diver, and on one of his dives something went wrong and he drowned. It was a horrible shock to all of us, but especially to his dear family. Several months after Dale's death I received a note of gratitude from his parents, not only for the sympathy card I had sent, but for that little plaque I had given Dale for his graduation. They had found that plaque with his other treasures when they were cleaning out his room. It spoke to their hearts through their time of sorrow.

Later, when our house burned to the ground, I was sifting through the ashes. My heart skipped a few beats as I found those two little plaques of mine, scorched but still readable. One now hangs in my bedroom, and one hangs here in my home office.

I have learned how true that saying is. *Lord, help me to remember that nothing is going to happen to me today that You and I together can't handle.*

Anna May Radke Waters

Gift-wrapped Words

Watch the way you talk. . . . Say only what helps, each word a gift. Eph. 4:29, Message.

THE YOUNG MAN ON the doorstep spoke to us gruffly. He was supposed to be welcoming us to his church, but he looked down and shuffled his feet. His words were well rehearsed but somehow flat and meaningless. I guessed he was really quite shy and felt uncomfortable about being the one to greet arriving guests. I smiled at him encouragingly as we shepherded our family through the church doors.

As we sat down, my young daughter turned to me and whispered, "What he just said, well, he tried hard, but it was like giving someone a lovely present in a brown paper bag instead of in pretty paper with a bow on the top."

I thought about what 12-year-old Bethany had said so eloquently, and she was right. I smiled as I thought about how she had expressed herself. Often the simplest gift can be memorable when it has been well presented. I once received a clutch of eggs from a friend who had placed them on a bed of hay in an old basket. She apologized that she didn't have any egg boxes. The little basket looked so adorable. It was a tiny gift, but it was made special by the way it was presented. It was a present I would never forget.

I remember another gift. It was my birthday, and we were living in America, far from home. Life had been a struggle; I had recently miscarried our first child. When I came home from work, there was a handmade cardboard box on my doorstep, decorated with stickers and ribbons. Inside was one doughnut with one birthday candle on it. Beautifully presented, it was a delight, another unforgettable gift. I'm sure I had other gifts for my birthday that cost far more than a doughnut, but 16 years later they are forgotten, and it's only the doughnut that remains, tucked in the tissue paper of my memories.

Our words are special. They can build up or tear down. We can say simple things and package them so that they are beautiful and memorable and encouraging, or we can package our words in brown bags tied with barbed wire, so that they are unattractive or even hurtful.

Father, help me to package the words You give me to say today so that they will encourage others and beautify their lives. Amen. KAREN HOLFORD

The Author of Love

Yea, I have loved thee with an everlasting love: therefore with lovingkindness have I drawn thee. Jer. 31:3.

WE HAD JUST FINISHED morning worship when my 6-year-old grandson, Christopher, said, "Grandma, my birthday will be here in a month; but I am sad because you are going to leave after my birthday and go back to Florida. I will miss you." As we talked, Christopher decided I shouldn't leave until two days after his birthday. Then we agreed we would visit every Friday night by telephone. If one of us wasn't home, we would visit the next day, later in the afternoon. When many miles separate me from my family and friends, how I enjoy phone calls rather than e-mails. I would rather hear their voices than read their messages.

What a joy and blessing to have the love of our children and grandchildren. Then I thought of our heavenly Father, who loves us so much. Do we love Him as we do our earthly family? Just as we look forward to visiting and talking with our children and grandchildren and to sharing our love, how much our heavenly Father longs to be included in our lives. Do we take time to visit with Him and tell Him how much we love Him and miss Him? Are we truly looking forward to His soon coming?

What joy it must bring to Him as we begin and end each day with Him in prayer and reading His Word. How He must miss us when we neglect communing with Him. What an extra delight it must be as we send up little prayers to Him all through the day. In this way we learn to trust Him with our lives, whether things are going smoothly or not.

My prayer is that I will continually show my heavenly Father my love for Him, just as I show my love for my earthly family. Then in the not-too-distant future I will have that privilege of telling Him, face to face, how much I love Him! How He too must long to gather each one of us to Him and show us all the wonderful things He has prepared for us. May each one of us plan for that great reunion on that wonderful day when we will be reunited with loved ones, never to be separated again.

PATRICIA MULRANEY KOVALSKI

A Ziploc Bag of Cheerios

They ate the food of angels! God gave them all they could hold. Ps. 78:25, NLT.

THE ENORMOUS MOVING VAN had just pulled out of my driveway when my little golden-haired neighbor came dashing across the lawn. "Goodbye, Glenda-mae!" She mouthed the words softly, trying not to cry. "This is for you." Reaching behind her, she pulled out all the heavy artillery of her 4-year-old heart—a Ziploc bag of Cheerios.

Trying to hide my own tears, I put her token of love in my purse for safekeeping. Her mother and I understood its significance and were moved. When Lilly and her parents had moved into the house next door, she was barely a year old. Her parents would bring her to visit at least once a week. She was a charmer. Sometimes she would even let me hold her and read to her. Sometimes she would read to me. Her chuckles were my delight.

Early one morning a while ago her mother had called in a panic. "I'm still on duty here at the hospital, and my husband has to leave for work. Can you take care of Lilly for me till I get home?" Minutes later the father gently laid his sleeping baby on my still-unmade bed and sped off.

I worried that the little girl would wake up screaming when she found herself in vaguely unfamiliar surroundings, but she simply smiled when the morning sun kissed her awake. After I lifted her out of bed, we prayed, washed, and went in search of breakfast. She didn't seem to want the orange juice, banana, or yogurt I offered. I opened another cupboard. Her eyes lighted up when she saw the box of Cheerios.

"Bowl," she ordered. I brought a plastic one. "Spoon." Her directions were minimal. "Milk" was her final request. And so our weekly ritual had begun.

Crunching on Lilly's Cheerios on my flight the next day, I thought about a line C. S. Lewis had once penned: "Pure and spontaneous pleasures are 'patches of Godlight' in the woods of our experience" (*Letters to Malcolm: Chiefly on Prayer,* p. 91). I knew I had experienced His light through Lilly that afternoon. For a second I imagined what the children of Israel must have experienced when they first tasted manna. Today's text underlines that experience through David's eyes—food for angels.

What could I do but thank God for showing me through a 4-year-old angel's model of generosity the blessings of giving what brings the most joy!

GLENDA-MAE GREENE

Go Away, Auntie!

As for me, I am in your hands; do with me whatever you think is good and right. Jer. 26:14, NIV.

I LOVE MY 2-YEAR OLD niece, Rezeile. However, because I live and work on another continent, I see her only once or twice a year. This does not enhance a good niece-aunt relationship. Yet there were times I thought she liked me. Whenever I talked to my mother on the phone, Rezeile would take the receiver and talk to me. She would even sing a song or two.

Then my husband and I had an opportunity to stay with them for a few months. The first couple weeks were days of cajoling and sweet-talking Rezeile to like me. I was only remotely successful.

I would have liked to hold her cute little hands and take her for a walk or cradle her and put her to sleep, but she rebuffed me with "Go away, Auntie." I wished to braid and fix her long hair. But as soon as I asked her if I could do it, her answer was "Go away, Auntie." It was a childish rejection, yet it caused me considerable frustration.

Then it was on one of those extraordinary days that it happened! Only Rezeile and I were at home. There was no one else to prepare her food, comb her hair, or walk her to the backyard to feed the chicks. She let me take her by the hand, and we strolled down the lane singing, "Let us go for a walk today." I was having fun!

There are times I refuse to hold on to the hands my heavenly Father extends when He knows I need them. I become self-sufficient or rely more on my own strength. I listen to other people for guidance instead of going into His Word. Yet when all these things don't work, I reluctantly submit to my Father's bidding. In spite of this, He is thrilled by my action and willingly forgives me of my childish stubbornness.

Today, Father, I am in Your hands; do with me whatever You think is good and right. I do love You and want You to know it. It would be so satisfying if You and I could go for a walk today, hand in hand. MERCY M. FERRER

More Than a Guess

But the very hairs of your head are all numbered. Matt. 10:30, NKJV.

I TEACH SECOND GRADE. One of the chapters in the classes's math book introduced the concept of estimating groups of items, such as beans or blocks. We also began learning about the place value of digits. Passing around a bag of small blocks, I asked my class to estimate how many blocks were in the bag. And, I reminded them, an estimate is just a good guess, a "guesstimate." I watched patiently as the bag passed from one small set of hands to another—some students struggling with the temptation to count them. When everyone had finished writing down their estimate and the blocks were poured out and counted, we discovered that there were 103 of them. No one had guessed the exact number, but one student had come close. For second graders, the idea that they weren't right, even though it was just a guess, can be very disappointing. One student tried unsuccessfully to erase her estimate, write in the correct number, and claim that she had made the perfect guess.

Watching this lesson develop, I thought of my heavenly Father, who knows the exact number of hairs on my head. He doesn't have to estimate or guess about how many strands of hair I have. He doesn't have to guess about what's best for me. He always knows. As adults we are sometimes like my second graders. We try to do things our way and are often disappointed when things don't turn out exactly right. However, we can always go to God, trusting Him to know what's best for us. We are incapable, with our finite limitations, of knowing exactly what to do, and we should not let that disappoint us. We must ask God for the spiritual maturity necessary for an abiding faith and confidence in Him.

When we go to God, the guessing element or aspect is more than practically or virtually eliminated. It is totally gone, completely nonexistent—one that we don't even need to factor into our concern. Isn't that wonderful?

Lord, give me the strength to always seek You for all my needs and the wisdom to always trust Your knowledge in guiding my life. SHARON M. THOMAS

God's Creation

God saw every thing that he had made, and, behold, it was very good. Gen. 1:31.

THE WIND IS LOUD and noisy today as I tramp over ice and snow, using a ski pole for balance. Chunks of ice hit the ground like glass shattering, and clumps of snow drop on the road. The sun has come out after more than a day of storminess. We have had snow, ice, sleet, rain, and wind. One can only look with awe at what this conglomeration has produced, and we know that traveling about outside can be a bit uncertain or precarious.

The sun is trying to help us, but we live in a land of many trees here in Maine. It just can't find its way quickly through all the evergreen branches waving high above so that it can melt the ice and snow from our road. I glance down the streets and actually see bare spots on the road where the sun has found an open space to shine. We are patient and know that after a lot of sunshine the earth under the branch's shadows will eventually get warm, and we too will have melted driveways.

I come inside and enjoy my lunch, watching the birds at our feeders. Even Mr. and Mrs. Cardinal have come today, making bright-red splashes on the white snow. I watch my lazy cat stand in front of the glass doors, spying on our contingent of squirrels and chipmunks. They ignore her, even though she seems to be saying, "Why don't you come in where it's very warm? There are even electric blankets my people leave on sometimes." They look at her with no interest and are content in the snow, dressed in their beautiful winter fur coats. The cat quietly leaves, and the next time I see her she is in the bed under the covers, her place on cold days. "Lumping," we call it.

I too yawn and murmur something about a nap in this weather and tiptoe upstairs to join the cat.

Out of that storm came a pristine beauty. Almost everything was covered with ice or snow, all sparkling under the sun like precious jewels scattered abroad. God's nature is so very beautiful, summer or winter. Winter is like a fresh beginning that God gives us with His wonderful grace. The snow is as white as anything can possibly be, and that is the way our heart can be as we accept the offer of forgiveness and repent. Our God is so great, and wherever we live there is beauty He has planned and made for us, His children.

Dessa Weisz Hardin

Night at Nandyal Station

Speak unto the children of Israel, that they go forward. Ex. 14:15.

AROUND MIDNIGHT WE REACHED the station of Nandyal, a small town in a sparsely populated jungle area on the rail line between Bangalore and Vishakhapatnam on the coast of Andhra, India. I awoke when the train halted for its scheduled 10-minute stop. I looked out the window to check where we were, then turned over and went back to sleep.

An hour later I awoke to find we had not moved. *Must be engine trouble,* I thought, and went back to sleep. A couple hours later I awoke again, and still we were in Nandyal. By this time the platform was empty except for some soldiers. I went back to sleep.

By 6:00 a.m. we were still at Nandyal. Unable to sleep longer, I got out my Bible and journal to have my morning devotions. This train trip was a parable of life. The engine for my life's journey is my will. It is my will that pulls me forward or, if it is malfunctioning, allows me to stay put. I jotted down the many things that can halt us in our desire to move forward in our life's journey: death of a loved one, disappointment in a relationship, ill health, criticism of others, natural disasters, financial setbacks, or failure at work.

As I sat there at the Nandyal station, the lesson seemed so clear to me that something needed to be done about the engine. It is our choice to hook up the engine of our will and to choose to move forward. Many stops in life are inevitable, but we don't have to stay put. By God's grace He can help us to choose to move forward.

About that point in my meditation the train indeed began to inch forward. It was only as we neared the next station that the news came that it was not engine trouble at all. Extremists of the People's War Group had blown up the engine of a goods train and a building of the railway station in the next town. That's why the soldiers were there all night protecting our train! That's why the delay. It wasn't the fault of our engine at all. The way wasn't clear, but now it was, and we could move forward.

Sometimes we have to wait awhile, but sooner or later God will say to us, as He did to Moses at the Red Sea, "It's OK now. The way is clear. Start your engine. Move forward." DOROTHY EATON WATTS

Unity in Diversity

How good and pleasant it is for God's people to live together in unity! Ps. 133:1, Clear Word.

THEY CAME FROM VERY different worlds, even though both had been born in the United States. He was the youngest of a blended family of 19 children. She was the third child and first girl of six children. His mother had died when he was only 14, and his father had ruled the family with an iron hand. Her father had left the home (never to return) when she was 5 years old, and her single mother had struggled to keep her family together.

They met in their late teens when both were students at the same school. He was attracted to her because of her work ethic and frugal ways. She had hoped to continue her studies and perhaps become a nurse or even a doctor. However, they joined their lives in marriage when she was only 18, ending her formal education. They had a good foundation because they were united in their love for God and their determination to serve Him wherever He would lead.

Four children came to bless their home. He continued his college education while she cared for the family and struggled with poor health. This was during the Depression years, and the pressure of supporting a family became too much. Just short of receiving a college degree, he discontinued his studies. Music was very important in their lives, and she often sang while going about her household duties. He gave organ and piano lessons.

She was a gourmet cook and never missed a chance to attend a cooking class to brush up on her skills, sharing food with family and friends. Sometimes he would disappear into the garden or the basement while she enjoyed entertaining the guests.

Travel was one of her great joys, especially during her later years. Sometimes she would leave her sickbed when she heard of an upcoming trip; it seemed to be healing for her.

During their last few years she was completely blind and he was very deaf, but they were devoted to each other through more than 74 years. I married their second son, and for almost 40 years I observed this couple.

Thank You, Father, for this living example of unity in diversity. Teach us to be loving and accepting of others, even when they are different from us.

BETTY J. ADAMS

Unseen Wounds

Jesus answered them, "It is not the healthy who need a doctor, but the sick." Luke 5:31, NIV.

IN MY DEPARTMENT AT the library, people are always hurting their hands. We put metal strips in the spines when preparing the books to go on the library shelves. The strips will set off our security alarm if someone tries to steal a book. They're sharp, and it's easy to cut oneself on them.

When I was doing a computer check on some books that a coworker had processed, I wasn't surprised when I noticed blood on a couple books. It got all over my hands, and I washed the book covers and disinfected my hands. I thought the problem was solved.

As I returned the books to the woman who had processed them, I noticed more blood on the book backs. I washed the books and my hands again. "Did you cut yourself when you were putting the strips in?" I asked her. "I keep getting blood on the books, and I don't know where it's coming from."

She did a quick inspection of her hands, but she wasn't cut. Then when she examined my hands, she found the problem—a tiny puncture wound on one of my fingertips that was bleeding.

The wound was so small that I hadn't felt it and couldn't even see it, yet it yielded quite a bit of blood before I found it and applied pressure to make it stop. If I had realized sooner that I was hurt, there wouldn't have been such a mess to clean up.

It's easy enough for me to call on the Lord in times of trouble. Even people who have never set foot inside a church suddenly start praying when a loved one is ill or dying. When things get out of control, when we feel helpless to solve a problem, turning to a higher power comes naturally.

But when things are going great, when the sun is shining and all's right with the world, we may not even realize that we are quietly bleeding from unseen wounds. My need for God is constant, in good times and bad. He knows what I'm going through. He is the Great Physician who can heal all the hurts that other people can't even see. Recognizing my own needs is a first step toward becoming all that I can be. GINA LEE

Now Is the Time

It is time to seek the Lord. Hosea 10:12, NIV.

BUT I DON'T WANT to do it now!" Melissa was sprawled on the sofa, a toothpick between two teeth. She stroked the cat rather diffidently. "I can write the report later. I've got puh-LEN-ty of time." (My young friend dragged the word out.)

At her age we all thought we had plenty of time. Now we wonder how it went by so quickly. Aloud I said, "Today you were given 86,400 seconds." Her eyes turned to look at me, interested but noncommittal. "How many of those do you have left before bedtime?" I continued. I could almost see the wheels of her mind doing cartwheels. Melissa hit the floor running and headed for the calculator.

The sound of her voice was punctuated by the occasional whirring of the machine. "If I count from midnight to midnight—and bedtime is 10:00—that leaves two hours' worth. And . . . I have 7,200 seconds left today," she sang out, obviously pleased with her problem-solving ability.

How could I explain the principle of first things first, of not putting off until tomorrow what can be done today? "How much of your report can be completed in 7,000 seconds?" I asked.

More whirring of the calculator, although I had no idea what numbers she was punching in. Melissa came into the kitchen and draped her growing self over the high stool. "Probably half of it," she responded honestly. "So," she continued mischievously, "I'm waiting for you to point out that some more interesting opportunity might pop up in the next day or two, and if half of my paper is finished, I might be able to take advantage . . ."

Her voice trailed off as I burst out laughing. Melissa headed for the study. Smiling. She'd figured it out all by herself and made her decision.

I sank down on the couch, reached for a magazine—then changed my mind. There were a couple things I needed to do now. And at least one of them involved my spiritual life.

"But seek first his kingdom and his righteousness, and all these things will be given to you as well. Therefore do not worry about tomorrow, for tomorrow will worry about itself. Each day has enough trouble of its own" (Matt. 6:33, 34, NIV).

ARLENE TAYLOR

Looks Can Deceive

And Jesus answered and said unto them, "Take heed that no man deceive you." Matt. 24:4.

WHILE I WAS VISITING a very dear friend who was very ill at home, I noticed a leaf from a beautiful schefflera plant on the floor. The leaf appeared as though it had potential for growth, as it still looked very green.

All of a sudden I had a liking for the schefflera plant and wanted one. With this desire in mind I decided to take the leaf home and plant it, hoping that someday I'd have a plant. Without a second thought I made my way to the leaf.

I had a wake-up call when I picked up the leaf and felt it. It was artificial! That potent-looking leaf was hard, green plastic; and, of course, so was the plant. I couldn't believe my sense of touch, because the leaf looked so real. The thought of having a schefflera plant vanished from my mind completely.

I told my friend what I had planned to do with the leaf and how disappointed I was. She looked at me and simply smiled.

That experience taught me an important lesson: It is not always sensible to want what other people have, because what seems so real might be fake.

Many of us have a habit of wanting things that other people have, because we like what we see. Often we want things we really don't need, but we act as though we can't do without them.

We want the same style of clothes that other people wear and the same kind of food that they eat. And you know what else some of us want? We want the same kind of music that they sing and the same houses, cars, furniture, clothes—and plants.

We must be very cautious with that habit, because we may be disappointed after we get those things. What's more, God may not want us to have them.

There is an old adage that goes "All that glitters is not gold."

Father God, please cause us to want everything You have because You are real and true. As a matter of fact, You are altogether lovely. CECELIA LEWIS

My Not-Listening Servant

Speak, for your servant is listening. 1 Sam. 3:10, NIV.

OH, LOOK!" I IMAGINE God pointing to a dot on the universe map. The angels in heaven draw near to see what He is so closely observing.

"Sally j. said her prayers, and we were about to talk, but she rushed off to live her life without hearing My part of the conversation. When I answered, wanting so much to give her advice, she was listening to the radio. Sometimes the noise is too loud," He says. The crowd grows quiet as He speaks, waiting for His next words.

"She thought she heard Me, but it was a song, telling her to go her own way."

The heavenly cherubs shake their heads. They know God's voice so intimately, so "heart-known," that signals are never mixed, messages never missed.

"Later I spoke again when I hoped she would be willing to hear, but she is so worried about her daughter's school play that I didn't get through."

The listeners exchange knowing glances, communicating without words.

"This servant of Mine, Sally, has much love, but needs guidance. She depends on a daily list she makes without consulting Me. I could save her time and energy." His loving voice has everyone's attention in heaven, yet somehow this one puny human has endeared herself to His heart in such a sweet way.

"She's so into her family. She loves them very much. All her hopes are for her children to love Me," He tells them, "and to have them live their lives as I guide." He's quiet as the angels consider her conflicting actions.

"Isn't that just like a . . . a . . ." He trails off like someone searching for the right words to speak.

A cherub rushing by with a playful puppy chips in her two cents' worth: "A single mom?"

God smiles. His love emanates throughout heaven, right down to Small Town, Planet Earth, and into Sally's heart. Sally J. Aken-Linke

Face to Face

Then we shall see face to face. 1 Cor. 13:12, NIV.

AS JIM MATHER SLUMPED listlessly into a chair in my office, I scanned his record and noted that he was experiencing multiple, varying, and rather undefined ailments, some indicative of depression. And he did look downcast and distressed as I inquired regarding his well-being.

"Well, ah da' know," he mumbled almost sullenly. He launched into the disgust and pain he felt over disturbing and destructive incidents occurring regularly in our area. "Can't make much sense of it," he muttered. "Da' know what ta make of it. 'Fraid it'll only get worse."

"Do you think this may be telling us something, Jim?" I asked. I continued by saying that before Jesus comes again there will be trouble on this earth, but in the middle of my sentence Jim interrupted with "Sometimes I wonder if He isn't here now."

I responded by saying that Jesus told us He will come and every eye will see Him.

"See Him? H'mmm," Jim mused. "Actually see Him?"

While completing my work I assured Jim that Scripture says, Yes, Jesus will come, and we will see Him face to face. Then I asked him what he thought it would be like to look into Jesus' face.

"Ya actually think face to face?" Jim queried. "Face to face! That's somethin' I need to be thinkin' 'bout." Jim's face seemed to have softened a bit to radiate some warmth and enthusiasm. He rose to leave, grasped my hand, and exclaimed, "Face to face! Thank you. This is a good day, a wonderful day!"

For Jim and for me, this indeed was a good day. What will Jesus' face be like? The disciples viewed it at the Transfiguration (Matt. 17:2). It shone as the sun! Daniel envisioned it (Dan. 10:6, NIV) and said it was like lightning, with "eyes like flaming torches." Jacob saw God face to face, and his life was preserved (Gen. 32:30).

Scripture and my feeble imagination provide me with a picture of a face from which emanates warmth, comfort, hospitality, and selfless love. It is alert and active and invigorating— He is the Creator. My most delightful picture is that of a face glowing with indescribable joy when sin, sorrow, and death are forever banished from the universe.

To see Jesus face to face! The glorious acquisition of eternal joy!

LOIS E. JOHANNES

A Single Woman's Prayer

I will instruct thee and teach thee in the way which thou shalt go: I will guide thee with mine eye. Ps. 32:8.

ALL RIGHT, LORD, HAVE it Your way! For years I've prayed to meet the right companion. But Your plan for me is to remain single and be a career woman, right? If that's Your will for my life, I'll accept it and be content."

After that prayer I asked the Lord's help to remain cheerful and happy in my singleness. I ceased praying for a companion and reconciled my thinking to remaining alone for the rest of my life. Yes, I dated a few men, but none of them seemed my type or suited me. Once I realized the fact that God's plan for my life was to be a career woman and not a homemaker and mother, I faced each day convinced that I'd remain alone, and I was determined to do my best.

However, God had another plan—a surprise! God's timing isn't always our timing. When His timing was right, a coworker introduced me to her former roommate during a trip we were both taking to the Holy Land. After arriving home, this new friend and I kept in touch. She invited me to her home one weekend. Conveniently, she also invited a certain young man and introduced us. We enjoyed dinner together as we visited. After conversing with this young man, who was near my age, I discovered that we came from similar cultural backgrounds. We continued dating and found that our likes, dislikes, and values were alike in most cases.

After we had dated for several months, he asked me, "How would you like to plan a wedding during Christmas vacation?"

I thought a moment and said, "Probably Thanksgiving would be better. November is less likely to have snow and icy roads than December. That would make my move to your home less difficult, don't you think?"

Since my husband-to-be was a teacher, Christmas or Thanksgiving vacations were the only options for a wedding during the school year. We agreed that Thanksgiving Day would be best for our wedding. As of this writing, we have enjoyed nearly 33 years of togetherness.

Thank You, Lord, for always guiding, directing, and teaching me to fully trust Your leading in my life. Please help each reader to find that same assurance, that total peace in You.

NATHALIE LADNER-BISCHOFF

Journey to a Strange Land

For God did not give us a spirit of timidity, but a spirit of power, of love and of self-discipline. 2 Tim. 1:7, NIV.

I HAD BRAVELY DARED TO take the trip alone. The other missionaries who were staying where I was on this short vacation would go later, but I was eager to see what I had come for while I had the time.

With prayers for safety, I boarded the local minibus with all the local passengers. The driver let me sit in the front to take pictures with my small camera. His kindness made me feel safer. The people seemed friendly. I had a card of introduction to the place where I would stay. It was for my safety and comfort, and I was welcomed kindly.

I set out to walk the trails in the first village. I had been told to buy one of their beautiful caps, usually handmade by the local women. So when I came upon a small shop, I bought one and joyfully wore it on the trail.

I was greeted by friendly people all along the way; it is not very often that they see an American! A group of five women came toward me, all wearing their colorful handmade caps. They stopped, looked at me, and smiled, talking among themselves, motioning to me about the cap I was wearing, and shaking their heads no. I took the cap off to study it, whereupon they each, in turn, tried their own cap on me and stood back for approval from their group.

Finally they all agreed upon the best one for me and motioned that it was mine. I was amazed and offered them the one I had purchased, but they shook their heads. They didn't want it because it was poorly made! Laughing, we all enjoyed the moment of understanding as they waved goodbye and went on their way.

I happily admired my lovely handmade Hunza cap with its brightly multicolored tiny stitches of hearts and flowers so closely covering the round pillbox cap. I still have it.

I learned to love those people in one short day, and all my fears and anxieties melted away. I carried away many precious memories from Hunza, including an assurance of God's care and the fearless love of simple rural people in a faraway place who share God's love.

Dear Lord, keep us humble, sharing Your love without fear.

BESSIE SIEMENS LOBSIEN

My First Encounter With a Deer

The angel of the Lord encampeth round about them that fear him, and delivereth them. Ps. 34:7.

IT WAS A GORGEOUS DAY for the winter season. As I walked out of the office to my car, a warm, gentle breeze blew on my face; it felt refreshing after being cooped up in my office for 10 hours. I relished every moment of that rare winter day.

Because of the nice weather, I decided to do my grocery shopping that evening. I got in my car and headed for the store. By now it was getting darker, and as I happily drove down a main road, I suddenly saw a deer dart in front of my car. In a split second another deer followed the first one. I was going at least 40 miles an hour, so I couldn't brake in time. I heard a big bang on the front side of my car and I knew that I had hit the deer and that my car would be dented. I immediately looked in the rearview mirror to see if the deer was lying on the road, but there was no sign of any deer.

Although I was shaken, I kept driving, praying that my car would not break down. As soon as I pulled into the grocery store parking lot, I got out and checked the front of my car, expecting to see a big dent. I praised God when I saw that there was not even a scratch! I knew my God had sent His angel to protect me and my car from that deer.

I've heard of many deer incidents that have caused a lot of car damage, and even bodily injuries. There is no way we can be prepared for a deer, because it can unexpectedly dart in front of the car. Our only security is in our heavenly Father.

I always pray before I start driving, and this has become a habit with my family. We always thank God when we reach home safely. God has given us the assurance of sending His angels to protect us at all times. I am reminded of today's text. We can always know that God is taking care of us, no matter what happens.

Father in heaven, who sends the angels who surround us, You have delivered me. I thank You. Guide and bless each of us this day; this is a day of promise, but we don't know what may cross our path. Please stay close beside me.

Stella Thomas

In the Midst of the Storm

So do not fear, for I am with you; do not be dismayed, for I am your God. I will strengthen you and help you; I will uphold you with my righteous right hand. Isa. 41:10, NIV.

I WILL NEVER FORGET THE CALL. I had been waiting for it all day. So when the nurse on the phone asked if there was someone who could sit with me when she told me her news, I knew my worst fears had been realized. The lower half of my body went numb as she talked.

I dialed my nurse-husband's number. "Honey, the test results are in. I have breast cancer. Stage 2. Will talk to you later. 'Bye." I could say no more.

The storm clouds billowed. A lumpectomy and a mastectomy followed. The cancer cells had spread to my lymph nodes. But the waves got rougher as I faced the next phase—chemotherapy. It turned my life upside down for six weeks. And that is where, in the eye of my storm, I met my Best Friend. When hunger, weakness, and nausea seemed to overwhelm, I could feel His arms around me and hear Him whisper, "This is just a test. Everything will be all right. I will walk beside you."

A church sister went with me to a breast cancer survivors' support group. I learned there that I was not alone. The women were gentle, but I did not return. The reports of the devastation they were experiencing at home—unfaithfulness, divorce, domestic abuse, unruly children—were as toxic as any of my medicines. My situation was so different at home. My husband of 17 years was very supportive, a true testimony to our marriage vow of togetherness "in sickness and in health." And I had a Best Friend.

But my story does not end there. Four years later there was an unbearable pain in my chest. Had the cancer metastasized? I needed to know. I learned instead that I had been put on the wrong medicine. Now I had both congestive heart failure and diabetes. I was petrified by the thought of diabetes, the illness that had stolen my mother's sight. I could only pray, "Lord, if this is what it takes to bring me closer to You, give me the strength."

With a new wellness regimen, I focused on staying worry-free, eating right, and walking and praying with my Best Friend for an hour each morning. Four months later I had a CT scan. There was no problem. There was rejoicing throughout my praying community. We had braved the storm with my Best Friend at my side!

MONICA JACKSON

He Is My Refuge

Though I walk through the valley of the shadow of death, I fear no evil; for thou art with me. Ps. 23:4, RSV.

I KNOW WHAT IT IS to be depressed, the gut-wrenching kind in which symptoms are so numerous and severe that you're afraid you're going to die—then almost hope you will.

I was 42 years old when I experienced those first panic attacks. Thinking it was the aftermath of the hysterectomy I'd had at age 37, I returned to my gynecologist, who put me on a program of hormones and nerve pills. But my health continued to deteriorate, until I finally hit rock bottom and wavered in that limbo for nearly 10 years. During this time I was unable to shop in malls or supermarkets, and getting caught in a traffic jam nearly sent me over the edge.

In time I became housebound. No one could come to my home, not even my own children; nor could I travel the few miles to visit them. When some friends dropped by one evening, I hurried out the back door as they came in the front. I could not even tolerate my two young grandchildren, whom I adored. When they came one day, I fled to find refuge by curling up in a ball in a corner of a small cabin we had on our farm.

I would have given almost anything for a good night's rest; instead, I walked the floor, night after night, or sat in darkness in my chair. Realizing that life was hardly worth living as it was but not ever considering an alternative, I dismissed my doctor and clung to the Lord, the Great Physician.

I picked out special Bible verses that I repeated again and again. The Lord's Prayer and Psalm 91 were among my favorites; they became my hope and stay.

Then I discovered that I had a chemical imbalance, precipitated by an extreme diet I'd been on for many months. When I experienced the signs of anorexia and was unable to eat, I called out to the Lord and He heard my cry. With a new diet (this time not to lose weight but to rebuild my sick body) minus all the sugar and sugar foods I'd consumed for so long, I gradually became a new person. Today I'm in better physical and emotional health than when I was ages 42 to 52, and I give God the glory.

"It is good for me that I have been afflicted; that I might learn thy statutes" (Ps. 119:71).

Clareen Colclesser

The Matching Rugs

In all your ways acknowledge Him, and He shall direct your paths. Prov. 3:6, NKJV.

MY DEAR FRIEND ETTA had been living with her parents in their home until they passed away. It was a very humble little home, but everyone was welcome there, and she usually had many guests on Sabbath, even if there was just a pot of beans to share. Everyone in her little country town was somehow affected by her love.

Now Etta was alone and on a fixed income with nothing for frills. Not only was Etta on a fixed income; she had osteoporosis, so she was not physically able to do many things. The old house needed fixing up, but there were no funds. Etta's church family put their heads together and decided something must be done.

One day Etta decided to visit her daughter in a neighboring state, and that's when her church family went to work. They painted her little house, inside and out; fixed the floors; and totally remodeled her kitchen with brand-new cabinets, new Formica countertops, and new vinyl flooring. There was a winter's worth of wood for her wood-burning stove, all cut and stored in the woodshed, and all of her garden had been harvested and placed in her food cellar. When Etta came home, she was totally shocked.

I happened to call her that evening from 400 miles away, and she told me all about it. I was so excited, we just rejoiced together. Then I said, "Only one thing bothers me. I wish I could have been a part of this. I feel so left out." I asked, "Do you have any little throw rugs for your kitchen?" She assured me that she didn't but that two would be nice—one by the door and another by the sink. So I told her that I needed to know her colors and that I was going to get those rugs for her.

Instead of telling me what colors she had, she giggled and said, "I am not going to tell you my colors. I am just going to let the Lord guide you in the purchase of these rugs, and I know they will be perfect." I was a little intimidated by that, but sure enough, when I went shopping I was totally impressed to buy two certain rugs, which I promptly mailed to her.

When I heard from her, all she said was "They are perfect." God did show me which ones to buy. Praise His Name! He cares about every little thing that concerns us.

ANNA MAY RADKE WATERS

We Are Safe in His Hands

My sheep hear my voice, and I know them, and they follow me: and I give unto them eternal life; and they shall never perish, neither shall any man pluck them out of my hand. My Father, which gave them me, is greater than all; and no man is able to pluck them out of my Father's hand. John 10:27-29.

DEAR JESUS, WE ARE so sorry that we weren't able to have worship this morning, but I'm glad that You will still receive us. Please keep us in Your hands today, for whatever is in Your hands is safe from all harm." As I concluded the prayer in the car, I fastened the seat belt, backed down the driveway, and went on my way with my two teenage children. I was taking my son, Deneil, to high school classes, and my daughter, Deidre, to university classes at the university where I work. After driving for about three minutes, we heard a very loud and frightening shattering sound as I passed a car going in the opposite direction. I knew something had happened but didn't know what it was. I stopped, and so did the other car.

As the other car backed toward me, I noticed that one of my side mirrors was missing. The holder for the mirror was still in place, but the mirror was gone. Right away I concluded that the other car's side mirror must have hit mine, and it must have fallen and broken on the road.

When the other driver finally reached me, he explained that in his effort not to hit two pedestrians, he seemed to have moved over too much to my side of the road. I told him that I was glad he hadn't hit the pedestrians and that he shouldn't worry about my mirror. I would get myself another one. We parted peacefully.

As I prepared to drive on, my daughter glanced down and said, "Mom, your mirror is right here at my feet." I could not believe it. My car is a small two-door vehicle. That mirror had flown past my son in the front seat and fallen at my daughter's feet in the back seat; it was not broken, chipped, or scratched; nor had that flying mirror hurt either of my precious children.

I pulled off the road, stopped the car, and thanked God for keeping us in His hands. Whatever is in God's hands is safe indeed.

JACKIE HOPE HOSHING-CLARKE

The Missed Train

Behold, I come quickly: blessed is he that keepeth the sayings of the prophecy of this book. Rev. 22:7.

WE DROVE TO THE STATION where we take the train to work every morning. When we parked, the time on the car radio read 6:52. I knew the clock was two minutes fast, so I said to my husband, "It is really 6:50."

Since the train arrives and we board at exactly 6:55 every morning, I calculated that I had five minutes—two minutes to stop by the restroom, one minute to slide my transit card through the turnstile, and two leisurely minutes to wait for the train.

After attending to my physical needs, I leisurely walked to the turnstile. Then I stopped and stared. The train was in the station, closing its doors and beginning to pull out. It was leaving me!

What had happened? I had calculated my strategy down to the minute. Evidently this train had come early the one morning that I needed it to stick to its schedule. Because of the change, I was left behind.

As I passed through the turnstile and slowly walked down the corridor to wait for the next train, I began to speak to myself aloud. "That is the same way it is going to be when the Son of man appears in the clouds," I mused.

Some of us have waited and waited so very long that we think that we have time. We think we have the events all calculated out, but "in such an hour as ye think not the Son of man cometh" (Matt. 24:44). We could be surprised and unprepared.

O Lord, this experience has been a sobering lesson to me this morning. I have to stay ready and prepared at all times. I can't afford to miss the "heavenly train."

"But the day of the Lord will come as a thief in the night; in the which the heavens shall pass away with a great noise, and the elements shall melt with fervent heat, the earth also and the works that are therein shall be burned up. Seeing then that all these things shall be dissolved, what manner of persons ought ye to be in all holy conversation and godliness?" (2 Peter 3:10, 11).

DARLEEN E. SIMMONDS

Alex's Choice

Choose for yourselves this day whom you will serve. . . . But as for me and my house, we will serve the Lord. Joshua 24:15, NKJV.

OUR 8-YEAR-OLD GRANDSON, Alex, likes few things better than spending a weekend at his dad's home on the west coast of Florida. His other set of grandparents, with whom Alex resides, live in the center of the state, with no place to fish close by. At his dad's he can toss in a fishing line from the backyard.

Since I knew this to be true, and knew that his dad is his very favorite person, I was quite surprised recently when he debated whether or not he really wanted to go for a planned visit. He confessed there was a carnival in town, and he really would like to go. When I suggested, "Fine, you can go to your dad's another time," he would not agree to that, either. "I really do want to see my dad, but I want to go to the carnival, also," he said.

Finally, when I needed to elicit a reply, I asked, "Which is more important to you, seeing your dad or going to the carnival?"

He immediately replied, "Seeing my dad."

Grandma Dot said, "So there's your answer—Grandpa and I will take you over to your dad's." Indecision over, happiness reigned.

Alex's dilemma is not unlike ours. Of course we wish to be with our heavenly Father for always, but sometimes we have trouble making choices. We know a certain course of action or chosen activity could lead away from our Father. Yet we vacillate. We might say, "This one time it will be OK." Or "It really isn't that bad." Or even "Everyone else is doing it." We determine that nothing will come between us and our Father, or we toy with the world's allurements until we lose our interest in spiritual things.

One of my favorite authors, Ellen G. White, says in *The Ministry of Healing:* "God has given us the power of choice; it is ours to exercise. We cannot change our hearts, we cannot control our thoughts, our impulses, our affections. . . . But we can choose to serve God, we can give Him our will; then He will work in us to will and to do according to His good pleasure. Thus our whole nature will be brought under the control of Christ" (p. 176).

DOROTHY WAINWRIGHT CAREY

Lunch Table Lessons

In every thing give thanks: for this is the will of God in Christ Jesus concerning you. 1 Thess. 5:18.

AS I HAD LUNCH one day with friends, we talked and laughed a lot about ourselves and how the years had changed us and our outlook on life. Just before leaving, one of them said that her children had come to visit and cooked a birthday dinner for her. After the dinner they sat around her and asked what she had learned during her 50-plus years. She said it ended up as a praise session on how the Lord had blessed her.

I thought about what I learned in my 63 years. I can say I've learned a lot. My lessons have included academics and areas in the physical, social, religious, economic, and family arenas, but I would rather focus on Jesus and how He has blessed me. Jesus loves me with an unconditional, everlasting love. He went to Calvary just for me. Jesus can solve any problem I have. He knows what is best for me. Even when I don't thank Him, He continues to bless me. If I fail to ask, He forgives. When I promise and default, He gives me another chance. He surprises me in ways I would never think of. Each day that I awaken is a testimony to His blessings. I'm able to read my devotionals and Bible and study my lessons. I am able to attend church as a free citizen.

I have never been hungry, naked, or homeless. And God has blessed me to do those things that I enjoy. Except for a few "intellectual interludes," which many of us have, I still have a good mind. My only son is self-sufficient. My 87-year-old mother still recognizes me. My aunt, almost 100 years old, who still recognizes my voice, can hold a good conversation with me. I'm still enjoying marriage after more than 43 years with my husband. My in-laws, aunts, nephews, nieces, cousins, and godchildren all show their love to me in various ways. I am blessed to have friends so very dear. They are my sisters who have shared life's problems, sorrows, and joys with me. They are here when I need them.

If Jesus can give me all these things—and even more—there is no doubt that He loves me. So I will show my love to Him through my daily life, giving back to others some of the blessings I have received. One of the most profound lessons I have learned is this: I'm still here because God isn't finished with me yet. I can never love Him as He loves me.

Marie H. Seard

Family Resemblance

So God created man in his own image, in the image of God he created him; male and female he created them. Gen. 1:27, NIV.

I JUST VISITED THE TWO youngest members of my church family, Joshua and Hannah Ashley, fraternal twins. They're only 3 months old, but already they have grown so much since I first saw them in the hospital when they were just 24 hours old. The twins were the tiniest, most precious little people I had ever seen in my life.

It's been so neat to watch their progress over the past three months. Little arms and legs getting plumper and stronger. Facial features and expressions becoming more defined. Little eyes that seem to be able to focus on you more and more. I'm sure Hannah deliberately turned her eyes toward me when I was holding her and talking to her this morning. Six weeks ago I'd spent some time with them. The following weekend their parents brought them to church for the first time. When I picked Hannah up and spoke to her, her eyes flew open. Her mom thought she recognized my voice. The possibility of that actually being true at 2 months of age and after just a few hours of interaction gave me a huge lump in my throat.

They've recently started smiling, and today, when I was talking to Joshua, he had the hiccups. He'd hiccup, then smile; hiccup, then another sweet smile. It was so cute that he totally captivated his parents and me for several minutes.

While driving home, I reflected on the wonder of it all. Their mom, Joelle, has told me some of the ways Joshua and Hannah are different from each other, even though they're twins. It's more than who wears the pink and who gets dressed in blue. For example, it's dainty little Hannah, not her big brother, who lets out a gusty belch when you burp her. And it's Joshua who wakes up and demands to have his diaper changed, while Hannah sleeps blissfully on.

It amazes me how they've been their very own little persons, their own distinct personalities, from the very beginning. It got me to thinking that if God went to all that trouble to make each one of us so totally unique, so special, we really don't have any business trying to be like anybody else. Jesus never followed the crowd—He followed His Father. It seems to me that's what we ought to be doing too.

TOYA MARIE KOCH

Prayer Changes the Face

Then shall ye call upon me, and ye shall go and pray unto me, and I will hearken unto you. Jer. 29:12.

THE DAY BEFORE I was to be baptized I realized that I hadn't told my husband, who didn't share my spiritual beliefs, about my decision. As he was lying in bed reading, I said to him, "I have something important to tell you." I could tell by the look on his face that he expected the worst. I said, "I'll be back in 10 minutes; don't fall asleep." Then I phoned my mother and sister and asked them to be praying nonstop for the next 20 minutes. I told them of my plans to tell my husband of my decision and that I expected a negative, volatile reaction of some sort, judging by his outbursts of rage over the ever-present "paraphernalia," as he called my spiritual books and magazines.

His demeanor was sad and nervous as I sat down on the edge of the bed. "What do you want?" he grouchily asked. As I was explaining what I had decided to do, his face suddenly changed to a real sense of peace, even relief, as though a problem or burden had disappeared, or the "big bomb" was not going off. He actually heaved a sigh of relief and said, "Oh!"

From the time I had reentered the room I had sensed a warm closeness filling the room. The air seemed to contain tiny dust speckles, similar to the effect you get when you look through sun rays. I knew the room was filled with the Holy Spirit, and I felt as though the angels' presence was warming and filling the air.

Through my family's prayers and God's guiding hand, my husband's heart was softened and filled with gentleness and love. He knew nothing of the changes in the room, but I did. It was an amazing phenomenon. In the dictionary it says a phenomenon is a fact or event or circumstance that can be observed, something extraordinary or remarkable.

That is what happened, God. You caused a phenomenal change to take place. I do thank You. That's what prayer can do. You were true to Your Word once again.

VIDELLA MCCLELLAN

My Garden

Show me Your ways, O Lord; teach me Your paths. Lead me in Your truth and teach me, for You are the God of my salvation; on You I wait all the day. Ps. 25:4, 5, NKJV.

GARDENING IS ONE OF my favorite hobbies. I am always excited even thinking about what will become of the new flower or vegetable seeds that I plant. When the tulips or daffodils come out in the spring, I feel elated to behold the beauty that those bulbs bring to the surroundings. The hardship of planting, watering, and weeding are forgotten.

Even though I have many perennial plants in my garden, I have a reserved place for annual flowers because I enjoy the changing flowers and colors, watching the plants grow as I water them day by day. Last year, just before the winter season started, I planted about 250 tulip bulbs, and this spring I am waiting excitedly, wondering how those bulbs will color my garden.

I've learned many lessons in life through my gardening experience. Take weeds, for example. You don't need to take care of them—they flourish wildly without your care. There was one weed that grew robustly by our first-floor bedroom window. I did not pull it because I wanted to know how far it could grow without any care. That little weed surprised me. It grew so tall that it was almost level with the second-floor bedroom window. And it looked healthy and green, even without any water or any care.

Our hearts are our garden. The weeds are the "little" imperfections or "dents" in our lives. The weeds may show up in the way we see others or in the importance we give ourselves. Or they could be the little judgmental attitudes we have, the unwillingness to help others. Maybe it's our indifference and unconcern toward an erring soul. Whatever they are, we need to weed them out, because they can grow and soon they'll be hard for us to control. God is there to help us perfect our character. All we have to do is ask Him.

May our prayer be that of David: "Show me Your ways, O Lord; teach me Your paths. Lead me in Your truth and teach me; for You are the God of my salvation; on You I wait all the day." Jemima D. Orillosa

God Knows

Devoting herself to all kinds of good deeds. 1 Tim. 5:10, NIV.

HAVE YOU EVER HAD that nagging thought that you should do something special for someone? You ask, "Why has the Lord placed this person on my heart today?" That's what happened to me, and it was about a person I hardly knew.

My son, Robby, had just started taking piano lessons a few months before from a woman down our street. After his half hour lesson he was always all smiles, and he had a teacher's note telling me how well he was doing. One Tuesday, however, he came home right away with the message that his piano teacher was sick, really sick.

I knew a little about Jeanne. She worked at an insurance company, was in her late 30s, was married, had a 15-year-old daughter, and was pregnant. I concluded that morning sickness must be getting the best of her. *I'll pray for her,* I thought. But as I prayed, the Lord kept impressing me to make her a get-well gift.

I didn't have many extras in the house. My husband was in between contracts, and we were pinching pennies. However, I found an unused basket and put in a can of soup. The basket sat there for a few more days. Every time I glanced at it, the Lord gave me another idea of what could be placed in it. By the time Tuesday came, it was bursting with surprises—body splash, herbal tea, a prayer book, snowperson note cards, and a get-well card.

Robby was delighted to run this special gift to Jeanne the night of his next lesson. When he returned home, he told me how she had loved the gift and had a note in his folder for me. It read: "That was very nice of you. The basket is lovely. Our family has been going through a lot of hard times right now. Last Tuesday we lost our baby. Then I had surgery on Friday. I'm OK, at least physically. Thanks again for your prayers and thoughts."

I had no idea of the suffering she was going through, but the Lord did. He uses His followers to care for His flock.

Won't you join me in praying, "Lord, use me today"? KAREN PHILLIPS

The Disappointing Towel

"For I know the plans I have for you," declares the Lord, "plans to prosper you and not to harm you, plans to give you hope and a future. Then you will call upon me and come and pray to me, and I will listen to you." Jer. 29:11, 12, NIV.

ON ONE OF MY TRIPS to conduct training for a group of family ministries leaders, I was surprised to find that towels were not provided with our accommodations. So we stopped at a store to pick one up. My favorite brand wasn't available, so I settled for a larger-than-usual bath towel in a lovely shade of pink and for a very reasonable price. After I had my shower that evening, I wrapped it around my body. It was soft and full of promise. But after rubbing it over my body, I was as wet as before! How disappointing! This large, soft towel in my favorite color couldn't fulfill its practical function of soaking up water, something it was expected to do.

I had a dysfunctional towel, looking so beautiful yet totally useless when it came to doing the job for which it was designed. The towel was probably a lot like the salt that Christ talked about in Matthew 5:13-16: "You are the salt of the earth. But if the salt loses its saltiness, how can it be made salty again? It is no longer good for anything, except to be thrown out and trampled by men" (NIV).

The few verses following bring up another analogy of a lamp that is lighted so everyone can benefit from its illumination. Lamps are not lighted to be concealed. Think about function and use. As Christians do we function in the way that we were designed to? Are we willing to submit to being used by the Lord as He desires? Or are we as disappointing as the towel that refuses to soak up any water, the salt that's lost its saltiness, or the light that's hidden from sight?

Christians who serve as ambassadors for Christ need to be presentable and look good from the outside, but that is only one small part. The more important question is the usefulness of each individual. It's only when we're willing to turn our lives over to the Holy Spirit, allowing Him to work through us, that we become efficient witnesses for Him.

At the beginning of every day we would do well to pause for a few moments, before the hustle and bustle begins, to request the Lord to use us as He will so we can be thirsty towels, salty salt, and prominent lights that will shine so that others may see.

SALLY LAM-PHOON

Good Job, 'Lala

Let brotherly love continue. Heb. 13:1.

BARAKA AND MALALA ('LALA), my two youngest grandchildren, are a real source of joy to me. To give their parents a break, we sometimes have them over to spend Saturday night. They are always elated to spend time at Nana and Poppy's house. Baraka, who is 5, is a typical little boy, full of energy. 'Lala, my 2-year-old granddaughter, gives him a run for his money. Even though I'm thoroughly exhausted when they're picked up on Sunday evening, I've enjoyed them so much that I don't mind.

I love the hugs and kisses I get from them, and the many different "Nana, what's . . . ?" and "Nana, let's . . ." They make me feel so special. On their recent visit, before my son-in-law dropped them off, I asked if 'Lala needed to be gotten up to go to the bathroom during the night. He told me that they normally took her before bed and again about 1:00 or 2:00 a.m. After their hugs and kisses and "I love you"s to their father, Stephen was off.

During the next several hours we played, had snacks, and read a bedtime story. Soon they were bathed, in their beds, and settled down. I checked on them, off and on, to make sure they were OK. About 2:00 a.m. I took 'Lala to the bathroom, then back to bed. Then about 8:00 a.m. I took Baraka. As I put him back I whispered for him to be quiet and not wake 'Lala. In the next half hour the house was astir, as my husband had to attend an early meeting at church. I got up to see him off. After breakfast I had planned a trip to the mall with the children so they could ride the carousel and train and visit the pet shop.

Soon after Poppy left, Baraka was at our bedroom door. "Nana, I took 'Lala to the bathroom, and when she finished, I said, 'Good job, 'Lala!' and I put her back in her bed." I commended him enthusiastically for being a good big brother. I was thrilled that he, even at a young age, was taking care of his little sister.

Then I thought of heaven. What a grand get-together it's going to be when Christ gathers His elect from earth! I thought of the Big Brother we have in Jesus, and how He takes care of us. I don't know for sure, but when He returns, even though He has done all the work and made the provisions for our salvation, I believe He's going to shout to us, "Good job!" May we all be ready.

GLORIA J. STELLA FELDER

Comfort in His Words

God is our protection and our strength. He always helps in times of trouble. Ps. 46:1, NCV.

MOM! MOM, YOUR DOCTOR is on the phone," yelled my teenage son from the next room.

I awakened from a light sleep and reached for the receiver. "Yvonne? I apologize for calling you so late, but this is the best time for me to get back to patients." I looked at the clock and realized that it was 10:30 p.m., and then repositioned myself to listen to her next words. "I got your test results back, and your Pap smear was positive. You need to come back right away for further examination and testing."

It was only after she hung up that the depth of her words hit me. *Positive Pap smear? Did she really say positive?* I had never had a positive medical test. In fact, I had never been sick. Now fully awake, my mind shifted in another direction. *What if I have cancer? What will become of my children? What will become of my aging parents?*

I dropped back onto the pillow and shut my eyes, but sleep failed to come. A knock at the door again aroused my thoughts. "Mom, are you all right?" asked my son, Darien. "I couldn't help wondering why your doctor was calling."

I assured him that it was nothing to worry about and asked that he keep me in his prayers. Darien eased out of the room, and again I closed my eyes, hoping to fall sleep. When it was apparent that sleep would not come, I turned on the light and asked the Lord to give me some words of comfort. As I leafed through the Old Testament my fingers immediately rested on the Psalms, where I read Psalm 46:1. Meditating on these words, I closed my eyes and fell into a deep sleep. No matter what the next round of results would bring, I could put my health, teenage children, and aging parents all in His care.

God is indeed a wonderful God! The next round of tests did reveal an abnormality that required some surgery, but things worked out fine. From this small experience I learned one of the best lessons in life. He is truly our protection and strength, and He does indeed help in time of trouble.

Father, thank You. Thank You for always being there for each of us each day. YVONNE LEONARD CURRY

The Pedicure

I will remove the heart of stone from their flesh and give them a heart of flesh. Eze. 11:19, NRSV.

LET ME TELL YOU about my feet. They were covered with a lot of hard skin and calluses, making them rather unsightly. Unfortunately, the worse they got, the more reluctant I was to seek help. But finally I decided to have a pedicure.

To break the ice, I joked to the pedicurist that I don't look after my feet well because I can't reach them! She laughed and replied, "That's why I'm here!" First she soaked my feet in warm softening solution. Then she took my feet in her hands and gently removed all the calluses and the layers of hard skin on the heels. She trimmed and smoothed the sharp edges on my nails that were digging in and hurting me. Finally she massaged my feet with a moisturizing cream. Looking up at me, she smiled. "Does that feel better?"

"Oh, yes!" I responded.

The work of the pedicurist reminds me of the work of Jesus in my life. There have been times of deep turmoil, an inability to cope in certain situations, the need to deal with some very painful memories. But rather than turn to the source of all comfort, I actually neglected Him. I stopped praying and reading the Bible. A hardness developed around my heart. The harder my heart became, the more difficult it was to seek help. As with my feet, I didn't seem able to take care of anything. And then, like the pedicurist, God said to me, "That's what I'm here for. To ease the pain and relieve the pressure." First He immersed me in a softening solution. A verse of Scripture someone read, a line from a hymn, a thought in a sermon, and the softening began. Then He took my heart and gently removed the layers of hardness. He trimmed and smoothed the sharp edges that had been causing me so much pain. He massaged and nourished my soul with the "balm of Gilead" (see Jer. 8:22). Then He asked me, "Does that feel better?"

"Oh, yes!" I exclaimed. The wonderful thing about Jesus is that He is never unreachable. He reaches out with tenderhearted compassion. "I have loved you with an everlasting love; I have drawn you with loving-kindness" (Jer. 31:3, NIV).

VALERIE FIDELIA

Wings Over My Head

Ye have seen . . . how I bare you on eagles' wings, and brought you unto myself. Ex. 19:4.

THE *CHOP-CHOP-CHOP* of yet another helicopter interrupted my concentration. I marveled at how often they passed over our retirement complex. We were new in this quiet town, comprised largely of hospital employees and medical students, with a higher-than-average number of senior citizens. We lived within easy walking distance of three hospitals, which explained the helicopters' frequent trips over us. They were en route to one of the two helipads atop the medical center close by. There white-coated personnel rush gravely ill or injured patients of all ages to a waiting staff inside. I have observed these whirlybirds land atop the medical center, and once I watched one drop down ever so gently on the hospital lawn.

Even as I write, I hear the soft whir of wings above me, and I offer a short prayer. But this has not always been my custom. When we arrived here a few years ago, I viewed these flying objects as unwelcome invaders from outer space. They were not that disturbing, but I was unaccustomed to their sound. Over time, though, I became immune to their sound and scarcely noticed when they flew by.

But one day something spoke to my heart. Perhaps it was the Holy Spirit. I suddenly began to realize the urgency of those wing-topped mercy machines scurrying across the sky. *But for the grace of God,* I thought, *I could be that patient hovering between life and death.* I breathed a prayer on that person's behalf.

Since that day I have vowed to stay tuned to that familiar purring of wings. I stop whatever I'm doing and send a prayer heavenward that the precious cargo within will reach the helipad in time, where the efficient staff of attendants await them. And staying tuned to the sound of those flying helicopters helps keep my own relationship with heaven strong.

One day soon I expect to hear a sound far more beautiful, a sound sure to capture our full attention. It will be the whirring of angel wings, and music surpassing anything our ears have ever heard. Then, joy of all joys, these white-robed angels will transport us—frail, flawed, and hurting humanity—to that glorious living cloud. There our Great Physician will welcome us, and we will forever be made whole. But staying tuned with heaven makes all the difference.

LORRAINE HUDGINS-HIRSCH

A Little Child Shall Lead Them

Unless you change and become like little children, you will never enter the kingdom of heaven. Matt. 18:3, NIV.

OUR YOUNGER SON AND his wife and two daughters, ages 5 and 1, came to live with us for almost a year. Sarah, the older child, often accompanied us on our walks. She had lived most of her life in the city, so we took her on walks into the nearby countryside. On one occasion we stopped to watch a big green frog in the grass. It looked at us; then, with a mighty leap, it was gone. Sarah was so excited to see this. Another day we visited a nearby creek and saw the salmon jumping their way up to their spawning ground. We were able to explain to Sarah the life cycle of the salmon. Her excitement was intense, and she couldn't wait to get home to tell her parents what she had seen. The red-winged blackbirds and the robins in the park were equally important to Sarah, and she always wanted to rush home and tell someone about what she had seen. Her enthusiasm was infectious, and she brought new insight to her grandparents. She was even enthusiastic about the horse chestnuts we found on the ground, and we were able to tell her about the game of conkers we used to play with them when we were children.

I had forgotten, or maybe never realized when raising my own children, how much enthusiasm a child can have. I was reminded of the verse "Unless you change and become like little children, you will never enter the kingdom of heaven." I had always thought that meant that we should be meeker, more trusting, as a child is. I now believe that the enthusiasm of a child is what's so often lacking when we become adults. When I discover some new treasure in the Bible, do I get excited about it and can't wait to tell others about it? When I see some evidence of God's love and design in nature, do I excitedly rush to share what I have seen with others? Do I want to share with intense enthusiasm the greatest good news of all with my family and friends? I fear not. I've learned a lot by having two of my granddaughters living with us. I know more clearly what Jesus meant when He told us we need to be more like children.

Give me the enthusiasm and excitement of a child over spiritual things, Lord, I pray today.

RUTH LENNOX

Confronting the Hard Questions and Prevailing

Who is this that cometh up from the wilderness, leaning upon her beloved? S. of Sol. 8:5.

I HAVEN'T BEEN WRITING ANY devotional material for almost a year and a half. The reason is that I'm working on a secular book I believe God wants me to write; however, it goes against all my ideas of the writing I want to do for Him. I have half-written children's Bible stories all over the room, as well as some exciting end-time events studies I thought my heavenly Father would be more interested in. But it appears that before I can settle down into a life of religious writing, He has let me know that this secular book is to keep me from forgetting where I came from. It's like the demon-possessed Gadarene (Luke 8:26-39). After being delivered from his bondage, after being miraculously healed and restored to his right mind, the man wanted to go with Jesus and travel in His religious circle. Jesus told him to go back to his home and "tell how much God has done for you" (verse 39, NIV).

Even today the religious writing life seems more appealing than going back and being reminded of my former degradation. I think of God as too holy to ask me to write a secular book. Does one still obey God, even if others might not understand? These are the hard questions I face alone while struggling to understand God when He acts contrary to my perceptions.

The day came, though, when I reached page 100 of the book. I knew what an impossibility I had achieved—it was a milestone worth celebrating. But being alone and in poverty, I knew that no one was proud of me or cared. The only party I'd be having would be a pity party. But that afternoon a Muslim neighbor, who had heard I wasn't feeling well, dropped off some money and a bag of groceries, including a half gallon of Friendly's ice cream, saying she had been wanting to give me something. She didn't know about my writing or about the milestone that day. But God knew and decided it was a cause for celebration.

After I had had some ice cream, I went to the mall—only He and I knew what we were celebrating. If I had entertained any doubts about continuing with this book, they were dissolved as we celebrated in secret that day. I was smiling to myself the whole time at the mall and whispering thank-yous to Him in the blush of our new relationship. He's the Lover of my soul. He can be your lover, too.

Aleah Iqbal

The Good Samaritan

"Because He loves me," says the Lord, "I will rescue him; I will protect him, for he acknowledges my name." Ps. 91:14, NIV.

WE HAD RECENTLY ARRIVED at our second missionary relief assignment to Ulaanbaatar, Mongolia. While returning from one of our evening walks, my husband, Gerald, stepped on a hot-water system hole. In an instant he fell in up to his waist. The cover of the hole had flipped open and shut, hitting his shin just below the knee. Gerald kept himself up by placing his hands on either side of the hole and asking me to hold him under his arms to keep him from slipping farther in. I looked around for help and noticed a well-dressed man a few yards ahead, standing near his car. I tried to get his attention, but he was looking the other way. For an instant he turned in our direction, and I waved my hands, signaling that I needed help. With his help we were able to pull my husband out of the hole. There was a nasty gash on Gerald's shin, and the sock and shoe on his left foot were soaked with blood.

The Korean man quickly summed up the situation and dashed to his car, returning with an emergency first-aid kit. He took out a large sterile cloth and bandaged the wound. He and his Mongolian secretary, who knew English, led Gerald toward the man's car, insisting that they take us to the hospital. The secretary explained our problem to the staff on duty, and Gerald was soon hurried into the emergency room, where nine stitches were needed to close the gaping cut. I thanked God that there were no broken bones. The good Samaritan and his secretary waited at the hospital with us, then took us home.

We were in a foreign country and did not know the language. Even if I could have walked back to our home where the church office is located, there would have been no one to help. The staff had gone for the day. The mission office was closed. Every night the two of us were left by ourselves in the three-story apartment building. Had the accident happened a few seconds later, the good Samaritan and his secretary would have driven away.

God in His mercy had provided the help we needed at the right time and the right place. There is a scar just below Gerald's knee to remind us of God's constant care over His children. BIROL CHARLOTTE CHRISTO

Forgive and Forget

For I will forgive their iniquity, and their sin I will remember no more. Jer. 31:34, NKJV.

I GLANCED AT THE LIST of invitees to the spring seminar. Instantly I felt a degree of discomfort. On the list was the name of a colleague with whom I previously had had some less-than-amicable encounters. After many years of covert—and often overt—mistreatment, I had developed a distinct dislike for this individual's behavior. In fact, her behavior had caused me many sleepless nights. With the passing of time, however, I thought I had forgiven her. It's not always true that absence makes the heart grow fonder—it certainly wasn't true in this case. My reaction made me realize I had not completed the formula—forgive and *forget.*

I remembered how hard I had tried to resolve things by myself. Believing that love conquers all, I had made a concerted effort to show love, kindness, and respect in a demonstrable way to this person. Nothing had worked. Ultimately I had concluded that this was a "cross" I had to bear. I also had decided to leave matters in God's care. It appears that God had been waiting for me to surrender my problem to Him, because almost immediately He had provided relief beyond what I had asked or hoped for. Quite unexpectedly my colleague had been transferred to another city, thereby minimizing personal contact. This had brought me much relief and peace of mind. What a blessed God we serve! Now I could forget as well as forgive.

I thought I had forgiven my colleague, yet each time we meet the old feelings of hurt come rushing back. The problem for me is the forgetting, which must inevitably accompany the forgiving. I know I can't claim forgiveness from God, whom I can't see, if I'm not willing to forgive a colleague, whom I can see.

Dear Lord, today I petition You to please take this unforgiving heart of mine and give me a heart like Yours, a heart filled with love, compassion, and forgiveness. Teach me not to dwell on the slights and perceived hurts that may come my way. Help me always to be mindful of the ultimate price that was paid by You. You separated Yourself from the Trinity. You joined humanity. You laid down Your life for me so that I may obtain forgiveness of my sins. Thank You for the assurance of forgiveness and also for Your promise to forget my sins.

Avis Mae Rodney

March 21

Disastrous Decisions

There is a way that seemeth right unto a man, but the end thereof are the ways of death. Prov. 16:25.

IT WAS LATE AFTERNOON and the sun was already dipping behind the mountains, so we thought we should start our descent before it got too dark.

Hiking in the hills behind the biblical town of Berea, we soon realized that we didn't know how to find our way back. We decided to search for a small stream that we knew would eventually lead us out of this densely wooded area and into the more open foothills. From there we could easily get our bearings. But where was that stream?

We stood quietly and listened, hoping to hear water splashing over rocks. But there was complete silence. Deciding to follow a small path, we soon came to a place where it divided. The path to the left was a little wider and seemed more open than the one on the right, which was half covered with briars and nettles. My husband and I chose the path to the left, but surprisingly, the rest of the group turned right. We set off again, sure that the others would soon have to turn around and follow us. Within moments, however, we lost both visible and audible contact with them.

As the path became narrower and more overgrown, we had to acknowledge that there was no way we could get through. We had to turn back. Wearily we retraced our steps to where the paths had separated, and took the path to the right. After slipping and sliding down the steep incline, we eventually reached the stream. From there the descent was relatively easy.

This simple experience really brought home to me the words of today's verse. If we hadn't turned back, we would have been lost in the darkness (without sufficient clothing to withstand the rigors of a March night on the mountainside), simply because we had chosen the wrong turn. The path that had seemed right to us was so very wrong.

It is easy to make similar mistakes in our spiritual walk if we aren't closely following our heavenly Guide. The consequences are incomparably worse and can easily result in our spiritual death unless we realize our mistake in time and retrace our steps. Even when we're entangled in the briars of sin, blundering along in darkness without the warmth of Jesus' love to protect us, we may feel we're on the right path, but "the end thereof are the ways of death."

REVEL PAPAIOANNOU

The Still Small Voice

Take not thy holy spirit from me. Ps. 51:11.

IT STARTED OUT AS ANY ordinary day for me—devotions and thanksgiving to God, preparation for the 10-minute drive to work, then taking that drive. And, as usually happened, the stress started early on because of too many things to do.

While busily engaged in a class discussion with my students, I was interrupted by a young beautiful Creole woman. She came in unannounced, uncaring that I was busy. Trying hard not to hide my annoyance, I frowned and stared her down. "It better be a good one," I said.

When she didn't answer immediately, I thought, *Doesn't she know that I'm teaching my class? Surely she can see and hear well.*

"I came for some of those books that you gave my teacher," she finally said.

Books? What books? My face must have looked blank.

"They are called Amazing Facts," she continued, ignoring my expression. "My teacher let me read hers, and I want copies of my own."

I did remember sharing some tracts with her teacher, who was a substitute for me. She spoke of the blessings from reading "such inspiration." She left them on her desk in full view of her students and shared them when asked.

"Stop by in the morning for yours," I heard myself say. She left, and I returned to the discussion until the lunch bell.

Sitting alone at my desk, I revisited the conversation with my visitor. *Lord, I mused, is this why I picked up the Amazing Facts packet this morning on my way out the door? Were You telling me in Your still small voice to be prepared to share my faith today?* But I had quickly returned them to the nightstand by my bed.

Take not Thy spirit away from me, I humbly prayed. *Give me other chances to hear Your sweet small voice.* MARGARET B. LAWRENCE

Do Not Worry

But seek first the kingdom of God and His righteousness, and all these things shall be added to you. Therefore do not worry about tomorrow, for tomorrow will worry about its own things. Sufficient for the day is its own trouble. Matt. 6:33, 34, NKJV.

I WAS WORKING FOR A well-known bank in Tulsa, Oklahoma, many years ago and faced a situation that only God could handle. I attended a different church at the time, and kept the holy days that are listed in Leviticus 23.

It was early spring when I began asking for the eight days I would need off to observe the Feast of Tabernacles. All through the year I talked with my supervisor, and she told me that she wouldn't let me off but that maybe I could transfer to another department. I talked to people in personnel from time to time and did everything I knew to do. About a week before I was to leave for the feast, I again talked to personnel and was told that if I didn't show up for work on Monday, I wouldn't have a job. I left their office very discouraged but very determined to obey God.

It was Friday, and as I left work I cleaned out my desk because I would be leaving that evening for the feast and knew I wouldn't have a job when I returned. I tried not to worry about what I would do when I returned, but I must admit I did worry, as I was single and had no other income. But I decided to follow God in what I believed.

After returning from the eight-day feast, I went into the bank to get my last check. Amazingly, I was given the opportunity to interview for two jobs that had become available while I was gone. I went home after the interviews to wait a week for them to make a decision. In the meantime I planned to go out to look for work. But within an hour the bank called and offered me one of the jobs. It had better hours and paid more money than the previous job had. What an awesome God we serve!

Since that time God has led me into another church, and I have been a baptized member for three years now. God continues to bless and lead. We don't need to worry as long as we put God first. I put God first with the knowledge I had at the time. We need a correct understanding of God's Word, but even more important, we must be willing to put Him first.

Donna Cook

God Helped Me Find Work

God is our refuge and strength, a very present help in trouble. Ps. 46:1.

GOD HAS NEVER PROMISED that the lives of Christians will always be trouble-free. But it seemed as though we were having more than our share when exactly one year after my mom-in-law had her aorta replaced, she was diagnosed with cancer in three areas: a kidney, one lung, and her brain.

Carl and I felt crushed. For the next year, until her death, the illness pretty much dictated our lives and schedules. I knew I needed to be home more, so I gave up some of my clients that I cleaned for part-time. I also stopped papering and painting. I took care of Mom from early morning until our daughter, Julie, came home from school in the afternoon. My husband then took the night shift alone.

My having to cut my workload hurt us financially. "Lord," I pleaded, "I need something I can do while I'm here with Mom, or while Carl and Julie are around to look after her." We needed about $50 more each week to make ends meet.

A day or two later I spotted an ad in the paper: "Musician wanted for small church on Sundays and choir night on Wednesday." I called the number and went to the pastor's house to audition, playing the piano and organ and singing. Pastor Thompson and his wife, Kathleen, hired me immediately. The salary was $30 a week.

A second ad stated: "Family needs someone to do laundry for them weekly. Will pay $1 for each piece ironed." I phoned them, learning that the family wore mostly natural fabrics and that I would be able to earn up to $30 a week starching and ironing their clothes. They would bring the basket of garments to me, then pick them up when they were ready. I could do this work either at our house or at Mom's trailer, which was in our backyard.

Although Carl's mother lived only five more months, the laundry job lasted until we moved to a different area three years later.

I still do the music at West Augusta Methodist Church. God not only helped us with our short-term difficulties, but showed He cared for our long-term well-being, too. I still feel grateful for how wonderfully He answered our prayers.

BONNIE MOYERS

March 25

Transformed: Seeing as Christ Sees

And we, who with unveiled faces all reflect the Lord's glory, are being transformed into his likeness with ever-increasing glory, which comes from the Lord, who is the Spirit. 2 Cor. 3:18, NIV.

IN ORDER TO BECOME all that I can be in Christ, I am determined to see myself as Christ sees me—not only human in all my frailties, but with all my potential. I will develop my understanding of what that means and how it can be translated into reality.

Today I see myself as empowered to will and to do. God gave me the power of choice to use for Him. He also gives me mental and emotional vigor. He shows me each day the picture of myself that He has of me.

What do I think He sees when He looks at me, His very own daughter? I am self-disciplined; I attend to the concerns of the day. Then I relax at the end of the day, knowing that what I've done has been enough, that He can take it from there, because He will be awake all night anyway.

I am purposeful. God keeps me focused on what is important to accomplish for today. My job is to put my hand to the task and do my best, always listening for Him so I can respond as He directs.

I am unhurried but efficient. Hurry blinds me to God's voice. Efficiency makes me effective, yet gives me peace to pause and listen to Him.

Sometimes there's a scared little child inside me who needs comforting and reassuring. God lets me feel this way to draw me to Him. When I sense that child's needs, I pause and feel myself in the shelter of God's arms, looking out at a scary storm, knowing that I'm completely safe in His embrace. I'm completely loved and accepted just as I am. After all, He made me, so He must have wanted someone just like me.

Empowered, self-disciplined, purposeful, unhurried, efficient, loved. That's the picture I see God showing me of myself today.

What do you think God sees when He looks at you, another of His special daughters?

Thank You, Lord, for Your glorious, transforming love. RHONDA BOLTON

The Precious Blood

The blood of Jesus Christ His Son cleanses us from all sin. 1 John 1:7, NKJV.

Shepherd the church of God which He purchased with with His own blood. Acts 20:28, NKJV.

THE TELEPHONE SEEMED TO BE ringing urgently as again and again it pealed, almost insisting on being answered. With a groan I picked it up, reluctant to be interrupted on a Friday evening. It was our local blood bank, and the voice on the other end was kind but very persistent.

"There's been a massive pileup on the freeway, and we need blood right away. Can you and your husband come in this evening?" When I said I didn't think we could, she begged, "Please, the blood you give could save a life." I glanced at my husband, who smiled and nodded.

The blood bank was only a few minutes from our home but in an out-of-the-way location. We knew about where it was, but still had to search before we found it. Soon we were settled on reclining chairs; the nurse swabbed our arms and slid the needle in. "It won't take long now," she said with a smile. "After some juice and a snack, you'll be able to go home."

I leaned my head back on the pillow and grinned at my husband. "Look at the sign across from us. It says, 'Give blood, the gift of life.' "

"Remember in Genesis 9:4 the people were warned not to eat the blood of animals because the life was in the blood?" Brett asked. "The blood dripping from our veins into these bags may save a life, but the blood Christ gives will save lives, and nothing we do of ourselves can. This evening we thought we were too busy to come in. We often think we're too busy to take the life-giving blood from our Savior. We think we're too busy to spend time in study and prayer, when that is how we're filled with His refreshing Spirit. It says in 1 John 1:7 that the blood of Jesus cleanses us from all sin, and in Acts 20:28 that He purchased us with His blood."

"Blood is the gift of life, isn't it?" I said to my husband. "But unless one takes the blood the giver offers, the person will die. Just as with Christ and us. Unless we willingly accept His life-giving blood to cover our sins, we will die. Nothing is more important than the life from Jesus."

My husband smiled and replied, "Sometimes it seems as though we're searching, as we did for the blood bank this evening. But He is always there. He never leaves us or forsakes us. And we'll never get lost if we just keep our eyes on Him!"

CHERYL HURT

Divine Encounters

Jesus suddenly appeared on the road behind them. When they realized that someone was there, they invited this Stranger to walk along with them. Luke 24:15, Clear Word.

IT WAS A GORGEOUS Easter Sunday. I wondered if I should do our usual two-mile ditch walk alone or go with my husband later. After an instant prayer for guidance, I felt compelled to go. A springtime profusion of color flooded my senses. The birds were singing their mating melodies. The great blue heron, great egrets, brilliant goldfinches, and bluebirds were some of the dozen species I viewed as I walked.

However, this story actually began five months earlier. I had been walking alone and felt a little apprehensive when I noticed a car with a single occupant parked at the end of my walk. On closer inspection I saw a woman and prayed that God would allow me to talk to her. However, she dashed from her car and down the path beside the stream. I continued on the levee above. All of a sudden she sprinted up the almost-vertical bank to walk beside me.

We discovered that her mother and my husband were both due to have hip surgery. She had come more than 100 miles to see that her mother's needs were met. When we reached the end of the ditch, instead of turning back she continued on into my neighborhood. She told me that the church of her childhood didn't encourage Bible reading, but in recent years she'd been thrilled with the Bible's message. In fact, she'd been sitting in her car reading the Psalms as I walked up. How I praised God that He had given me this opportunity to share my life and faith!

Now, five months later, it was Easter, and as I approached the end of my walk, a woman walked briskly up beside me. When we looked at each other, she beamed and asked me how my husband was doing. I immediately knew it was Gretchen, the same woman I'd met so many months before. Our visit was much briefer, but I knew that God had arranged this encounter.

Jesus, Gretchen and I may never meet again on this earth, but I pray that we can continue our walk with You and each other in the earth made new. Please keep me alert to any other witnessing opportunities.

DONNA LEE SHARP

Not an Orphan

He chose us in Him before the foundation of the world, that we would be holy and blameless before Him. In love He predestined us to adoption as [sons and daughters] through Jesus Christ to Himself. Eph. 1:4, 5, NASB.

MY MOTHER PASSED AWAY peacefully in her sleep on Easter Sunday morning. She had suffered with congestive heart failure and lived with an enlarged heart for almost 10 years. Breathing, something we do without a second thought, became so very labored for her that she sometimes had to gasp for air. During her last year the doctors told us that it was just a matter of time—four days, four weeks, four months, or four years—and we needed to prepare ourselves for the inevitable. We lived with that uncertainty for a long time, counting each day Mom was with us as a blessing. Every morning it became a daily routine to check to see if she was breathing, and, during the day, if we didn't hear her groaning because of her discomfort, someone would run upstairs to check on Grandma.

The dreaded day eventually came, and Mom died peacefully in her sleep, at home, on Easter Sunday morning. What a glorious day to rest in the Lord. In the midst of all the tears, prayers, laughter, singing, and funeral arrangements, it struck me that I was now an orphan. My father had died 11 years earlier, and my grandparents had predeceased him. Isn't an orphan someone who has no mother, father, or legal guardian? Well, I decided, I now qualified. Both my parents were now dead, which made me an official orphan.

With that realization I began to feel somewhat lost, abandoned, and very much alone. Words cannot describe the void I felt when my mother was no longer around. She was my buddy, my confidant, my shopping partner, my consultant, and my Rock of Gibraltar. What was I going to do without her? Who would tell me to slow down, to take it easy, and to relax? As I contemplated my major loss, a passage of Scripture came to me, letting me know that I'm neither alone nor an orphan, for I belong to God. "You have received a spirit of adoption as [daughters] by which we cry out, 'Abba Father!'" (Rom. 8:15, NASB). What joy filled my heart to know that my heavenly Father chose me, and I belong to Him. He chose you, too. We're not alone. I'm so glad I'm a part of the family of God!

Sharon Long (Brown)

Light

You are the light of the world. . . . Neither do people light a lamp and put it under a bowl. Instead they put it on its stand, and it gives light to everyone in the house. Matt. 5:14, 15, NIV.

IT WAS 4:30 IN THE morning. I was awakened, and my mind was so full of turmoil that I couldn't find sleep again. It was too early to get up, but I was wide awake. I usually fall asleep again if I read a bit. Often just a page or two will be enough. The new Christian women's magazine was on the floor at my bedside. *If I turn the light on, it will disturb my husband, and he needs his sleep.* I turned over again. *I'll put a towel over the lamp, and then I'll have just enough light for me and it won't make any difference to my husband. A light just for me.*

The magazine was so interesting that I didn't fall asleep after the first page. I continued reading for quite a while. Then I started coughing. I'd been ill, but my cough was already gone. I reached for my cough lozenges. *I'd better blow my nose as well,* I thought. But my handkerchief smelled funny. *Smoke? How on earth?* I looked up at the wall to which my lamp was attached. The towel was burning! Bright flames were reaching for the wallpaper. I snatched the towel down quickly and watched as black flakes of charred material gently floated through the air toward the floor. The towel was still burning, so I quickly folded it up until the flames died out. Only then did I realize that the whole bedroom smelled of smoke. Now I had to open the door to the balcony in order to get rid of the smoky odor.

I suppose it really isn't good to cover up a lamp. It is meant to light up the darkness. Jesus mentioned in one of His sermons that nobody would be so stupid as to light a lamp and then cover it up. I had done that. How stupid I had been! And so now I have learned from my little fire accident that I should not try to keep my light to myself!

Christians are told to let their light shine. We shouldn't let it be covered by our worries, squabbles, stress, or moods. Just as the moon reflects sunlight, we can shine only when we let God's light shine on us. May God help us catch and reflect the light of His love. If we give God our burdens, He will make them disappear so that nothing will cast a shadow on our light.

Hannele Ottschofski

The Plums Are Secure

God is our refuge and strength, a very present help in trouble. Therefore will not we fear. Ps. 46:1, 2.

MINUTE GREEN PLUMS HAD appeared on our plum tree for the first time. I was thrilled to see them—tiny and precious. Every day I examined them just to see if they were holding on to the branch.

One night, apparently out of nowhere, a fierce storm sprang up. Severe winds howled outside. The wind slapped against the window and sent the curtains flying in all directions. Leaves and trees swayed at the force of the wind.

I was so worried that the tiny plums would all be blown off and destroyed. They were just too small to withstand the heavy winds. We had waited so long for the plums to appear, and now they would be destroyed before they had time to mature. My heart sank as I thought about it.

Early the next morning I hurried out to investigate the damage. I couldn't believe my eyes! I invited my husband to come and do his own inspection. Not one of the precious plums had been shaken from the branch. There were leaves strewn all over the place, but the tiny plums were undisturbed. I couldn't explain it, but I was happy and thanked God for protecting them. I had worried and feared for nothing.

Clearly it was a miracle—something like my life. The fierce winds of life's challenges and trials are inevitable. Sometimes we're tossed to and fro. We feel vulnerable and wonder, *Where is God?* But in the morning, when we can see the effect on our lives, we can truly say that we are better off. God has protected and brought us through. We are safe and sound.

Each experience gives us the opportunity to truly thank Him and to see the evidence of His presence in our lives. Life's challenges might temporarily block our view of God and His love, but in the end we'll be happy to confess that through it all God kept us safe in His hands.

Vow that you will make God your refuge. Vow that the storms of today will not sever you from His secure love. He has promised you enough strength for today. He will never fail you.

GLORIA GREGORY

Reaching Out to the Community

God so loved the world, that he gave his only begotten Son. John 3:16.

THE EXECUTIVE DIRECTOR HAD asked me, "Will you give us just five hours a week to start a most needed health-care program in our community? Our adults and youth don't respond anymore to government health workers. Some would rather die than seek medical attention."

It was fun working with them as I blended my ideas with their plans. I was able to reach the people and help them, to enhance life within the boundaries of accepted cultural practices.

The director had first asked me to work five hours a week. Then she increased the hours to 10, then to full-time, and many times to overtime. A few months later she asked me to coordinate the health clinic, and she added the hypertension program. When the medical clinic stabilized and the program expanded, she begged me to direct the alcoholism program.

They were interesting and exciting positions for a new, inexperienced graduate. Some days I had to work in the field, training the community health representatives. Other days I had to do outreach with them. We found some senior citizens with blood pressure as high as 240/110. Other clients had leg wounds with visible maggots crawling in and out of the open skin.

At one time the country director of nurses asked me to help her give TB medicine to a man who could not be confined, and the country nurse had been unable to track him down. He wouldn't consider any treatment.

I looked for the man by biking up and down the street, finally spotting him at the back of a liquor store, scanning the garbage. I tried to persuade him to go with me to his chicken coop home so I could give him his shot of streptomycin. But he refused to go home, asking me to give him his injection while standing behind the liquor store. That was the only way to accomplish that assignment, so I did it. I was hesitant, though, fearing someone might see me and conclude I was dispensing illegal drugs. That place is registered in the United States statistics as one of the top 10 cities in crimes because of heavy drug traffic.

Jesus completed His purpose when the Father sent Him to save us from sin. Regardless of what others thought or said, He followed the plan of salvation, risking all so that we may have life. When I completed my assignment, I understood a little better how He too completed His.

ESPERANZA AQUINO MOPERA

Under His Wings

He will cover you with His feathers and hide you under His wings. Ps. 91:4, Clear Word.

A SPRING STORM DROPPED GRAPE-SIZE hail on the roof of my car as I drove into the retreat center in the mountains of northern Idaho. It reminded me of the storms that had blown through my life during the past year and why I had come to this place to find some comfort and healing in time alone with my Lord.

The sun broke through the clouds as I checked my car roof for hail damage. The white hailstones covering the ground sparkled like diamonds. I looked up to the mountain trail where I had often gone hiking before, and decided to go for a walk before I checked into my room.

The smell of the wet woods, the pine trees, and the new spring flowers filled my lungs and infused new energy into my soul as I climbed up the steep path. *Dear Lord,* I prayed, *last time I was here I felt like Elijah when he was fed by the ravens. What do You have for me now? I want a deeper sense of Your presence in my life. Please reveal Yourself to me in a way that meets my heart's need at this time.*

Farther up the trail I noticed a grouse sitting right in the middle of the path. I cut a wide detour around the bird, half expecting it to run as I got closer, but it just sat there, motionless. Fifteen or 20 minutes later, as I was on my way back, there was that grouse, still sitting. I concluded that the hailstorm must have stunned or wounded it. I knelt down and reached out my hand. "Little bird, are you hurt?" I asked softly. The bird started, and as she moved, a dozen or more adorable baby grouse poured from under her wings. They scuttled off into the bushes to hide, with Mama right behind them.

I get the message, I whispered, tears filling my eyes. *You want me to snuggle under Your wings during the storms that threaten to destroy the peace in my soul.* I almost felt His breath on my shoulder. Since it was just the two of us there in that wooded sanctuary, I began to sing an old hymn that had just taken on a new meaning for me: " 'Under His wings I am safely abiding; though the night deepens and tempests are wild, still I can trust Him; I know He will keep me; He has redeemed me, and I am His child.' " My heart was light as I ran down the path still singing, " 'Under His wings my soul shall abide, safely abide forever.' "

CINDY WALIKONIS

The Poison Asps

Death and life are in the power of the tongue: and they that love it shall eat the fruit thereof. Prov. 18:21.

I DREAD JULIA'S VISITS. Apart from the weather, there is nothing one can discuss with Julia. Clothes? She lives in a holy atmosphere far above such mundane matters as adorning the body. House? She thinks it wicked to spend a lot of money on a place to live when many in the world have neither shelter nor food. Cars? The car she once bought from another Christian turned out to be a lemon, and it has left her permanently bitter.

But it's the church that really gets Julia stirred up. Not the actual bricks and mortar, you understand (although sometimes she has decided views about them, too). It's the people who comprise and run the church, both laity and leaders.

"*Him* for conference president? Not if you knew some of the things he's done. My father knew him at college."

"Yes, she teaches a good Bible lesson and the children all love her, but she wears all that fake jewelry. Such a bad example."

"Yes, Blankville church members are friendly, but they don't know much about the Bible. Ask any of them to explain Daniel 11 or Revelation 13, and they wouldn't have a clue."

"Sure, Donna is reliable, and she does a great job with the youth. But I heard that last year, when she took them camping . . . "

I always feel a great sense of relief when Julia gathers her robes of righteousness about her and departs. There must have been people like her 2,000 years ago, because she reminds me of what Paul says in Romans 3:13: "The poison of asps is under their lips."

Poor Julia; she is telling on herself. Only people with extra-low self-esteem are as critical of others as she is. Her caustic comments are not making one iota of difference to the ones she criticizes. All she is doing is souring her own character and ruining her walk with Christ.

Dear Lord, please show me some way to help Julia. And as we begin a new day, please control my thoughts so that I will speak only kind, loving, helpful words that will encourage those I meet along life's way. Thank You. Amen.

GOLDIE DOWN

Bluebird Babies—Spring Is Here!

The flowers appear on the earth; the time of the singing of birds is come. S. of Sol. 2:12.

BIRDS HAVE ALWAYS FASCINATED me, especially since the time I earned my bird honor while teaching students in a church-related school. We set up a bird feeder outside the schoolroom window and proceeded to learn about the different birds and how to identify them. One of my first-grade students learned to spot the blue jay very quickly. When he saw a cardinal, he immediately thought it must be a "red jay."

When we retired to Tennessee, one of my first projects was to ask my husband to set up a birdhouse so I could watch the birds raising their babies. That first year our birdhouse included two sets of chickadee babies and two sets of titmouse babies. The second year a pair of bluebirds examined the birdhouse and sat on top of it, but finally decided it wasn't built right for them.

I mentioned the bluebirds to one of our neighbors. I said, "I surely wish I could have some bluebirds nest in our birdhouse." She told her husband, and it wasn't long before she brought me a surprise. He had thoughtfully built me a proper bluebird house. We painted it red, and sure enough, that very spring we had two sets of bluebird babies in the new birdhouse. I keep a pair of binoculars on top of my microwave oven, so I am ready to watch more closely all that goes on in the bluebird neighborhood.

I've often pondered why the birds affect me and others. I believe it's because they bring hope. We live in an area where many of the birds migrate, leaving us during the weary days of winter. The birds are a harbinger of spring, along with flowers, new bird babies, gardens, and green lawns. Winter snows can be beautiful—or deadly. But spring suits almost everyone.

When we think of such things as September 11, 2001, we think that our world is getting old, dangerous, and deadly. We long for a new earth, new bodies, and a closer life with Jesus, our Savior, who has promised us no more sorrow, no more tears, no more death (see Rev. 21:4). He has promised to come and live with us forever. My prayer for you today, dear reader, is for a walk of hope that will eventually lead us home to heaven.

LORAINE F. SWEETLAND

My Visit to Khuma

Have no fear. . . . When you pass through deep waters, I am with you, when you pass through rivers, they will not sweep you away. . . . For I am the Lord your God, the Holy One of Israel, your deliverer. Isa. 43:1-3, NEB.

THE VOICE ON THE other end of the phone line spoke in a different dialect. I had to ask her to repeat what she said in order for me to understand. She sounded so excited that she'd finally made contact with me. Her name was Adelaide, she said, and she told me she'd bought the woman's devotional book *This Quiet Place.* She saw that I was a contributor from Cape Town, and she wanted to tell me how my stories had uplifted her spiritually. She asked if I would correspond with her.

In her letters Adelaide intimated that should she be spared to see her sixtieth birthday, she'd like me to celebrate with her. After we had corresponded for three years, the time arrived for me to go. I traveled by bus on an overnight journey of 17 hours to meet her at Klerksdorp in the North-West province. When we met personally for the first time, she hugged and hugged me.

She lived far out of town in Khuma township. I hadn't known where I would be going or what the conditions would be like. It was a different culture, and they spoke the Xhosa language, a language unknown to me. We had to take two taxis to reach her home, where she made me feel so welcome, special, and comfortable for the duration of my stay.

I arrived on Friday, the celebration was on Sunday, and on Tuesday I was to leave Khuma by 3:30 p.m. At 2:00 p.m. an electric storm broke loose. Lightning streaked, thunder rumbled, rain poured in torrents, and hail pelted the windowpanes. Fear gripped me. I looked out the bedroom window. The red ground had become a white carpet. How was I to get out of there? The only thing I could do was pray.

The storm stopped at 3:00, but the red gravel street now resembled a river of blood. How was I to cross? My feet would get soaked. I sent up another prayer: "Please, God, You opened the Red Sea for the children of Israel to cross; perform a miracle for me, too." There was no time to waste, so I bravely walked across to the other side of the street. My shoes and feet were dry! Surprised? Yes! God answered my prayer, instantly and miraculously.

I was once again reminded that God's promises never fail.

PRISCILLA ADONIS

From Dingy Cream to White as Snow

Though your sins be as scarlet, they shall be as white as snow. Isa. 1:18.

I WAS GOING TO ENJOY my newly decorated home. From a dingy cream and golden oak decor, it had been transformed into a California garden home with bright white walls, window coverings, and a sofa that looked out on a retreat room of plants and flowers and, beyond, a yard of orange trees and dark-pink crepe myrtle trees. It was the carpet that I worried about. When it had been laid and I saw it for the first time, it seemed to be much whiter than the sample I had picked out.

But now I was going away for the weekend, leaving my newly decorated house in the capable hands of my house sitter. I was prepared! I had directions! "Don't allow Sheba [my black Doberman] to lie anywhere but on her blanket. Feed her dog crackers in the kitchen, not on the carpet."

There were more instructions. "And don't eat spaghetti with tomato sauce in the living room; and no grape juice, either! And remember to take off your outdoor shoes."

Then just before my house sitter could say, "Forget this job; I'm going where people have deep-green or black carpet," I said, "Don't let anything happen. But if it does, there's a remedy." I brought out my trusty sponge that takes up everything, a roll of paper towels, spray spot remover, and a white powder that makes the carpet new again.

It wasn't until I had finished the demonstration that I realized the significance of the object lesson that had taken place. God says to us, "Don't mess up your life. I want you to be productive and happy. Don't make bad choices! But if you do, there's a remedy. There's forgiveness." He says, "Behold, I make all things new" (Rev. 21:5). And there's more: "Though your sins be as scarlet, they shall be as white as snow; though they be red like crimson, they shall be as wool" (Isa. 1:18). From the dinginess of sin, He can turn us into something wonderful, white as snow.

And yes, in case you're wondering, everything went fine that weekend.

EDNA MAE GALLINGTON

Mixed Blessings

Behold, I send an Angel before thee. Ex. 23:20.

IT WAS THE SPRING of 1990, and I was overwhelmed. I desperately needed to talk to someone, someone who was understanding and trustworthy. I turned to my pastor. My car was being repaired, and I had no transportation when I phoned him. He said he'd meet Sonny, my special-needs child, and me in a few hours. As we walked, I shared with Pastor Hessel my concerns.

We were nearing the Treasury Branch Mall entrance when the pastor commented, "The love you have for little Sonny—I've never seen this dimension of love before!" What an impression that statement made on my weary mind as I carried 3-year-old Sonny in my arms. Those were special words God meant for me to hear.

Soon the floodgates opened, and I began to pen my personal journal, *Dimensions of Love.* A few weeks later I wrote my first devotional. Are you prepared? I ended the article with this prayer: "On bent knees I will become prepared for what lies ahead for me, and I ask for the strength, the patience, and the wisdom I'll need. A new dimension of love has been shown me, beyond that which I can describe. It is a love so pure yet so fragile—like the child that it adorns. My prayer, for this child's sake, is 'Please, Lord, make and keep me prepared, and bless the precious understanding few who help me along the way.'" In writing and in absolute sincerity I had placed my mind, heart, and soul upon the altar.

By midsummer I was having an emotional breakdown, and I spent two weeks in the hospital. I listened when Pastor Hessel counseled me to seek professional help, because I knew he loved me, and I love and trust him. Since then, family and friends have reached out to me with cards and poems. Often friends leave cards of encouragement in my church mailbox. Every card given is sincerely appreciated. My friend Dianne once gave me a card with a special poem about how acts of kindness become treasured memories. Once again special words from a precious friend came precisely when I needed them. At times I get very discouraged, and I cry to the Lord, "Please come quickly, Lord; not all prisons have bars and locked doors."

May you be blessed as you reach out to someone who has a need of *your* special touch.

DEBORAH SANDERS

Grace

For we have not an high priest which cannot be touched with the feeling of our infirmities. . . . Let us therefore come boldly unto the throne of grace, that we may obtain mercy, and find grace to help in time of need. Heb. 4:15, 16.

ONE MORNING DURING A Bible class discussion the leader asked us to share a time in our lives that another person had interceded for us, a human comparison to Jesus interceding before the Father on our behalf. The story I shared was from my childhood.

I suppose I was about 11, and my sister was about 10. I told my mother a lie about my sister. It was meant as a prank, a joke. It was a terrible story, but in my innocence I didn't see the seriousness of my words, and therefore I didn't for a minute expect a negative reaction from my mother. Alas, she didn't see it as remotely funny, and the punishment of a whipping was swift and severe for my sister. Shocked into action, I quickly confessed my sin and told Mother that I had lied. She didn't think that was funny either! With the look of a forthcoming whipping in her eyes, she advanced toward me. And then an amazing thing happened. My sister, still stinging from her own unfair punishment, said, "Please don't punish her!" Mother conceded that since my sister had been the one unfairly accused and punished, Mother would honor her request and not give me the whipping I so justly deserved.

What a picture of God's mercy! Before that class discussion the event had been just another memory from my childhood. Now it has taken on new meaning. It is what Jesus is doing even now for me. Unjustly accused and, oh, so very unfairly punished, He has gone to heaven, to the right hand of God the Father. Still stinging and bruised from His own unfair punishment, He is saying, "Father, please don't punish her. She didn't mean it." And God, who loves more than all the parents who ever were, is replying, "You were the one unjustly accused and unfairly punished. I will concede Your right to decide."

I don't know if I have ever adequately expressed my thanks to my sister for interceding on my behalf. Perhaps I should make another attempt. But I have been grateful ever since. It is unlike human nature to do things like that. Right at that moment she was emulating Christ, helping me to understand grace a little better. RACHEL ATWOOD

Declare God's Loving-kindness

It is good to give thanks to the Lord, and to sing praises to Your name, O Most High; to declare Your lovingkindness in the morning, and Your faithfulness every night. Ps. 92:1, 2, NKJV.

I HAD JUST MADE A mistake by mailing a letter with a 33-cent stamp when it should have been a 34-cent stamp. It wasn't a big deal, but I decided to go back to the small contract postal station to retrieve the letter. When I arrived, several people were waiting to be served, so I joined the queue. While awaiting my turn, I heard people complaining because there were neither 34-cent stamps nor one-cent stamps available. One of the women said she'd had to use two 20-cent stamps to mail her letter. She rattled on, questioning why the main postal system had decided to change the postal rates when the post office personnel weren't ready to cope with the change. That comment seemed to open the hornets' nest. Others joined with their different complaints, seemingly adding more fire to the heated complaints. One person suggested that the United States of America was becoming like a developing country. I couldn't take the unreasonable complaints any longer. I had just visited the country of my birth, and perhaps these people didn't know what they were talking about.

Trying to be very polite and tactful, I mustered up my courage and said, "I'm not a citizen of the United States, although I'm a legal resident here. I'm thankful that I live here where I enjoy so many things I don't have in the country of my birth. We've a comfortable home here; we enjoy the abundance of food. We've lots and lots of clean water in this place called America. Above all, we enjoy peace."

It was amazing how positive words and comments changed those people's outlook. In a short time, after my few words, the people began to say how great America was. Then one of them thanked me for my positive attitude. God must have put those thoughts in my mind and helped me to be courageous, for the people appreciated what I said.

O God, You have been merciful, kind, and faithful to me. I'm just a tiny speck on Planet Earth, and yet You care. Please help me to appreciate Your blessings and to speak up and share with others when given the opportunity. Give me courage and a positive attitude to influence others for You.

OFELIA A. PANGAN

My Precious Birthday Gift

For God so loved the world, that he gave his only begotten Son, that whosoever believeth in him should not perish, but have everlasting life. John 3:16.

IT WAS MY BIRTHDAY, and I was pregnant. I had expected the baby to arrive two weeks earlier, but she had decided to follow the pattern of her siblings before her. They had waited an extra two weeks, and so delivery was always through induced labor. The day before my birthday I'd gone to the clinic, where I'd been given some drugs to induce the labor, but to no avail.

I was not particularly looking forward to any celebration. How can one celebrate with a big tummy? All I wanted was for my baby to come out so that I could be free. As I woke up that morning I felt weak and decided to go to the clinic. I got there about noon to complain about my weakness. My nurse wished me a happy birthday and jokingly said that maybe God wanted me to have a birthday gift. I didn't take her seriously.

Since I'd been induced the previous day with no results, I didn't expect there would be anything more that could be done. My doctor asked me to go into the labor room, where he put me on drips. Within five hours my little girl was born at exactly 6:25 p.m., thereby becoming my special birthday gift.

Today as I write, she is in her late teens. In all the years since her arrival we have celebrated our birthdays together. She is fearfully and wonderfully made. She resembles me physically to the point of easy recognition by those who knew me when I was her age. That, dear readers, is how great our God is.

There are many special gifts that can come to one in a lifetime, but none, in my opinion, can exceed the gift of another human being. There is, however, another special gift for you and me, another person who is better than even my daughter. That is the gift of Jesus Christ. John 3:16 tells us that God so loved us that He gave us His Son, Jesus Christ, so that through Him we can have the gift of eternal life.

Father, I thank You for the birthday gift in the person of my daughter—she is so special to You and to me. I especially thank You for the gift of eternal life through Jesus Christ, my Lord and Savior. BECKY DADA

The Unwanted Visitor

They conceive evil and bring forth iniquity. They hatch vipers' eggs and weave the spider's web. Isa. 59:4, 5, NKJV.

WE HAD VISITORS COMING FOR afternoon tea. I'd met the elderly couple only briefly, but when we women know someone is to visit, what do we all do? Clean, clean, and clean some more. I dusted and swept, wanting everything to be just right. I washed my best tea set and polished the silver sugar basin. Most important, I did a lot of baking. I made fruitcake, Melting Moments, and chocolate-chip cookies. I sliced tomatoes, ready to put on cracker biscuits.

Finally everything was finished, but I wanted a table centerpiece. As I'm always loath to cut flowers from my garden, I looked around for an inspiration. There was a small potted plant on the patio, a cactus with pretty bright-red flowers. Exactly what I wanted! The pot itself was a bit dirty, though, with a spiderweb on one side of the plant. I carried it into the laundry room and put it down in the tub to clean. Something cautioned me, so I found my garden prong and used it to remove the web. Then I saw it. The bright-red stripe. The biggest redback spider I've ever seen came out from the base of my plant and started to crawl slowly across the bottom of the tub. (Highly poisonous, redbacks can be found anywhere in Australia. The spiders are black; the distinctive red stripe gives them their name.) Racing into the kitchen, I grabbed the insect spray and sprayed the redback with one hand while turning the hot-water tap on with the other.

A neighbor had been bitten by a redback spider sometime before while sitting on our patio with me. She had ended up in the hospital for a night to be given antivenom. That episode had taught me to be more aware, so my husband and I spent many hours spraying, cleaning, and checking for spiders.

Now, with the redback truly dead, I completed the task at hand. I cleaned the potted plant by washing the pot and cleaning the leaves.

Satan is like that spider. He's always there, hiding, ready when and where we least expect it, to come out and attack us with the poison of sin. Thankfully, there are sprays and antivenom for sin, too. May we always be vigilant and prepared with Jesus.

LEONIE DONALD

The Gift of Memory!

I thank my God every time I remember you. In all my prayers for all of you, I always pray with joy. Phil. 1:3, 4, NIV.

I RECENTLY RECEIVED THE SAD news that a dear friend and colleague was now suffering from Alzheimer's disease. Her once-sharp memory had slipped into oblivion. Her ability to articulate the gospel and to share from the depths of her heart were gifts she had given so generously. I miss her on the ministry trail.

With her on my mind, I've made it a special point to thank God for memory and memories. Just this afternoon, while pulling weeds from my large patio pots, I plucked a marigold blossom and crushed it between my fingers. Then, while drinking in the fragrance, I let my mind take me back to my grandma Jennie's flower garden that always had room for marigolds. I thanked God for her precious influence in my life and for marigolds to remind me of her.

During the past couple weeks the wild blackberry bushes along the road leading to our home have been bent over with ripe fruit. One day I couldn't resist them and, after tying a small bucket to my belt, I began wandering down the road. Soon I had gathered enough berries for a cobbler, a family favorite. But while I stood in the tall grass on a humid summer day picking blackberries, my memory took me back to a Michigan woods and hot summer days of berry picking. Grandma's endurance far outweighed mine. As a child I had endured berry picking; as a grandmother I enjoy it. It's a longstanding family tradition—briars and all!

Recently my daughter, Heidi, said she wanted to preserve tomatoes and applesauce this fall. I'd already seen the jars lined up on her garage shelves, awaiting their hot-water bath that will seal the fruit and preserve it for coming months. No, she won't need to refer to a recipe book. When she was young, I passed on to her the recipes, much as Grandma had done for me a generation earlier. Precious memories help to perpetuate family traditions.

The Holy Scriptures declare, "I have hidden your word in my heart that I might not sin against you. . . . I meditate on your precepts and consider your ways. I delight in your decrees; I will not neglect your Word" (Ps. 119:11-16, NIV). Let's exercise our minds by hiding God's Word in our minds and hearts and thanking Him for life's sweet memories. ROSE OTIS

A Lesson in Faith for Me

All things work together for good to them that love God, to them who are the called according to his purpose. Rom. 8:28.

I'D RECENTLY HAD AN OPERATION to replace my right knee. When I was released from the hospital, the doctor told me to be very careful and not to fall. After several weeks at home and a therapist coming in, I experienced terrible pain in the knee again. When I went for a checkup, the doctor told me I would probably have to have surgery to straighten the knee and tighten the ligaments.

I came home that afternoon feeling down but praying that somehow God would fix it so I wouldn't have to have another surgery. In the meantime, two birds had left droppings on my front porch. It was a mess! I decided to take a chance and take the hose, which was only a few steps away, and wash off the porch. Knowing I was not well or very steady on my feet, I prayed, and proceeded to do the task that would take only a few minutes. All went well until I was putting the hose back. Then I felt myself falling.

I began calling to my neighbor for help. No one heard me, so I sat there for 45 minutes. As I sat, I prayed, *Lord, You said that all things work together for good for those who love You and trust You, but I don't understand what is happening to me. Where is the good in this?*

A neighbor drove up the street, but didn't hear my call for help. Then another neighbor, who lives across the street, heard me and came over to help. She was a small-built woman, so I asked her to get my son, who lives about three blocks away. By then the first neighbor heard what was going on and came over. Together they helped me up and into the house and made sure I was OK before they left.

When I phoned the doctor to tell him what had happened, he asked me to come in right away. After taking X-rays of my knee, he said, "It looks like you won't have to have that surgery after all; your knee is back in place." The good that I could not see in the fall, God saw and allowed, for He had His own way of answering my prayer—a way I would never have expected.

Lord, help me to remember that Your time and ways are so different from mine. Please give me the faith and patience to wait on You and to trust Your promise, for indeed all things do work together for good to them that love You, to them who are called according to Your purpose. MARGURITE HILTS

The Circus

They shall see the Son of man coming in the clouds of heaven with power and great glory. Matt. 24:30.

I REMEMBER WHEN THE CIRCUS would come to my town. It was an exciting event. Posters were nailed to telephone poles, barns, or buildings. Excitement mounted, especially on the day the caravan arrived. There was always a parade, led by the steam calliope that snorted and spit and filled the air with music. It was so loud when it passed that we had to cover our ears.

Horses, elephants, animals in cages, and funny clowns passed by on Main Street, irresistibly inviting us to the circus. Canvases were unrolled and became the huge big top. Smaller tents formed the midway. For a small fee we could see the animals up close in their brightly carved and colored cages in one of the tents. There was the sideshow of strange marvels: a two-headed baby calf preserved in formaldehyde, a fat woman bigger than anyone we knew, a bearded woman, a man with a horse's tail, and a woman with a baby growing out of her chest—both of them dead and dried up like a mummy. There was a man with tattoos over his entire body, a strong man who could lift fabulous weights, and a woman's head without a body, all camouflaged with mirrors. It was all so exciting to a child.

The day of the circus found us inside the big tent, waiting eagerly for the performances to begin. The ringmaster announced each act. The plumed horses galloped around the rings with pretty women balancing on their backs. The trapeze artists performed from their high perches and swings, floating through the air with the greatest of ease. It was so exciting! Our necks ached from looking up.

All too soon the performances were over, and the crowd dispersed. By morning the tents were packed away and the circus people, the animals, and the now-silent calliope had gone from our town.

God has posted His signs of a coming event for all to see. He shows us strange happenings in world events and in His Word. He wants us to be watching and waiting with excitement until the main event becomes a reality.

His caravan will be the noisiest, most spectacular event since Creation. No one will miss it, for every eye will be fixed on that wonderful event.

LAURIE DIXON-MCCLANAHAN

Prayers of Desire

And it shall come to pass, that before they call, I will answer; and while they are yet speaking, I will hear. Isa. 65:24.

ON THE FIRST OF APRIL I was impressed to pray until camp meeting in July for a used set of *Testimonies for the Church.* I felt that someone must have an extra set they weren't using. I decided I would ask as many people as I could to pray, and would have it announced in church.

On April 5 four of us got together at my sister's place and prayed my "prayer of desire." In 1985 I'd had a brief spiritual experience and had purchased a new set of the books but had read only a few pages. Soon after, I had sold them at a discount for some much-needed cash. My sister had told me more than once not to sell them. She had said that perhaps one day I would need them again, but I had assured her that I would not.

On April 8, at our women's prayer group, I shared how the Spirit had impressed me to pray for the books. I explained how I'd gotten rid of mine and of my newly revived desire for spiritual nourishment. If I could not get a used set, I told them, I would have to buy new books. So I asked that my request be put on our prayer list, and my finger tapped on the list to emphasize my point.

While I was speaking, the woman of the house walked over to her china cabinet (I thought she was being rude) and opened the doors. There, on the top shelf, was the exact set of books I wanted. She took them down and put them on the table in front of me. She said she had inherited them from a friend and had put them away, thinking that someday someone would need them. God had been planning ahead for my prayer to be answered.

Even before we ask, He is willing and happy to fill our needs. I know He impressed my friend to save them. He knew that I was going to have a change of heart and that I would want those books again one day. I was filled with joy. It is indeed true that "it shall come to pass, that before they call, I will answer; and while they are yet speaking, I will hear" (Isa. 65:24). It happened for me. And God provided even more than I asked, as another friend gave me a different set of books for spiritual nourishment as well.

God gives us blessings, full, heaped up, and overflowing.

Vidella McClellan

Ketchup Day

By the seventh day God had finished the work he had been doing; so on the seventh day he rested from all his work. Gen. 2:2, NIV.

WHEN I WAS YOUNG and people asked me, "How was your weekend?" I usually had something interesting to report. Time off from work meant time spent away from home. I might have gone ice skating or to a dog show. I might have gone to street festivals, arts and crafts displays, or antique stores. I was always ready to go to the beach or try out a new restaurant.

Today things are a lot different. My weekends now are all about to-do lists. I judge my days off according to what I can get done, not how much fun I have. Every time I run an errand in town, part of my mind is lingering on the undone chores at home.

Sometimes I take a day off work to celebrate "Ketchup Day." This is a holiday I invented, and it occurs several times a year, whenever I feel completely overwhelmed and my to-do list is out of hand. Ketchup Day is a day I set aside to catch up on chores—ironing, weeding, or organizing closets. The day leaves me feeling in control of things again and with a lot less clutter in my life.

I think of the Sabbath as the ultimate Ketchup Day, blessed by God. When the world was created, God set aside the seventh day as a Sabbath, a holy day of rest. People who keep the Sabbath refrain from working on that day, but the Sabbath is about what we do, not about what we don't do. The Sabbath is about a special time set aside so we can catch up with our Maker.

During the week our time spent with the Lord may be limited by the pressures of a full-time job or raising a family or trying to do both at once. Prayers and tempers may be short as we rush around with our lists of chores and errands. But on the Sabbath we put our lists away. The things that seem so important during the week are no match for a day spent focusing on our spiritual well-being and using our quiet time to catch up with our Lord. Taking time to be with Someone you love is a great way to spend your day off!

GINA LEE

Preparation Days

But as it is written, Eye hath not seen, nor ear heard, neither have entered into the heart of man, the things which God hath prepared for them that love him. 1 Cor. 2:9.

AT SOME POINT IN LIFE each of us has had to make preparations for some occasion: our wedding day, work, church, graduation, a child's first day at school, or a funeral.

Through our years together my husband and I have told each other some of our life's experiences. The experience that stands out so vividly in my mind as he shared it with me was the preparation he had to make as a young man drafted into the United States Army. He had to prepare himself mentally for telling his parents and then having to leave home. He recalled how his mother had reacted upon hearing the news. She had looked at him, put her hands on his shoulders, and said, "Son, sit down." And in a soft voice she had said, "Son, you always have to put your entire trust in God, because He's the one in control of you and the United States Army, and He'll send you back home." These words, he said, had been the crowning act of his preparation.

He had survived World War II and embarked on another day for which he had to make preparation—asking me to marry him. He recalled that his feelings were quite different. He said he had decided to tell both parents at the same time, but decided to mention it to his dad again. His dad had reminded him of the marriage vow, saying, "Remember, son, for better or for worse." And then had come the question: "Son, do you really love this young woman?" His reply had been yes, and when my husband passed away we had been married for 53 years.

Just as my husband's dad asked him, "Son, do you really love this young woman?" Christ is asking each of us, "My child, do you really love Me? If so, what preparations are you making to show you really love Me? And what measures are you taking daily to ready yourself for My return?"

Thank You for loving me so much, dear Jesus, and for making provisions for me and others so that we'll be ready for those mansions You have prepared. I can hardly even imagine the fantastic things there will be—but I know You, so I know it will be wonderful.

Annie B. Best

Seek and You Shall Find

Search the scriptures; for in them ye think ye have eternal life: and they are they which testify of me. John 5:39.

MY HOUSEKEEPING CHORES OF vacuuming and dusting are often neglected because of an overbooked schedule. At other times lesser priorities, such as my relaxing hobby of needlework (hardanger in particular), take first place. When I know company is coming, I do a touch-up job. Infrequently I do a thorough job of moving furniture and getting into the corners with the vacuum cleaner, and polishing the fine wood carvings of the coffee table with a Q-tip dipped in lemon oil.

One morning I determined to clean every nook and cranny in my condo. I have an oversized upholstered chair that's my favorite for relaxing. It's big enough to slouch in for a nap or to curl up in to read or solve puzzles while munching on popcorn. It was time this chair got vacuumed. So I lifted the cushion to vacuum any popcorn bits that might have fallen down the sides.

What a surprise! In the center of the seat were two golden loonies (Canadian $1 coins). There is no way these could have fallen out of someone's pocket. Had that been the case, the coins would have been near the edge. Someone must have deliberately placed them under the cushion. I had no clues to guide me in detective work to solve the mystery of "Who dun it?" I couldn't remember when I had last vacuumed under the cushions, and neither could I remember which of my guests had sat in that chair. I have done some quizzing, but to no avail. Had I vacuumed more frequently, I might have discovered the one who brightened my day.

This experience made me think of my Bible study habits. How often do I neglect studying God's Word? How often do I hurry through my devotions? I may oversleep and have to rush off to work, so I promise myself—and God—that I will do it in the evening. When I come home from work and finish eating supper, washing the dishes, and sorting through the mail (or going to an emergency meeting), I'm too tired to concentrate. I vow to do better tomorrow.

How is it with you? Faithfulness in Bible study will help unearth special promises, words of encouragement, hope for the future, or "just what I needed for today." Then, by sharing what we read in God's Word, we may brighten someone else's day, just as two golden loonies brightened mine.

Edith Fitch

The Natural Order of Things

Seek ye first the kingdom of God, and his righteousness; and all these things shall be added unto you. Matt. 6:33.

FOR AS LONG AS I can remember, music has been what makes me tick. Music has been where I've turned for comfort and fulfillment. During the time we were searching for answers to what was happening to our daughter Morgan, I escaped into my songwriting and singing in order to gain some sense of peace. But there was none to be found.

We received the diagnosis of autism spectrum disorder—finally a name for what was turning our family upside down. Early intervention was important, but finding that intervention was yet another maze. Almost two years passed, and Morgan wasn't getting the help she needed.

One morning, following a week of what we call "Morgan's Bad Hair Days," I sent the girls off to school and sat down for my devotional. I poured my heart out to God. I was exhausted and at the end of my mental rope. I told God I was ready to do whatever it would take to get my daughter back. I would lay down my music if that was what I needed to do. God knew my heart and knew I meant it. I had to get my priorities back in order.

God heard my prayer. After that tearful, soul-searching half hour I opened my devotional. The title for that date was "The Power of Music." When I gave my music to God, He gave it back to me. Right then I made a promise to make my music for Him and to do it with a purpose.

Things fell right into place, as they always do when we put the kingdom first. We had to move because the help for Morgan was not available where we lived. We prayed every step of the way. We found out about Vanderbilt's TRIAD Department that specializes in autism treatment. Rudy found a job at a dealership in Nashville. Our house sold in six weeks, while other houses in our neighborhood had been on the market for more than a year.

John Rees, owner of GodsChild Records, asked me to come on board with his label after hearing some of my work. John's wife, Holly Lu, is a warrior for special-needs advocacy. She has given us a wealth of information and support. A coincidence? I doubt it!

Morgan is doing much better. Not all days are perfect, but I'm glad they're in God's hands. And I'm finally finding that peace that passes all understanding (see Phil. 4:7).

TAMMY VICE

Make Me a Living Rainbow, Lord

I do set my bow in the cloud, and it shall be for a token of a covenant between me and the earth. Gen. 9:13.

IS THERE ANYONE WHO ISN'T fascinated by the sight of a rainbow? With their spectrum of colors they do indeed capture our attention. I'm sure that's why the rainbow is used as a logo for many businesses. The artwork induces a cheerful feeling in the beholder.

Why are we so taken with this phenomenon? The wooing factors seem to be the gathering together of all the basic colors and the vastness of the bow—in addition to its elusive end. Ah! To catch a rainbow!

For me the most beautiful aspect of the rainbow is that it's a symbol of the promise from God. We writers have tried in vain to describe the essence of the bow. Artists work diligently in various mediums to capture the awesome sight, as do photographers—but in the end all these efforts are only poor reflections of the original.

A Japanese description of the bow is that it's "the floating bridge to heaven." I like that! It's like a connection to His covenant with us humans.

Remember the children's song "Jesus Wants Me for a Sunbeam"? That's how I feel about the rainbow. I'd like to be a living rainbow to attract others to Him. But we don't have to be big and showy to do that. Just as rainbows are found in places other than the sky, I can be like the tiny surprise rainbow that is found in the water dance of a fountain, or the spray of a water hose, or a wave breaking against a jutting rock, or the spill of a waterfall, or even a single raindrop.

"Yes, Lord, make me as a rainbow raindrop, if nothing else, to bring joy to others—to bring glory to You."

There is yet another rainbow I want to see, the one that Bible writers Ezekiel and John wrote about. John called it a jewel: "There was a rainbow round about the throne, in sight like unto an emerald" (Rev. 4:3). If there's any rainbow-catching to be done, that's the one I plan to touch!

I have a suggestion: The next time we see a rainbow, why not renew our personal covenant with Him? That will make us all living rainbows!

BETTY KOSSICK

Poor Pansy

The Lord will guide you continually, and satisfy your soul in drought, and strengthen your bones; you shall be like a watered garden, and like a spring of water, whose waters do not fail. Isa. 58:11, NKJV.

GROWING GOD'S GARDEN" was the theme of the one-day women's retreat. Beginning with a nature study and display of birds' nests, the day continued with a focus on growing as a Christian woman in the same way a garden grows. As a parting gift we were each given a small pansy to be planted in our flower garden. The cheerful pansy would remind us to grow where we are planted.

I chose a plant with a bright-yellow blossom that was healthy and showed promise of vigorous growth. Arriving home that evening, I placed it on the lid of the wastebasket in our breezeway. There I left it for several days, alone and neglected. Days later I saw how it longed for water. The stem and leaves were wilted, and the pretty yellow flower had bowed its head as it thirsted for living water. I had forgotten to care for my poor pansy.

As I held it over the sink and poured water into the pot, the thirsty soil drank in every drop. Watching the water soak in, I realized that the plant needed to be in a container where it would be able to draw upon a continuous supply. Putting the little pot into a glass of water has ensured that the plant can continue to drink. The poor pansy can once again hold its head up high. Planting it in the rich soil of my garden will allow it to grow and sink its roots deep in the ground to draw in the needed moisture.

I ask myself, *Are there times when I've neglected my friends and left them, struggling, as they've longed for a drop of the water of kindness and cheer?* Sometimes I too feel lonely and neglected. The cure for those moments of loneliness is to pick up the telephone and call a friend or neighbor. Often I discover that I have chosen to call a friend who, like me, is feeling lonely or is struggling to hold her head up in the midst of problems. In return for speaking words of encouragement, I receive a good watering for my soul's garden that encourages me and restores a zest for living.

Evelyn Glass

Snuggling Up with God

He gathers the lambs in his arms and carries them close to his heart. Isa. 40:11, NIV.

WE HAVE LONG PADDED pews in our church, and although they are not as comfortable as they might be, they offer some distinct advantages. When we have lots of friends who come to church with us, we can just keep squashing up close until everyone has a seat! When we clean the church, it's much easier to sweep around the pews than around lots of chair legs. But the best thing is that it's easier to snuggle closer than when we're sitting on individual chairs.

My two youngest children are boys, and when they come to sit next to me in church, they want me to sit between them. My daughter, Bethany, is older now, and she always wants to sit with her own friends in the next row. In some ways that's good, because I have only two sides to me, and my pastor-husband can't always sit with us.

Even though Nathan and Joel are 10 and 13, they like to cuddle close to me, especially during prayer. For three years I was quite ill and couldn't kneel easily for prayer, so I stayed seated. The boys would snuggle in close to me, and I would put my arms around them. I suppose I thought they would grow out of it, but they didn't. I began to wonder whether I was doing the right thing or whether I should make them kneel to pray, even though I didn't kneel.

Then one day a woman in my church said, "I love the way you cuddle your boys during prayer! It's such a lovely idea. Just think; whenever they pray, they will remember the feeling of being loved, feeling safe, and being held close to your heart. That's just the way God wants us to feel when we talk to Him."

I'd never thought about it like that. And yes, she was right! To this day my boys are still snuggling up to me in church during the prayer. I don't stop them, and I don't feel bad. As we snuggle together, I think about God snuggling me, too, and somehow that opens up a whole new dimension to my prayers.

Today, when you pray, imagine yourself being held close to the heart of God, soothed, safe, and loved. Talk to Him as you would if He were right there, snuggling you close, and then experience His love for you in a fresh new way.

Karen Holford

Girdles and Answered Prayers

Call unto me, and I will answer thee, and shew thee great and mighty things, which thou knowest not. Jer. 33:3.

FOUR MONTHS AFTER GIVING birth to my first child, I still struggled to get rid of 10 extra pounds and a very unattractive tummy. For weeks I had watched commercials about a new "miracle" girdle that would make my bulk disappear in 10 days.

Finally I mustered up enough courage to go down to the store and check it out. My cousin, who was also trying to lose some weight after her second pregnancy, accompanied me. The agreement was that I would use it first; if it worked, then she would try it. We found the store, and I stood in front of the display case trying to decide whether I should invest that much money in a girdle I wasn't sure would do the trick. The salesperson, noticing my dilemma, walked up and began reciting the benefits of the particular brand I was staring at.

I tuned her out momentarily while I read the information on the box. Still trying to make up my mind, I examined the girdle from every possible angle and tried to imagine whether it would really fulfill all its promises. Then I turned to the salesperson, looked her straight in the eye, and asked, "Does this thing really work?"

She gave me the most earnest look and nodded emphatically. "Yes; yes, it really works."

My cousin watched in confusion as I thanked the woman and walked away empty-handed. I waited until we had gone a safe distance; then I explained. "That girl in charge of selling the miracle girdle is about 20 pounds overweight! If she believes so much in the product she represents, how come she hasn't tried it?" Or had she?

Back home that evening I replayed the situation in my mind. Sometimes as Christians we are the worst possible advertisement. If prayer is so wonderful, why do we waste so much time running ahead of God and fretting over the inevitable, when all He asks us to do is to place it—whatever it is—in His hands and let go?

Prayer works! "O taste and see that the Lord is good" (Ps. 34:8). Then, when others ask the reason for the lightness in our steps, we can be living testimonies of how much God desires to bless us, if we only ask.

DINORAH BLACKMAN

Just When One Needs Him Most

May our Lord Jesus Christ himself and God our Father, who loved us and by his grace gave us eternal encouragement and good hope, encourage your hearts and strengthen you in every good deed and word. 2 Thess. 2:16, 17, NIV.

The waiting area was all but deserted as a purple streak caught my eye. From my seat in the nearby food court I could hear her pleadings in frantic disbelief that she would not be boarding the plane. She leaned heavily on the counter to catch her breath after running to the gate. Bags lay sprawled where she had flung them. Alternately she berated the gate agent and herself for missing her flight. Instinctively I prayed for this woman, hoping she could still make it; but alas, she turned away and sat down.

As I munched my fries and scanned the other travelers, I asked God to show me someone who was still on His side. God's answer surprised me. Have you ever been called to interact with a stranger when you were some distance away? Have you thought, *Isn't intercessory prayer sufficient?*

After thinking, *You want me to do what?* I shrugged. Well, what did I have to lose? Disposing of my remaining fries, I approached the angry woman prayerfully. By now she was on the phone, cursing and sobbing her story into some familiar ear. There was nothing she could do till later that night. I waited till she finished, then respectfully told her I had heard her plight. As she started to pour out her story again, I stopped her and asked if I could sing her a song. She was a bit startled, but agreed and offered me a seat next to her. I sang a modified version of the hymn "Just When I Need Him Most," personalizing some verses for her situation. What a grand moment! She wiped her eyes, and I sat reveling in God's grace that had empowered me for this unique mission.

We talked freely then about her life, her concerns, and God's promises. She pulled out a pocket New Testament that she was actually carrying with her! She was the one who was still on God's side, one who needed God to intervene and remind her of His love so that she could trust Him, even when she'd missed her plane.

You may be surprised by God's answers to prayers today! Whatever He prompts you to do, faithfully go for it! What do you have to lose? He is with us just when we need Him most!

Janel Raelene Palmer

A Leap of Faith

Now faith is the substance of things hoped for, the evidence of things not seen. Heb. 11:1, NKJV.

MY HUSBAND AND I TRAVEL for both business and pleasure, and whenever we're visiting in another city, one of our favorite tourist attractions is the local zoo. Recently we found ourselves in beautiful San Diego, home of a world-famous zoo, so we took time off to enjoy a day there. We purchased passes on a tour bus, and as we rode among the various animal pens and viewing areas, we noticed that the kangaroos were housed in an area with a low, three- or four-foot retaining wall and a shallow ditch just inside the wall. Since the kangaroo is known as quite a strong jumper, I asked the guide how they kept the animals in the low enclosures.

"The animals will not jump if they cannot see the ground outside the pen," he answered, "so as long as they can't get close enough to the fence to see the ground, they don't try to jump out."

Such a small impediment to freedom, yet it might as well have been a mile high! The animals stayed in their prison because they couldn't see solid footing outside.

I saw many more sights that day, but that one scenario has remained with me. How many times have we not acted because we couldn't see the ground ahead? Are we stuck in ruts because we're afraid of failing? Do we doubt that God can catch us if we fall?

I have discovered that sometimes when I'm afraid to move forward with a new project or to try something different, it's because I haven't committed it to God and gotten His approval on it. It may be something that would not be in my best interest. But usually fear of the unknown is the culprit, a doubting of myself.

The most reliable and effective way to conquer doubt is with action. Our first steps may be tentative or wobbly, or may even seem insignificant. But the best way to accomplish a task is to make a start, even if we can't see the way ahead clearly. As we begin to move forward, our doubts begin to disappear. Courage—maybe even confidence—will begin to replace the fear. Not only will there be pride in the accomplishment, but the desire to accomplish more will become part of us. Let's not let fear and uncertainty paralyze our actions. Take a leap of faith, and fly! FAUNA RANKIN DEAN

Papa's House

Let the children come to me. Don't stop them! For the Kingdom of God belongs to such as these. Luke 18:16, NLT.

FIVE WEEKS AGO MY husband and I left for what we thought would be a two-week vacation. We drove to the coast to visit our son and his family, who had recently moved there. During their first two months there they lived in four different locations: two weeks of house sitting, then 10 days at a friend's house, then two nights in a motel, and finally a month in a small suite. It would be September before they could take occupancy of their country home.

Everyone was feeling stressed, especially our 2-year-old granddaughter, Meagan. She was no longer the happy little girl we had known. By her frequent outbursts and temper tantrums it had become obvious she was all out of sorts. My son had to begin work immediately, so his wife had to deal with their child alone. It felt as though she needed a break, and when I offered to stay an additional two weeks, my daughter-in-law accepted gratefully. That meant my husband would have to return home alone.

Two weeks later we were all together at our house for the long weekend. Our granddaughter had taken the flight well, but how would she react to having to sleep in yet another strange bed? That first night she sat up, looked around, and said, "Papa's house," then lay back on the pillow and fell asleep. The next day she sat quietly through church with her uncle and aunt.

It was a beautiful fall day, so we decided to have our Sabbath meal on the new deck. While my daughters-in-law and I made dinner, Meagan was busy playing with her stuffed animals. It had been two months since her auntie and uncle had seen her, so she was showered with a lot of hugs and kisses. I was amazed at how content she was, even though our home was unfamiliar to her. My husband came to the conclusion that she was happiest when she had all her relatives around her. All too soon the weekend was over, and everyone had to leave.

"Children know when they are loved," my doctor told me that week at a routine visit. I was reminded of how the children loved to be with Jesus. The disciples wanted to chase them away, but Jesus invited them to come to Him. He took them on His knees and blessed them. They were content. They knew they were loved. Do we?

VERA WEIBE

The Lord Is My Shepherd; I Shall Not Want

Whom have I in heaven but thee? And there is nothing upon earth that I desire besides thee. Ps. 73:25, RSV.

MY 8-YEAR-OLD DAUGHTER doesn't like change. Having the furniture or window treatments changed is very stressful to her. Her older sister often complains that she quotes Psalm 23 to bolster her need for everything to remain the same.

One afternoon I took her with me as I did some last-minute errands at the mall. Pausing at a department store, I stopped by a very attractive display of china settings. A clear little voice beside me murmured, "The Lord is my shepherd; I shall not want."

I got the message and moved on. A shelf of scented candles caught my attention. As I reached for a particularly lovely one, again I heard a gentle whisper. "The Lord is my shepherd; I shall not want."

And so it continued throughout the store. With her not-so-subtle assistance, I left the store empty-handed. When we went to the pet store, however, it was a very different story. We had to get something for the dog, a new toy for the bird, and a maze for the hamsters. Her list seemed endless. "What about 'The Lord is my shepherd; I shall not want' verse?" I had to know.

"But Mommy, I am their shepherd. They need these things. They depend on me." Her little voice was insistent. I realized that her argument, though self-serving to the situation at hand, had a broader application. I remembered a quote from *Thoughts From the Mount of Blessings:* "Whatever spiritual blessing we need, it is our privilege to claim through Jesus. We may tell the Lord, with the simplicity of a child, exactly what we need. We may state to Him our temporal matters, asking Him for bread and raiment as well as for the bread of life and the robe of Christ's righteousness" (p. 133).

My little daughter had reminded me that just as she felt the pets depended on her for their care, protection, and entertainment, so we must depend on Him to meet all of life's perplexities. More important, we must make Him first, last, and best in everything. Because He is our shepherd, despite our wants we have need of absolutely nothing.

Father God, help us in all our choices to give You absolute control. Remind us to trust in Your ability to manage, and to give up the management of even the most trivial things to You.

JANET M. GREENE

Stuck in the Mud

He brought me up also out of an horrible pit, out of the miry clay, and set my feet upon a rock. Ps. 40:2.

MY HUSBAND, RON, and I had just spent a glorious day at Point Calimere bird sanctuary on the eastern coast of India. Thousands of waders, ducks, storks, and herons filled the coastal wetlands. Masses of flamingos grouped together, turning the water pink. When they all took flight at once, it was enough to take our breath away. In the sunshine their wings sparkled white, pink, and black against the blue sky.

To get a closer look, we had walked on the mudflats, and by the time we reached the car I noticed that my shoes were caked in mud. I was tired, though, and didn't want to walk the few hundred feet to the shore to wash them off. Near the car, not more than 20 feet (six meters) away, was a pool of water, or so I thought. I stepped into black mud that acted like quicksand, sucking my feet down. When I tried to pull one foot up, the other went deeper yet into the muck and the mire. I could see nothing to grab. I saw no way out of the mess. "Help me!" I screamed.

Manuel, our driver, got to me first. From the solid ground of the narrow pathway he bent over and took a firm hold on my right arm and pulled hard. In moments I was standing on rocky ground once more.

Now I was dirtier than ever. I went to the shore and tried to wash off the sticky mess, but it wouldn't come off. I had to change my clothes, socks, and shoes before I could enter the car again. The white socks I had been wearing were black. I couldn't imagine any detergent that would get them white again, so I threw them out. My jeans still have stains up to the knees.

I will be very careful from now on where I go to wash my feet. Things are not always as they appear to be. The quick fix is not always the best fix. These, and many other lessons, I jotted in my journal that night.

Probably the clearest parable for me, though, was that when those times come in life, when I get caught in the miry mudhole of sin, there is no way I can get out by myself. I will perish without help. It is when I call out "Jesus, help me!" that He reaches out His arms of love and sets my feet again on the solid rock of His salvation.

DOROTHY EATON WATTS

Cherish the Moment

Bear one another's burdens, and in this way you'll be doing what Christ Himself would do. Gal. 6:2, Clear Word.

THE SECOND TUESDAY OF each month, when the Christian women of all faiths in our area meet together for a luncheon, is a special time for many of us. There is always a guest speaker with an inspiring message, a special feature, and musical selections to uplift us after the meal. It is a time of friendship and fellowship.

I often sit with the same women each month, but one day someone new sat next to me. We always wear name tags, and I quickly noted that we shared similar first names. As we visited, we found that we both had spent some time living in the same foreign country. She and her husband were planning to build their retirement home in the near future. She was such a pleasant person, and the others at our table enjoyed getting to know her also. This was her first time to attend the Christian Women's Club luncheon, and we were happy that she had chosen to sit with us.

She didn't say anything about her health, but I noticed she was walking with a cane. When we lined up to get our food at the buffet table, I helped her walk, as it would have been difficult for her to carry her plate while using her cane. She graciously accepted my assistance, but it was all very low-key. It wasn't until we were almost ready to leave that I learned she was Catholic, while I am Protestant, but that didn't lessen our newly found friendship. I couldn't help hoping that she would sit at our table again the next month.

The days sped by, and it was almost time for our luncheon again. As I was glancing over our local newspaper one day, for some reason I found myself scanning the obituaries. *That's good; no one I know,* I thought. But then as I looked closer, I saw the name of my new friend. What a shock! We had had no idea that she was terminally ill, and perhaps even she had had no idea that she had so little time left. At the next luncheon I shared this sad news with my other friends at the table, and it was sobering to all of us. We hadn't known that we would never have the opportunity to fellowship with her again. We just hoped that our time together had been a bright spot in her life, as it had been in ours.

Lord, help me make the best use of each moment is my prayer today.

BETTY J. ADAMS

The Yellow Pansy

"Many women have done excellently, but you surpass them all." Charm is deceitful, and beauty is vain, but a woman who fears the Lord is to be praised. Give her a share in the fruit of her hands, and let her works praise her in the city gates. Prov. 31:29-31, NRSV.

THERE THEY WERE AS I turned into the parking lot: a mass of purple-faced pansies, blowing in the spring breeze. And one bright-yellow face nodded from the middle of the bed.

I had to smile; it seemed so out of place. And yet so beautiful—so noticed. As I drove on I thought about people who seem so out of place, so noticed, and yet so beautiful.

I thought of special-needs children. As I have watched them, sometimes in person, sometimes on television, I have noticed that they so often have such beautiful smiles and attitudes. I've watched them in the Special Olympics, so happy with their effort. I wish the other Olympic contestants were as happy. I have heard more than one parent say how special these children are, so loving, so patient, so like a yellow pansy in a field of purple.

I thought of other people who have stood out in the crowd, willing to be different and make a difference—Joan of Arc, Rosa Parks, Sacajawea, Helen Keller, or Aung San Suu Kyi, and so many more who are unnamed and unsung. I think of the thousands of women in the nineteenth century who opposed alcohol in their towns and homes, bringing about the blessing of prohibition. When these women faded from sight, prohibition was overturned.

In the same century there were the women lobbying for women's suffrage, giving women in the United States the right to vote. Many of these same women campaigned for better schools, prisons, mental health care, and welfare legislation. What a difference people can make when they are willing to stand up and be noticed.

There are, of course, women in the Bible whose remarkable actions have been recorded for our encouragement—Deborah, Ruth, Esther, Jael, the daughters of Zelophehad, all the Marys, Priscilla, Phoebe, and Lydia. How glad I am that they, and many more, found a place in Scripture.

How about you—how about me? Are we willing to stand up, stand out, and be noticed if it will make a difference for others? Yes, we might look out of place, but I think we will actually be in exactly the place God created us to be.

ARDIS DICK STENBAKKEN

Our Woolly-haired Angel

God is our refuge and strength, an ever-present help in trouble. Ps. 46:1, NIV.

THE PLAN WAS TO SPEND the night in Atlanta with some family friends and board the plane the next morning for Barbados. The trip had been planned for several months, and we were excited and eagerly looking forward to seeing my parents and family. The day before the trip the car was checked, and the mechanic assured me everything was OK for our four-hour trip.

We were about an hour and a half from our destination when the car began to slow. I kept pressing the gas pedal, but the car came to a halt. My three daughters and I were scared—the night was pitch-black. We prayed for the Lord to send someone to help. I opened the hood and flagged passing vehicles, but they zoomed on by. No one seemed to care. In desperation I decided to walk to the nearest exit to get help; I told my girls to stay in the car and not to open the door for anyone. My second daughter, afraid to let me go alone, came with me. We flagged motorists, but they whizzed by, almost blowing us off the shoulder of the road. We walked and prayed. Suddenly a truck stopped, and we saw a big, burly man with white wooly hair walking toward us. He shouted, "Woman, are you crazy? Don't you know it's dangerous to be walking on the highway at night?"

He offered to take us back to our car to see if he could fix the problem. When we returned, another truck was parked behind our car, and the driver was looking under the hood. The two truck drivers conversed about what to do; then the wooly-haired driver told us that the other driver would help us. We thanked him for rescuing us. The other truck driver took us to the nearest telephone booth to call AAA. When we arrived at the service station, the mechanic said that he had planned to leave earlier, but for some "strange" reason he hadn't.

The truck driver stayed with us until the car was fixed, then drove behind us about five miles to make sure everything was all right. We never received a bill from the mechanic. In the midst of our fear and worry, God provided the right people at the right time and the right place to assist us. My girls experienced firsthand that God answers prayers. He is truly our present help in time of trouble.

Shirley C. Iheanacho

Living Water

Whoever drinks of the water that I shall give him shall never thirst; but the water that I shall give him shall become in him a well of water springing up to eternal life. John 4:14, NASB.

IT WAS THE KIND of hot, steamy Madagascar morning that makes tempers soar with the rising mercury. I could see the owner's guard and his wife having an animated "conversation." I realized that this was no ordinary marital chat. Mild-mannered Dominick was being verbally harangued while giving Gina the silent treatment, further fueling her ire.

It wasn't a pretty sight, this public display of an obviously private matter. Then again, their tiny thatched hut did not afford the space to rant indoors. Gina finally left for the market with a dramatic flounce, and our yard was quiet once more.

An hour later I tried to concentrate on my devotions as a rhythmic *clip, clip* floated through the open window. Dominick was cutting the owner's grass with pruning shears. The reminder of his presence turned my prayers in a more specific direction.

"Lord, I don't know what's wrong between Gina and Dominick, but please help them to make up soon. I have no idea how to be a witness here. How can I show Your love when I can't even speak to them?" My prayer drifted off in frustration as the clipping continued below.

"Give him a drink of cold water." It was as clear as if someone had spoken aloud. I started to laugh at the very simplicity of the idea. Of course! On a sweltering day like today, who wouldn't appreciate cold water?

I savored the unusual awareness that God had answered my prayer so quickly, so specifically, so—practically. Minutes later I headed to the front yard, pitcher of ice water in hand. "Dominick, this is for you," I said in halting French, setting it down on a nearby step. He smiled a shy grin but continued on with his work.

Several hours later, when I returned from town, Dominick bounded around the corner and said, "*Merci!*" With a smile he handed back the now-empty pitcher, then rushed off to hoe.

God had no great drama in mind. This was no life-changing event. But though he doesn't know it, Dominick sipped from Living Water that day, and I hope to pour out more for him in the months and years to come.

Kimberly Baldwin Radford

The Hummingbird

Eye has not seen, nor ear heard, nor have entered into the heart of man the things which God has prepared for those who love Him. 1 Cor. 2:9, NKJV.

I LOVE WORKING IN MY YARD. My husband and I should have had sprinklers put in several years ago, as they would have saved us a lot of time. We thought about it every time we saw neighbors adding the convenience to their landscaping, but for various reasons we put off the easier watering method and continued to care for our lawn with a garden hose.

I'm glad we made the choice to remain "old-fashioned," because now that I'm nearly retired, I enjoy my early-morning and late-afternoon times when I watch the grass absorb its refreshing drink, opening its long spires to the gentle sunshine and water. It seems to turn a little greener right before my eyes.

It was on one of these mornings, while I was watching this interesting change take place in the grass, that I heard an unfamiliar whirling sound. I held the flow of water steady while listening closely to the curious sound. What was it, and where was it? Within seconds I realized it was at shoulder level, coming from my right. Slowly I turned my head to look at a precious ruby-throated hummingbird, its little wings beating several hundred times per minute, while it hovered about four feet away from me.

I was so pleasantly surprised that I started gently talking to it. "Hi, sweetheart; you are so pretty!" Instead of being frightened by my voice, the little hummingbird decided to move in closer to get a better look at me. Soon it had maneuvered itself to within a couple feet, and I had to resist the urge to reach out and touch the petite form. All too soon the magic ended, and my little friend flew up and away.

God taught me a beautiful lesson that morning. I had had a minuscule glimpse of heaven. There the living creatures will entertain us unafraid. The beautiful birds will light on our shoulder; gentle lions and good-natured tigers will come in answer to our call. Our little ones will play with sweet-tempered bears and feed grapes to friendly crocodiles. Angels will answer our many "How?" and "Why?" questions. Best of all, Jesus will be there.

Lord, haste the day! MILDRED C. WILLIAMS

Our Heavenly Father's Dairy Bar

How often I have longed to gather your children together, as a hen gathers her chicks under her wings, but you were not willing. Matt. 23:37, NIV.

ACCORDING TO LA LECHE League International (LLLI), breast-feeding is an art form; hence the title of their book is *The Womanly Art of Breastfeeding.* As the breast-feeding mom of 3-month-old twins, Joshua and Hannah, I hardly think of myself as the artist extraordinaire. In fact, our "feeding frenzies" (as my husband and I affectionately call the children's six-plus meals per day) are anything but artwork.

After experiencing this art form, I think LLLI should rename their book *The Godly Art of Breastfeeding.* Although the image of our heavenly Father breast-feeding His children may seem unnatural, I'm convinced that He has created this miracle as yet another unique insight into His relationship with His children—an infinitely brilliant metaphor.

As I scoop Hannah and Joshua up to the dairy bar, I'm reminded that it is God who initiates our relationship. In our fragile and vulnerable state of sinfulness He first loves us, and then His kindness leads us to repent, reconciling us by His grace into a relationship with Him. What a simple, saving message just from drawing my children up onto my lap!

Sometimes during a feeding our babies respond to their hungry stomachs with red faces, clenched eyes, gaping mouths, and furiously wagging heads, as if to declare war on the very solution to their hunger. Likewise, our hearts cry out in emptiness, yet so often we stubbornly refuse to submit to the peace that can be found from the infilling of God's nourishing Spirit. I know how I long to lead my children to peace. How must God feel?

Occasionally one of our sweet babies will insistently search for food in the opposite direction of the prize. It's not until they've fussed and cried that I can guide them back in the right direction. How many times has God opened my eyes to reveal that I've wandered off course and am in need of a grace-filled about-face?

God longs to gather us under His wings, to mother us. Through the godly art of breast-feeding, God daily reveals to me that we are like vulnerable, stubborn, wandering babes in need of the sustaining power of our heavenly Father's dairy bar.

JOELLE ASHLEY

Be Not Weary in Well Doing

And let us not be weary in well doing: for in due season we shall reap, if we faint not. Gal. 6:9.

ONE SUNDAY AS I stepped into Daisy's home I sensed an unpleasant atmosphere. In tears Daisy complained about her family. Being her neighbor and friend, I could well understand her problem. After teaching school, Daisy would come home to continue teaching students who needed extra help. Day in and day out she worked hard to make ends meet. She was happy to earn a little extra to support the family. However, on this particular Sunday something had gone wrong. She could contain herself no more. As a result, she blurted out her disappointment. It seemed her husband had not seen the importance of having a celebration for her forty-fifth birthday, which had occurred the past week without any special attention from him. She had even bought a cake to make it easy for him. Dwelling on this disappointment, she felt rejected, and this made her think that all her hard work for the family was in vain and not worth doing.

Do other mothers sometimes feel like Daisy? Is it worth sacrificing our time and energy for the family when even on our birthday no one seems to care for us? As I pondered the role of a mother, I again read Proverbs 31 that outlines what I think God expects of us. From my analysis I found there are at least a dozen expectations.

After this analysis I thought to myself, *Is it possible for me to reach this goal? It seems insurmountable to me. The expectation is too great even to attempt.* However, I decided that according to the chapter, there will be good results if I try to perform my role as God expects: "The heart of her husband doth safely trust in her, so that he shall have no need of spoil. . . . Her husband is known in the gates, when he sitteth among the elders of the land. . . . Strength and honour are her clothing . . . she shall rejoice in time to come. . . . Her children arise up, and call her blessed; her husband also, and he praiseth her. Many daughters have done virtuously, but thou excellest them all. . . . She shall be praised. . . . Her own works praise her in the gates" (Prov. 31:11-31).

God, in His love and concern for mothers, wants our value to be "far above rubies" (verse 10). So it is not too hard when He says, "Let us not be weary in well doing: for in due season we shall reap."

ANNIE M. KUJUR

God's Exuberant Joy

Let the heavens rejoice, let the earth be glad; let the sea resound, and all that is in it; let the fields be jubilant, and everything in them. Then all the trees of the forest will sing for joy. Ps. 96:11, 12, NIV.

SOMETIMES I WONDER IF the psalmists were bipolar. They exhibit such mood swings, from deepest despair to exuberance! But I love the way they portray a God who is willing to absorb our despondency and then fill us, and all of nature, with the lightness of His joy.

The great naturalist Loren Eiseley tells of being caught on the beach in a sudden rainstorm. Seeking shelter under a large piece of driftwood, he found himself facing a tiny fox kitten, too young to know fear. Playfully it challenged him to a game of tug-of-war with a chicken bone. From that entertaining encounter he discovered that at the core of the universe "the face of God wears a smile."

Well-known Christian author Philip Yancey describes making friends with three fox kits near his home in Colorado one summer. They followed him everywhere, enchanting him with their playful antics and offering "a thrilling flashback to Eden, when fear had not yet arisen."

I will never forget one early Sabbath morning when I was walking in the beautiful botanical gardens near our home in Maryland. As I entered the herb garden, I saw a big black crow sitting on the edge of the drinking fountain, looking for all the world as if it were waiting for someone to come along and give it a drink. I paused a moment, then slowly approached, talking to it in a quiet, friendly tone. It watched me curiously as I drew closer and tentatively reached out to turn on the water. For several seconds it put its beak in the stream of water, then lazily flew away, squawking its thanks!

My smile of pure delight echoed the smile I felt deep inside. For just a moment I too knew the joyous thrill Adam and Eve must have known. A great hunger awakened in me for a world of innocent pleasure, the day when we can forget our bitterly won knowledge of good and evil and enjoy our status as creatures of our God and King, knowing, enjoying, and worshiping Him.

Dear Creator-Father, thank You for offering to blow away the dark clouds of sin and guilt and fill our hearts with the sweetness of Your joy and freedom! Maranatha!

CARROL GRADY

A Memorable Day

He shall give his angels charge over thee, to keep thee in all thy ways. Ps. 91:11.

IT WAS A BRIGHT, SUNNY spring morning as I readied myself for a shopping trip near our home in a small town in Illinois. After my husband had left for his work and our son had gone to his school, I straightened up our home so that all would be tidy when I came back. After checking our downstairs bedroom, I turned to leave the room. With a backward glance I stood in the doorway to be certain that all was finished and that I hadn't forgotten anything.

Suddenly a loud, ominous noise exploded the silence. As I looked up toward the source of the sound, a large section of the bedroom ceiling suddenly bulged. With a crashing and thudding, many large, heavy pieces of plaster and lath boards dropped to the floor, missing me by scant inches!

Momentarily stunned, I contemplated the disastrous scene. It was a miracle that I hadn't been injured. Immediately I offered a prayer of thanks to God for protecting me from harm. Still shaking, I notified our property manager about the incident.

I rested a few minutes in the living room in an effort to regain my composure. Then I took a shovel and began the arduous task of cleaning up the room once more, this time of its pile of debris. After I had finished cleaning the second time, I resolved not to worry so much about the little things, and went on my short journey very thankful that I could do so!

That evening I announced to my family, "I had a harrowing, life-threatening experience today!" As I recounted the experience to my family, we all gave special thanks to God for His wonderful protection for each one of us all the days of our lives. It certainly had been a memorable, unforgettable day for me. So often we forget to give thanks.

Dear heavenly Father, thank You so much for Your daily watch care, protection, and guidance over us. You constantly amaze us with Your goodness and love. Draw us near to You now with Your protecting arm, and grant us Your peace according to Your will. In Jesus' name, amen. ROSEMARY BAKER

Bareheaded

But the very hairs of your head are all numbered. Matt. 10:30.

I KEPT LOOKING THROUGH MY concordance, trying to find an encouraging text for a woman—me, actually—whose hair was falling out by the handfuls. With most chemotherapy patients, day 14 after the first treatment is the most common time to start losing hair. And losing it I was! I first read, "Then shall ye bring down my gray hairs with sorrow" (Gen. 42:38). Yep, I was just about to give in to sorrow. In Psalm 40:12 David stated that his iniquities were more than the number of hairs on his head. If that was true with me, I'd soon be perfect.

Fighting depression and panic, I put out the hair-loss word—via e-mail—to some of my closest supporters. Their reactions soon filled up my e-mailbox. A former student wrote, "You've always been such a beautiful woman. I'm sure that losing your hair won't make any bit of difference. You'll just have fewer obstructions to letting your spirit shine through." Another reminded me: "With or without hair, you'll still be everything you are now. Church member and musician, wife, mom, friend, special daughter, and caregiver. None of these roles requires hair!"

A former colleague encouraged, "You are a beautiful blond, and you'll be an even more beautiful bald, because there's no dimming that light that shines from within! You're His girl, His beloved daughter. I can almost hear Him laughing in delight at the marvelous surprises He's planned for you, just around the corner!"

My son responded, "Mom, it's good you have a well-shaped head. [How would he know? He'd never seen me bald.] I'm sorry that I'm not there to sweep the hair up after you."

I looked out the window. In spite of the drizzly day, I began to smile at all the encouragement God was sending me through some of His own. Maybe having a lot of hair wasn't such a big deal. After all, even though Absalom had the most beautiful head of hair in the world, it still couldn't save him. And didn't Christ promise that His Father would always be aware of each individual's hair count—whether it was 40,000 or a measly four? That meant He'd be with me through this humiliating ordeal.

Turning back to the computer screen, I read the last sentence of my son's e-mail: "I hope that you are able to rest in Abba's arms."

And I was.

CAROLYN SUTTON

A Time to Wait

The Lord is good to those who wait for him, to the soul that seeks him. It is good that one should wait quietly for the salvation of the Lord. Lam. 3:25, 26, RSV.

THE FIRST TWO TRIMESTERS of my pregnancy were filled with anticipatory joy. Watching my abdomen grow, feeling the knobs when I palpated my abdomen, and eventually feeling the first movement of life were all signs of life, and I enjoyed every moment of it.

Then came the third trimester, and with it the aches and pains, slowed movements, and arching back. The last three months turned into an everlasting wait. The wait itself felt like a burdensome weight. Oh, how I longed to put it down! Many nights I wished that the baby would come then, that very night.

What if the baby had come when I'd wished it to? What if nature hadn't taken its course and the baby, too, had gotten tired of waiting and had come prematurely? What would have been the chance of its surviving?

I look back at my impatience and thank God for not answering all my prayers immediately but answering by asking me simply to wait. Even a short waiting period can seem so long. But there is a time for everything.

Sometimes we are impatient with God and want Him to come now because we think that we're ready. We want Him to come now because we want an end to the lawlessness and pain. Yet there are so many people who aren't ready for His return.

While we wait let's delve into His Word and keep learning about Him. We need to identify our talents and abilities given by God and use them to be a blessing to someone. Maybe God is waiting to give us an opportunity. Maybe the wait is to develop our patience.

Today let's prepare ourselves to wait patiently on the Lord. Let's do all that is within our power to hasten His return. Let us, one sister at a time, share with others His love and His willingness to take us home to be with Him. Take comfort in His words: "Rest in the Lord, and wait patiently for Him" (Ps. 37:7). For God really is "good to those who wait for him."

Gloria Gregory

Prayer Plant

We must always give thanks to God for you, brothers and sisters, as is right, because your faith is growing abundantly, and the love of everyone of you for one another is increasing. 2 Thess. 1:3, NRSV.

GIFTS FROM MY MOTHER-IN-LAW are always lovely, but I keep on appreciating the prayer plants that she gave me several years ago. Loving and leaving plants is part of my destiny, it seems, so these two new plants that were shared with me when we started over in Oregon are special.

Somewhere I read how to care for them. Once a year, the experts said, repot them in a larger pot and fertilize. But three years had gone by, and mine still grew. Every year they would lose leaves and grow new, fresh ones, and I'd determine to repot them soon, but I still hadn't found the time to do it.

Finally, last week, as I was repotting outdoor plants, I remembered my neglected prayer plants. Bringing them out to my potting area, I looked in vain for larger pots. Finding none, I used several flimsy smaller ones. When I took the plants out of their pots, I could see they were root-bound, with roots growing extensively outside the bottoms of the pots.

H'mmm, I thought, *these poor plants sure need room to spread out.* I separated the different shoots and the little bulbs that would make new plants, and put each one in a new pot. In each of my original pots I put back a single healthy shoot. I'd made six new plants from my two prayer plants!

How often I do the same thing spiritually. I put off prayer time and devotions. In the meantime I run hither and yon, working hard, but all on my own. Root-bound—that's what becomes of me when I'm not plugging into the Source. What little good works I do are never up to my real potential, because they're done in my own power, without prayer. But with prayer comes sharing, and with sharing comes multiplication of effort and growth.

Now I have the privilege of sharing my new prayer plants and their spiritual lesson with my friends. Next year I plan to care for my prayer plants in a more timely manner and have more to share. And I will be sure not to forget where my power to share comes from! Becki Knobloch

Surprised by Joy

You will go out in joy and be led forth in peace; the mountains and hills will burst into song before you, and all the trees of the field will clap their hands. Isa. 55:12, NIV.

IT WAS WITH SADNESS THAT the midwife pronounced the newborn baby girl "dead on arrival." The baby was wrapped in a blanket and placed in a corner of the room. Arrangements had to be made for her burial. Her father, who was working overseas at the time of her birth, would not have the opportunity to see his baby girl. An elderly neighbor who had come to cheer the young mother proceeded to unwrap the tiny bundle. The baby sneezed. This, I am told by my mother, was the start of my struggle for survival.

As a premature baby who was born at 7 months, I lived in a developing country with limited medical facilities, and with parents who had even more limited financial ability to access what medical services existed. Life was difficult for the family.

I recall that as a young child there were always issues about my health. I contracted most childhood diseases and was labeled a sickly child. It is of little wonder, therefore, that I cried with joy when I celebrated my twenty-first birthday—the age of majority in England, where I lived at the time. You see, I never expected to live to adulthood.

I was surprised by joy when I became a mother, not once but twice. Each milestone in my life has been celebrated with inestimable joy because of the realization that I have been given another chance at life. This might in part help to explain the unquenchable desire I have to live life in a hurry.

Each morning gives us all a chance to start anew. This new day and the unspeakable joy it brings is a free gift from our Savior, given to us with love. It is ours for the taking. We need only to invite the Lord to be part of our day. Allow yourself today to experience the presence of our Savior. Ask Him to grant the desires of your heart. "Take delight in the Lord, and he will give you the desires of your heart" (Ps. 37:4, NRSV).

As sinners we do not always truly know what those desires are. We must, therefore, trust Him to reveal that truth to us. Then wait patiently. You too will be surprised by joy!

Avis Mae Rodney

Remarkable Resemblance

Your love for one another will prove to the world that you are my disciples. John 13:35, NLT.

MABEL WAS IN HER 90s when we met, and her mind was sharp. I was a volunteer working in the extended-care unit at the hospital. She wanted her family to know her life story, so she asked me to help her to write her genealogy.

I felt blessed by being asked, and I made writing her story a priority. When Mabel's daughter and family came from Florida to visit, I politely excused myself so that they could visit privately. Mabel insisted that I not go. "You are always here for me; they are not. Please stay," she said. I felt awkward.

I told Mabel many times that if she ever needed me she should just call. Only once did she phone me. It was the evening before Easter Sunday. She told me that she thought she was dying and asked if I would please come quickly. Mabel and I talked and prayed together, and I was home by midnight.

Sonny, my autistic son, was very special to Mabel, and it made her happy when I brought him to visit. It was on Sonny's seventh birthday, a Saturday, that Mabel passed away. Unaware of that, I went to get her for hymn-sing the following Wednesday morning and saw that her nameplate had been removed from the wall beside her door. My heart sank, and I asked the nearby nurse, "Is Mabel gone?" She looked up from her cart and replied, "She passed away shortly after you left her on Saturday afternoon."

Surprised, I said, "I wasn't here on Saturday. You must be mistaken!" I repeated myself three times, but she seemed not to hear me. I was so overwhelmed that I phoned my mom to tell her what had happened.

Angels are spiritual messengers sent from God to protect and comfort the heirs of salvation. I decided God must have sent a guardian angel to be at Mabel's side for the last few minutes of her life, as no other family or friends were there. If you can feel the presence of holy angels surrounding you, then how safe you must feel, even at the time of death.

DEBORAH SANDERS

Well Done

Well done, thou good and faithful servant: . . . enter thou into the joy of thy lord. Matt. 25:21.

MY HUSBAND RECENTLY TOOK OVER the family room in our basement and remodeled it as his own little electronic sanctuary. Since this was his project, I had little to do with the rehabilitation, other than to help select colors and a few furnishings.

My profession as an interior designer keeps me in close contact with others in similar fields, so I consulted with painting professionals as to the best paint to use, explaining the existing paint and the end result we hoped to achieve. Armed with proper paint, brushes, rollers, tape, and drop cloths, I relayed the information, step by step, to my husband.

My husband, older and more perfectionistic than those who had advised me, experimented, then decided that since the room was already painted, priming was unnecessary. I came home from work several days later to a beautifully and carefully painted room and a tired but happy husband, proud of his accomplishment and the haven he was creating for himself.

Once the carpeting had been installed, I inspected this newest phase of development. I noticed, however, that small bits of paint were peeling off the trim. Not wanting to cause conflict in my happy home, I cautiously began questioning my husband as to the steps he had followed in applying the paint.

We would both learn in time that the walls were fine without primer, but the trim work was another story. As predicted by the experts, the trim needed the primer to make the new paint adhere to the old. As a result of my husband's neglecting that step of preparation, the new paint is easily removed with the slightest bump or scrape.

So it is with our lives. We all know the proper steps to a better life with Christ. We have the directions clearly written in God's Word, and we have the experience of others to guide us, but too often we choose to ignore this advice. On the outer surface all may be well, and we may appear to have a relationship with Christ, but it's the preparation of our hearts and the end result that must be considered.

If we choose to live outside His guidelines, we will indeed suffer the consequences of never hearing Him say to us, "Well done."

PAULETTA COX JOHNSON

Innocence

Truly I say to you, unless you are converted and become like children, you shall not enter the kingdom of heaven. Matt. 18:3, NASB.

ONE DAY I WAS playing doctor with Brandon, my 3-year-old grandson. As usual, Grandma was the patient and Brandon was the doctor. When the novelty wore off, he packed up the instruments and headed toward the room in which the toys were kept. About halfway across the room he turned back toward me and said very seriously, "I'm not really a doctor; I'm just a kid!" I was struck with his honesty. He didn't want to deceive me. This small boy did not want Grandma to assume he was something he wasn't.

Now, three years later, Brandon was twisting Grandpa's arm to play Candyland. Since it is usually Grandma who plays the games, Grandpa had no idea as to the rules. It wasn't long before Brandon shouted, "I won! I won!" Then he added, "I cheated! I cheated, and I won!" The honesty is still there.

As children grow, many are tempted to deceive so that they can win. They enjoy the praise a winner receives. If you catch them cheating, they try to deny it, because they know that punishment may be the result. But worse than that, they feel the loss of respect that others have for them. Adults have a look of disappointment on their faces, and other children are likely to refer to them as a "cheater."

This little grandson of ours is so openly honest, but we do realize it's probably only a matter of time before Brandon will attempt to deceive. After all, we live in a sin-damaged world. Our prayers are that God gives him the strength of character to always be honest.

Wouldn't it be a wonderful world if everyone were as honest as a child? We would be able to believe all politicians, all news commentators, and all used-car salespeople. How easy it would be to make decisions if we knew that all the information we had received was the truth.

God wants the people in His kingdom to be honest and trustworthy. Jesus came to our world to reveal the character of the Father. There are many facets to God's character, and Jesus demonstrated that honesty is one of them. The lesson we need to learn from the little ones is that our characters need to reflect the honesty we see in them. JUDY HAUPT JAGITSCH

Go to the Master Gardener

With men it is impossible, but not with God: for with God all things are possible. Mark 10:27.

ONE OF MY FAVORITE fruits is the persimmon. When I learned that my friends had successfully grown a persimmon tree in Virginia, I grew two trees.

The first spring one tree had many little developing fruits. I was very excited and hopeful. I thought I would have an abundance of persimmons come winter. It was worth the $70 that I had invested in the trees. I bragged to my friend, who said, "My trees have a lot of developing fruit too." But as the summer progressed, most of the persimmons began falling off.

Nearly every day I anxiously counted how many persimmons were left hanging on the tree. By the end of summer the more than 50 potential fruits had thinned out to three—and then one.

One day I checked the last persimmon that was ripening, but I didn't pick it. I waited for it to become fully ripe. When I returned, the fruit was gone. I found it on the ground; the precious fruit had been pecked by a bird. I was so disappointed.

Three springs later I counted more than 500 persimmons starting. I consulted someone who had more experience to find out what to do to keep them connected until ready for harvest. The expert said, "Go to the nursery pharmacy and get some spray." Another consultant said, "You have to thin them out. Get rid of quite a few of them to allow more room for the others to grow." An agriculturist said, "It takes five years to stabilize persimmon trees before they can fully bear a fair number of fruits."

I started to pick out what I thought needed to be discarded. One fruit out, one fruit remaining. One fruit thrown, one fruit left. Before I could finish thinning properly, a storm began approaching. So I knelt between the trees and prayed, "O Lord, I have done all I can. I have consulted the experts and the professionals. I will leave this matter to You now. Please do what you want. You are the Master Gardener. I leave this matter in Your care at Your own time."

Today the fruit is getting ripe. I will be able to harvest abundantly. God is so good! One call to the Master Gardener was sufficient. He does what is best, and I know He will do the best for us who will trust in Him as well.

Esperanza Aquino Mopera

A Mother's Love

Being confident of this, that he who began a good work in you will carry it on to completion until the day of Christ Jesus. Phil. 1:6.

AS A CHILD YOU SOMETIMES wonder why your parents chastise you so often. I never understood why Mom would reprimand me when I did something unbecoming. I never understood why she wouldn't allow me to visit certain places that my peers liked to visit. Once in a while she would allow me to venture out according to my desires, but, to my horror and surprise, it was as distasteful, painful, and even embarrassing as she had predicted.

Later, when I was grown up, I began to realize how much love was intertwined in all those reprimands. If Mom hadn't steered me in the right direction, I would probably be lost spiritually today. During devotional time she used to mention her 12 children by name, even though most of them had grown and married. It just hit me one day during my college years that there was certainly something to what she did for us. So I took time to write her a thank-you letter. I told her that if it weren't for her pleading for me each day, I wouldn't be what I am today. I even thanked her for those reprimands that I had hated so much. I thanked her for showing me so much love as she nurtured me into the beautiful young woman that I am today. I thanked her for being there for me when I needed her. I thanked her for being an exemplary mom. It was then that I realized the art of love and the time she had invested to mold me into what I am today.

There is only one day in a year to thank all the mothers, but mine is a blessing each day. Yes, mothers are so special. To have a God-fearing mom is the most wonderful gift.

Just as my mother did her part, God is working on me each day. Sometimes I have a rebellious spirit, but I thank God for that still small voice, pleading with love each time, each day. Sometimes situations turn sour and I wonder why. But I now know that I'm under His wings every day. Someday God will be there to answer all those "whys" that I have. I wait for that glorious morning to tell Him thank You, face to face, and that I am what I am because of Him.

SIBUSISIWE NCUBE-NDHLOVU

The Amazing D

For the Lord God is our light and protector. He gives us grace and glory. No good thing will the Lord withhold from those who do what is right. Ps. 84:11, NLT.

IT WAS MY FINAL YEAR in college. My advisor did one last check of my transcript to ensure that all requisites for my graduation were accounted for. "One thing is still missing," he told me. "It's the same thing that's been missing for the past two years." My heart sank, as it had each time he had reminded me. "You are still missing one credit of physical education, and you must register for it this quarter." His baritone underlined the time frame as he handed me the schedule.

My eye-hand coordination is virtually nonexistent, so I had never excelled at sports. "What about badminton?" My professor pushed his wire-framed spectacles up his nose as we looked for a class I might pass. "I know you can do that. It's fairly straightforward. My daughters love it."

I signed up for the course. The first class went well as we learned the rules of the game. At the second class we went to the court. Things went smoothly until I discovered that ducking the shuttlecock as it was volleyed over the net was not acceptable. I had to return it.

"You cannot shut your eyes each time the birdie comes your way," my classmates advised me kindly. Nevertheless, I still flinched each time it was my turn to return the serve.

I came to dread Tuesdays—the only day we were on the court. Valiantly my instructor tried to give me tips to improve my game, but still I had problems. It was clear that chances for any improvement on my part were few. Hopes for passing the class and graduating dimmed.

Just before graduation the final grades were published. Hesitantly I walked across campus to scan the physical education roster. I could not believe my eyes! I had passed that badminton class. With a D, but I had passed!

That long-ago experience gave the bumbling student a new perspective on the grace Paul talks about. "For by grace you have been saved through faith, and that not of yourselves; it is the gift of God, not of works, lest anyone should boast" (Eph. 2:8, 9, NKJV). That's what is so amazing about the gift of grace!

Thank You, merciful Savior. Your fleet-footed pursuit of this unworthy, procrastinating sinner mystifies me. You bring me such goodness that I can never praise Your name enough! GLENDA-MAE GREENE

A Forever Friend!

The poor is hated even of his own neighbour: but the rich hath many friends. Prov. 14:20.

MANY YEARS AGO SHELLIE STEIN was not on my favorite persons' list. I really did not know her at the time, but for a while I let my perceptions keep her at arm's length. Years have passed since then, and I cannot even remember anything that was particularly wrong with her. As I look back, it seems silly how much validity was put into a first impression. I realized early on that my initial perceptions could have cost me a valuable friendship. I'm thankful that my perception changed, especially because Shellie is one of the best friends I have, and through her friendship I have seen how Jesus is a forever friend.

Shellie has helped me personally more than I could ever repay. I remember when I had my first child. My husband and I were lost. It took both of us to change her diaper. The little 8-pound thing sure could wiggle! So we needed help when it came to the "how to" of bathing. Shellie came right over and showed us how, without making a big deal about our lack of parenting skills. She also has the uncanny ability to organize information and numbers in her head. She never fussed when I depended on her information base, even when I would ask for the same piece of information again and again. A few years ago when I was going through a particularly stressful time, she listened to me, never uttered a judgmental word, and encouraged me.

Although we have relocated and I miss her dearly, she is not far from my heart. She is like a sister to me, and I appreciate our weekly contacts by phone or by e-mail. Shellie is one of those special people who is blessed and seems always connected to God. I appreciate her spiritual coaching, and it's comforting to know that she's praying for me. I hope I can be a friend to her and others as she has been to me.

People such as Shellie remind me of how Jesus was on this earth. He is not only our Savior but a friend. The examples of how He helped others shows us His unconditional love. He is a forever friend who is only a prayer away. Jesus is always by my side, even when I make mistakes. I am truly blessed!

MARY WAGONER ANGELIN

Right on Time

Listen to my voice in the morning, Lord. Each morning I bring my requests to you and wait expectantly. Ps. 5:3, NLT.

I HAVE JUST EXPERIENCED THREE wonderful, positive answers to prayer in my life. We had laid our plans for the women's ministries program at our annual camp meeting, and now there was only a week to go. There were still myriad little things to be done to ensure that everything would run smoothly. How we were praying for God's special blessing on each woman who would come to the tent!

Some weeks earlier I had sent our order to Bangladesh for beautiful cards with cross-stitched panels from Pollywog handicrafts so that we could sell these items. This would help support the women who made them half a world away, enabling them to buy food for their children. The year before, Pollywog products had been a great success, and we hoped they would be again.

The only problem was that it was just a little more than a week before camp meeting was to start, and the Pollywog order hadn't arrived. On that particular Thursday morning I took my request to the Lord and very boldly asked Him to please have the Pollywog goods delivered that day. Then there were so many other things to do that I promptly forgot about the matter.

A couple hours later, as I was busy with correspondence, the doorbell rang, and my husband opened the front door. As I heard the door close again I called out, "Is that my Pollywog order?" and he answered, "Well, yes, it is." I then told him of my request made just that morning.

Another answered prayer was the exciting telephone conversation with a dear friend who had been struggling with trauma for three months but had now turned the corner.

Third, I decided to clean up a basketful of ironing and had just ironed the collar on the fifth shirt when I felt compelled to phone someone whom I knew was having a spiritual battle. So I simply left the shirt and the iron, walked to my desk, and took out the phone book to look up the number; just then the phone rang. I was stunned to hear the voice of the woman I was about to call. As we shared this experience, we were sure that God wanted us to have a chat about Him. Right then and there we did. As I prayed for this special person at the end of our talk, our faith in God was greatly strengthened.

Is God with us each day? Oh, yes! I've just had three proofs.

URSULA M. HEDGES

Between Life and Death

The spirit of God hath made me, and the breath of the Almighty hath given me life. Job 33:4.

JANUARY 1986. I SAT staring as the doctor from the Mayo Clinic reconfirmed the diagnosis I'd received a month before. I had primary pulmonary hypertension, an incurable lung disease that becomes progressively worse very quickly. He said I had, on the average, six months to two years to live and probably not more than six years at best. He said my only chance was to have a heart-lung transplant, and that I should get on the waiting list as soon as possible.

It was as though I had turned to stone and couldn't seem to get up to leave the doctor's office. I was so glad my sweet Manna had come with me and could help me get back to the hotel. Once we got to the hotel, the first thing we did was to pray.

I'd had great difficulty breathing for two years, but since I had asthma, we thought that was the culprit. It was not.

Whatever would I do now? I planned to quit my job, which was far too demanding anyway, but my husband was not well either, so I worried. My regular doctor at home assured me that no one could really say for sure how long I had, and encouraged me to keep working as long as I could.

With great difficulty and much prayer I was able to stay at my job for six more years. All that time I prayed that God would heal me. Then I asked myself, *Why would He heal me when others pray and still die? Why do I deserve to be well any more than anyone else?*

God did do something for me, though. No, I didn't get a transplant, nor was I healed. I still struggle to breathe every day. I shake three rugs, sweep half the floor, and then must rest. My work must be done in bits and pieces. I'm thankful I need oxygen only at night, and we do travel quite often.

I feel so blessed, because this is 17 years later as I write. But my life did change in 1986. I know more than ever that every day is a bonus. For some reason my illness has stabilized, at least for now, and I hope I won't let a day go by without doing something to help someone. Praise God that I can breathe at all! When I was ready to give up and things seemed hopeless, He was—and is—always there.

DARLENE YTREDAL BURGESON

Comfort One Another

That their hearts might be comforted, being knit together in love. Col. 2:2.

I WAS ONLY 18 YEARS OLD when I became pregnant with our first child. Harold and I rented a small two-bedroom furnished house, and with a borrowed bassinet we awaited the birth of our baby. It was an uneventful pregnancy until the final week. Believing the baby was overdue, the doctor decided to induce labor. So it was on November 12, 1941, that I gave birth to a beautiful 7-pound-15-ounce baby girl. But for reasons even the attending physician could not explain, our daughter was stillborn.

When I arrived home from the hospital two days later, no mention of the baby was made. The bassinet, baby clothes, and all other reminders were stashed away in boxes and drawers.

I didn't see my baby while in the hospital, and it wasn't until the morning of the graveside service that they brought her to me. The funeral director laid the little white casket at the foot of my bed, and it was then that I wept for this tiny person I would never get to hold.

I was very young when all this took place, and years later as I was once again reflecting on the events of that sad day, one thing besides mourning the death of my child kept going through my mind: I had been left to grieve alone. Neither my husband nor any other family member even came to my room to share in my sorrow.

It wasn't until years later, after I became a nurse, that I was able to understand better the true meaning of compassion and sympathy during times of illness and death.

My family wasn't being callous that day in 1941; they just didn't know how to approach such a delicate issue. For them it was easier to close their minds and hearts to all the sadness than to face up to reality. They thought it would ease my pain, when in fact it may have prolonged it. What I perceived to be a lack of sensitivity to the situation at hand was their way of masking their own feelings. After all, they were hurting too.

In time we were able to experience the needed healing process, and later on we were blessed with two healthy children, a boy and a girl.

As it says in Deuteronomy 31:6: "It is the Lord your God who goes with you; he will not fail you or forsake you" (NRSV). Others may fail, but God never does.

Clareen Colclesser

Vegetables of the Spirit

But the fruit of the Spirit is love, joy, peace, patience, kindness, goodness, faithfulness, gentleness, and self-control. Gal. 5:22, NIV.

HAVE YOU EVER WONDERED why God commanded us to have the "fruit of the Spirit" and not the "vegetables of the Spirit"? It got me thinking about the differences between the two.

Most vegetables, such as cabbage, cauliflower, carrots, onions, and broccoli, are annual plants. They must be planted each year. They bear one crop and then die. Their roots are shallow compared with a fruit tree's. When planted, many of the seeds are either trampled on or fall on rocky soil. Or they are choked by other plants. They are easily damaged by lack of water, too much or too little sun, weeds, or poor maintenance.

Fruit trees, such as apple, pear, peach, banana, date, and fig, take several years to mature. Most trees don't even bear fruit for three years, or more, after the tree has been planted. Its roots are as deep and wide in the ground as the tree is above the surface. It survives through seasons of snow, ice, and bitter temperatures. A piece of fruit also has seeds to enable more trees to grow.

I can see why God wants our Christian life to bear fruit! When we first come to a life in Christ, we are mere saplings; but as we grow, we become more grounded in God's Word and our prayer life. This enables us to bear fruit for the Lord. From this fruit, seeds are planted in others, and the Holy Spirit can work powerfully in them to become strong trees of their own. We can withstand great trials and unfavorable circumstances because we are grounded so deeply in our relationship with God. Even the tree of life and the tree of the knowledge of good and evil in the Garden of Eden were fruit trees.

Like vegetables, fruit trees can be in danger of disease, drought, or not producing. The Bible says, "The ax is already at the root of the trees, and every tree that does not produce good fruit will be cut down and thrown into the fire" (Matt. 3:10, NIV). If we choose to bear fruit for the Lord, we must be deeply rooted in Him. With the Master Gardener's hand caring for us, we can bear on our tree all nine fruits found in Galatians 5:22: love, joy, peace, patience, kindness, goodness, faithfulness, gentleness, and self-control.

KAREN PHILLIPS

The Alternative

Out of the mouth of babes and sucklings hast thou ordained strength because of thine enemies, that thou mightest still the enemy and the avenger. Ps. 8:2.

THIS MANY YEARS LATER I cannot remember what the crisis was or why it was so upsetting to us. I remember that my son, Drew, then 6 years old, was in the car as we were discussing how upsetting a certain situation was. My son sat next to me in his seat-belted car seat, listening patiently as Mama ranted on and on. He asked questions occasionally and listened quietly to my answers.

Evidently the problem revolved around a situation in which someone had really messed up, because Drew suddenly turned to me, his face aglow with the knowledge that he had the solution to the problem, and exclaimed, "Isn't it wonderful that no matter how badly we mess up, God always has an alternative?"

His perspective caught me off guard. My breath caught in my throat, and I had to fight the tears in my eyes as we continued down the freeway. Proverbs 23:15 flashed into my mind: "My son, if thine heart be wise, my heart shall rejoice, even mine."

When I could speak without crying, I answered him the only way I could. "Yes, Drew, God always has a preferred plan for our lives. But no matter how badly we fail and divert that original plan, God does have an alternative, and that failed circumstance can still be to God's glory and the happiness of the person who messes up.

My son nodded gravely. There was no reason to continue the former conversation. He had solved the problem with his child's insight.

He had also taught his mother an important lesson about God's grace, love, and support of His creatures as they go stumbling through life, making mistakes and errors and failing at so much that they try. It really is wonderful that no matter how badly we mess up a situation, God always has an alternative.

Dear God, thank You for the wisdom of babes. And thank You for having an alternative ready when we mess up. Amen.

DARLENEJOAN MCKIBBON RHINE

Expectations

Be wise about what is good, and innocent about what is evil. Rom. 16:19, NIV.

OUR TEAM CAME IN third!" Melissa's face was the very picture of distress. "Third! We were so sure we'd win," she continued, her voice a wail. "We'd even talked Josh into taking the last leg!" Moisture that looked suspiciously like tears gathered in her preteen eyes. I knew there'd been months of planning and months of track meet practice.

"Once upon a time," I began, "a cactus was transplanted to a swamp." I watched her interest spark. "A passerby, noticing that the plant was beginning to rot (to say nothing of listing dangerously to one side), commented, 'They don't grow cacti like they used to.' "

Melissa's infectious laugh bubbled into the air. "Oh, I can just picture that poor little cactus!" she exclaimed. (Her ability for mental picturing is amazing.) "It was in the wrong environment. How could it be expected to flourish?" (Her love of big words continued unabated.)

"My point exactly," I replied.

Melissa's brows curved in momentary puzzlement. "Oh! You mean that Josh is a long-distance runner, and we expected him to sprint for the relay!" The girl was quick. We ended up having one of our special conversations, the memory of which I'll cherish forever. We spoke of the power of expectations and how Josh had finally agreed to do his best for the team effort, "even if it's not my forte," as Melissa quoted. We discussed the way in which our culture typically rewards outcome and ignores effort.

"Josh really deserves an A-plus for effort," I commented. "Especially for trying so hard in an area outside his innate giftedness." And we talked about winning as doing one's absolute best versus winning as coming in first.

"Excuse me for a minute." Melissa hopped up. "I've got to call Josh." The words floated back over her shoulder. "Our team really did win—we all did our absolute best!"

I remained curled up in my favorite chair, listening to the lilt of her voice as she chatted with Josh. And I thought about expectations. Mine, as well as those of others—and of the Lord's expectations for us. "Seek good, not evil, that you may live" (Amos 5:14, NIV). Fortunately, with God's help, that is always within our ability to achieve!

ARLENE TAYLOR

Jesus Loves Me, This I Know!

I have loved you with an everlasting love; I have drawn you with loving-kindness. Jer. 31: 3, NIV.

I HEARD A STORY ONCE of a woman who left her husband and traveled to a far country. At last her money ran out, and all her friends except one turned away. Soon there came a letter from her husband saying that since she had been gone so long she could now take off the wedding ring. She took off the ring for the first time since her husband had put it on her finger, and she laid it down on a small table. The friend picked it up to look at it. Suddenly he said, "Look! Have you read what is inscribed inside this ring?" For the first time the woman read the inscription inside: "Always remember two things: I love you, and the name of the bank."

The woman packed her bags and returned to her loving husband, who was waiting with open arms. There she found his true love again; he had been waiting for her return to him and their lovely home. They had many more happy years together, according to the story.

I found a lesson hidden there. I miss my dear late husband. He left me the little home and income I have because of his love, the love he learned from God. I can claim the promise in Isaiah 54:5, 6: "For your Maker is your husband—the Lord Almighty is his name—the Holy One of Israel is your Redeemer; he is called the God of all the earth. The Lord will call you back as if you were a wife deserted and distressed in spirit" (NIV).

Those words in the ring, "Always remember two things: I love you, and the name of the bank," sound rather like the promise inscribed in God's Word. He has ever-accepting love and the name of the bank of heaven. And the bank of heaven is always full. He is preparing mansions there for us!

I can claim those promises every day as I develop a relationship with Jesus, my Lord; His true love never fails. He draws me to Him with His loving arms around me. I never want to lose my awareness of His everlasting love for me. Inscribed in His hands are the marks of His true love for every person on earth. That love transcends all circumstances!

BESSIE SIEMENS LOBSIEN

The Beautiful World

The heavens are telling the glory of God; and the firmament proclaims his handiwork. Ps. 19:1, RSV.

IT WAS A BEAUTIFUL SUNDAY morning in spring. I was at Brookside Gardens in Wheaton, Maryland, with a friend, enjoying the gorgeous tulips in many colors. I cannot even explain the majestic beauty of the flowers, each petal so perfectly shaped and each color perfectly blended.

We sat down on a bench to drink in the beauty and watch the people, young and old, male and female, exclaiming their joy as they beheld bed after bed of gorgeous tulips and breathed deeply of the sweet smell of the flowers.

We also saw an elderly couple helping each other so they could bend to touch and smell the delicate and beautiful creations. We saw others enjoying just walking under the trees.

Two cute little girls, probably 5 and 6 years old or so, were busy jumping and hopping around, contented in smelling the flowers and pretending they were actresses posing for the camera in front of the beautiful backdrop. As the girls jumped around enjoying the beauty around them, we noticed the doting mother, smiling as she watched her daughters having fun.

If we take time to go out of the closed environment of our houses, offices, and classrooms and enjoy the beauty of nature that God has so wonderfully and carefully made for each of us, our doting Father, who loves us very much, smiles from heaven, happy that we took time to enjoy the beauty that He gave us. I imagine His smile as He sees us enjoy a walk in the woods, touch the fertile ground, and plant a delicate flower or place a seed. I can almost see His smile as He sees us pause to pat our dog or to hear a bird sing or to watch the changing colors of a rainbow or a brilliant sunrise.

Someday, of course, we want to see our Father in heaven, and there we will in reality see Him smile as we enjoy all the things He has created and planned for us. But let's take some time today to enjoy and thank Him for the beauty of nature that surrounds us.

Father, please help us to take time to feel Your love through the bounties of nature during this season. JEMIMA D. ORILLOSA

Peace and Contentment

You will keep him in perfect peace, whose mind is stayed on You, because he trusts in You. Isa. 26:3, NKJV.

EVERY YEAR, WITHOUT FAIL, a pair of mourning doves builds its nest in a trellislike structure we built to help a gourd vine climb every summer. As soon as the foliage of the vine becomes thick enough to camouflage the birds' nest, the mourning doves busy themselves, making their nest in which to lay their eggs and raise the young ones. As soon as the nest is built, the female dove sits in it for two weeks while the male dove hunts for food. It has been amazing to watch the two birds take care of each other while they are in the process of raising a family.

One day after the gourd had grown and produced some long, edible gourds, we wanted to take one. The gourd that my husband decided to pick was so close to the nest that he thought the female dove would protest. By this time the two young birds had already hatched and were being nurtured. The father dove was watching closely, perhaps wanting to know what my husband would do. After all, he was to take care of his family. Without complaint or protest the mother bird sat there quietly. We thought she was a perfect picture of peace and trust. Did she know that we were not going to hurt her and her young ones? Did she understand that we care enough to protect them from the two or three neighborhood cats that usually prowl around our backyard? Did she know by instinct that we were there to truly protect them? Her peace and trust really impressed me.

Here were God's creatures, "ordinary" mourning doves, that showed trust in humans who had the power to annihilate them. Oh, that we women could show this same trust in our loving, caring God who created us after His own likeness! Could we as God's daughters display the same peace and contentment and trust in Him? So often a little problem ruffles our feathers. Can't we trust the One who made us and knows our frame? Isaiah 26:3 says that God will keep us in perfect peace if our mind is stayed on Him. Psalm 91:3, 4 says, "Surely He shall deliver you from the snare of the fowler. . . . He shall cover you with His feathers, and under His wings you shall take refuge" (NKJV).

Yes, just as those mourning doves trusted my husband, you and I can trust our heavenly, powerful Father.

Ofelia A. Pangan

Where Is God?

In whose hand is the soul of every living thing, and the breath of all mankind. Job 12:10.

WHILE VISITING THE DINOSAUR museum in Drumheller, Alberta, Canada, I marveled at the lovely displays of fossils—extinct fish, insects, and dinosaur figures, some reaching up to the second-floor ceiling and stretching many car lengths. There are videos and science displays of how the remains are found, preserved, mounted, and labeled. I marveled at the plush carpeting, expensive gift shop, restaurant, and well-put-together educational place.

The lack of belief in Creation was verified near the end of the exhibits. There was a wall-to-wall display almost two stories high and equally wide. Displayed on it were about eight figures, approximately 10 feet tall, depicting how the human race supposedly began.

It started with a birdlike creature that evolved to walk on the ground but still seemed pretty birdlike. Then came a creature that gradually looked like a monkey and that began to walk more erect, followed by an ape, and then a caveman. After more evolution the caveman became a modern man. No credit was given to the God of Creation, the one responsible for all we are and have.

My heart was heavy. As we were about to exit the building, I glanced up, and there, around a curved corner, in large print, was written only this text: Job 12:8. I assumed they at least in part had recognized a greater Creator. They had not left me totally disappointed.

When I got back to the motor home, I looked up the verse and came to the realization that they did not know the God of Creation by taking that verse alone. My spirits fell a little again. The verse read, "Or speak to the earth, and it shall teach thee: and the fishes of the sea shall declare unto thee." I was puzzled. How could they show that we evolved and still say that the earth shall teach and the fish shall declare? I continued to read further, as I felt there was something in this experience for me. When I read verses 9 and 10, I was thankful for the God I know. I said to myself, *They should have posted verses 9 and 10.* I'd like to think someone made a mistake in choosing which verse they put on that wall.

This also makes one think about how often in our lives we forget to give God the credit for the wonders He performs in our lives, families, and communities each day. Let's be careful to give Him all the praise. VIDELLA MCCLELLAN

May 28

Lines of Communication

Evening, and morning, and at noon, will I pray, and cry aloud: and he shall hear my voice. Ps. 55:17.

AS WE SAILED INTO THE port of Copenhagen I glowed with excitement. *Surely I'll find a way to communicate with family members back home without having to pay $15 a minute* (the rate for a phone call on the ship), I reasoned. I'd been gone a few days and missed talking to my family. My goal was to touch base before engaging in any activities.

Various shops along the dock posted signs advertising where to fax, e-mail, or buy phone cards. Prices ranged from $3 to $32 to send an e-mail.

When I saw this I felt very special. I generally pray about almost everything, and this was certainly another answer to prayer. An e-mail for three bucks! For less than $10 I could e-mail both my sisters and my son.

Quickly entering the shop to inquire about the actual existence and legitimacy of this operation, I discovered it was indeed real. Everything was exactly as advertised. Why $3 here and $32 a few doors away? Once I was convinced and confirmed, all else was history.

Thumbing through my address book brought me to the realization that it definitely needed to be updated. In my excitement I searched desperately for e-mail addresses, but to no avail. What a rude awakening! With a six-hour difference in the time zone between the United States and Europe, my sisters and my son would probably be at work or asleep at a reasonable time for me to call them. An e-mail or fax would have been the perfect means of communication. I learned that it is imperative to keep my address book updated.

There are lines of communication open that connect me to my heavenly Father. He's given me a personalized directory that never needs updating. I can reach Him through fasting and praying, Bible studies, my Sabbath school lessons, songs of praise, a teacher's meeting, worship services, and even being alone in my closet.

I can call at any hour, day or night. He can be reached faster than by e-mail, fax, phone, or telegram. There are never any busy signals, He is always available, and there is never a charge.

CORA A. WALKER

Say It Now

A word aptly spoken is like apples of gold in settings of silver. Prov. 25:11, NIV.

YESTERDAY I ATTENDED THE funeral of a lonely 69-year-old unmarried woman who had been our church organist for as long as anyone could remember. Muted music, beautiful flowers, and soft lighting heightened the solemnity of death—until the officiating minister announced a "Memories of Margaret" segment. Then people surged forward.

A tearful student came to the microphone and mumbled between sniffs that Miss Margaret had never gotten cross with her, even when she hadn't practiced, but had lovingly told her that to succeed she must work harder at her music lessons. A much younger single woman, an associate organist, made us all smile as she told how the two of them used to get together to talk about men and music. Then a classical pianist said that when she had learned that Miss Margaret particularly admired Bach, she came to church early on Friday evenings and the two of them played Bach for pure enjoyment.

"Margaret didn't wear the latest fashion in clothes," said a neighbor, "but she always wore a smile. Her kindness and love for God showed in her face."

Then the minister testified to Margaret's willingness to do anything she could for her Lord. "You could rely on her at work bees. She walked miles on ADRA appeals, for the Red Cross, or distributing evangelistic advertising. When her poor old feet hurt, she changed into slippers and kept on going."

One time he was to conduct a wedding and, at the last minute, found that neither party had arranged for music. Quickly he had called Margaret. She knew she would receive no remuneration, but at the appointed time she was at the church playing appropriate music. She played on and on and on until the bride, who hailed from a country where time means nothing, arrived without apology—two and a half hours late.

As we listened to these oral tributes, I wondered how many of the speakers had expressed appreciation to Miss Margaret for her music, her kindness, and her missionary work while she was living. How her tired old eyes would have glistened behind her spectacles.

Dear Lord, help me to show Your love by speaking words of appreciation and encouragement to those around me. And thank You for all You do for me. Amen.

GOLDIE DOWN

Inspiration From a Graveyard

When the perishable has been clothed with the imperishable, and the mortal with immortality, then the saying that is written will come true: "Death has been swallowed up in victory." "Where, O death, is your victory? Where, O death, is your sting?" 1 Cor. 15:54, 55, NIV.

IT WAS SABBATH AGAIN! Another bright, lovely, and serene day had dawned. A day for physical rest, yes, but even more for inspiration and blessings.

At 8:30 a.m. my husband and I packed our books and lunch in the car in preparation for our 20-mile journey to church, our first time to visit that particular church in Jamaica. As we traveled along the lonely, winding roads, we tried to take in the awesome scenery. In the middle of nowhere we discovered an old abandoned church with its unkempt graveyard. We decided to stop on our return journey.

When we stopped at the old churchyard later, we noticed tombs of various shapes and sizes. We hastened toward a dilapidated structure. Inside, the air was musty, and the fixtures, apart from a few remaining plaques on the walls, had long since disappeared. The sunlight, however, streamed through the tattered roof, as if God's Shekinah glory were shining through.

We proceeded to read the plaques that were dedicated to veterans who had given service. One read: "In memory of John Stowe for 31 years of service. 'And I [John] heard a voice from heaven saying unto me, Write, Blessed are the dead which die in the Lord.'" I was immediately overwhelmed, and I cried out, "Yes, write!"

I then hurried outside to gain more inspiration. We read the various epitaphs, the earliest of which dated from 1858. One read: "Nothing in my hand I bring/Simply to Thy cross I cling." Another: "Jesus Christ, the same yesterday, today, and forever." Envisioning the glories that await the saints of all ages, dead or alive, and thrilled at the expressions of hope and assurance, I just burst out singing, "'O that will be glory for me, glory for me, glory for me; when by His grace I shall look on His face, that will be glory, be glory for me.'"

Are we ready for the glorious appearing of our Lord?

Bula Rose Haughton Thompson

Up, Up, and Away

For he shall give his angels charge over thee, to keep thee in all thy ways. They shall bear thee up in their hands. Ps. 91:11, 12.

THE HOUSE WAS A FLURRY of activity as we hurried to get ready for our emergency trip. Friends arrived to take us to the airport. My mother had died at home in her sleep; we had held a memorial service the following Wednesday. Now we were on our way to Montreal for the funeral on Sunday, as that had been our home before I'd moved west to Alberta. Mom had followed and had lived with me ever since that time. Nine of us got into the two vans, and we were on our way. My oldest son, at 16, was his usual cool self—on the outside. This was his first plane ride, and I knew he was anxious, as he didn't know what to expect. He'd had stomach pains during the night because of his nerves.

We got to the airport early and passed the time browsing in the airport shops and counting heads to make sure we didn't lose any of the younger children, my grandchildren. Although the purpose of our trip was a sad one, there was excitement as we boarded the plane. My son watched eagerly as the flight attendant demonstrated the safety procedures. He even checked the pocket of the seat in front of him to ensure that the card with the relevant information, and the air sickness bag, were there. Reassured that everything was in place, he settled comfortably in his seat next to his twin sister and younger brother.

We each offered silent prayers and settled in for the four-hour flight to Montreal. As I looked around at the other passengers, I wondered how many of them were Christians and had prayed for traveling mercies. Some were sleeping; others were working on their laptop computers; some were reading; and some were watching the in-flight movie. The passengers didn't seem to have a care in the world. Their fate was in the hands of the pilot and the crew.

I was reminded of the text that says that the prayers of the righteous avail much (James 5:16). I felt confident that our prayers had covered them as well as ourselves, and that God's will would be done on the flight. Their fate may have been in the hands of the pilot and the crew, but I knew ours were in the hands of God. If God is for you, who can be against you?

SHARON LONG (BROWN)

A Place of Its Own

And if I go and prepare a place for you, I will come again, and receive you unto myself; that where I am, there ye may be also. John 14:3.

WHEN WE MOVED INTO our new house, friends gave us several floral gifts. My sister-in-law and her husband sent a huge bouquet of spring flowers that graced our dining room table for more than a week. For my birthday a good friend and a member of one of my prayer circles each brought an exotic anthurium lily that flourished in our screened porch. The women's ministries department of our church gave us a pot of gorgeous orchids that bloomed in the living room for more than six months. Another friend from my other prayer circle brought two blooming rosebushes—one pink and the other red—that we planted in our front garden.

The pink rosebush thrived, putting out bloom after bloom all summer. The red bush, however, put out only one rose. Soon its leaves began to wilt. It looked as though it was going to die. "Perhaps you have it too close to your sprinkler," a friend suggested, uprooting it gently and planting it in a different spot. Within a week it was putting out new leaves. Soon tiny buds and then new blooms signaled its vibrant life. It had found a place of its own, one better suited to its unique needs.

Sometimes we spend too much time in the wetlands of despair. We stop growing and begin to wilt. Ellen G. White penned a precious promise to help us deal with situations such as this: "When we really believe that God loves us and means to do us good we shall cease to worry about the future" (*Thoughts From the Mount of Blessings,* p. 101).

The floral offerings also symbolize our different gifts. Some gifts, such as a vibrant smile, are as beautiful and short-lived as cut-flower arrangements. Others, like a fervent prayer, are as long lasting as the beautiful anthurium. God remembers and uses them all.

When we spend time in the sunshine of His loving watch care, we begin to grow and thrive as my rosebush did. God loves us so much that He wants us to find our own place in this world and in the garden that He has prepared for us.

Thank You, Master Gardener, for sunshine to bless our lives and for gifts to share with others. Thank You for preparing a place for us here and in the world to come.

CAROL J. GREENE

Could It Have Been an Angel?

The eternal God is thy refuge, and underneath are the everlasting arms. Deut. 33:27.

ONE DAY WE WERE taking care of Carly, a bright little 8-year-old girl, in our home. We decided to let her help deliver fresh roses from our garden to a couple dental offices near us. She was wearing a cute little hat from Washington, D.C., and with her smile and the flowers, she was a happy child to see.

On the way back from making the deliveries, we decided to stop and see the city rose garden. Since it was June, the roses were blooming their hearts out. We walked all around the gardens and had a glorious time. We even saw a special cherry tree that was 155 years old—a large, majestic tree with branches reaching out and seeming to invite adventurous children to climb among them. Our little friend would have loved to do just that, but of course it was against the park rules.

We next took a nice walk along the river, being careful not to get too close to the edge. But we all peeked down to see the moss, or "hair," swinging in the clear water. After a while Carly and I decided it was time to get up, and we began to climb the steep bank. Little Carly had no problem, but I struggled, even with my husband's help. When we were about three feet from the grassy area, a man rushed over and said, "Here, I'll help you. Relax, and I'll get you up." Then he lifted me in his strong arms as if I were a feather. It was a thrill to feel his strong arms. I had never felt such strength. Later, as we walked along, I was in awe and wondered if the man had been an angel. What a memory of God's care to cling to!

Thinking back on my life, I'm sure many times God has sent His angel to save me; sometimes I haven't even known it. But one time, while I was driving alone in my car, another car coming in the opposite direction pulled directly into my path. All I could think of was Lord, save me! Suddenly the other car swerved away, as if pulled by strong angel arms. Shaken but unharmed, I offered a prayer of thanks to God right then and there for saving my life.

Dear Lord, thank You for the promise of Your everlasting arms to help in times of need. I want to feel Your presence at all times, always remembering Your blessings.

FRIEDA TANNER

The Legacy of Prayer

"As for me, this is my covenant with them," says the Lord. "My Spirit, who is on you, and my words that I have put in your mouth will not depart from your mouth, or from the mouths of your children, or from the mouths of their descendants from this time on and forever," says the Lord. Isa. 59:21, NIV.

LEAVING AN INHERITANCE FOR one's descendants is one of the interlocking themes of the Bible. Yet many of us mothers are fearful for the fate of our children. We try to make them good through the multitude of our words of advice and by our watchfulness. But words—or even our enveloping love—seem futile. So what kind of spiritual inheritance can we leave?

With surprise and delight I found the simple answer. Our prayers. Prayers are never lost but prayed again in heaven by our Intercessor as He pleads for His beloved. John 17 shows that Jesus prayed for all the future generations of believers. That prayer is still being prayed—and answered! The same is true of the prayers of mothers. Blessed is the young person who has an inheritance of prayer—praying parents, grandparents, and great-grandparents.

Soon after our oldest grandson was baptized at age 11, our son and his wife added a room to their house so that Tommy could have a bedroom of his own. At its completion we had a special dedication service, dedicating the room and its use to the Lord. Tommy's parents and my husband and I filled the room with prayers and songs, asking the Holy Spirit and the angels to dwell there continually, protecting the mind of this young man who was so special to us all.

Did God hear our prayers? Yes! Those prayers are still being prayed in heaven. Tommy, now 18, is attending evangelism school and preaching the Word of God. Our privilege as parents and grandparents is to continue in prayer for him, holding him up before the Lord.

Prayer is a legacy that cannot be destroyed by fire, flood, or theft. When we pray for our children and grandchildren, those prayers will continue to be answered down through the years, even after we are dead. "This is what the Lord says: 'Restrain your voice from weeping and your eyes from tears, for your work will be rewarded,' declares the Lord. 'They will return from the land of the enemy. So there is hope for your future,' declares the Lord. 'Your children will return to their own land'" (Jer. 31:16, 17, NIV).

CARROL JOHNSON SHEWMAKE

A Dock of Angels

Nebuchadnezzar said, "Blessed be the God of Shadrach, Meshach, and Abednego, who has sent his angel and delivered his servants, who trusted in Him." Dan. 3:28, RSV.

I DON'T REMEMBER HOW OLD I was at the time. I do remember vividly the events of the day. We had spent an afternoon boating and waterskiing on the lake with our Pathfinder Club. One boat headed back to the lake's boathouse to load the boat and to take kids home. I was in the second boat with seven others. The two Pathfinder leaders in that boat decided to stay on the water a little longer. Several people skied, and we were enjoying the late-afternoon sun when the clouds began to roll in. Soon the wind began to blow. The adults in our boat became concerned, as we were several miles from the boathouse. One of them began to slowly drive the boat in the right direction as the wind became stronger and the waves became bigger. The other adult soon had us bailing the water that was gushing over the sides. The sky turned black, and the rain began to come down. I remember one of our Pathfinder leaders saying, "Keep bailing, and pray that God will get us safely to shore!"

Suddenly the boat driver said, "Look! There's a private dock." He turned the boat as the waves seemed to become even more choppy. Soon we were tying up the boat securely and scrambling up to the safety of the wooden dock. We walked up the path to a house on the side of the hill. Our Pathfinder leader rang the doorbell and explained to the homeowners that we had been caught in the storm and had tied our boat to their dock because we couldn't make it back to the public docking area. We asked to use their phone to communicate with the rest of our group. The people were very helpful, providing us the use of their phone and a dry place to wait. But, they explained to us, they had no dock. Our Pathfinder leader said, "Well, it must be your neighbor's. Anyway, we are so grateful that the Lord provided us a safe place to tie up and get the children to safety." But the homeowners insisted that there was no dock along the lake below their house, even though all eight of us had clearly seen it and walked on it.

And sure enough, when the storm was over and our leaders went to retrieve the boat, there it was on the sand—no dock was to be seen. Surely we had been accompanied by angels that day—a dock of angels!

SANDRA SIMANTON

Living Perfume

But thanks be to God, who always leads us in triumphal procession in Christ and through us spreads everywhere the fragrance of the knowledge of him. For we are to God the aroma of Christ among those who are being saved and those who are perishing. 2 Cor. 2:14, 15, NIV.

I AM A BEAUTIFUL BOTTLE of perfume whose contents are unique and special. I have my own fragrance and the liberty to chose what to do with it. I can give joy to people as I give off the delicate aroma of flowers and ripened fruit, or I can transmit the strong odor of an old perfume to those around me.

My culture, skin color, height, or social position do not matter. What is important is that I am the fragrance of life, a sweet and good perfume. My life is my witness.

God, who also likes perfume, planned to make the plant kingdom a storehouse of delicious perfumes in which we find the delicate fragrance of roses, lilies, and jasmine; the strong aroma of anise, nutmeg, and cloves; and the sweet smell of mangoes, pineapples, and peaches.

The sweet perfume can be compared to private prayer; it is as essential as food, water, air, and sun in our lives. The strong aroma is compared to the daily study of the Bible and the spiritually inspired writings. The pleasant smell and calming effect and beauty of the fruit are the acceptance of one's self, leaving feelings of inferiority aside.

The odor of old perfume can be unpleasant, causing nausea and making people stand back. It is the characteristics of a complaining, proud, and insecure woman. The woman whose aroma reinvigorates is willing, attentive, simple, and balanced.

The size, shape, or color of the container is not important. More important is being a good perfume of God, taking the aroma of love, joy, and peace to others.

I am a beautiful bottle of perfume. I will choose to be a sweet fragrance in all places and circumstances.

IVONE FELDKIRCHER PAIVA

A Silly Goose?

But ask the animals, and they will teach you, or the birds of the air, and they will tell you; or speak to the earth, and it will teach you, or let the fish of the sea inform you. Which of all these does not know that the hand of the Lord has done this? In his hand is the life of every creature and the breath of all mankind. Job 12:7-10, NIV.

HAVEN'T YOU HEARD THE expression "you silly goose"? Well, I've come to the conclusion that a goose is perhaps one of the wisest creatures in the universe. We have a very large population of Canada geese here in our area. Mainly, I suppose, because Nashville is surrounded by the Cumberland River and Old Hickory and Percy Priest lakes. The geese have a sanctuary here. They are protected, and many of them remain in our area year-round.

Since we have a two-acre lake in our backyard, we have the opportunity to be hosts to all kinds of waterfowl. Canada geese have learned that Farmer Al feeds grain to horses there each day and that these horses are very messy eaters. They leave scattered grain all around, thus feeding many wild birds in plenty. We've always enjoyed watching the habits of the geese and have observed so many interesting things about them. Did you know that they set the perfect example of family life?

Number one, they mate for life. If something happens to their mate, the remaining goose will stay with the flock, alone, but still surrounded by the other geese. Have you ever watched them take to the air? They follow close behind their leader in perfect formation. I have never observed them fighting over who goes first or sparring to be the leader. If one of the geese is in trouble and falls behind, the others never leave it alone. I saw a goose with a broken wing. The rest of the flock left, but one pair stayed behind to be with the injured goose. What a support system! And we call them silly geese!

Perhaps we should spend more time observing the goose. Humans could learn some valuable lessons about family life, about commitment, and about caring for one another if we would just observe geese. Sometimes God's lessons are taught in very simple ways in nature.

Barbara Smith Morris

Eyes for Seeing

How great is God—beyond our understanding! Job 36:26, NIV.

IT SEEMS THAT I'VE always had trouble with my eyes. When I was born I nearly lost my right eye when the doctor poked me in the eye with forceps as he pulled me out. The eye was saved, but there was damage to my face under my eye, so people are always asking me how I got a black eye.

At first I wore glasses, but now I have contacts. I'm not brave enough—or rich enough—to try laser surgery. I've never taken my eyesight for granted, but I didn't usually think of my eyes as being particularly vulnerable, either—until my run-in with a yucca tree.

For those of you who don't live in a dry climate, a yucca is more cactus than tree. It grows very tall and has long, spiky leaves. I was weeding around the base of a yucca when a leaf stabbed me in the eye.

The pain made me fall to my knees. I opened the eye, but my vision was hopelessly blurred. I ran into the house, afraid to look in the mirror, sure I would see a bloody mess. When I did look, there was no blood. The eye was just a little red and teary. I realized that my sight was blurring because my contact lens had fallen out.

I went back outside and retrieved my contact. When I took it to the bathroom and poured disinfectant on it, the liquid went right through it. I held it up to my good eye and discovered that the yucca had punched a big hole in it.

Human beings can be remarkably strong and resilient creatures, but the truth is, we are all vulnerable. When I saw the hole in my contact, I thought how easily that could have been my eye. Our lives are often at risk—a slip in the bathtub, a piece of food going down the wrong way, a careless driver, and our lives can be over.

We could live in fear, but I prefer to live in gratitude. Knowing that life could end at any moment makes it that much more precious. Those of us who are blessed with eyes for seeing have all of creation to explore. God has spared my eyesight once again, and I enjoy simply being quiet and looking at the beautiful vistas around me—including my yuccas. But now I wear safety glasses when I work around them! GINA LEE

Almost Left Outside

Therefore be ye also ready: for in such an hour as ye think not the Son of man cometh. Matt. 24:44.

RECENTLY I MADE A TRIP to the hair supply store. Because it was Sunday, I knew they would close early, at 6:00 p.m. I left home about 4:30 and made this the first stop. I arrived about 4:45, picked up the item I needed, and browsed for a few minutes before getting in line to be checked out.

As I waited, I noticed that the person in charge told an assistant to lock the door, then let the customers out as they completed their purchases. I thought it rather strange, since the store wouldn't close until 6:00. As I inched forward in the line, I saw people trying to enter, only to be turned away. It was too late. One woman pleaded through the glass door, "Please, I need to purchase only one little thing!"

But the person in charge said, "No, we are closed." The woman continued to beg but was repeatedly denied. Disappointed, she finally walked away, as did the others who had sought entrance after the door was locked.

When I reached the counter I asked the cashier, "What time does the store close?"

"Five o'clock" was her prompt response.

"Every Sunday?" I asked in surprise.

"Yes," she said, "every week." I had almost missed out, thinking that I had more time. Had I not made this my first stop, I too would have been turned away.

As I walked to my car to leave, I was reminded that by God's grace I need to set my priorities straight and make first things first. What a tragedy it would be to miss out on heaven and be left standing outside because I put less important things first, thinking I had more time.

Dear God, please help me live as though You are coming at any moment. Help me to get ready, be ready, and stay ready, for at such a time as I may not expect, You may surely come. GLORIA J. STELLA FELDER

Well-watered Gardens

The Lord will guide you always; he will satisfy your needs in a sun-scorched land and will strengthen your frame. You will be like a well-watered garden, like a spring whose waters never fail. Isa. 58:11, NIV.

PERENNIAL FLOWERS DECK my backyard. Growing flowers provides me an ongoing labor of love, teaching me valuable everyday lessons of life.

To prepare my flower beds I first remove several inches of heavy, stone-embedded clay, shovelful by shovelful. Next I apply rich topsoil. After preparing the soil, I select each plant with great care. Because my yard is shady, I choose my flowers accordingly. The colors, heights, and varieties also need my consideration.

I carefully nest each precious plant. After setting each bleeding heart, hosta, coneflower, or pink pearl, I nurture it as I would a baby, fertilizing, watering, and weeding as needed. Mulch helps keep the moisture in the soil. Once a plant is established, the maintenance need is reduced.

When a plant becomes overgrown or if I want to start it in another location, it must be taken apart. To do this I often thrust a shovel into the middle of the plant, cutting roots and all, and take part of it to another spot to be planted. Other times I dig up the entire plant and separate it into various parts to make more plants. Because of their hardiness they are able to withstand this separation process. My efforts are rewarded by rich, colorful blooms.

You and I are much like the flowers in my perennial garden. The Master Gardener lovingly cares for us with infinitely more passion than I care for my flowers. Using the shovel of love, He endeavors to remove the hard clay from our hearts. In its place He puts sensitivity, gentleness, and humility. The fertilizer of His Word guides, leads, and directs.

Regardless of our race, color, size, or shape, when we yield to His will He places us in just the right location to thrive. As the plant's roots draw nutrients from the soil, so prayer draws us to the Divine Gardener. He, in turn, empowers us to develop characteristic like His own. Just when we need it, He applies the water of encouragement in many different forms. In return, He asks us to advance His kingdom by beautifying and watering well the garden He's placed us in.

MARIAN M. HART

God Spoke to Me!

Before they call, I will answer; and while they are still speaking, I will hear. Isa. 65:24, NKJV.

I'VE HEARD PEOPLE SAY, "God told me such and such" or "God spoke to me." Now, I've questioned that, thinking that they were bragging, imagining, or making up things! Now I'm not so doubting, because yesterday God spoke to me!

A few days ago a friend brought a situation to my attention. Two of our other choir members always seemed to find time to talk together after choir practice. They were usually left standing in the parking lot as the rest of us drove away into the darkness. As I thought about it, I was impressed how inappropriate it was for two married people (but not to each other) to spend this time together. My friend and I began to pray for God's guidance and a solution. We planned to meet in five days to talk about it.

As the day arrived, I talked to God: *I can't hear You; could You talk to me and give me some direction?* Within the hour another friend called. We talked for a while, and then I shared my need for God's answer for this situation. She advised, "You need to talk with the woman; tell her how special she is to you, and of your observation and concern. You need to say, 'This is not what God would want you to be doing; it may be a problem to your marriage.' "

I suddenly realized that God was speaking to me by impressing my friend with His thoughts as she talked to me! She mentioned the council given in Matthew 18, then prayed with me. What a peace came over me as I determined to follow God's leading in this situation.

That evening following choir practice I asked the young woman to stay so we could talk. When we were alone, I began by telling her how special she was to me, then expressed my concern for her and the danger she was putting herself in. She said, "You are exactly right! I don't need to be doing that anymore."

God had given me words to say and had been preparing her heart to receive them. She was humble and accepting of my words. Together we talked with God and asked Him to help her follow through with her decision to break off the relationship. In tears we hugged each other.

I knew that God had spoken to both of us and that He would continue to speak.

SHARON FOLLETT

The Forgotten Glasses

For the Lord does not see as man sees; for man looks at the outward appearance, but the Lord looks at the heart. 1 Sam. 16:7, NKJV.

MY HUSBAND, RON, AND I were driving home after visiting his father in the hospital. The doctor had told Ray that he had internal bleeding and severe liver problems. The physician believed that he had less than two years to live. Ray hadn't given his heart to the Lord, and my pastor-husband had tried to share the love of Jesus with him, but Dad was not interested.

As we drove I suddenly exclaimed, "Stop! I forgot my glasses in your dad's room." We made a U-turn and headed back. Ron waited for me in the car while I retrieved my glasses.

I breezed in and picked up my glasses, smiled, and said, "I need these for driving." Ray's eyes caught mine—he looked as though he had been crying. "Ray, are you OK?" I asked.

"Nicole," he said, "I don't want to die."

Only God could give the words that I needed to say after his vulnerable declaration. After a quick, quiet prayer, I said, "You know, you can have eternal life. We're on this earth for only a while; and yes, you may die. But God has another plan, and He has given us some awesome promises. If we believe in Jesus as Lord and Savior and believe that He has died to set us free from sin, we will have eternal life."

My heart was overwhelmed. What an awesome privilege and responsibility we have as Christians to share the good news, especially with someone terminally ill and whom I love.

"Ray, would you like me to pray on your behalf, and pray the sinner's prayer?" He nodded with agreement, and I prayed: "Dear heavenly Father, please come into Ray's heart, and forgive him for the wrong that he has done. Cleanse him of all the unrighteousness, and help him to be ready when Jesus comes to bring us home to a better place. Comfort and stay close to him. Please, Jesus, surround him with Your love so that he will trust You and not be afraid."

When I looked at Ray with tears in my eyes, I saw he was sobbing and wiping his eyes as well. He looked at me and simply said, "I believe."

Ray died about a month later. I praise God that my forgotten glasses helped me to minister to my father-in-law so he could see the light of God's love and forgiveness, and believe.

NICOLE PARADIS-SYDENHAM

I Want to Run Again

And when he comes, he will open the eyes of the blind, and unstop the ears of the deaf. The lame man will leap up like a deer, and those who could not speak will shout and sing! Springs will burst forth in the wilderness, and streams in the desert. Isa. 35:5, 6, TLB.

IT WAS THE LAST FRIDAY night of camp meeting, and my husband asked if I could meet with him in our cabin after the meeting. "The wife of one of our pastors has been battling multiple sclerosis for years and has asked for anointing," he explained.

My immediate response was no, because I had a handbell practice scheduled. Then it occurred to me that because this was Cheryl's first camp meeting and she didn't know many people, perhaps she needed me.

The evening speaker had shared experiences from his own years of struggling with fibromyalgia. At times the pain had been unbearable. Long plane flights had been the worst. During one of these lows he had decided to ask for anointing. Following the anointing service, he had been pain-free. He went on to say that he had been pain-free ever since. If God could heal the guest speaker, could He not do the same for Cheryl? That's what prompted her and her husband to request anointing.

Surrounded by a small group of friends, Cheryl prayed first. Looking heavenward, she said, "Jesus, this is Cheryl." She listed her blessings, then got to the point. "I have to be quite frank with you, Jesus; I'm tired of this disease. I'm tired of putting on a brave front all the time. I used to be a runner, and I want to run again."

Then we all prayed, and at the appropriate time the visiting pastor placed oil on her forehead. Fervently he prayed for healing for Cheryl.

The next day I scanned the crowd, looking for Cheryl. As the morning service ended I saw her a few rows behind us. She made her way toward me without a cane or a leg brace. A smile lit her face. Tears of joy filled my eyes as I gave her a hug.

Two months have now passed since that weekend. *How has she been doing?* I've wondered. *It would be wonderful, Lord, if she were healed; but if not, I pray that she will be at peace, knowing that one day, when Jesus comes, she will indeed be able to run again.*

VERA WIEBE

Ask in Prayer

And all things, whatsoever ye shall ask in prayer, believing, ye shall receive. Matt. 21:22.

THE SITUATION COULD NOT BE ignored or put aside; it was getting desperate. It was Thursday, and Alice and Art needed a ride home from camp meeting on Sunday. We'd known Alice and Art when we went to the same church, but our paths hadn't crossed recently. They had moved about 30 miles away and attended church near their home. My friend, Mary, told me of their situation, not knowing that we already knew each other

Their car had taken them up the California coast to camp meeting. It had even taken them to Fortuna on Tuesday for shopping and laundry. Several miles from the campground, however, the engine had thrown a rod and would go no farther. Ruined, the car had to be towed to a junkyard. This left them with no way to get home. They didn't panic, but quietly asked the Lord for help. They told a few friends about the problem and kept praying that a positive answer would come.

As Mary and I walked slowly and talked, Alice happened to walk toward us, and we all stopped to talk. When she inquired, "How are you?" I decided to be direct and skip the "Fine, just fine" answer. I told her that I had a pinched sciatic nerve in my back that was triggering some unpleasant pains not only in my back but down my thighs and legs. "Oh," she said, "I can help take care of that for you. Come over to my tent tomorrow."

My husband and I discussed the need for Alice and Art to get home and thought it would be very workable to have them ride with us. The next day I arrived at her tent with a plan: we could trade transportation for massage therapy. Alice was very happy to accept our offer, and she made my back feel more stable and alleviated a lot of the pain. We both knew it was an answer to our prayers.

On Sunday we drove the 300 miles home. We thoroughly enjoyed the trip, the conversation, and the stop for dinner. When we arrived, Alice massaged my back again, making me feel much better. Alice and Art were safely home before dark, praising the Lord and thanking us profusely.

LILLIAN MUSGRAVE

Dazed in the Maize

But he that shall endure unto the end, the same shall be saved. Matt. 24:13.

TWO FARMERS WHO LIVE three miles out of town plant 10 acres of corn every year. Then they have a maze tilled in it for tourists to find their way through.

An aerial view of the maze showed the outline of our province—Alberta. Within its boundaries was the design of the provincial shield, showing snow-peaked mountains, rolling foothills, the prairies, the parklands, and stalks of grain. Also included was the wild rose, the provincial floral emblem.

My sister and I accepted the challenge of wandering through the labyrinth from start to finish. After paying the entrance fee, we were given a choice of passports to help guide us through. These passports offered a series of questions with multiple-choice answers. When we reached a numbered marker in the maze, we were to stop and answer the question matching the number on the marker. All goes well if one knows the answer to the question. The answer we chose then told us which path to take—to the left, right, or straight ahead.

With the corn towering eight to 10 feet tall, there's no way to peek over the top, and the stalks were planted so closely we couldn't see through. Many times we came to dead ends or returned to the marker we had just left. We'd then choose a different answer to the question and move on. We climbed the lookout tower at one point to see if we were anywhere near the end. Surely we had walked several miles and should be almost home free! Not so. On we went with determination.

At one place we were totally confused. There seemed no way to get out of the circuitous maze. Throughout the maze were "rescue guides" for those who might despair, get claustrophobic, or simply be lost. We sought a tip from a guide. Finally we found the exit and rejoiced that we had done better than the one-hour average.

Our journey in life is like a maze. If we study and follow the instructions of our passport, the Bible, we can reach our goal of heaven. There will be detours, but don't be discouraged. There will be dead ends, but don't give up. Seek advice and counsel from guides along the way. They may be your pastor, a family member, or a friend. Let's be like Abraham, who looked for a city whose builder and maker is God.

EDITH FITCH

Who Knew!

Before I formed you in the womb I knew you, before you were born I set you apart. Jer. 1:5, NIV.

A RANDOM SMILE AND A casual hello were exchanged amid the clanging of slamming metal school lockers. It was here that I first became aware of a high school classmate. We had attended different elementary schools, and our neighborhoods were miles apart. We never shared any classes during our four years in high school. We seemed to have nothing in common. I heard from other students that my locker acquaintance excelled in art class. But it was only in the hallowed halls of South High that our paths had any reason to cross. But who knew?

Upon graduation I enrolled in business college. Marriage and a secretarial position soon followed. Then a daughter was born. My thoughts turned toward God. I remembered the church that my mother and her sisters had attended. I reasoned it might be a good place to start. But who knew?

As I entered the foyer, an outstretched hand took mine in a warm welcome. We both smiled and instantly recognized each other as former high school classmates with adjoining hall lockers. The hows, whys, and whens spilled forth. She had married into a family that attended this church. I was returning to the church of my mother. Our firstborns were both daughters and close in age. The distance between our homes was now amazingly close. We became fast friends. Weekly phone calls and afternoon lunches cemented a beautiful friendship.

I was privileged to be part of the early years in her newspaper writing adventures. Who knew where it would lead when I drove her to meet her writing and interview assignments for a small Ohio country newspaper? Our Lord knew! She became a professional writer and journalist for more than 30 years and is still going.

And who knew she would find merit in this late-blooming writer, this grandmother's memory stories and poems? She now drives me, not in a car, but with encouraging words. Yes, my dear friend Betty is also my mentor. But best of all, we are sisters in Christ with bright rainbow threads woven into a tapestry that has lasted more than 50 years. Yes, He knew!

Dear Lord, never let me pass up an opportunity to extend a smile and a hello, however casual it may be. It may be the beginning of a lifetime friendship. Amen.

MARIANNE TOTH BAYLESS

Light Brings New Perspective

The Lord turns my darkness into light. 2 Sam. 22:29, NIV.

WHILE WORKING FOR A Christian bookstore I needed to assemble a display for camp meeting. It would be a nice eye-catching display holding some great sales on kids' music. I glanced at the pieces and figured, *This will be easy.* Of course, I was trying to put this display together quickly, which meant I didn't take time to read the directions and only glanced at the diagrams. I tried putting the ends together first. Wrong! Sides first? No. It was time to read the directions. Sure enough, the box part went together fairly easily then, and it even attached to the stand. But before attaching the top to the stand, I had to make the compartments to hold the various CDs and cassettes. This was the biggest challenge. Turning the display a different way, I still couldn't figure it out. My emotions were rising now, and I was referring to the directions and diagram often.

A coworker came to help, but shrugged and left after a few tries. I was still trying various ways to get the compartments to take shape—even using force wasn't helping. Another coworker arrived. After assessing the problem, she tackled the display with determination. I told her all the things I had tried so she could profit by my mistakes, but my advice fell on deaf ears. Isn't that the way we are? We keep trying something that we've already been told doesn't work. She announced, "I never give up until it's done right." That sounded good to me.

I kept saying, "We really need a fold at this spot," but there didn't seem to be one. Conclusion: the directions were wrong or the manufacturing was wrong. It couldn't be us! I walked to the other side of the room and looked at the section one more time. Guess what? In the light from that angle there was a faint fold line—yes! Right where I kept thinking one had to be.

How like my own life. I want the results to be different, but I'm not trying anything different. When I quit focusing on the problem or situation and begin to see things in a different light, things look different. The pieces fit better as I learn to let God shed His light on my life. Reading God's message from different books in the Bible or different versions of the Bible can bring me new light too. Light does bring new perspective.

LOUISE DRIVER

Nudges

I will instruct you and teach you in the way you should go; I will guide you with My eye. Ps. 32:8, NKJV.

WHEN I WAS WORKING at a Christian high school, my husband and I always gave each graduating senior a little plaque or wallet card that read: "Lord, help me to remember that nothing is going to happen to me today that You and I together can't handle." Year after year we gave each graduate the same gift, until the plaques were no longer available.

We received many words of appreciation. Some years later, when one of our graduates lost his life in a drowning accident, his parents told us how they found the plaque among his things and how much it meant to them.

In the class of 1984 there was a young man whom I shall call Bob. As soon as Bob graduated he went into the Navy and lived the life of a sailor. He used to call me now and then from Saudi Arabia or France, or wherever he happened to be, and let me know he was carrying that card in his wallet. However, he wasn't living a Christian life.

Some time passed, and Bob was discharged from the Navy. He moved back to our area and married a woman with children. He started coming to church by himself and sitting with us because his wife believed differently than he did. One Sabbath morning he pulled out that little card from his wallet to show me he still had it. Then, out of the clear blue, I asked, "Bob, have you ever thought of being rebaptized?"

As soon as I had said it I wondered where that thought had come from. He looked at me with tears in his eyes and replied, "Yes, I have; how did you know?" I hugged him and told him to be sure to let me know when the occasion would be, because I would be there for sure.

While on vacation I felt impressed to call home and get our messages off the answering machine. There was one from Bob to tell us that he was going to be rebaptized and hoped we would be there for the occasion. What a thrill to see that baptism!

What an even greater thrill to know that it was God who directed in giving those little plaques and wallet cards and that it was God who told me to ask Bob if he had ever thought of being rebaptized.

ANNA MAY RADKE WATERS

Before They Call

Before they call I will answer; while they are still speaking I will hear. Isa. 65:24, NIV.

IT WAS IN A BORROWED book that I read a unique prayer that has forever changed my thinking. Let me tell you about it. We were preparing for a long journey to a niece's wedding where I was to recite some poetry, so I practiced and polished my lines. As we were about to leave, a friend dropped a packet of yellow guavas into my hand. "For the trip," she explained. I adored these pink-fleshed, yellow-skinned delights, and I was truly grateful.

At lunchtime we stopped to eat the lunch that I had prepared and, of course, enjoy the guavas. Now, if I failed to explain that this delectable fruit has small, white, iron-hard seeds, I shouldn't have. I stopped eating suddenly and painfully, sending my tongue to explore for damage. It was worse than I feared. A hard seed had lodged between my front teeth, shattering the filling and splitting one tooth into a V shape. My first reaction was to break into tears and beg my husband to take me home. How could I recite with a yawning gap in my front teeth? To complicate my problem, it was Good Friday. I knew dental help would be all but impossible.

It was then that I recalled that unique prayer. The two men with me waited for my outburst, but the prayer words flowed into my mind like calming balm. "Thank You, Lord, for solving this problem. It is too big for me; I gladly hand it over to You and trust You."

When we arrived in Queensland, Hazel, my sister-in-law, asked incredulously, "Edna, whatever have you done?" I explained, and hastened to say, "I'm trusting the good Lord to solve the problem, Hazel, because I don't know if anyone else can."

Hazel paused. "Just this morning as I read the paper I saw a box advertising an emergency dental service over Easter." She ran to find that address. "Let's hop into my car, and we'll go." I imagined one more problem as we drove along: *What if there is a long queue, and I don't get in before sunset? What shall I do?* Then I rebuked myself and said again, "Thank You, Lord, for solving this problem, too. It's too big for me. I'm trusting You."

There was no queue. I proposed that the dentist put in a temporary filling to save time. He smiled and assured me he would do better than that. And he did. God had provided the solution long before the emergency arose, and I thank Him every time I tell the story. EDNA HEISE

Happy Father's Day

Honor your father and your mother, that your days may be long upon the land which the Lord your God is giving you. Ex. 20:12, NKJV.

I LOVE TO READ FOR a few minutes before I fall asleep, so I usually have several books stacked on the headboard of our bed. Darrell jokingly teases that I should be afraid lest they fall on me during the night. Last week, while leaning out one window to wash the outside of the other, I leaned against the headboard and caused it to fall. I thought I would quickly repair the damage and go on with the day. However, it wasn't quite that simple. I needed help to lift the headboard.

When Darrell came home for lunch, he helped me do the heavy lifting, and I assured him I would finish the repairs and all would be well. As I started to work I found that I couldn't do the necessary repair. When he came home for supper, I told him I hadn't been able to complete the job. My loving husband gathered his tools and without any comment went to do the necessary repairs.

Never did he scold or tell me that I should have been more careful. He simply repaired my mess. Those who know Darrell know that he loves a good joke or humorous story. Now he has the basis for a good story— he delights to tell how my stack of books caused the headboard to collapse. We laugh together and enjoy the humor of the situation.

The headboard incident reminds me of how often he has done similar things through the years, not only for me but for our children. As a husband and father he has patiently worked to make life better for each of us. When we've made mistakes, he has loved, forgiven, and helped to make things right—all done with a spirit of cheerfulness.

Our home has been blessed because we have a husband and father who is patient, kind, and loving through every situation. Dads care for their families, laugh with them, and make each day better than the day before. Repairing things when accidents happen is only one way they do this. They are also repairers of hearts, helping to heal the little hurts that we each experience.

I like to think of a heavenly Father just like that, don't you?

EVELYN GLASS

Security of a Profile

I have loved you with an everlasting love; I have drawn you with loving-kindness. Jer. 31:3, NIV.

I HAVE A DAUGHTER WHO is young and beautiful and has a heart the size of Texas. Although she is very caring and kind, she is bluntly honest, so you always know where you stand with her.

Last year I got married for the last time in my life. It was a fun and unique wedding. It began to rain just as we got to the part where John sang "Let It Be Me" to me. My best friend moved behind us with a large umbrella to protect us from the rain, which was now coming down at a pretty good pace. Everyone said, "It's a wedding we'll always remember."

Last month my daughter flew in from California to visit me and help pack up some old mementoes and condense my 17 years of raising children alone after a sad divorce. John and I were moving, and I needed the help and the moral support.

Amber and I ended our fast-paced, exhausting week relaxing with tea and laughter and a collage of photos to scan and share. One of the photos from the wedding shows my chubby little cheeks glistening with rain. Another shows me lovingly watching John sing his song to me.

"Ugh! I hate that one." I shook my head. I've always been overweight, but this showed my double chin, and because I was laughing, it squinched up my eyes and made my cheeks look fat.

"No, I love this one!" Amber insisted. "Mom, don't you know how much security I find in your profile?" She laughed at my reaction, forcing me to sober up and listen. "Since I was a baby I saw that profile from the opposite seat in the back of the car. And you usually sat me beside you when we went out to eat. Your profile is probably the side of your head I've seen the most."

She was right so far. All of her childhood I had had to work in town, so we would drive 17 miles to the sitter's. In the car we'd chat, tell stories, sing songs, read to each other, and share school stories and heartaches while eating lots of platters of nachos and drinking large glasses of tea. And although I would turn to look at her, a lot of the time the side of my face was truly what she saw.

It still isn't my favorite photo by any means, but the lesson is much larger than a simple 4" x 6" photograph. I'll never be a pretty, petite woman like my daughter, but I have the blessed assurance that I am loved deeply and have given a child the security of a mother's profile. SALLY J. AKEN-LINKE

Choose Not to Remember

I . . . am he who blots out your transgressions . . . and remembers your sins no more. Isa. 43:25, NIV.

THE LINES WERE LONG and the day was hot in the small country post office. Traveling through town, I had dashed in to mail a package.

I tried not to listen to the conversation that was developing near the front of the line, but the post office was small and the voice was loud. A woman had come in and recognized another woman, whom she obviously had known from work some time in the past. Evidently it had been quite some time since they had met last. The first woman walked over to the second woman, who was standing in line with her teenage son, and began telling her—in a loud voice—about all the unpleasant things that had happened since they had last seen each other. The woman in line didn't say much.

After some time of this, the loud-voiced, negative woman, who seemed to have worked in personnel in a hospital, turned her attention to the teenage boy. "You remember when we kicked your ———?" she said crudely, loud enough for all of us to hear. By now she had everyone's attention—in both lines.

"No, I don't," replied the boy.

"Of course you do!" she replied.

"No," said the boy again, steadily returning her gaze.

"You have to—you couldn't forget that."

He looked at her a moment, then said slowly and deliberately, "I choose not to remember," and he turned and walked out the door.

There was silence in the post office. No one said a word. I almost expected applause to break out. But in our hearts we gave him a standing ovation.

We can't help sometimes what happens to us in life. We can't always keep from making dumb mistakes. But we can "choose not to remember" and go on down the road of life toward better choices. God doesn't remember either.

EDNA MAYE GALLINGTON

A God Who Cares

Cast all your anxieties on him, for he cares about you. 1 Peter 5:7, RSV.

ONE WARM SUMMER NIGHT my dad decided to treat my sister and me to dinner because Mom had to work. We decided to go to Taco Bell and enjoy a yummy, if unhealthy, dinner. We enjoyed our burritos and chalupas and just having some classic family fun. After satisfying our stomachs with Taco Bell gourmet, we headed out the door for Baskin-Robbins for some ice cream. We all got double scoops and enjoyed every single bite.

When we got home, I was just finishing my ice cream when I remembered my retainers. Where had I put them? I looked around the kitchen and in my room; then I remembered. I had put them on my tray in Taco Bell and hadn't picked them up!

"Dad, my retainers!" I exclaimed. "I think I left them in Taco Bell."

"Stop playing," my sister said, not believing me.

"I'm serious! I put them on the tray, and I think I threw them away by mistake."

"Then let's go back to Taco Bell," my sister suggested.

Although I was afraid it was too late—we had left an hour before—all three of us raced to the car and straight back to Taco Bell. As we arrived, the trash was just being hauled out by one of the workers. I raced in and breathlessly asked if I could look for my retainers in the trash bags. He gave me an understanding look and offered to help. Luckily the retainers were near the top, and I found them within 10 minutes.

We walked out of Taco Bell laughing. What an experience! On our way home I whispered a prayer of thanks. It amazed me how God had answered a prayer that had never been prayed. God had made sure that the worker had waited just a little bit longer to take the trash out. God had cared for something very small compared to all the other problems of this world.

How God cares for and loves us! How important we are to Him. I know that sometimes we feel small and unimportant. Sometimes we feel that God won't bother Himself with us because our problems are a speck of grain compared to famines and earthquakes. But if He was willing to answer a prayer never spoken, don't you think He is willing to answer yours? If He cared enough for my retainers and me, don't you think He cares for you?

CRISTINE JEDA ORILLOSA

Peace for My Troubled Soul

Before they call, I will answer; and while they are yet speaking, I will hear. Isa. 65:24.

SUNDAY MORNINGS I USUALLY linger under the warm blanket because it's the only day I don't have to rush to get dressed for work or church. This particular Sunday I decided to go downstairs for my devotional time. As I sat on the sofa, thoughts that had nothing to do with devotions began racing through my mind. I became overwhelmed in my search for answers to challenges that seemed to consume me, and I began to drown in my own cistern of despair and self-pity. Many times in our Christian walk Satan succeeds in taking our focus away from Jesus, depriving us of sweet communion we can have with our loving heavenly Father.

As I opened the devotional book *Fabric of Faith,* the page happened to open to the reading for March 5. I was about to turn to the current date when my eyes caught the heading, "For Women Who've Fallen and Can't Get Up." The text read, "You will be secure, because there is hope" (Job 11:18, NIV). I had been wrestling with issues that had disturbed me for several weeks. How heavily the burdens weighed on me! As I read the devotional thought it seemed just for me. It spoke of feeling heavy laden and how a talk with God about my big and little concerns could make a difference. Those words were a source of encouragement.

I meditated for a few moments, then turned back to the current day's reading. Again Jesus spoke to my heart: "Before they call, I will answer; and while they are yet speaking, I will hear." God was saying that He knew what I was going through and that He was there to strengthen me. As I was about to close the book, my eyes glanced across the page. Almost staring at me were these words: "Come to me, all you who are weary and burdened, and I will give you rest. Take my yoke upon you and learn from me, for I am gentle and humble in heart, and you will find rest for your souls" (Matt. 11:28, 29, NIV). What a blessing to have a friend and burden bearer such as Jesus, who loves and cares about me! I am grateful to God for the precious words He sent to cheer me up when I was in the valley of despair.

Today, if you are walking through the arid deserts of your life, don't give up; take courage, look up, and go forward confidently in the knowledge of God's supreme and abundant love. He is always there, waiting to carry your burdens if you will let Him. SHIRLEY C. IHEANACHO

The Morning Glory

How you have fallen from heaven, O morning star, son of the dawn! Isa. 14:12, NIV.

MORNING GLORY. WHAT A beautiful name for a flower! It is funnel-shaped and has no separate petals. The scientific name is *Ipomoea.* (Sweet potatoes are members of the same family. They originated in the West Indies but are widely grown throughout the tropics and subtropics.) The morning glory gives a blaze of purple color to our hedge, which is a Cape honeysuckle *(Tecomaria capensis).* The flowers grow high up on the hedge; they open early in the morning and close late in the day.

However, despite its beautiful name, the morning glory is a poisonous plant. It's also an irritant and is toxic. It can cause stomachache, nausea, blurred vision, and hallucinations.

The morning glory sends out tendrils that twist tightly around the hedge. You have to have lots of patience and time to unravel and untwist each tendril, which seems to grow many yards long. Many times the branches of the hedge break off when you try to loosen them from the morning glory's firm grip. The morning glory that has been removed has to be destroyed; otherwise it will grow elsewhere. You must wash your hands thoroughly to remove the sticky substance it gives off; otherwise your hands will itch and get a rash.

How the morning glory plant reminds me of Lucifer! The name Lucifer means "shining one," son of the morning. What a lovely meaning to his name! He was once an exalted angel in glory, created in heaven. He was so handsome (more beautiful, even, than a morning glory) that he became proud of his beauty and desired to be like the Most High. He was cast out of heaven with those angels who believed his lies. Satan is the father of lies, the great deceiver. He works so subtly to ensnare you in his clutches (like the tendrils of the morning glory) till eventually you cannot loosen his grip. Satan likes to take control. We must not let Satan gain advantage over us, for we are not ignorant of his devices (2 Cor. 2:11).

You need a gardener friend to break these tendrils of sin. Like the hedge, we can't remove the tendrils ourselves. Like the branches that break, we must be willing to surrender all to Christ. "But thanks be to God, which giveth us the victory through our Lord Jesus Christ" (1 Cor. 15:57).

PRISCILLA ADONIS

God Watches Over Us

I shall be safe. Ps. 119:117.

A FEW YEARS AGO MY husband and I drove from Brisbane to Adelaide, Australia, a trip that took two full days plus a night's stopover. I earnestly asked God for His protection. Not only was it holiday time with more traffic on the roads, but it was a distance of about 1,400 miles (2,250 kilometers). We left early and watched the sunrise. It was delightful to see God's creation evident everywhere. There was beauty in the willow trees hanging low over water and in a rock formation with boulders balancing precariously on each other. There was beauty as the hills gave way to flat, burnt-brown ground. Here the road, shimmering in the heat, seemed to stretch forever in front of us.

It was good to arrive safely in Adelaide, but the days went all too quickly, and soon we began the journey home. The return route was further inland, taking us first through the mining town of Broken Hill, an area of desolate dryness. We passed over bridges arching above completely dry riverbeds. We stayed overnight at a little town in the countryside, where the soil is so red that the redness is ground into the paving on the road.

We left early in the morning, and because it was just before daybreak, the next hour or so was like driving through a wildlife park. We encountered God's handiwork once more, this time in His animals. Foxes ran into the scrub. We slowed for cattle and sheep wandering over the road and had to stop the car a couple times as emus, large flightless birds, crossed in front of us. We spotted an eagle, many bush turkeys, and a large lizard lying on a log. There were flocks of brightly colored rosellas and galahs rising from the grass at the sound of the car. But what really slowed us were the kangaroos, dozens of kangaroos, from the big "reds" to the very young. They jumped in front of the car, beside the car, and behind the car. I sent more prayers heavenward, and many hours later we turned into our driveway. I thanked God for the assurance we have of knowing that God is only a prayer away, continually watching over us.

As we travel life's roads, Father, we ask for Your safety and guidance. We also ask that You open our eyes to the evidence of Your love and presence displayed along our route. LEONIE DONALD

Joy and Happiness for the Heart

Thy words were found, and I did eat them; and thy word was unto me the joy and rejoicing of mine heart. Jer. 15:16.

VIRGÍNIA IS A MARVELOUS woman! I perceived this when I first saw her. I had just become an announcer on the Radio Novo Tempo when she came to visit me.

She was enchanted with all that she had learned through the radio program and how much she had learned in such a short time. When this sincere, religious woman had received the diagnosis of a possible cancer, she had promised the Lord that if the examination came back negative she would spend one hour daily kneeling at the altar of her church praying, and she would dedicate her life entirely to helping the needy. And she was faithfully fulfilling what she had promised to God.

But upon discovering that Jesus desires that our religion be a relationship of spontaneous and personal love, Virgínia had come to ask me if God would forgive her if she exchanged the time of prayer at the altar for moments of devotion in her own home.

Every morning Virgínia woke up long before her family to spend time in communion with God, studying her Bible and praying. Then she copied Bible texts so that her children and husband could take these texts with them to school and work, so that they could have them handy and perhaps seek help in these verses if they needed them.

While she cleaned her house she missed having an intimate relationship with Jesus, so at various times throughout the day she paused from her work, went into her room, and knelt beside her bed to read some more verses and to pray again. She felt an indescribable pleasure during these moments of communion.

I thought about my devotional life. I didn't feel as she did. A few hours after my time of devotion I was not "missing Jesus." Why did she feel this way? After visiting Virgínia several times, I discovered that for 40 years Virginia had felt hunger and thirst for the Word of God in her church. Now the Bible was a true treasure and each verse a precious gem to her.

Lord, help me today to feel the same spiritual hunger and thirst. May the moments of communion that I spend with You bring me true joy, and may they lead me to desire Your companionship not only while I live on this earth but for all eternity!

SÔNIA RIGOLI SANTOS

Laundry

Do not worry about tomorrow; tomorrow will take care of itself. Matt. 6:34, NAB.

THE BATHROOMS HAD TURKISH toilets, the showers had no showerheads, and the computer tables were supported by crates. But there were nice things about the school that served as our excavation headquarters. Trees surrounded the courtyard, owls flitted from tree to tree after dark, and (best of all) our laundry was done for us. Rather than using pails of water to wash clothes stiff with ground-in excavation dirt, we took bundles of dirty clothes to the school laundry and, several hours later, received back huge piles of laundry, freshly washed—perhaps not shining white, but at least cleaner. I didn't mind sorting through 60 pairs of brown pants to find the two pairs I had worn to the tell. Faced with 100 shirts, I still smiled, happy that I hadn't had to wash my four by hand.

I was happy until one weekend when, looking for my clean clothes, I discovered that almost half were missing. Where were my faded T-shirts? And what about the long-sleeved shirts I wore to protect myself from the sun? I couldn't find a sheet, and, worst of all, my dig pants were nowhere to be seen.

I might have been phlegmatic about the situation, but I had recently thrown away two pairs of pants. After spending a week in the field dealing with sharp cobbles, I could no longer wear either pair with any semblance of modesty. What would I do if the rest of the laundry wasn't finished soon?

As I walked to the cafeteria for supper and to check once more for my lost laundry, I crossed the basketball court with John. "I'm missing things too," he reported. "A facecloth, three T-shirts, two short-sleeved shirts, and a pair of pants. With this rate of attrition," he added with a smile, "by the end of the excavation I'll be digging in my swim trunks and one of those Arab scarves—a kaffiyeh."

"Do not worry about tomorrow; tomorrow will take care of itself."

His lighthearted attitude broke through my worry, and I could see things in perspective once again. Nothing was lost; it was just late. As a worst-case scenario, I could reclaim my dirty clothes and wash them myself—or wear them dirty for another day's digging. Laughing, we entered the building.

DENISE DICK HERR

A Miracle Along the Highway

For he shall give his angels charge over thee, to keep thee in all thy ways. Ps. 91:11.

MY FRIEND'S DAUGHTER WAS going to be married in the city of Campo Grande, Mato Grosso do Sul, Brazil, where I had lived for almost eight years. My 16-year-old daughter and I very much wanted to attend the wedding and decided that we would go by car, just the two of us, in spite of my husband's advice that it would be safer to travel by bus.

We prayed that angels would drive the car for me and that God would give us His protection. We left very early in the morning so that we could arrive before dark. The trip would be approximately 400 miles (650 kilometers), and I was not acquainted with this highway and needed to pay close attention to the road signs.

We'd gone about 200 miles (325 kilometers) when I got confused and took the wrong road. Although we could still reach Campo Grande, this route was longer. But I didn't want to go back, and decided to continue on. So that we would not have to travel at night, I increased the car's speed. I really don't know exactly how it happened, but I swerved off the highway a little and the tire went onto the gravel shoulder. The car skidded toward the guardrail of a bridge. I pulled the steering wheel to one side, then to the other, and now the car was rapidly going in the direction of the guardrail. I heard my daughter desperately shout, "Mother!" and I yelled, "We are going to crash!"

The car went over some large rocks, rupturing both tires on the right side. No matter how much I turned the steering wheel, the car did not respond. It crossed over to the other side of the highway where there was no guardrail on the bridge, only some trees on a steep clifflike embankment, below which the waters of a river flowed. There was nothing more that I could do; I felt that we were going to die. In great despair I shouted, "God, not my daughter!"

The car stopped immediately. It was badly damaged and had to be towed, but we didn't suffer any injuries, not even a scratch. One of the police officers who filled out the accident report told us, "Your saint must be very powerful for you both to get out of this accident alive."

Through faith I could clearly see that the angels of God were there with us.

MARIA BALDÃO QUADRADO

June 29

The Grip of Love

The earth is full of his unfailing love. Ps. 33:5, NIV.

AT A LOCAL COUNTY FAIR my husband and I wandered through the barns to see all the animals and activities. The scents changed as we watched the sheep being sheared, the cattle being judged, goats being washed, and the swine snoring. Then we saw the horses.

Until this point I hadn't touched a single animal, but as we continued to go through the different horse barns, the urge was building. Unfortunately, the horses were positioned in their stalls with their tails toward the public! Finally we came to the racehorses, and their stalls opened to the outside of the barn, where they could stick their necks out over half gates.

I walked along in front of each one, stopping to talk, scratching an ear here, patting a neck there, and feeling their soft noses. Suddenly I met a horse that was different from the rest. I could tell he really enjoyed my attention, because he nuzzled up against me. As I started to move away from him, I discovered he had grabbed the front of my T-shirt and was holding it tightly in his teeth. The owner of the horse, who was sitting nearby, laughed when he saw my predicament. He said his daughter was responsible for teaching the horse that little trick, and it meant that he didn't want me to go away.

As I later mused on this incident, the hymn "O Love That Wilt Not Let Me Go" came to mind. I thought about the many times that God's love has grabbed me and held me captive. This year I've experienced God's love in so many ways. I've seen it in the light of a full moon in the crystal-clear blue-green waters of the Caribbean and in the changing shadows of Yellowstone canyon. I've heard it in the songs of crickets and frogs on a summer night and the low hooting of a great horned owl.

Don't you feel the love of God in the warmth of the sun, a colorful display of flowers, the affection of a pet, and the purity of freshly fallen snow? Nature has a way of gripping our hearts and pulling us to the Creator.

Lord, thank You so much for all You have given to show us Your love; help us to accept it and respond with love to You. DONNA MEYER VOTH

Night-light

Thy word is a lamp unto my feet, and a light unto my path. Ps. 119:105.

WE HAD MOVED A NUMBER of times already in the relatively short life span of our two boys. Brandon, the older, was 7 at the time and could already remember three moves. For Jonathan, then 4 years old, this would be his first memorable move. As we entered the front door on moving day he said simply and rather philosophically, "This is our new home now." With that little declaration he seemed to have closed the chapter on the former place and was off on an adventure to discover what secrets this new place held for him. That was not to be the case with brother Brandon.

As I tucked them in their makeshift sleeping bag bed amid boxes, Brandon was more than a bit concerned. He knew the old place with his eyes closed, but this new place would be different. How could he find me? In actuality, the place wasn't that big, but to a 7-year-old I guess it seemed as if we were a continent apart. That's when I called his attention to the night-light.

"Do you see that night-light?" I asked, pointing to the little light fixture I had plugged in. "When you go outside your door, there will be another. And when you get to that one, you'll see the glow of another a little way down the hall. Simply follow those markers that I've placed strategically along the way, and they'll provide you with a lighted path to me." That, along with a hug, seemed to provide the necessary assurance that he needed.

As I left the boys, following the path via the night-lights, I thought of how God has given me the same assurance. Although the path I travel may be new and unfamiliar and take unexpected twists and turns, though it may be filled with obstacles and challenges, He has marked out the path for me.

I praise You and thank You, dear Jesus, for providing the night-light of Your Word to direct me. May I remember and recognize the way markers that You have strategically placed in my life so that I need not feel lost. Help me this day to go forward with the confidence and boldness I need, because You are lighting and leading the way. Your Word is truly a lamp to my feet and a light to my path.

MAXINE WILLIAMS ALLEN

Struggle Brings Victory!

That is why, for Christ's sake, I delight in weaknesses, in insults, in hardships, in persecutions, in difficulties. For when I am weak, then I am strong. 2 Cor. 12:10, NIV.

LAST SUMMER I DECIDED that our white mailbox would look pretty with some purple morning glories climbing the post and covering the box itself. So I bought a package of seeds and soaked them overnight. I couldn't believe how quickly they sprouted once they were planted, and I was even more surprised by what natural climbers they are. Why, soon the mail carrier was greeted with a flourish of purple morning glories. The only downside was that I had to carry a bucket of water to them almost daily or they'd sulk.

Although I enjoyed them all summer, the next year I decided to plant new morning glory seeds where they'd have access to water from the sprinklers. Much to my surprise, I soon discovered that morning glories are not shrinking violets. With no encouragement of any kind, the seeds from the previous year began to fight their way up through the dry Virginia soil, and it wasn't long until the vines were reaching out to grasp the mailbox post once again.

By last week the determined ones had circled the mailbox and produced beautiful purple blossoms—without my help! *How had they done it?* I wondered. They'd had no encouragement; in fact, just yesterday the weather reporter said that we've been experiencing the worst drought in 40 years. I guess no one bothered to tell that to the morning glories! They had delighted in their weakness! They had not allowed my lack of support to discourage them. Any hardship my failing to water them had caused in their growth process had made them only more determined; in persecution they had become overcomers!

So we'll see what next year brings; but for this year they've taught me an important lesson.

I've heard it said, "When the going gets tough, the tough get going!"

God, give me the endurance of the humble morning glory! Make me strong when I'm feeling weak. When insults, difficulties, and hardships come my way, let Your healing balm sustain me. ROSE OTIS

Stain Removal

Though your sins are like scarlet, they shall be as white as snow; though they are red like crimson, they shall be as wool. Isa. 1:18, NKJV.

ONE OF MY FAVORITE desserts is a bowl of berries. Because fresh berries are very expensive and not grown where we live, I usually buy the frozen berry mix: marionberries, raspberries, and blueberries. While they're still frozen I add either a tiny scoop of ice cream or a spoonful of sweet coconut strips in coconut syrup as a topping for my berries.

One evening as I was enjoying a bowl of berries, my thoughts brought me back to a time some years before when an experience taught me a spiritual lesson.

It was one of those beautiful Sabbath days that we often have in Hawaii. Billowy cumulus clouds in an awesome blue sky hovered over the mountains, and cool breezes tempered the humidity. This was an even more special Sabbath, however, as it included a choral reunion of our church choir. Former members from all over the United States had flown in to sing a familiar Easter cantata that our choral director had chosen. The choir looked good in their "uniforms"—the men wore dark pants, white dress shirts, and a red tie; and the women wore long white muumuus. We sang our very best, and afterward we all had a bountiful and delicious potluck of multiethnic foods. It was then that I experienced an "accident."

I'd been eating some berries when someone called my attention to stains on my muumuu. To my chagrin, bright-red berry stains marred my lovely white dress. "Oh, no!" I groaned. "I hope it isn't ruined!"

I hurried to the restroom with doubts that such a deep stain would wash out.

Just then my friend Ardis said, "Wait; I'll get you some very hot water. It's the best thing I know of to get berry stains out." Sure enough, as Ardis poured the hot water over the stain, it disappeared. How thankful and relieved I felt that my dress was once more clean and white.

Our sins—yours and mine—are like that berry stain: seemingly impossible to remove. Only Jesus, our Savior, can wash them away so that the garment of our character will be as white as snow.

Thank You, Lord, for Your wonderful and powerful cleansing.

AILEEN L. YOUNG

Sunshine in My Soul

They all joined together constantly in prayer, along with the women and Mary the mother of Jesus, and with his brothers. Acts 1:14, NIV.

WE WERE STANDING IN church singing "There's Sunshine in My Soul Today," but I wasn't feeling very sunny. I was alone again, and it was a holiday weekend. The song also declared, "There's music in my soul," but there wasn't. It was more like the next line said: "And Jesus, listening, can hear the songs I cannot sing."

Just then a woman slipped into my pew, and I became aware that there were three of us, all women, in the pew, all by ourselves. I forgot about the rest of the song as I began to think of Jesus' ministry to women, women by themselves. In fact, as I thought about the women in Scripture, I realized how many of them were by themselves. Some were widows, and we don't know the marital status of others. Most women in Bible times were married (or had been). They married young, many by arranged marriages.

I thought of Anna in the Temple. Luke says she had lived with her husband seven years after her marriage and then was a widow until she was 84. She never left the Temple but worshipped night and day, fasting and praying (Luke 2:36, 37). That was a long time to be worshipping alone!

Then I thought of Jesus' mother. We really have no idea how old Mary or Jesus was when her husband, Joseph, died, but it may have been rather early in Jesus' life. But she continued to worship—alone. The last we hear of her is right after Jesus' ascension, when she met with the others in the upper room, waiting for the Holy Spirit.

Then there was the woman caught in adultery, Mary and Martha, the widow of Nain, and the woman at the well. And Lydia in Philippi, Phoebe, Mary, Tryphena, Tryphosa, Persis, Rufus's mother, Julia, and the other women mentioned in Romans 16. Did they have supportive families, or did they step out to worship alone? We have no way of knowing.

As I thought of these and other women, I realized that truly "when Jesus shows His smiling face, there is sunshine in the soul."

Ardis Dick Stenbakken

The Living Water

The water that I will give will become in them a spring of water gushing up to eternal life. John 4:14, NRSV.

ONE OF THE GREAT THINGS about living in Europe is the opportunity to visit places others only read about, such as Pompeii's pillared square. Of all the many wonderful sights, one simple object continues to haunt my thoughts: a short, hollowed-out Roman marble column in one of Pompeii's courtyard gardens. I had never seen a well like this, so tiny yet so useful. Only a bucket dipped down into the hollowed-out marble column—down deep into the earth—could bring its owners the cherished fresh water they so needed.

It amazed me that these people were alive and active when Christ walked the paths of Palestine. But they didn't know the Living Water, Jesus Christ. They were rich, in need of nothing. They cherished the water of the earth, decorated their homes with the colors of the seas, and worshipped the gods of passion and plenty. But one long-ago day all these things vanished in one giant volcanic eruption. Then there was silence where music had lived, darkness where light had danced. Life ceased for many and was twisted for others.

Their agony is preserved by volcanic ash for our wondering eyes to observe. But what about those who escaped, leaving their homes, possessions, family, and slaves behind? Where did they go? Did they make their way to places where Christ's friends would one day meet them? Did they finally taste of the Water of Life? Did they find Someone and something they could keep forever, without threat of natural disaster or impending wars? Out of all that tragedy and chaos, did even just one of them end up at the feet of Jesus?

I can't forget the feel of the fine marble edges of that Roman well under my curious fingers. It occurs to me that sometimes the worst events of our lives bring us unknowingly to the River of Blessing, the Water of Life.

Dear Father, in these troubled times open our eyes to the place we are right now. Let us smell the precious aroma of Your grace, taste the sweet kindness of the Water of Life, and hold tightly to Your all-encompassing arms. Let us laugh with joy at Your goodness and cherish the eternal, never letting it go for momentary pleasures. Amen!

NANCY ANN (NEUHARTH) TROYER

Coot Chicks and Currents

And if I go and prepare a place for you, I will come back and take you to be with me that you also may be where I am. John 14:3, NIV.

ONE OF OUR FAVORITE places to go as a family is to the park surrounding the large cathedral in St. Albans, England. The beautiful cathedral rises silently and elegantly at the top of the hill, and it glows rosily in the light of the summer evening sun. The gardens tumble gently down to a narrow river; large oak trees rise from the soft grass and the gatherings of flowers. We like to go to the park to feed the birds—Canada geese, ducks, swans, herons, moorhens, and coots. Even at my age it's fun to watch the squabbling beaks fight for some old stale bread.

One evening we were walking along the stream when we saw something in the water. From a distance it looked like a little black pom-pom. As we got closer we realized it was a tiny coot chick that had fallen out of the safety of its nest. We had seen the mother sitting on her large midstream nest with the other babies peeping out from under her wings. But this little one must have fallen overboard into the flowing water, and now it was paddling like crazy, with the tiniest little feet, trying to get back home.

To be honest, it wasn't doing very well. When it was trying its hardest, it managed to swim forward only a few inches; then it would tire and float back again. It looked so tiny, so fragile, so tired. Then we saw something else. Right behind the chick was its father, making sure that the chick wouldn't drift too far downstream, protecting it from danger, even though the little one couldn't see him.

I smiled. There was no need to worry anymore. Daddy was there.

I often think about that little chick, probably because there are many times when I feel as though I'm drifting further and further away from my comfort zone, my home, and my goals. As fast as I paddle, I just seem to float further out of control, pushed around by the currents of life. But I needn't worry, because Daddy's right behind me, keeping me safe, protecting me from danger, and preventing me from drifting where He doesn't want me to go. Sometimes I'm so busy struggling that I don't even notice how close He is to me. But it's good to know that He's there, and one day we'll make it home together.

KAREN HOLFORD

Witnessing Opportunities God's Sent My Way

Ye shall be witnesses unto me. Acts 1:8.

DURING A LARGE CHURCH conference in Toronto, Canada, my heart was deeply touched as I listened to many soul-winning experiences of people from around the world. I wanted to share my faith too. One morning I asked God to use me in some way to witness for Him. Amazingly, He provided opportunities right in my hotel room. Before going to Toronto we were told to leave a tip every day for the housekeeper. The first day I left a tip with a "Thank you and have a good day" note. When I returned to the room, there was a note on the desk: "I just want you to know how happy I am for your goodness. God bless you and your family. Thanks a lot. Lorna. Housekeeping staff."

The following day I left another tip and note. The reply note read: "Dear Guest, Thank you very much. Housekeeping staff, Myrna."

On July 6, when I returned from the meetings, another note from Lorna awaited me: "Dear Ma'am and Sir, How are you today? I believe always blessed by the Lord. Amen. Well, I write a letter to you because I want to ask a favor. Would you mind, ma'am and sir, to please pray for my husband to accept Him as Lord and Savior in His life? I ask this because I know that you are God's servant. Yesterday I didn't clean your room. I hope everything is OK. I'll be back Sunday. God bless, and thanks a lot. Have a wonderful and blessed weekend to both of you. Lorna."

I believe that my Bible and devotional book in the hotel room may have served as silent witnesses. Although I did not personally meet these individuals who left the notes for me, it seemed we knew each other through the little notes we shared.

Before returning home, I felt impressed to leave a note, some literature, and a devotional book for Lorna, Myrna, and Marcus, the bellhop (he was always so courteous and helpful). I wondered if I displayed such joy in service. I prayed that God would use the materials to touch these hearts. I also prayed that Lorna's husband would give his heart to Jesus.

I'm grateful to God for the people He's sent my way and for the opportunity to witness. *Lord, give me the zeal and passion to witness for You and to be a channel through which Your love can flow to others.* SHIRLEY C. IHEANACHO

The Yucca

Unto thee lift I up mine eyes, O thou that dwellest in the heavens. Ps. 123:1.

WE HAVE A YUCCA PLANT growing in our garden. A native of California, it is a stiff-looking plant growing erect with very large panicles (a branch raceme in which each branch bears a further raceme). The plant sometimes grows higher than four feet. The flowers are bell-shaped, creamy white, and scented.

Despite the plant's disadvantage of not getting full sunlight because of a hedge behind it, I was pleasantly surprised to see the yucca beginning to bloom again after eight years. I delighted in watching it day by day as the panicles took shape. Then I noticed that the yucca was trying to maneuver itself away from the hedge to seek more sunshine.

Every morning as I opened the door I stood and admired my yucca. As I admired it, this verse from Psalm 121 would come to mind: "I will lift up mine eyes unto the hills, from whence cometh my help" (verse 1). The yucca was so majestic, magnificent, and proud.

One morning my yucca plant was lying on the ground. Even the ants had attacked it for the sweet nectar. I called my husband to help me stake the plant so it could stand tall again.

We women can be compared to the yucca. We can grow in purity and grace, erect and tall. Some people admire us for certain qualities and characteristics. Sometimes, however, we become supercilious, characterized by haughty scorn or indifference toward others who don't meet our standards. "The Lord hates and cannot tolerate: a proud look" (Prov. 6:16, 17, TEV). "Pride goeth before destruction, and an haughty spirit before a fall" (Prov. 16:18).

Satan may come with some deceptive means to knock you down, perhaps something such as tempting you to be lax in your devotions. Maybe people, like the ants after the nectar, are passing juicy bits of gossip about you. Whatever has knocked you down, there is a Gardener who will come to your rescue to help you up again. Like the yucca, you cannot lift yourself up. You need the Gardener. He stands ready to help you now, if you ask Him.

O Lord God, we lift our eyes to the heavens, from where our help comes. Let us not be diverted by the glitter of Satan's deceptions. May we focus on You only.

PRISCILLA ADONIS

Fully Prepared

These ought ye to have done, and not to leave the other undone. Matt. 23:23.

CONFISCATED! CONFISCATED! CONFISCATED!" This was the security screener's answer to my plea to be permitted to keep my harmless little knife. I begged, I pleaded, but to no avail. "No, no! Confiscated!" was the reply. And the decibels kept mounting.

My husband and I, needing to take a break after a rather busy schedule, had decided to go on vacation to Jamaica, in the West Indies, shortly after September 11, 2001. Because of current business that needed attention, we had to make hurried last-minute preparations. As we talked with others, we were reminded of the possible dangers we might face and warned about including in our luggage innocent-looking items that could be considered as hazardous weapons and objects of terror.

At last the list of things to be done before we left was checked off: neighbors, relatives, and friends were notified; clothing was all packed; airline tickets and passports were in hand. We took off for the airport, confident that we were fit to travel, fully prepared.

We arrived at the ticket counter two hours before departure time. We were processed immediately and directed to the appropriate departure gate. At the security checkpoint the buzzer sounded as I went through. That's when the knife was revealed. I was directed into a closed-off aisle and ordered to sit down and take off my shoes and my hat as the security scanner carefully examined me. My shoes and hat were returned, but the knife was confiscated.

I missed my little knife! As I quietly mourned my loss, I reflected on the vanity of worldly possessions, cherished treasures. I realized that what had happened was the consequence of my neglecting to take the proper precautions and double-check my belongings for the trip. If I had checked, the little folding knife would have been safe in the luggage that I had shipped.

How often on our spiritual journey through life we neglect to check on people, heirs for the kingdom, precious treasures—our relatives, friends, neighbors, coworkers—who are trapped by the evil one. We have failed to involve them among those we should be preparing to take with us to heaven. Saved, not confiscated!

How about you? Are you carefully preparing for the journey, or is the business of life keeping you too busy? It's a sobering thought and can have serious consequences.

Quilvie G. Mills

A New Heart to Praise Her God

I will give you a new heart and put a new spirit within you. Eze. 36:26, NKJV.

IN THE EARLY 1990s I was very sick with heart problems. The official term was severe cardiomyopathy. I was told I had but a few months to live. My only chance of life would be a heart transplant. Despite the fact that I was 63 years old, three years over the age limit for such surgery, in July 1995 my name was put on the list, and only 11 days later I was notified that a suitable donor had been identified. Two teams were at work the day I received my new heart: the transplant team and the prayer team. It's a wonderful thing to be upheld in prayer by friends and family all around the world.

Life posttransplant has not always been straightforward. The anti-rejection treatment was not pleasant, but necessary. Suddenly, about a year after the transplant, I started experiencing blackouts and was told that my new heart was malfunctioning. "You need a pacemaker," the doctor advised. "It's the only thing that will save your life."

It was fitted, and I had another chance for life. Since then I've been fine and am still going strong at 70 years of age.

Following heart transplantation the medical team prescribes three essentials for physical recovery: daily doses of medication, diet, and exercise. If those of us with heart transplants stick to these essentials, we reap the health benefits.

I can assure you that there are benefits to be gained in our spiritual lives, too, if we apply the same formula: daily renewal of our commitment to a personal relationship with Jesus, a regular diet of feeding on His Word, and spiritual exercise though prayer and personal witness. These are the things that keep our spiritual heart beating strong and regular. If you've had a spiritual heart transplant, you'll want to follow the regimen.

Heavenly Father, give each of us a new heart today. A heart in tune with Yours. A heart kept healthy in a close relationship with You. A heart that will not reject Your call but will beat with the vibrancy of obedience to Your will. Amen.

NADEGE MICHEL

God's Unfailing Care

For he shall give his angels charge over thee, to keep thee in all thy ways. Ps. 91:11.

THE SUN SHONE FROM a cloudless sky, and the crisp mountain air invigorated us. My husband and I were eager to view the mountain peaks before the weather changed and the clouds settled on them. We had motored down from the warm subtropical area of Australia to holiday in the Australian Alps. As we aren't skiers and didn't have suitable clothing for alpine regions, we chose the warmer summer months for the visit.

We came to an area where the summits of the main peaks could be seen. A boardwalk had been constructed over the rocks and vegetation, and led to a vantage point where a panoramic view could be obtained and signs pointed to the various mountains. We reveled in the pristine beauty for some time before starting the return to our car.

On the way back I felt myself beginning to slip on the boards, and I remembered nothing else until my head cleared and I found myself lying facedown among the moss-covered rocks. My husband, who had been walking in front of me, heard a shuffle and turned. To his horror, he saw me spearing headfirst toward the rocks below and imagined a cracked skull, broken neck, or some other serious injury. How would he summon help to take me to a hospital? It was the off-season for tourists, no one else was on the boardwalk, and the road was hidden from view.

When I began to stir, he almost collapsed with relief. I felt no pain. When we examined my body, particularly my head and neck, there were no signs or feeling of injury. The thick moss on the rocks must have helped to save my head from serious injury, despite my feeling dazed for a few moments. With the help of my husband I climbed back onto the boardwalk without any effort or discomfort. We walked back to the car and marveled at the way God had sent angels to take charge of us. We praised and thanked the Lord that angels had hovered around us and protected me from any injury. We continued our plans for the remainder of the day, ever mindful of God and His protecting care.

As I look back over my life I wonder how many times You have sent angels to protect me from danger. Thank You, Lord. Joy Dustow

Great Reunion

Rejoice greatly, O Daughter of Zion! Shout, Daughter of Jerusalem! See, your king comes to you. Zech. 9:9, NIV.

WE WERE ATTENDING CAMP MEETING for the first time since arriving in the United States. Since we'd just arrived as students, we didn't think we would meet anyone from home. We were still enjoying the camp meeting services when we spotted familiar faces we'd known for years; some had been missionaries in Africa, some were college colleagues, and some were just friends. You can imagine the excitement that got under way that day!

Some who were missionaries while we were teenagers couldn't recognize us at first, but believe me, the old stories began to awaken those memories of long ago. We truly had a wonderful time catching up on so many happenings.

It reminded me of that great reunion we're all waiting for. Imagine how hard it has been for Jesus to be away from us for this long. I'm positive He has missed us a great deal. He promised that He will come back so we will be with Him forever in that home that He has prepared for each one of us. Our loved ones who are now asleep will be awakened by that trumpet sound. On that day there will be no more sorrow. All will be joy, because we will be changed. Yes, it may sometimes seem a long time before Jesus comes, but I'm sure it won't be long. There will be tears of joy when we meet one another—no more sad goodbyes. What a glorious occasion for all those who will have done His will!

The Bible says, "No eye has seen, no ear has heard, no mind has conceived what God has prepared for those who love him" (1 Cor. 2:9, NIV). What an exquisite artist! Imagine the joy we will all have sitting at His feet and catching up on the happenings of ages gone by. It will be a glorious occasion—the greatest camp meeting in history! We will meet long-forgotten friends and loved ones and rejoice forever.

I don't know about you, but I've made up my mind to be there by God's grace. His invitation is still open, so make up your mind while there is still time. I want to be there, rejoicing and meeting each of you.

Lord, help us to heed Your Word, and prepare us for that grand reunion.

Sibusisiwe Ncube-Ndhlovu

Making Footprints

Always be glad because of the Lord! I will say it again: Be glad. Phil. 4:4, CEV.

A LITTLE 2-YEAR-OLD BOY GIGGLES. His face is one huge smile, and joy bubbles up from inside, bursting into radiant exuberance. "See my footprints?" he shouts as he runs back and forth in a puddle, leftover evidence of a summer rain. His shoes slosh in and out of the water, absorbing as much water as possible. Again and again he jumps until he is completely covered with splashes of water.

Envying the fun, I join him. Laughing, we together fill the expanse of dry cement with little and big footprints. "I can make footprints too," I tell him as I also get splashed. "My footprints are bigger than yours!" His eyes are shining, and I have never seen anyone more happy and filled with life than this little person at this very moment.

"Hey!" he shouts once again, this time to a passing stranger. "Look at the footprints I made!"

As we say goodbye to the puddle that has entertained us for the past 15 minutes, all that remains is a sidewalk completely covered with tiny Pooh Bear running-shoe prints and women's size 9 Teva flip-flop prints. So proud of the sight of his own footprints and of his own ability to create them, this happy little person jabbers on about it to any new face we meet as the time passes. I have never seen him like this before.

Life is full of making our own footprints; often we find enjoyment at each step of the way. At other times it's easier to try to avoid the darkness of a problem—much like a puddle—by jumping over it. Yet to fully get through a difficult experience we need to trust God completely and jump fully into the puddles. He will lead us in making beautiful footprints as He teaches us more about Him. We need to be like the little boy who had no fear of jumping into a puddle and who is ever curious to see the pattern the footprints will make.

What an adventure! Let's not lose our sense of wonder at puddle jumping and leaving footprints! We can always be glad in the Lord. Let's rejoice as we look back to see where our Lord has led us. "I will say it again: Be glad."

ALANNA O'MALLEY

July 13

The Journey's Almost O'er

Blessed are they that do his commandments, that they may have right to the tree of life, and may enter in through the gates into the city. Rev. 22:14.

ON A HOT, HUMID DAY in New York I made my way up the stairs and out of the steaming subway. I'd gotten off the train two stops before the normal stop that lets me off a block from work. I wanted to purchase some special candy for my niece, Jeanine. This candy was a particular favorite of hers, but she hadn't been able to find it in California, where she used to live, nor in Huntsville, Alabama, where she attended school, nor in Maryland, where she now lived. I was going to see Jeanine that weekend, and I could not show up without it.

After buying the candy, I had planned that I'd board the train again and continue on to my job. But then I stopped at a nearby shoe store. When I came out onto the street again, I looked down the seemingly few blocks and thought to myself, *I don't need to take the train. I can walk to work; the distance is minimal.* So I started walking.

In the sweltering heat each block became longer and longer. Had I made a foolish decision? I pressed on. As I drew closer and closer to my landmark, the famous bull that sits in the middle of Wall Street, I began to take hope. I was almost there! I was going to make it.

When I had almost reached my place of employment, I stopped and looked back—back to where I had started my journey. How long the journey had seemed! But now that I was only a block away from my destination, it didn't look long at all.

That morning reminded me of my Christian journey. As I walk the Christian pathway from day to day, it sometimes seems too long, too tiring, too far to go. Then I look back and see where God has brought me from, then forward to where He is leading me, and I rejoice. The journey's almost over, and I'll soon reach my mark.

"Even so, come, Lord Jesus!" (Rev. 22:20). DARLEEN SIMMONDS

The Fountain of Life

Jesus answered and said to her, "Whoever drinks of this water will thirst again, but whoever drinks of the water that I shall give him will never thirst. But the water that I shall give him will become in him a fountain of water springing up into everlasting life." John 4:13, 14, NKJV.

AS I LOOKED OUT THE window one morning during my devotional time, I saw a hummingbird drinking from the feeder that hung on the porch. I thought of how much and how often the little bird has to drink just to survive. Each morning about daybreak the first little bird appears and feeds heavily to get off to a good start. Some days the birds feed heavily during the day, also. But every day they feed most the first thing in the morning and the last thing in the evening.

I thought of our need to go to our fountain of life—Jesus. Daily we need to begin our day by drinking in the living water that Jesus offers. We need the Holy Spirit to fill our lives so that we're able to endure whatever the day may bring. We need the spiritual energy that comes from spending time in prayer and study—drinking in that living water. If I were to begin the day on my own, I would be trying to handle the cares of the day on my own too.

Jesus tells us, "I can do nothing on my own" (John 5:30, NRSV). If Jesus can't do anything on His own, what makes me think I could ever do anything on my own? I need to drink of the Holy Spirit just as heavily as the little hummingbird does the sugar water. Before I retire at night I need to spend time with Jesus, to fill my mind and heart with the living water, to protect my mind from the evil one while I sleep, to keep him out.

Each spring I eagerly await the arrival of the hummingbirds. They send out a scout to find food; then the scout leads the others to the food source. I spend hours watching them as they dart from feeder to feeder, defending their territory. Am I as ready to defend the One who gives me the living water? Will I guide others to the Fountain so that they too may drink and live?

Thank You, Jesus, for the beautiful picture You have revealed to me through these tiny little creatures of Yours. Please help me always to be willing to lead others to the water of life, the living water. DONNA COOK

Fire Blessings

The wilderness and the solitary place shall be glad for them; and the desert shall rejoice, and blossom as the rose. Isa. 35:1.

MY DAUGHTER, MARINA, LIVES about an hour's drive from me. To reach her home in the California desert requires about 30 minutes of traveling through the Cajon Pass, a vast area of paved highways surrounded by desert cactus, trees, and shrubs. I grew up in Arizona, so I love the beautiful surroundings and have driven this highway enough times that the trip doesn't seem as long as it really is.

During the first two weeks of June this year the area was plagued by wildfires. No sooner had the firefighters extinguished one than another broke out, destroying everything the first fire had left behind. The pass had to be closed for several hours as the flames reached clear down to the sides of the highway.

About a month later my daughter and I had planned to entertain some friends at her home. Since Marina needed to take care of some appointments near my house a couple days after the event, we decided to share a ride to her house and then back to mine. As we rode along we chatted about our plans and how we were going to enjoy the time we'd be spending with family members and loved ones. But a few minutes into the pass we grew quiet as we looked at all the devastation that had taken place. Once-green bushes, shrubs, trees, wildflowers, and even the rocks were mere black skeletons and odd forms of charcoal.

Finally Marina broke the silence. "I feel so sorry for all those poor burned plants," she said. "They look so sad."

Some time ago I heard a talk given by a forest ranger. He explained that fires in the forests and fields are not totally bad. "The fire clears away the thick herbage and underbrush," he said, "giving room for some of the beautiful plants that many times we haven't seen in years."

How often God uses nature to explain His working with us! If we'll allow Him to, He will let the fires burn in our spiritual lives to destroy the weaknesses that have prevented His beauty from growing in our hearts.

Dear Lord, may we bloom this day, and every day, for You. Amen.

MILDRED C. WILLIAMS

Death Valley Angel

The angel of the Lord encamps all around those who fear Him. Ps. 34:7, NKJV.

DRIVING ACROSS DEATH VALLEY at high noon may sound questionable, but it was exciting! My friend Zlata and I had left our working husbands at home—by their choice—and launched our Out West Trip. We flew from Florida to Phoenix, rented a car, and began our adventure. There was so much to see and do and enjoy on our way to the northern California coast.

Our daily practice was to have prayer together, asking the Lord to send our guardian angels with us on the day's adventures. We knew that in order to experience all the natural beauty along the way, we would be in isolated places such as forests, beach coves, and whatever beckoned.

It was necessary to cross the Mojave Desert as we left the wondrous Zion National Park in Utah and headed toward southern California. The time frame turned out to be noontime—but the fact that it was July did not deter us! By following the "turn off your air-conditioning for the next 20 miles" signs and drinking lots of water, we expected that both of us and our vehicle would survive the heat.

All went well as we made frequent stops to admire a bit of flora and check out the view— until we came to a crossroad that wasn't shown on our map. We knew that to take the wrong turn in the middle of the desert, where we had not seen more than two cars during the past hour, could spell disaster.

We immediately bowed our heads and asked the Lord to show us the proper direction. As we opened our eyes, a car approached the crossroad from the opposite direction and stopped for no apparent reason. The driver didn't get out of the car, so Zlata and I walked over to him and asked for directions. He told us which way to go, and without further conversation he drove on.

A coincidence? Rather unlikely, given the precision timing and location. Whether he was really an angel or just a man God used to help out two women in need, we don't know. However, from that time forward as we thanked the Lord for the timely answer to our prayer, we referred to him as our Death Valley angel.

Dorothy Wainwright Carey

Steward of My Soul

Well done. . . . You have been faithful with a few things; I will put you in charge of many things. Matt. 25:23, NIV.

Settling into the café booth, I removed my coat and shoes. A glass of grapefruit juice proclaimed my right to occupy this space, at least for a while. It was nearly three hours until my connecting flight. Pulling out a ruled tablet and locating my glasses, I began to write. "Dear Melissa." The words flowed easily over the paper as I described the busy airport, including the hot-pink and lemon-yellow checkered décor of the café. I chuckled. Melissa would enjoy the description of her two least-favorite colors. (I could almost hear her exclamations: "You've got to be kidding! Give me a break!")

And then my pen slowed. Stopped. What to say in response to the voice mail she'd left on my cell phone? Then fragments of conversation from the next booth caught my attention. No, I was not eavesdropping—their voices just happened to be raised so they could hear each other above the rush hour clack and clatter. "Those are my three choices," the younger woman explained, "and I don't know which one to select." I stayed tuned in to hear her companion's response. What would it be?

The older woman's voice was softer and pitched somewhat lower, but I managed to pick up ". . . all three . . . fine options." A pause; then: "In those situations . . . I try to select the optimum choice . . . as steward of my soul." The younger woman nodded and smiled appreciatively. Almost absentmindedly I watched them check watches, collect belongings, put a tip on the table, and leave.

How often had I heard those words separately? Many times. But never before combined in that exact phrase: steward of my soul. What a concept! How often had I been faced with multiple options, any of which could be considered appropriate—even desirable? Many times. It happens to us all. But I'd never consciously made my decision in terms of the optimum choice as steward of my soul. H'mmm.

Here was the answer to Melissa's dilemma. I picked up my pen.

Arlene Taylor

Commitment

But one thing I do: Forgetting what is behind and straining toward what is ahead, I press on toward the goal. Phil. 3:13, 14, NIV.

SEVERAL YEARS AGO I had a great passion for interior decorating. I spent hours poring over my books and magazines with the pictures of re-dos and makeovers—all in living color for every room in the house.

But that was then. I was younger, and we moved more often. It was fun to decorate each "new" house, depending on my mood and our pocketbook at the time. This is now, and except for the stacks of magazines that I don't have the heart to part with, that great passion has been downgraded from one of picking out wallpaper and paint to just a lot of good memories. I guess you could say I now have a new passion: writing. Whether it's writing stories about my life (which is the only thing I know to write about) or sending letters and cards to family and friends, it seems I have to write.

I'm still a novice, but someone once told me I should get a computer, or at least an electric typewriter, as it would make my job so much easier. But I prefer my antiquated Smith Corona portable that I've had for years.

Another bit of good advice I received was that an artist should put something on canvas every day; likewise, a writer should write something each day, even if it's only a few lines. I believe I do that without even trying.

But I must admit that I'm not always as disciplined as I should be; I get sidetracked easily. Some days I find myself with more than one iron in the fire at the same time. There have been times I've had a story in the typewriter, and then I get stalled and tend to allow my mind to wander in a different direction. Perhaps it's just my age, another sign of senility creeping in.

When I was young I should have been concentrating on spiritual things. Now I find it's more difficult to focus on the more important issues of life. Proverbs 16:3 says, "Commit your works to the Lord, and your thoughts will be established" (NKJV).

Lord, help me to be the committed person You would have me to be so that I will glorify Your name and be a witness to someone each day.

CLAREEN COLCLESSER

Ringing Bells

Here I am! I stand at the door and knock. If anyone hears my voice and opens the door, I will come in and eat with him, and he with me. Rev. 3:20, NIV.

IT WAS A HOT NIGHT, and the window of the hotel room was wide open. In the early-morning hours I was reminded of the fact that the town was full of churches when the church bells started ringing. The believers were being called to early Mass. I turned over and slept on until the church bells started ringing again. I felt as if the bells were ringing for me. It was as if God were saying to me, "Wake up! It's time to spend time with Me!"

So I began to reflect on bells. Ringing bells have had various functions in past centuries. They can express many things: warning, joy, rejoicing, sorrow. Our hearing is connected with our emotions, and we have different kinds of feelings, depending on the occasion for which bells are ringing. The bell ringing at a funeral pierces our soul. The church bells ringing in London during the queen's Golden Jubilee expressed contagious jubilation. The victory bells after one of Napoleon's battles must have consoled the wives of the soldiers: *Maybe he is still alive.* In medieval times bells would awaken those in danger of fire or warn of the presence of the plague. The school bell sets the pupils free to enjoy their leisure time. The cowbells in the Alps are perceived in various ways, either as an annoyance or an enjoyment. In Africa a rusty truck wheel serves as a church bell, calling the believers to worship. A doorbell announces visitors. A bell calls the hungry family to the table.

Are we hungry for God's Word? Is there a bell that reminds us to come to God's table? Or do we prefer to stay hungry because we are too lazy to accept His invitation?

The door at which Jesus is standing and knocking because He wants to eat with us does not have a handle on the outside. There is no loud bell, no doorbell, only a soft knocking. God doesn't always call us with the loud ringing of bells. Our life is often so loud and busy that we can't hear the knock. And that's why we should become quiet—so that we can spend time with our Lord.

Hannele Ottschofski

A Stronger Arm

Ah Lord God! behold thou hast made the heaven and the earth by thy great power and stretched out arm, and there is nothing too hard for thee. Jer. 32:17.

I LOVE BEING A GRANDMOTHER. I live only six miles away from my two youngest granddaughters, and watching them grow fills me with pleasure and pride. Perhaps it's because I've gone over this road before and know the pitfalls to avoid. Or perhaps it's because I know that the total responsibility of rearing them is not mine alone. Whatever the reason, when I discover that I have to pick them up after school, it's impossible to wipe the smile from my lips. I so enjoy interacting with those young minds.

One particular Tuesday afternoon the 8-year-old decided she wanted to try a recipe she had seen on the Internet. Gravely collecting all the items for her handwritten recipe, she fetched a mixing bowl and wooden spoon. She motioned for me, her willing assistant, to preheat the oven.

Soon I could see the little head bent industriously over the bowl, as if she were saying to herself with each stroke, *I will make brownies. They will be wonderful. My mom will like them. My big sister will like them. Even the neighbors will want to taste a sample.*

Then I watched as her strokes slowed and finally stopped. "Grandma," she called. "This is hard; I need a stronger arm. Can you help me?" Again I was her willing assistant. Even at her tender age, Briana seemed to know that her success in baking required teamwork. She couldn't do it alone.

Munching on her tasty treat later that evening, I thought of the similarities between our relationship and the one I share with my heavenly Father. We are a team. My success in any endeavor is based on how closely I work with Him. I know He delights in my company—He has told me so on several occasions. I read it in Psalm 100:3-5 and in Isaiah 43:3, 4. I know He is always willing to help me (Ps. 119:173). But what is most significant is that His is the stronger arm in our partnership. I need to be aware of that and ask His assistance in everything I do.

Thank You, dear God, for Your promise. Regardless of the size of my need, I am always on Your mind and in Your hand. Help me to remember that.

CAROL J. GREENE

Give God Your Concerns

Cast all your anxiety on him because he cares for you. 1 Peter 5:7, NIV.

WHEN I TOLD A friend I prefer the word "concern" rather than "worry," she asked, "Is there a difference?"

"Well, no," I admitted, "but 'concern' sounds better to me."

Are you ever worried—no, concerned—about your marriage, children, job, finances, relationships, health, whatever? I know I've been. For example, a few summers ago the verse "An anxious heart weighs a [woman] down" (Prov. 12:25, NIV) fit me to a T.

I've had osteoarthritis for many years; and then osteoporosis caused me to shrink five inches from my once-5'10" frame. I'm sure that many folks can relate. I went to an orthopedic spine specialist who ordered a myelogram. I told a friend about it. "Oh, yes," she said, "you'll have that, and then another test, and then surgery!" Because her husband had just undergone all that, it didn't mean I would—and I didn't. *Praise You, Lord!*

I was put on a fitness program at a spine center gym. In spite of my strong feeling that there would be no surgery, I must admit to some anxious thoughts about the results of the myelogram. I found that such verses as "Cast your cares on the Lord and he will sustain you" (Ps. 55:22, NIV) and "The Lord is near to all who call on him. . . . He hears their cry and saves them" (Ps. 145:18, 19, NIV) were helpful.

Ruth Bell Graham, in her book *Legacy of a Pack Rat,* wrote: "According to the Bible, God responds to our sighs, our tears, our murmurs—even our longings can be interpreted as prayer" (p. 235). Then she quoted John Trapp: "The Lord is near to all who call on him: yea, he can feel breath when no voice can be heard for faintness" (comments on Psalm 145).

To "cast all [our] anxiety on him," we can pray, talking to Him as to a friend, for He is our best friend. It may be difficult to think of Him as sitting across the room from us or having a meal with us or riding in the car with us, but if we can see Him that way, we will feel freer to tell Him what is on our minds and hearts.

Praise You, Lord, that we can tell You everything: our aches and pains, our likes and dislikes, our troubles and temptations, our pleasures and joys, our longings and anxieties.

PATSY MURDOCH MEEKER

An Aerial View

And we know that in all things God works for the good of those who love him. Rom. 8:28, NIV.

BEFORE WE WERE MARRIED my husband belonged to a flying club. He lived most of his earlier years at the airport, observing as well as flying. When we married, I became interested in aerodynamics. Whenever you would engage my husband in a conversation, before long he would try to take you for a mental flight. We had four children, and he tried his best to get one or more of them interested in flying, but to no avail. Not one had the desire after flying once with us. As my husband has matured in years, his vision and blood pressure have forced him to stop flying. This, however, hasn't stopped his mental aeronautics. Every chance he gets—via television, books, magazines or videos—he flies.

After retiring we moved south, to a minifarm in the country. My husband had always said he would like to rent a plane and fly over our land so he could see the layout from the air. He never could get anyone to take him, but he didn't give up. He asked at our small county airport, as well as the neighboring one, but they said they didn't give rides or rent planes because of their insurance.

One day while we were outside working in the yard, an unfamiliar car drove up. A woman got out, introduced herself, and explained her mission. In her hand was a photograph of our land, taken from the air. I was really surprised. It was a beautiful picture. I quickly called my husband over from another area of the yard. He was just as surprised as I was once he was able to calm me down. We were looking at an aerial view of our land! An answer to a prayer! She showed us the different sizes we could purchase.

Yes, God does answer prayers in His own time and in His own way! Imagine our friend Jesus with His aerial view, sitting up high, looking at all His children. He has the ability to see and hear every little thing that we say and do.

My prayer is that the earthly view of our lives coincides with the aerial view that our heavenly Father sees from above. ELAINE J. JOHNSON

Belonging to the Family of God

Sing forth the honour of his name: make his praise glorious. Ps. 66:2.

I'VE COME TO KNOW many people in my work and travels. Now, looking back, reliving friendships or meeting old friends or acquaintances, I feel indeed privileged to be able to say, "It is wonderful to belong to the family of God."

I live in a retirement center that is also a service center. If one chooses to be occupied or is asked to do something that will benefit others, there's a satisfaction that you belong to the family of God and can still be of help to others.

When I meet folk who were at the same high school or college in the days of long ago, we reminisce. I feel I belong to a large family. I'm grateful for how the Lord has guided and led, given me health and energy and an ability to keep constantly busy.

Recently a young friend asked me if I would like to go on a trip to the coast. She needed to attend to some business and wanted some company for the long journey. I really felt privileged. We visited one of our other retirement centers where I know several folk. We met friends with whom I am still corresponding. We were invited for lunch after church the next day. There I met several more people I used to know in the days of yore. The blessing of the worship service and the blessing of the fellowship at lunchtime again brought the feeling of how wonderful it is to belong to the family of God.

At camp meeting time I really realize how big the family of God is. I see people with whom I once worked and am greeted affectionately.

None of my three daughters live near me. With today's business and expense it isn't possible to see any of them very often. So I value friends so much more.

What a blessed assurance it is to know that one day we who remain faithful and true will meet way beyond the blue with our heavenly Father and Big Brother, who is also our Savior. What a family! PHYLLIS DALGLEISH

The Little Piglet

If you ask anything in My name, I will do it. John 14:14, NKJV.

MY MOTHER PASSED AWAY A number of years ago. She and I were very close. She had come to spend the last few years with us, but lived separately in a small house with a garden of her own. One morning she was very upset to find her garden all messed up. She called me to see her garden and asked if I had any clue as to who had done the damage. I had no idea and felt sorry for her.

She replanted the uprooted plants and tidied up her garden again, but, sad to say, the next morning she found the garden messed up again. Mother was determined to find the culprit. The next day, after watering and weeding, she went inside and watched from the window. It wasn't long before she saw the culprit: a cute, chubby, little piglet, fully white, with pink ears and an upturned pink nose. It probably had strayed away from its mother and didn't know how to get back to her. It began to dig with its nose.

"Get out!" Mother cried as she ran and chased it with a stick. It disappeared behind the hedge, only to come out again later when Mother was out of sight. This continued for a day or two. Mother found it impossible to get rid of the little pig. I couldn't help her either.

Mother was very discouraged and made this problem a matter of prayer. She prayed earnestly, asking God to keep this pig away from her garden. One morning Mother excitedly called me to follow her to her garden. There, among the uprooted plants, was a dead piglet. I asked her what had happened.

She told me she'd been praying to God to remove the piglet. That morning, while it was still dark, she had heard dogs barking and the piglet squealing. And then all the noise had stopped. We felt very sorry for the little pig—it was just a baby without a mother. The answer had come in a way that none of us had necessarily wanted.

God gave His only begotten Son to die for the human race, although He cares very much about animals, too. Jesus' death was one that no one would have chosen. God heard Mother's request and kept His promise that He will give anything if we ask in Jesus' name. Oh, that more of us would believe His promise and go to Him when we are in any kind of trouble.

BIROL CHARLOTTE CHRISTO

Rotting Soles

Do not lay up for yourselves treasures on earth, where moth and rust destroy and where thieves break in and steal; but lay up for yourselves treasures in heaven. Matt. 6:19, 20, NKJV.

I SAT IN CHURCH ONE Sabbath morning, waiting for the service to begin. As I reached for a hymnal, I glanced at my shoes and smiled inwardly. The open-toed gray leather pumps were as perfect for today's outfit as they had been for the New York wedding I had bought them for more than 15 years before. I had not worn them very often since. In fact, when I had moved to Florida a few years after that wedding, I had kept the shoes in their box.

But there was one particular Sabbath morning that I had decided to wear them. Their tiny pink rosette bows were the exact color of the dress I wanted to wear. Imagine my horror as I sat in church and saw that I had somehow tracked the sand from the parking lot into the sanctuary. I moved my feet. More sand on the floor. Another movement brought even more of the gritty mess. Cautiously I lifted one foot, only to discover that the sole was disintegrating before my eyes. The other sole was the same. I still remember my son's muffled giggles as I stepped gingerly down the aisle after church.

"Dry rot," the shoemaker later explained as he replaced the sole. The finished product looked like new. It was restored.

Just as that shoemaker was able to restore that shoe that was destroyed by dry rot, so it is with the Lord who is willing to forgive us for all the sins we have committed. He will accept us as if we had not sinned.

It is very easy for my Christian life to disintegrate, just as that pair of shoes that had been left unused for an extended period of time. I know if I spend too much time doing worldly things and neglect to feed my soul with daily prayer and study of His Word, dry rot will set in. Rotting soles and dry rot of the soul. Ellen G. White reminds us, "You who in heart long for something better than this world can give, recognize this longing as the voice of God to your soul" (*Steps to Christ,* p. 28).

Lord, I recognize the longing of my soul. Please help me to focus on You daily, and not the things of this world. GLORIA HUTCHINSON

God's Geography

Trust in the Lord with all your heart and lean not on your own understanding; in all your ways acknowledge him, and he will make your paths straight. Prov. 3:5, 6, NIV.

I WAS SO EXCITED WHEN I got an answer from the German Academic Exchange Service— from the size of the letter I could immediately tell that it was an acceptance this time. Finally. I had tried a couple times before to get a scholarship so I could travel to Iceland, and now it seemed that all my plans would come true. I opened the letter with trembling hands. But what was this supposed to mean? It was an acceptance letter, all right, but it didn't say anything about Reykjavík or Akureyri. Iceland was not mentioned by even a single word. The location where I should spend seven months as a language assistant was called Tingsryd, Sweden. But this was just the first shock. When I read further, I began to understand that the school had applied, not for a language assistant with German as a native tongue, but for a French- or English-speaking person. What now?

All of a sudden I was filled with deep peace and reassurance when I remembered that I had given this whole matter to the Lord. I had prayed alone and together with my prayer group for months, so I could be sure that the Lord had taken the case in His hands—even though it seemed to me that He wasn't that up-to-date with geographical details. With this reassurance and a quiet heart, I began to write an e-mail to my potential supervisor in Sweden. I told her about my being a German and a Christian. The reply came quickly. My supervisor had also had some doubts about the whole thing and had prayed just the night before that she wished to get a sign from the Lord: the language assistant should be a Christian. Talk about direct answers to prayers! Of course I was thrilled to hear that she was a Christian, and both of us were sure that the Lord had led us together. Even though everything seemed to have gone wrong, this would still be right.

In retrospect I can add that the Lord has showed me in this experience how wonderful things can turn out if we give our decisions over to Him and trust the ways He leads us. Those seven months in Sweden have enriched and changed my life in a special way. Maybe God isn't that good in human geography (or so I had thought), but maybe we should trust in His divine geographics—He knows the right way for us!

SONJA KALMBACH

The Bow of Promise

If anyone serves Me, him My Father will honor. John 12:26, NKJV.

IMMEDIATELY AFTER GRADUATING with a two-year college business secretarial course, I was employed by Manila Sanitarium and Hospital as an administrative secretary. The hospital administrator was considerate of the limitations of a young worker. I looked forward to every phase of the orientation to my secretarial duties and found each working day full of surprises and new things to learn, for the hospital was growing by leaps and fast becoming a teaching institution.

Before long I was taking more and more medical dictation, in addition to my administrative secretarial duties. Medical terms and information fascinated me, so I spent most of my days off perusing the medical textbooks of my older brother, David. Because my training was in business, I had to develop my own shorthand characters for medical terms.

As the hospital patient count increased, so did the need for the medical staff to have their own full-time secretary. There was no choice but me. Mastering the medical language became my obsession and priority. I put my all into the challenge.

I read the *Journal of the American Medical Record Association* to keep abreast of medical records-keeping trends. In this journal I found a school for medical records training. I wrote for information, filled out the application form, and received their acceptance. However, I found I would have to take a class on Saturday. I took this problem to the Lord, and after deciding I would rather obey God's command, I wrote a letter to the school declining my acceptance.

Not very long after, I received a scholarship offer from Union College in Nebraska. A song of praise displaced my disappointment and filled my heart. The Lord also facilitated in the completion of the necessary papers.

One happy April day in 1958 I was on a ship sailing to California. David was living there, so I stayed with him and his family. He helped me board the train to Nebraska. As the conductor announced, "We are about to cross the state line to Nebraska," a bright rainbow appeared. As we sped toward the bow of promise, there was a palpable reverent awe among the passengers. I felt the Lord saying, "My child, I will be with you. I will lead you."

Thank You, Lord, for fulfilling Your promise to those who commit their lives to serve You.

CONSUELO JACKSON

Pockets of the Soul

Purge me with hyssop, and I shall be clean; wash me, and I shall be whiter than snow. Ps. 51:7, RSV.

LAUNDRY DAY WAS ALWAYS a challenge when my five children were young. If you are a mother, I'm sure you can identify with me. It was Thursday, time to do the children's laundry. I had four young boys and one baby girl, so the piles of dirty clothes on the laundry room floor were quite impressive. I put a load of white underwear, T-shirts, and socks in first, then sorted the pants and shirts.

I never knew just what awaited me when checking the boys' pockets, so I had learned to be careful. After a trip to the beach, pockets would inevitably be full of seashells and sand. More often it would be pockets full of rocks, marbles, toy cars, old keys, or rubber bands. One time I found a pocket full of worms! Even worse than the worms was the time I reached my hand into a pants pocket and pulled out dead bugs. I can still remember how I shuddered and screamed. I instituted a new policy: everyone was responsible for removing their "treasures" before putting their clothes in the dirty clothes hamper.

One time I failed to double-check the pockets of one pair of pants and gingerly put the load in the washer and then the dryer. When the dryer stopped and I started pulling out the clothes, there were stains of different colors on jeans and shirts. I was puzzled and continued checking until I found the empty crayon wrappers in the bottom of the empty dryer. I was amazed at how the crayons had completely melted into the fabric. I tried washing the clothes again with stain remover, but the crayon colors refused to come out.

We smile and chuckle over the things our children collect and hold dear, but aren't we just like them? Except that the things we sometimes hold on to are much more insidious: jealousy, greed, hurt feelings, an unwillingness to forgive and let go of past injustices. And just like the melted crayons, all these things we hold on to in our lives tend to color us and change who we are. The only way to get rid of those stains is to surrender our lives to Jesus and allow Him to cleanse us completely. CELIA MEJIA CRUZ

Princess

For thy Maker is thine husband. Isa. 54:5.

REMEMBER THE GLORIOUS DAY that Lady Diana said "I do" and became princess of Wales? As Charles and Diana rode in their carriage she looked like Cinderella. Many of us probably wished to be that princess. As we watched Diana growing more confident, becoming more active in humanitarian engagements, loving her children, and resisting royal protocol, some of us still wished we could live the life of a princess. Lovely clothes and shoes; traveling, skiing, and cruises; the lack of mundane housework; nannies to care for the children; and a palace to live in!

Soon we began to see the strain of royal life on Diana; she was sad, the activities were wearing on her, and her unfaithful prince was tearing her heart out. We began to realize that being a princess isn't always what it's cracked up to be. There are royal rules for everything: how to curtsy, sit, smile, walk, discipline, educate the children—and how to accept the other woman.

Guess what? My Bible says that Jesus is to be my husband (2 Cor. 11:2). He is the "Prince of Peace" (Isa. 9:6). This makes me His princess! Just think: I own the cattle on a thousand hills and have a mansion that my Prince of the universe has personally built and decorated for me. My wardrobe will contain more then I ever dreamed of, and each robe will have matching shoes! The banquets I attend will cater to world dignitaries, famous musicians, and people from all walks of life. My luxury cruises will be out of this world, stopping to visit faraway constellations. My perfect hairstyle will support a crown decked with stars. My Prince will give me gifts of gold and jewels. I won't wear them around fingers or neck—I will walk on gold and enter my kingdom through pearly gates. My children will be "children of the King," making them princes and princesses too. What more could I want?

While I was praying for the spiritual safety of my college-age children, my heavenly Father impressed me to make a picture of each child dressed in royal robes and crown. This will remind them of who they really are. I bought regal frames, and on the wide matting above my daughter's picture I boldly inscribed "Child of the King." Under that I wrote: "That makes you a princess; ask your Father daily for wisdom and grace to live up to your royal protocol."

BETH VERSTEEGH ODIYAR

Next-Day Delivery

Bring ye all the tithes into the storehouse . . . and prove me now herewith, saith the Lord of hosts, if I will not open you the windows of heaven, and pour you out a blessing, that there shall not be room enough to receive it. Mal. 3:10.

ONE YEAR I RECEIVED $150 for my birthday. Soon a not-so-civil war broke out inside me. My selfish side wanted to spend the entire amount on self. But the Holy Spirit reminded my selfless side that God comes first. When Selfish lost the battle, Selfless added $15 to the normal monthly tithe of $120.

The very next day, when my friend Sharon and I went to play tennis, she spotted two pug dogs running down the street, their owners nowhere in sight. Sharon seems to have a built-in radar for animals in need. Her family already had eight stray animals as pets, most rescued by Sharon and whoever happened to be with her. As Sharon, without hesitation, swerved her car across the oncoming lanes of traffic, I realized that the next "whoever" was about to be me.

We parked the car and ran down the street shouting, "Here, doggy, doggies!" We were finally able to capture them and waddle back to the car, each carrying a heavy and panting pug. The water bottles that we'd brought along were used to hydrate our thirsty new animal friends.

We put the dogs in the car and took them to Sharon's house so we could call the number on their collars. We informed the owners that we had their pugs safe and sound. They were so happy to get their pets back that they gave us a $300 reward.

Sharon insisted that I take half—$150. The Holy Spirit impressed me to tithe on my reward money, leaving $135, the exact amount, down to the penny, that I had given in tithe the day before.

We simply can't outgive God. He is faithful to reward our faithfulness, even when it takes some arm-twisting to make us faithful.

Thank You, Lord, for Your sweet Holy Spirit. We praise You for giving us the strength to pass spiritual tests, then lovingly rewarding us for passing them.

CLARISSA MARSHALL

Lost in the Dark

The Lord is my light and my salvation; whom shall I fear? Ps. 27:1, NKJV.

IT HAS BEEN A WONDERFUL experience and a privilege for me to travel to several countries outside of the United States. I enjoy traveling, especially seeing how people live in other parts of the world. But after a while I thought I had seen enough overseas. Why not focus my attention on traveling within the United States? Surely there was a lot here to be seen and explored.

One summer my friend Ruth, who is president of a club, invited me to join them on a bus trip from New York City to the West Coast, and I invited three others to come along. There were 35 men and women. Most of the women had traveled throughout the Midwest and East Coast before.

Of all the places we visited, one in particular remains clearly in my mind, not because of the scenic and awesome beauty but because of an experience I had. It was quite late when we arrived at the Grand Canyon in Arizona to settle down for the night after a long day of traveling. We had something to eat but needed ice for our drink. I volunteered to go and fetch some. Ice bucket in hand, I set out to an ice depot I remembered seeing on my way in. I succeeded in getting the ice because there was a light over the ice machine. When I tried returning to the place I had set out from, I noticed several streets branching off in different directions, each lined with rows and rows of apartment buildings.

I was in a dilemma. Which of these streets had I come from, and from which house? With my back turned toward the light, I was facing total darkness. No one else was on the street. Here I was, ice bucket in hand, lost in the dark. Fear gripped me. Just then I heard a voice whisper, "Fear not, for I am with you" (Isa. 41:10). I then realized I was not alone—my guardian angel was there with me. Miraculously, I was led down the right street and up a pathway to the right house. It was a relief when one of my roommates responded to my knock on the door.

As a result of that experience the plight of the "lost" has laid heavily on my mind. How terrible and frightening it will be to be lost when Jesus comes. Thank God that Jesus came to seek and save us. It is glorious to be found.

DOLORES SMITH

The Wind Chime Tie-up

I will praise you, O Lord, with all my heart; I will tell of all your wonders. I will be glad and rejoice in you; I will sing praise to your name, O Most High. Ps. 9:1, 2, NIV.

MY DELICATE LITTLE WIND chime had been softly tinkling its tunes in the summer breezes all summer long from its place on the front porch. It was made of 12 small metal cylinders hanging in two rows from a polished piece of ornately carved wood. It had three small metal disks, hung between each three sets of the long cylinders, that were suspended on sturdy strings and weighted down with polished oval wooden pieces. Even a soft breeze would swing the wooden pieces to and fro, hitting the hollow metal cylinders and causing them to put forth their charming melodious tones.

But one day in the late summer I realized I had not heard my wind chime, so I looked up at it. It looked normal until I took a closer look and saw that a little spider had deftly wound its strong web around, in, and out of the metal hangings of my wind chime. No wonder it couldn't make its lovely music by swinging in the breeze. It was bound up and unable to move. I quickly got a stool and brushed off the offending webs, taking the spider along with them. Once again I could hear my wind chime giving forth its delicate tones in the soft breezes. What a peaceful sound!

I thought of the webs we often find ourselves bound up with when we need to be singing praises to our Maker. Webs of being too busy, discouragement, worldly distractions, or just plain neglect can wrap us up until we can no longer praise.

I decided that I would watch closely to avoid any webs in my life that would keep me from praising my Lord each day, at every turn in my daily life. I especially want to share my praises with those around me, as my wind chime has done for me. Whether in speech or song, I will do more of that. I've found 75 verses about praises in the Psalms alone. You may have found more. And there are many more in other parts of the Bible.

Dear Lord, today I praise Thy wondrous works, as do Your angels and all the heavenly hosts. BESSIE SIEMENS LOBSIEN

Wisdom on the Tarmac

He that covereth his sins shall not prosper: but whoso confesseth and forsaketh them shall have mercy. Prov. 28:13.

THE DOORS OF THE airplane were shut, and my seat belt was fastened. But still we sat. "We are waiting for an airport vehicle to come to push us away from the gate. We should be on our way in a few moments," the pilot explained.

I watched as the small airport vehicle arrived and got connected by a long rod to the front of the plane. Ever so slowly that small vehicle pushed the huge 747 away from the gate until we were in a position to move forward. Once the ground crew was out of the way the pilot slowly moved the jet forward, taxiing down the runway, gathering speed for takeoff.

A sudden insight made me smile. Sometimes you have to back up to move forward. Had the pilot moved forward without first moving back, we would have gone nowhere that day, and great would have been the damage to plane, building, and, possibly, lives.

How often I've wanted to push forward, when to do so would be disaster. I need to back up first, correct my mistakes, and then move forward. How often a relationship could not move ahead until I was able to go back and say, "I'm sorry."

I thought of the times when I was a young girl learning to crochet. Sometimes I took too many stitches or not enough. My mother would look at my work and say, "Dorothy, rip it out to the place where you made the mistake. Correct it, and move on. Only then will you have a satisfactory piece of work." I hated going back, of course, but she was right. Since then I've ripped up many a project and begun again at the point of my mistake, correcting it and moving on.

An article in a newspaper once caught my eye. It was the photo of a cat on the top of a telephone pole and a firefighter climbing the ladder, reaching for it. The cat could have backed down, but like so many of us it didn't want to back down from its position. That cat, like the airplane (and, too often, like myself), needed help to back up so it could move forward.

Dear heavenly Father, help me today, when I have made a mistake, to be willing to acknowledge I'm headed in the wrong direction. Help me to confess my sins, to back up with Your help, to say I am sorry, and then to move on.

DOROTHY EATON WATTS

August Wedding

Who comforteth us in all our tribulation, that we may be able to comfort them which are in any trouble. 2 Cor. 1:4.

IT WAS OUR DAUGHTER'S wedding day! She called her fiancé at 8:00 that morning to remind him what to bring. The phone rang. No answer. She tried again at 8:30. Still no answer. His sister had flown in and was staying with him, so we began to be worried because of a large fight he'd had with her three days earlier.

Another try at 9:00 without response. Now we were all worried! We drove to the apartment and tried the door. It was locked, and no one was home. We finally located a caretaker who told us he couldn't give us a key. We begged and cried, explaining the situation, still hoping they'd show up. The wedding was scheduled for 4:00 p.m. What could we do? Finally, at 11:00, the caretaker agreed to let us in, but only if he accompanied us. Nervously, breathless and scared about what might await us, we followed him.

Everything was gone! The closets were empty. They had even taken our daughter's car. A book on demons and an inexpensive coiled serpent ring were left. How ominous they seemed! Then we saw his Bible. A note beside it read, "Please forgive me. I am not ready for marriage."

Our precious Tami was crushed. The bottom fell out of everything. The lovely wedding dress would never be worn, the cake never eaten. It was like being in the middle of a nightmare. Things just couldn't be this bad. How could we contact all the guests, and how would we comfort our daughter?

We made a frantic to-do list. The bakery said they could freeze the cake. The florist used the flowers elsewhere. Neither sent a bill. My poor husband stood at the church to meet people, many from long distances, repeating the sad story again and again.

I can't describe the grief we all felt. We couldn't make any sense of it, but we prayed for them both. Tami's fiancé had planned to be baptized the week after the wedding, and she had planned to be baptized with him. The next week Tami was baptized alone. God, in His loving care, gave her the courage and strength to go on.

Isn't it wonderful that we Christians have a Bridegroom who really will come?

DARLENE YTREDAL BURGESON

The Chasm

I will give of the fountain of the water of life freely to him who thirsts. Rev. 21:6, NKJV.

I STOOD ON A RUSTIC bridge gazing into the chasm below. Mountains dressed with evergreens formed a backdrop while the air, pregnant with moisture, tingled my nostrils. Straight ahead an icy stream hurtled its way from a snow-covered mountain, gathering speed as it washed through the chasm. I saw huge boulders, lying in the path of these glacial waters, that had been changed in shape and size by this powerful rushing stream. Large holes appeared in some, while others showed smoothed edges from years of perpetual weathering. Other rocks, away from the edges of the torrent, lay covered with moss.

I pondered this spectacular scene, fascinated by the power of nature. I was visibly affected by the power of this body of water, carving, molding, or reshaping the objects in its pathway. Things outside its pathway remained unchanged, with roughened edges and covered with lichen or moss.

The spiritual lesson became clear. God's Word is called the Water of Life. Without it our lives are like the stones outside the pathway of the stream, stagnant and unpolished, with roughened edges or covered with moss. It takes a powerful agent to apply the needed abrasive.

I thought of the words of Jesus to the Samaritan woman. "But the water that I shall give him will become in him a fountain of water springing up into everlasting life" (John 4:14, NKJV). Jesus offers not a singular drink of water but a perpetual artesian well that has the power to mold, shape, and polish the edges of my character. Water, in this verse, is a picture of the spirit of Jesus working in us. He is not working to save us, because that work has already been done by His death on the cross.

He is working to change us.

God has promised to "let him take the free gift of the water of life" (Rev. 22:17, NIV). I must truly thirst for this change, this new life offered to me. I must spend time with His Word and allow the rich current of His love to mold, change, polish, and fashion me.

Lord, I thirst for the refreshing draught of Your Water of Life. Come into my soul, wash and purify me. Thank You, God, for this rich object lesson today.

JOAN MINCHIN NEALL

The Birthday Cake

I love the Lord, because he hath heard my voice and my supplications. Because he hath inclined his ear unto me, therefore will I call upon him as long as I live. Ps. 116:1, 2.

MY DAUGHTER, VONI, WAS celebrating her twelfth birthday and was busy in the kitchen making the birthday cake for her party. She preheated the oven, prepared two boxes of mix according to the directions, and within minutes had the cake in the oven. She had asked to make her cake herself and was eager for it to bake. I realized as I passed the oven that it was set at only 325 degrees. I raised it to 350. Voni protested, "But you always put the oven lower because our oven bakes too hot."

"I know," I agreed. "I do set it lower, but not by 25 degrees." I went to the living room to relax. She stayed in the kitchen to watch the cake. Twenty minutes later she flopped on the sofa and announced that my husband had come through the kitchen and turned the oven down to 300 degrees because the cake was baking too quickly.

"What!" I yelled, running to check the cake. The middle section jiggled, but the outer section looked done. I wished I had told her to use two small round pans instead of one large sheet pan. "I don't know about this cake," I said apprehensively. Seeing her despairing look, I sighed, set the oven to 350, left the kitchen, and whispered, "Lord, help!"

Ten minutes later the cake still jiggled and the top was getting too brown. I covered it with foil and lowered the oven temperature, and it continued baking. Finally Voni took it from the oven, exclaiming, "Looks OK to me." The cake had indeed baked a total of one hour and 15 minutes. I didn't think it was OK, but I forced a smile. After the cake had cooled, it was difficult getting it out of the pan. Once frosted, though, it looked beautiful, with no hint there had been any problems. During the party friends gobbled cake and more cake. Voni beamed from ear to ear, a dramatic change from the worried girl hours earlier. When she heard that my rather picky friend had commented, "This is the best cake I ever had," she was ecstatic and proud of her accomplishments. Her cake, despite numerous mishaps, had turned out fine after all.

Thank You, Lord, for caring about a birthday cake and the emotions of a 12-year-old and for answering my cry for help. I will call on You for the big things in my life too and know You will hear and answer just as faithfully.

IRIS L. STOVALL

A Cleanup Job

Wash me, and I shall be whiter than snow. Ps. 51:7.

IT WAS ONE OF those days when I had to wonder if I'd ever see my kitchen counters again! Tomatoes from the garden were at their peak, demanding my attention. They, along with yellow squash, zucchini, green beans, okra, and bell peppers, covered the counters. Besides that, the ancient refrigerator in the garage just had to be defrosted, which meant emptying it, turning it off, and carrying kettle after kettle of hot water from the kitchen down the steps to put in the freezing compartment. In spite of the fact that it had been recently cleared, it had thick layers of ice, taking a lot of time and effort to melt.

At last the tomatoes were peeled and stewed with celery, onion, and green pepper; some had other veggies added for soup. The cartons were filled and stowed in the freezer to make a hearty supper to be enjoyed when the snow falls and the cold winter winds blow.

Next came the cleanup job. The ice and water from the fridge were disposed of, the insides wiped dry, and the contents replaced. The kettles were washed, along with the other cooking utensils, and all the produce was put away. Finally the counters were visible again, and I could breathe a sigh of relief.

There are other cleanup jobs that need to be done. As a Christian, I wonder what kind I need. Not physically, as I take care of that daily, but spiritually and mentally, which can be harder to do. I think of the three monkeys with their mottoes "See no evil, hear no evil, speak no evil"; in today's world this can be a problem. The temptation to see and to hear evil surrounds us, even though we don't choose it. Then there is the temptation to pass on that juicy tidbit of gossip we picked up. Our only safeguard is to allow the Holy Spirit to guide us and to be willing to follow where He leads, to ask for His presence to be with us daily.

Speaking of daily—there's a basket of tomatoes waiting in the kitchen right now, this time to be canned. There are jars to wash and sterilize; the canner to bring in and fill with water, tomatoes to wash, scald, peel, cut up, and cook; and jars to fill and process.

Yes, it's a lot of work, but won't all the work be worth it when the snow falls and the cold winter winds blow! Mary Jane Graves

Children of the Living God

You are all children of God through faith in Christ Jesus. Gal. 3:26, NLT.

ONE OF MY FRIENDS has traced his genealogy back to distant relatives of George Washington and Abraham Lincoln, as well as Robert E. Lee. He is thrilled when he traces the paths to one of these distant relatives.

I teasingly asked him one time, "Are you still willing to speak to us 'common folk'?" He assured me he is. Reading about his amazing discoveries has given me an enthusiasm to see if I can find anything about my own family tree.

I work on genealogy sporadically when meals, housework, church work, other volunteer work, my husband, my 98-year-old mother-in-law, and three dogs don't require my attention. I presently am working on my husband's side of the family tree. The most recent discovery is Brigadier General James Reed, who fought at Bunker Hill and Ticonderoga. I now have a picture of this man who is my husband's fourth great-grandfather, as well as a picture of a monument dedicated to him at Fitzwilliam, New Hampshire.

I wonder what it is that God has placed within us that makes us want to know who our ancestors were, where they lived, and what they were like. For me, personally, it is a desire to know more about my mother, who died at age 30, and my grandmother, who died at age 62. I was too young to remember much about either one of them. For my mother-in-law it is a desire to know more about her father, who passed away when she was only 1 year old. For others it may be a desire for the status of being related to someone who is thought of as a great person, whether president or otherwise. We get a vicarious thrill just thinking about the relationship. Adam and Eve would be the father and mother of us all if we had the ability to trace our roots back to that distant time, but even the Internet and genealogy Web sites aren't quite that good.

The greatest thrill of all should be that we are brothers and sisters of Jesus Christ and sons and daughters of the living God who created us and redeemed us. We can be children of His forever if we choose to follow Him.

Father, what a privilege it is for us common folk to be able to speak to You. We ask for You to speak to us. I thank You that we are all children of the living God.

LORAINE F. SWEETLAND

Bloom Anyway

Let us stop just saying we love people; let us really love them, and show it by our actions. 1 John 3:18, TLB.

DEADHEADING LILIES. It can teach one a lot!

It had been several days since I'd had a chance to step into my garden, enjoy the beautiful flowers, and, of course, deadhead the lilies. Even without turning to look at them, I knew the Asian lilies were in bloom; their heavenly fragrance was everywhere. As I worked my way around to every blooming plant, examining the intricate markings, enjoying the wonderful colors of the flowers, and picking off the dead, dried-up blossoms, the thought occurred to me—no one had been in my flower garden for several days to enjoy the exquisite beauty of these exotic flowers. No one had enjoyed their heady fragrance as it perfumed the surrounding air. No one had appreciated the efforts these plants had made to make the place where they bloomed into a pleasant, beautiful spot where one could stop and refresh one's eyes. And yet they bloomed anyway.

I wonder—do I bloom "anyway" in my own little world? Even when no one is around to see my good deeds? Even when no one cares what I may have done that day? When I see the opportunities presented to me, opportunities to share love and compassion to others, do I bloom anyway, acting upon my Christian experience and knowledge?

It really doesn't take much to bloom where one is planted, to perfume one's surroundings by showing God's love through our actions. Perhaps it will mean extending a hug to a hurting or lonely person; writing a note of appreciation; flashing a contagious smile; sharing how God has worked in one's own life with someone who may be struggling; or extending the hand of friendship to a new church or community member. It may mean taking a meal to one who is ill or homebound; making a telephone call to one who may be discouraged; encouraging a child for a job well done; or simply doing random acts of kindness. Everyone, no matter how poor or wealthy, can do these things. And the rewards? The "fragrance" of knowing that one has lightened the load of another is reward enough.

Do you bloom where you are planted? What if no one sees? Bloom anyway!

Barbara J. Reinholtz

A Run-down House

For ye are bought with a price: therefore glorify God in your body, and in your spirit, which are God's. 1 Cor. 6:20.

MY NEPHEW BOUGHT A HOUSE in a respectable part of town, but it had no appeal to me. Tufts of grass struggled to survive in a dry lawn. Weeds thrived along the weathered fence and bordered the sidewalk. Some grass managed to wedge through the sidewalk divisions. An untrimmed rosebush stretched to the eaves on one corner of the house. A few brave flowers competed for sunshine and moisture among the weeds in the flower beds. Low junipers with many winter-killed branches lined the front of a stone wall.

The one attraction to the yard was a giant maple tree. It would provide cooling shade during hot summer days. But its beauty couldn't dispel the fact that there would be buckets of leaves to rake every fall.

The inside of the house had its failings too. The stench cut one's breath. The owner had lived with his best friend, a Labrador. The carpet was worn and stained from doggy accidents. Added to this were stale tobacco fumes. The walls were grimy, and the windows had never been washed. The wallpaper was peeling in the bathroom.

This place looked like hard work and little satisfaction to me, but my nephew and his wife could see potential. The junipers were removed, the rosebush trimmed, the lawn watered, the weeds pulled, and the fence scraped and painted. Inside, they removed the carpet and installed hardwood in the living room and laid new carpet in the bedrooms. A French door expanded the look of a small room for an office. Fresh paint brightened all the walls. The windows were washed inside and out. How cheery the place began to look.

I'm so glad God sees potential in me. He bought me with His blood while I was yet a sinner. I'm still not perfect, but with His help I'm making progress in my Christian walk. I need to be faithful in my housecleaning. Am I putting the best thoughts in the library of my mind? Am I feeding my body temple with healthful food? Is my heart dedicated to His service?

Someone said: "I'm not perfect, but God ain't done with me yet!" Let each one of us allow God to work in our lives today and every day.

EDITH FITCH

Mom's Flower Garden

The grass withereth, the flower fadeth: but the word of our God shall stand for ever. Isa. 40:8.

MY MOTHER LOVED FLOWERS and always kept plants inside the house and on the front porch. I recall, however, that the pride and joy of her outdoor life was that small flower garden on the side of the house where she knew the names of each flower.

There were times growing up that I disliked knowing spring would soon be coming, because Mom would begin talking about plans for her flower garden: what kind of flowers she would have and how many. I knew full well that when spring and summer came I had an outdoor job—pulling weeds and grass from her flower garden.

Spring and summer came, and, sure thing, Mom would call to me, saying, "Annie Belle, let's pull weeds today." *Why did she have to say those words?* I thought with a groan.

One day, with a bit of an attitude, I grumbled in Mom's hearing, "I don't see why I have to pull dumb weeds all the time." In her soft voice she explained to me that her beautiful flowers (she called each one by name) would not be as beautiful if she didn't keep the weeds and grass pulled out. The weeds would stunt the flowers' growth, causing them to die.

Many years have passed, and I have surprised myself by having a small flower bed, although not a garden like Mom's. As I pull the weeds from time to time, my thoughts go back to Mom's telling me, as she called the flowers by name, that weeds would stunt the growth of her flowers, keeping them from growing to be beautiful. I began thinking of myself and others whom God has created as being His flower garden of diversities; He knows each of us by name—not only our names but the number of hairs on our head. My thoughts began to focus on my spiritual life, and I compared it with a spiritual garden and asked myself the question Are there weeds growing there, such as pride, envy, gossip, or evil thinking, that need to be pulled out so that my spiritual garden will grow and not become stunted?

Mom relied on rain to water her flowers, and we must rely on God for the Water of Life.

So I'm thanking You again, dear Jesus, for making me one of the flowers in Your garden of human diversity. Help me to keep the weeds pulled so that I might continue growing in love for You and do Your will. ANNIE B. BEST

Out of the Mouth of Babes

God hath chosen the weak things of the world to confound the things which are mighty. 1 Cor. 1:27.

I CANNOT HELP RECALLING some of the remarks and prayers of children, which help me to understand God better. One evening my husband took the family out to dine in one of the posh restaurants in Delhi. But in the midst of our enjoyment, suddenly our son, who was only 5, blurted out, "I don't think Jesus is happy to see us here." Taken aback by this remark, we hurriedly finished eating and left. We left behind the wild music and dance.

One night I was really annoyed because our son was having bedwetting problems every night. While trying to fall asleep again, I suddenly heard these words: "Mommy, I am sorry that I did not sleep right away. I was telling Jesus about my problem." With that he tiptoed back to his bedroom. What a lesson to learn.

Two toddlers named Anu (Hindu) and Ali (Muslim) embraced each other with a grin from ear to ear as they came toward me. In unison they introduced themselves in just three words, "We are brothers." I thought, *If we would practice our religion like Anu and Ali, there wouldn't be any fights between the Hindus and the Muslims, or, for that matter, between any other people.*

One morning in my home school I made little Esther repeat the prayer after me: "Dear Father, thank You for the nice day; thank You for food; thank You for flowers and for birds. Bless us today. In Jesus'. . . " Suddenly little Esther added, "Thank You for the pretty butterfly You sent into my room this morning." The "weak thing" had reminded me to thank God for the little joys.

It was time for our evening family worship. The children were always delighted to hear the Bible stories and take part in praying. I asked the two little Muslim girls who lived with us what they would like to ask God for in their prayer. Anaita, who was 8, excitedly said, "I want to ask God to take me to the moon." And little Vaisa, who was 5, seriously said, "I do not want anything special. I just want to be with Jesus." What a lesson to learn from the children!

Therefore Jesus Christ admonished us, "Except ye be converted, and become as little children, ye shall not enter into the kingdom of heaven" (Matt. 18:3).

ANNIE M. KUJUR

Master of the Sea

You are mightier than all the breakers pounding on the seashores of the world! Ps. 93:4, TLB.

ON A RECENT VACATION I enjoyed a relaxing few days exploring the waterfront walks of the Australian coastal town of Port Macquarie, located at the mouth of the Hastings River. With sunlight sparkling on the water, children playing happily on the beach, and recreational and fishing craft bustling about it, was an idyllic setting. But the peaceful scene carried reminders of past tragedy.

Beside the pathway near the breakwater was a row of plaques (I counted 17), each one representing a ship that had come to grief. Sailing ships, a paddle steamer, and various other trading vessels had been lost near that spot while battling to negotiate the narrow channel from the open sea into the safety of the river. *Being at the mercy of the wind and waves, without recourse of an engine or any of the safety devices we now take for granted, must have been a fearsome experience,* I mused. But if I had been tempted to think that the elements can be controlled by modern technology, the evening news brought stark contradiction.

Just a little farther along the coast huge seas whipped up by gale-force winds had ripped the keel from a giant racing yacht. Its stability gone, the craft capsized—only two of the crew members had been plucked from the ocean alive. Not so long before this, and more embarrassing than tragic, a British Royal Navy vessel, fitted no doubt with all the most up-to-date navigation equipment, had run onto rocks close to Lord Howe Island. A multmillion-dollar salvage operation followed.

Navigating the seas of life is no less fraught with danger, whether from unexpected storms of adversity, inattention, overconfidence, or failure to follow the guidance of our heavenly Pilot. How wonderful it is to know that our God is in control and can still bring us home safe, just like the storm-tossed sailors described by the psalmist: "Then they cry to the Lord in their trouble, and he saves them. He calms the storm and stills the waves. What a blessing is that stillness, as he brings them safely into harbor! Oh, that these men would praise the Lord for his lovingkindness and for all of his wonderful deeds!" (Ps. 107:28-31, TLB).

JENNIFER M. BALDWIN

Collecting for Charity

God loveth a cheerful giver. 2 Cor. 9:7.

MY COUSIN AND I WERE spending the day collecting for ADRA, a charitable organization that provides hands-on help both home and abroad. We were posted at entrance gates to the Brisbane Exhibition Show—an annual event that runs for eight days each August. This event attracts on average 50,000 people daily, so we knew we were in for a long but hopefully rewarding day.

And what a kaleidoscope of people went through the gates! There were older couples; there were lots of parents with their very excited children; there were teenagers. Some people were well dressed, their hair beautifully coiffured, trousers with a permanent press, shoes polished to perfection. Then there was the opposite end of the scale. People in not-so-clean, sometimes crumpled clothes. But everybody had the happy look of anticipation of a fun day ahead. A fun day at the show. So as the crowds entered I held out my collection tin, and the coins went in. Smiles abounded.

Especially delightful were the times young mothers would give their toddlers some coins to put in my collection tin. The little ones would hesitantly put their hands forward as I bent down to their level. As the money clanged into the tin they would giggle and then instantly look around for the security of their mother.

The hours passed; we had lunch and then moved to another entrance. As the afternoon wore on, young people began pouring in, ready for the evening's entertainment.

Three young men in jeans and soiled T-shirts bought their tickets and walked toward the entrance gate. One had very long hair pulled back in a ponytail, showing several earrings in one ear. As he passed me he put several coins into my tin. I thanked him, we exchanged smiles, and he headed after his mates. But after only a few steps he hesitated, turned back to me, opened his wallet again, and pulled out a $10 note. "Here," he said as he put it in the slot.

I had expected nothing from them, but was so mistaken. As I thanked him again I thought of the text "Man looketh on the outward appearance" (1 Sam. 16:7). What a lesson to me! I had done exactly that—judged on appearance. How thankful I am that our loving God looks on the heart.

Leonie Donald

August 14

Forbidden Fruit

They shall plant vineyards, and eat the fruit of them. . . . They shall not plant, and another eat. Isa. 65:21, 22.

I WANTED TO LISTEN TO the evening news on television. There was a news item about a man who had been robbed. He had bought some packets of watermelon seeds and planted them. When they started bearing fruit, he calculated how much he could sell his watermelons for and how much profit he would make. The watermelons grew very large and luscious; they yielded a very good crop. The next morning he would take his produce to market.

However, in the night, while he was sleeping, enemies came and plundered his land. The watermelons that were not stolen were smashed. He was totally devastated.

Similarly, we have a loquat tree that bears large, sweet, juicy fruit. Because we live next to a park, children constantly come to raid the tree. We had to have steel gates erected to keep intruders out.

My neighbor had a huge avocado tree. One day while they were resting, some naughty children jumped over their wall. The avocados were already big but still grass-green. The children cleared the tree to the last avocado. Because the fruit was still too hard to be eaten, they smashed the fruit in the road.

We frown at such activities of delinquent children who are tempted by our fruit. In this life there are also other forbidden fruits that we see and sometimes desire. The fruit looks so tempting. As women, temptations also come our way in various forms. Satan tempted Eve; she admired and then desired to taste the forbidden fruit. Satan is more experienced now, shining up apples of sin, making them look very attractive. He then whispers, "Just one bite will be all right." Satan is a liar. He will lead us into very serious trouble.

I am so glad that in the new earth there will be no liars and no thieves. "And there shall in no wise enter into it any thing that defileth, neither whatsoever worketh abomination, or maketh a lie: but they which are written in the Lamb's look of life" (Rev. 21:27). "Blessed are they that do his commandments, that they may have right to the tree of life, and may enter in through the gates into the city" (Rev. 22:14). PRISCILLA ADONIS

What a Good Idea!

For his Holy Spirit speaks to us deep in our hearts and tells us that we are God's children. Rom. 8:16, NLT.

HE LOOKED POOR AND NEEDY. Always I had an impulse to place money into his hand, so I did. He had the warmest hands. Graciously I accepted the kiss that he always placed upon my hand in return. He was nonverbal, and this was his way of saying thank you. The sight of him walking the streets created a mental picture of what my own son's life could be like. Sonny was still young (age 5) and the scope of his mental disabilities uncertain. I had an overwhelming attraction to this man that I could not ignore.

It was summer 1991, and I made the following comment to my husband: "I wonder what that man [I didn't know his name] does with the money people give him? I hope he buys food with it."

"If it really concerns you, why not just take him to lunch whenever you get the chance," my husband remarked. What a good idea!

The very next day I saw him on the sidewalk. I ran out of the store where I was shopping. In my makeshift sign language I asked him to have lunch with Sonny and me. We had a lovely lunch in the co-op cafeteria. Every eye in the place seemed to be upon us. He would point his finger at the staring people, then smile at me. I was comfortable dining with him and happy that he had accepted my invitation.

Together we crossed the street. The man surprised me with a little kiss placed upon my cheek. I smiled at him, and we parted. I went back to the store where I'd been shopping; the clerk had seen us at lunch, and she informed me that my guest's name was Indian Joe.

Several months later I began volunteering at the Salvation Army soup kitchen and thrift store where Joe was a regular. The staff shared with me the things they knew about him. The last gift I gave Joe was two bowls of my homemade soup, served at the soup kitchen several days before he passed away. At his funeral I couldn't control my tears—I loved this man our community named Indian Joe.

Words are not always necessary for good communication. Love speaks plainly as well.

DEBORAH SANDERS

Enjoy the Journey

Let love be genuine; hate what is evil, hold fast to what is good; love one another with brotherly affection; outdo one another in showing honor. Rom. 12:9, 10, RSV.

IT WAS A CLOUDY SABBATH; actually, it had started to rain and then stopped. After a potluck lunch we were all determined to take the walk that had been planned. Sherry had invited the group to visit her small church and then go for the afternoon walk. There were 17 of us who braved that cloudy, almost black-cloud afternoon.

The walk took us through woods and on to waterfalls. We followed the red marks on the trees that led to the falls. It was not a very easy walk, because one had to hop and jump to cross the creek a number of times or pass over on a rickety log. There were times when we had to bend low to pass under the half-fallen trees. Some people in the group got tired easily; some were scared to cross the stream, and others were worried the rain would fall and soak us. However, some of us enjoyed the walk tremendously because we focused on the walk and not on the obstacles in the way. Even the crossing of the stream with just a rickety log to pass over was a thrill to us.

Another thing that made the walk enjoyable for me was to see and watch the group help one another. In crossing the stream, Jamie and Sheila would position themselves so they could give a hand. Sherry would turn back and ask George how he was doing or whether Ceazar was fine with his sandals. Danny would wait for George; Bob directed the way; Doug and Sue went ahead to see whether the way was muddy or not. Howard kept the conversation going while Ana and I kept commenting on the beauty of the place, and the young people energetically ran through the difficult paths and across the challenging stream.

I can't help linking this with our journey toward heaven. If we don't focus on the obstacles that are planted by Satan—hardship, failures, hurts, or troublesome people—we will enjoy the journey with our family, friends, and acquaintances. And if we care for each other, it will make our journey even more meaningful and endurable.

Lord, today help me to enjoy the journey with You, and help me to be mindful of those who need me. Use my heart, Lord, to love those who need love.

JEMIMA D. ORILLOSA

Entering the City

Blessed are those who wash their robes, that they may have the right to the tree of life and may go through the gates into the city. Rev. 22:14, NIV.

EAGER TO MEET MY husband after six months of separation, I joined one of the queues in the arrival hall at Heathrow Airport. Soon it was my turn, and the immigration officer demanded my travel documents. I gave her my passport and my husband's admission letter from Newbold College. "Your visa, please," she said.

"That's all I have," I replied.

She laughed and asked, "How can you travel all the way from Africa without a visa?"

"I thought the admission letter could cover my two little girls and me; so I came just like that," I replied.

"I am sorry, ma'am; you cannot enter England with this," she said. She gave my passport back to me and called the next person. She had finished with me.

Now what? I asked myself. As usual, I quickly turned to my reliable heavenly Father for help. After a short prayer in my heart, I sat on a chair and attended to my 9-month-old baby while my little girl of 4 stood by.

After everyone had left, the chief immigration officer came and inquired about my presence there. I told him my story, and he ordered that my husband should be paged. My husband came within minutes to talk to the officer, who then allowed us to enter with a promise to report at the home office later for a proper visa.

Many are sent back to Africa because they do not have visas. Why was I allowed to enter? Was it because of my little girls? Or because I was a woman? No! Their father did it.

Likewise, our heavenly Father has provided us with our "visas"—the white robe of His righteousness. We must be careful that we do not allow our robes to be stained by the world. It is our duty to keep them washed through regular contact with Him. Otherwise, when we arrive at the gates of the heavenly city, we will not be allowed to enter.

Our Father, please empower me to remind others about washing our robes in Your Son's shed blood and to get ready to enter the gates of the city when time is no more.

MABEL KWEI

An Angel Appeared

The angel of the Lord encampeth round about them that fear him, and delivereth them. Ps. 34:7.

EVERY MONDAY, WEDNESDAY, and Friday I took my husband to dialysis for his usual four-hour treatment. One very hot summer day we were on our way when the car started acting up. I had just turned onto the freeway when the engine began to stall. It was a bad spot, with lanes changing and merging. I needed to get over two lanes in order to go straight.

"Lord, I need Your help," I quickly breathed. The car picked up speed and seemed to run smoothly.

I made it to our exit, but when I came off the freeway and drove to a red light, I had to stop. The car died right there. I got out and walked back to a pickup that had pulled up behind us and told the young driver of my plight and that he'd need to go around me. He said that when the traffic cleared a little he would get around in front of me and pull me across the intersection with a pull strap that he had.

In a little while he was able to pull up ahead of me, and when the signal changed he pulled us across and down about a block to where the car would be out of the way. This young man got out and unhooked the truck from my car. I told them that I was taking my husband to dialysis and that he was to be there at 4:00; it was now 3:40. I thanked him for helping to rescue us and assured him that our son would arrive shortly, as my husband had called him on the cellular phone. I asked him if I owed him any money.

"No, just help me sometime when I'm stranded by the side of the road," he said.

"You've got it," I assured him.

Before he drove away, he remarked that he hated leaving us in so much heat. However, that's not the end of the story. Within about five minutes he was back with two ice-cold bottles of water for us. I couldn't believe it. That water tasted so good as we waited for our help to come!

I could feel the very hand of God working through this young man, an angel in disguise.

Lord, help me to be of service this day, and let me help others as You would lead me to do! Thank You, Lord, for being with us every day—all the time.

ANNE ELAINE NELSON

Where Were You?

He will be with you, He will not leave you nor forsake you; do not fear nor be dismayed. Deut. 31:8, NKJV.

SUMMERTIME BRINGS CHANGE to my regular routine. I get to babysit my one and only grandchild, Megan, a big 7-year-old bundle of energy. Our special days together are the Wednesdays between when her parochial school lets out and when school begins again.

I was there when she was born, and we have been bonded ever since. I have enjoyed watching her grow from the simply crying, eating, and sleeping of her baby days to her walking, feeding, and dressing herself. Now she is constantly chattering and challenging both me and her environment. It's wonderful!

I pick her up at her home and drive her to my house. We share breakfast together, followed by a loose routine of activities. She enjoys her quiet time, during which she likes to color, write, teach my collection of stuffed animals, or some other activity of her own choosing. If I am going to be out of her immediate sight, I tell her where to find me. But one morning I assumed she would be so busy that I could slip into my master bathroom. When I came out I sat in my bedroom, leaving the door open so as to be easily seen.

A few minutes later I heard a frantic voice, and a troubled little girl appeared in the doorway. "Nana, where were you? I couldn't find you, and I looked everywhere." As she fought back the tears she asked, "Where were you?" Obviously she hadn't checked the master bathroom.

"Megan," I soothed her, "Nana would never leave you here by yourself. Don't worry. Even though you may not see me, I'm here." I watched the worry lines erase from her face, and a sweet smile appeared.

Then I realized that the same promise God made to Israel through Moses in today's text He has made to each of His children. How often does He look at our troubled or tear-stained faces while reassuring us that through all of the troubles and trials of life He is there for us and with us? Even though we do not always sense His presence, He is there!

Dear Lord, please put Your loving arms around us today, reminding us of Your faithful love and care. Amen.

Mildred C. Williams

Detour to Refuge

The Lord is a refuge for the oppressed, a stronghold in times of trouble. Ps. 9:9, NIV.

The Lord is our refuge and strength, an ever-present help in trouble. Ps. 46:1, NIV.

WHILE DRIVING THROUGH BUSY streets recently with my granddaughter, we saw "Work Ahead" and "Detour" signs. She, like most 6-year-olds, wondered why we needed to turn. Trying to get her to understand, I stated, "If you are going this way and find out the road is rough and rocky or the wrong way, you don't keep traveling that way, but immediately turn and go the right way, which will be safer."

After navigating the detour for a bit, I saw that it was time to turn at my destination. I moved over to the center lane to prepare for my turn. Again, her curiosity wanted to know, "Why are we sitting still in the center of the street with cars going all around us?" I then explained that the turn lane is like a refuge, and no other car can bother me while I am in the refuge; as long as I stay here and wait for the light to change, I am safe.

Her questions reminded me of the highway of life. Jesus is so sweet—all through my life He has been there to detour me from dangers seen and unseen. And just when things seem unbearable He puts me in a refuge to shield me from certain dangers.

I no longer stress about trivial things. Sometimes I have gotten off my schedule—such as getting to the airport—because I misplaced my keys or ticket; I had to stop and take valuable time to search for the items. Perhaps the Lord allowed this to happen to help me avoid a possible vehicle accident. I have had sleepless nights on occasions, later to find the stove left on or a door not secured, my sleeplessness saving us from possible danger. Sometimes the Lord has a special thought that needs cultivating in the early hours, and He wants to commune with me while my mind is still fresh; for this I am grateful. Detours are not always a bad thing.

Do not be dismayed at whatever happens on the road of life, as God will take care of you—in the appointed time, in the appointed way, which may not necessarily be your time, but it is on time; or your way, but it is the right way.

Dear Savior, thank You for being there for me all the time by detouring me from danger and being my refuge on life's highways. Amen. BETTY G. PERRY

Exercise and Sins

Let us lay aside every weight, and the sin which so easily ensnares us. Heb. 12:1, NKJV.

I AM IN THE PROCESS of losing weight. I must admit that I should have safeguarded myself in the first place, because the process is not easy. Not only must I struggle to get out of bed in the mornings and head to the gym, but I must also discipline myself to do my exercise routine on the treadmill and with the weights. If only I had not eaten so much! If only I had not eaten and gone straight to bed after those heavy meals. And those so-called comfort foods of September 11 have really produced some discomfort. If only I had resisted the snack machines! OK, I did not, so I have to do this. It's amazing how easily weight can creep up on you.

One morning while doing my treadmill routine, I realized that there are a lot of similarities between losing weight and giving up my pet sins. Indulging in what is wrong can be very enticing and attractive. *Only one piece of chocolate,* I say to myself, but the melting of the Godiva in my mouth makes it difficult to resist the other piece. *OK, I guess two pieces won't hurt.* And soon I have eaten all four pieces. I then feel guilty for indulging in something that I know is unhealthy as well as fattening.

It is the same thing with sin. *Just this once,* we say, and sooner or later it becomes a habit. Habits are very hard to break. If you have ever tried to give up something, you know the struggle. Some days you seem to overcome the temptations, but on other days you just give in and return to the same old habit. However, it becomes much easier to resist the temptation when we prayerfully and earnestly ask God to help us stay strong. But we must put forth the effort. Then we will find that the need to indulge in a sinful practice does not have such a stronghold on us. It is like exercising. The more I exercise and feel the results, the easier it is for me to get out of bed, because I know that the reward is great.

Lord, it is always difficult to bring my body under subjection, spiritually or physically. But I know, Lord, that You are willing to work with me to achieve all my goals, because You wish above all things that we prosper and be in good health. You also want to see me in Your kingdom, and I know that You will do everything that lies in Your power to get me there. Help me to stay focused on eternity.

ANDREA A. BUSSUE

A Pricking Brier

And there shall be no more a pricking brier . . . , nor any grieving thorn of all that are round about them . . . ; and they shall know that I am the Lord God. Eze. 28:24.

OUR FRIEND WAS BEING transferred and asked us to keep her cactus plant. Her mother had given it to her, told her that the plant would produce a very beautiful flower, and asked her to take care of the plant and to wait for the flowers to bloom.

Missing her mother and remembering her promise, she thought of me, as it was not possible to take the cactus with her. She also asked me to wait till the flowers bloomed.

My husband and I planted the cactus in the flower bed next to the road in front of our house. It grew to a height of more than seven feet. It had many swordlike leaves all around its trunk. Whenever I went near it, I got a poke or two on my arms. So did other people. We began to hear unpleasant remarks about our plant and even suggestions to cut it down. Because of my promise I begged my neighbors to be patient till the flowers grew on it, and then we would cut it down.

Four years passed by, yet there was no sign of flowers. Instead, many new shoots grew at its base; they poked us when we weeded. Finally I wrote to my friend that we would like to cut it down. So we began the task of removing the offensive plant. My husband had to hack the main trunk and remove the stump and all the new shoots. To our surprise, we found numerous large roots under the topsoil stretching to the end of that bed. We pulled them all, making sure not a bit was left. Later we set fire to the pile. Yet out of those charred roots new shoots began to appear again and again. It took me a whole year to destroy the plant completely.

Sin is as stubborn and hurtful as the cactus. We have to pay dearly for its promise of any reward. We are glad of the promise that God will destroy sin completely, leaving neither root nor branch behind (Mal. 4:1). We are also looking forward to the new earth, where there will no more pricking briers or thorns to trouble us.

I pray that God will uproot every sin, every inclination and tendency to sin, from my life. I want Him to clean me thoroughly from every bit that may lie hidden in the dark recesses of my mind. May God then see only the beautiful fruit of the Spirit growing in my life. BIRDIE PODDAR

The Trusting Bird and the Christian Cat

Trust in the Lord with all your heart and don't depend on your own understanding. Prov. 3:5, Clear Word.

BUDGIES ARE MOSTLY HAPPY little birds, full of important chatter. My pretty green Regie was no exception; from the moment we removed his cover in the morning, life seemed a song of joy.

The porch offered a protected outlook over the backyard, and often his chatter would attract other birds to his cage, where they picked at seeds that Regie appeared to scatter purposefully.

His favorite attraction was the family cat, Muffin, who for hours would sit close to the side of the cage. This was an invitation for Regie to peck and pull at the cat's tail and extract hairs—much closer to his face than I thought safe.

Muffin and Regie often studied each other intently, and as I watched I questioned what a cat's and bird's thoughts might be, but the cage barrier never prompted an answer—until one day.

I was taking Regie outside to clean his tray when the whole bottom of the cage fell out, including the bird. As he flew off chirping, I could only helplessly watch, realizing that the chances of his recapture were near to hopeless.

I reassembled his cage and followed the chirps to the front of the house, where I could see him high in a tree jumping from branch to branch enjoying his freedom. Minutes seemed like hours, and I knew that one wrong move could send him farther away. Frantic, I silently prayed that God would spare my feathered pet.

Then it happened; Muffin came and sat watching me. I groaned, for he was the last creature I wanted around right then. But I was wrong, for Regie sighted the cat and flew right down to Muffin's paws. What I expected didn't happen, and while in trust Regie chatted happily to the cat, I promptly caught him and returned him to the cage. What relief!

Surely God works in mysterious ways His wonders to perform. It reminded me of the wonderful pictures of heaven, where all beasts will be at peace with each other.

My cat and bird gave me a meaningful object lesson that day about God's peace, which He extends to all who put their trust in Him. LYN WELK

Seize the Day

This is the day the Lord has made; we will rejoice and be glad in it. Ps. 118:24, NKJV.

I REMEMBER TRANSLATING THE phrase "seize the day" in my Latin class in high school, but now it is well known in English and can also be literally translated "capture the day."

I think of this often when talking with women who are discouraged by the circumstances of their lives so that they tend to see only gray skies and negativity. The enemy is very busy going around like a roaring lion scaring us silly, and sometimes he seems to take a bite out of us.

God has told us that He is the "I Am." Whatever I am experiencing today, He is here with me. He does not call Himself "I Was"; because yesterday is past, I can safely leave it with Him. Tomorrow is not yet mine, so my worrying about it is useless. He does not call Himself "I Shall Be." However, He does say, "I am the same yesterday, today, and forever" (see Heb. 13:8), and "I am with you always, even to the end of the world" (Matt. 28:20, TLB). He is the great I Am, ready to be with me, steady me, strengthen me, and bless me today. Surely that is sufficient to give me joy and a positive attitude.

I have a wonderful professional friend who was experiencing one trauma after another. One dark, stormy day as she was driving home she asked God to give her a little something positive as a symbol of His love and care. Almost immediately the clouds parted a little and the sun filtered down in a blaze of diffused beauty. She knew that God would see her through.

This morning a dear 18-year-old girl who has developed a wonderful trust in God rang me to tell how she had been walking along a path by the ocean, and there in the low bushes she had spotted a couple delightful Australian blue wrens with their cheeky long tails twitching as they hopped about. "The thing is, I had asked God to please give me something special in nature to show His love," she said, "and I knew the blue wrens were the answer. You would have just loved seeing them!" I certainly would have, because I too had fallen in love with blue wrens and bought some delightful prints of them to frame for my study wall.

You have only today. Live it positively with God. Make it a party with Him. He is delighted to be there with you, always present, always the I Am.

URSULA M. HEDGES

The Power of Words

A word aptly spoken is like apples of gold in settings of silver. Prov. 25:11, NIV.

ONCE UPON A TIME there was a little girl who dreamed of being a gymnast. She was very happy practicing the moves she saw on television. But then one day her mother sat her down for a serious talk. The mother told her daughter that she could never be a gymnast. Only small, thin girls could be gymnasts, and she was quite likely to be a very big girl by the time she was a teenager.

The woman who told me this sad little story was in her 50s, and she had grown up to be a large woman, just as her mother had predicted. She had married and had a child and worked in an office. She was satisfied with the sedentary lifestyle she had adapted to after her mother crushed her dream. But not pursuing her love of gymnastics had left her with a sense of failure and bitterness.

No doubt the mother thought she was being helpful by telling her little girl that obesity ran in the family and she should just accept it. But I wonder how many well-meaning parents crush their daughters' spirits by insisting that they face reality.

I was reminded of the power of words when I paid a visit to my hometown and saw a good friend I had not seen in a year. While we were sitting in her kitchen she remarked that I looked younger, thinner, and healthier. I perked right up. She said this several times in the course of the conversation. Each time I felt better about myself, and when I left her house I left with a smile on my face and a sparkle in my eye—no doubt actually looking younger, thinner, and healthier!

Our words are more powerful than we realize. They can influence someone to pursue their dreams or to give them up. This is a power we all have over our loved ones—the power to help or hurt. The power of words.

I want to use my power to help, not hurt. I want to use my power to encourage the people I care about. I want to build them up with my words and prayers. I especially want to use my words to help the children in my life to soar toward their dreams. As a Christian, I can do no less. GINA LEE

Musings With Mugly

Watch and pray, lest you enter into temptation. The spirit indeed is willing, but the flesh is weak. Matt. 26:41, NKJV.

MY CALICO CAT SNUGGLED close to me on the couch. She was totally relaxed and content—until the wind blew some water from the sprinkler into the window near us. Oh, what was that terrible noise? Was it real danger? Mugly settled down as I calmly explained the situation to her. No need to fear. Everything is OK. Horrors, there it was again. Panic time for sure! More soothing words and some rubs under her chin restored peace. This happened several times, but each time she seemed less disturbed.

Sitting with her, I thought how very much this parallels Satan's temptations and attacks. At first we are alarmed, even frightened. Gradually, however, this concern is less pronounced. Remember when profanity began hitting the TV channels? How startling and disgusting this was! As this accelerated we became more accustomed to it. Certainly it remains offensive, but no longer as shocking—unless we deliberate on it.

I explained to my Mugly that she was correct to be startled by noises and events that were not expected, and that being so could keep her safer. Again, I reflected on the necessity to stay near to Jesus in order not to be caught in a trap set by Satan. I need to remain alert and not be lulled by the voices both in and out of the church that say, "Oh, it's OK. You don't need to be concerned about that—it is just a small thing."

Then I remembered the song from the children's cradle roll class that admonishes little eyes to be careful what they see, little lips to be careful what they say, and little feet to be careful where they go. It is important. I need to guard the avenues to my soul. Just as Mugly feels a measure of safety near me, I know I have a heavenly Friend who indeed has the power to help me guard the avenues of my soul and keep me safe.

Dear Father, help me to remember that it is the little things that make up my life, and it is important to be careful what I see, hear, and do, and where I go. You do love me, and I do not want to disappoint You by being careless in my actions and thoughts. Thank You for caring so much. Amen.

Dorothy Wainwright Carey

The Body of Christ

There are different kinds of gifts, but the same Spirit. There are different kinds of service, but the same Lord. There are different kinds of working, but the same God works all of them in all men. 1 Cor. 12:4-6, NIV.

LAST SUMMER WE TOOK a trip to Canada. We enjoyed visiting with relatives and spending time as a family. We spent several days in the spectacularly beautiful mountains of Banff and Jasper national parks, and we enjoyed hiking the trails and taking lots of pictures.

One afternoon we set out on a trail above Lake Louise on Fairview Mountain. The hike was a rather strenuous one, and I quickly became aware of just how out of shape I was compared to my young, active children. The trail on the side of the mountain was a series of switchbacks. My daughter would dash ahead along the trail to the next corner of the switchback and encourage me. "Come on, you can make it, Mommy. Keep on; you're almost there!" My son walked along slowly beside me offering his own style of support. "Are you OK? Do you need water? Do you want to lean on my walking stick?" It was fascinating to see the different gifts displayed by my children in responding to the situation. My daughter is an encourager. She has the ability to use her words to urge others on, to encourage them in their efforts. My son is a caretaker, a nurturer. He worries about how others are feeling and wants to be able to meet their needs.

The experience reminded me of 1 Corinthians 12, where Paul describes the different spiritual gifts as parts of the body, each with its particular function within the body of Christ. Some are good at public speaking or teaching; others have the gift of hospitality; still others have the gift of peacemaking. There are those with the gift of compassion, perception, or encouragement; there are those who can plan and organize; others are helpful and dependable. Each of us, whatever our talent, is a needed part of the body of Christ. As Paul put it: "Now you are the body of Christ, and each one of you is a part of it" (verse 27).

Perhaps you feel you have no special ability or talent to put to use. Or that what you can offer is so small that it doesn't really matter. Be assured that your Creator, the one who bestowed on you your unique gifts, longs to show you ways to use them! Ask Him to open your eyes to the opportunities around you today. You'll be amazed at what He can do through you!

SANDRA SIMANTON

My Life—A Living Miracle

You will protect me from trouble and surround me with songs of deliverance. Ps. 32:7, NIV.

TODAY I WRITE THIS because the Lord performed a miracle in my life. He saved me and brought me back to life. I have collected the information from those who took care of me. My son, Tlaunga, and I were returning from town. My son was driving the motor scooter, and I was sitting behind him, when the horrifying accident took place. As we were heading toward our home, a speeding truck hit our scooter. From that moment on I did not know what happened to me or to my son. After hitting us, the truck left. The Lord sent strangers to take us to the nearest clinic.

Tlaunga had several cuts and wounds and lost his middle finger on his left hand. After recovering from a painful surgery he was released from the hospital. The nurse who saw me lowered from the truck wrote, "You were held by shoulders and legs and looked limp. You looked gray all over, and I feared that it was a fire accident, but there was no smell of anything burnt. But later I found out that you were covered with black mud from the roadside."

I had a head injury and was vomiting blood. When the doctors arrived, they started first aid, while other teams cleaned up the three-inch-deep wound that was filled with mud and blood. They immobilized my legs and hands, which had sustained multiple fractures. The doctors immediately moved me to the nearest hospital with better facilities, where my dreadful head injury could be treated.

One of the doctors involved in giving me first aid wrote, "We were shocked to see you in such a condition. You were unconscious, not responding to any stimulus. Your legs were broken and swollen." That day many prayers were said on my behalf. The doctor continued: "If you were to ask me if I believe in miracles, I would say yes, because I witnessed the miraculous way in which the healing power of God has been demonstrated in sparing your life."

I was told that my relatives and neighbors had already planned for my funeral in case it was God's plan that I not gain consciousness. Yes, it was none other than the healing hand of the Lord that touched me and restored me to life.

As I look back I can only thank the Lord for His merciful hand. Today I realize that each day is a miracle. The Lord is great. There is no one else who can do such miracles. My life is a living miracle of deliverance!

LALNUNMAWII COLNEY

God Is Just a Prayer Away

Casting all your care upon him; for he careth for you. 1 Peter 5:7.

I HAD TO QUIT COLLEGE because of finances. But I so wanted to finish my course that I decided to go back and try again even without any money. All along the way in the bus, I talked to the Lord. *Please touch the heart of the director of finance to allow me to enroll.* When I was accepted, I knew for sure that God had answered my prayers.

But it was not easy. One time I felt my stomach asking for food, but I had many assignments to finish. Also, my purse was empty. Again I talked to my loving Lord. *Lord, help me to survive.* Just then the bell rang, and it was time for me to go to my classes. As I went downstairs, I saw something—it looked like folded money. I stopped and looked around. No one was near, so I picked it up. I slowly counted: it was 2,000 pesos. I took a deep breath. *Maybe this money is for my tuition fee.* I closed my eyes and thought, *What shall I do with this money? Shall I return it to the owner? Or shall I keep it? But I do not know the owner.* I finally decided to go see my home dean, returning all the money I found.

The day after that incident, I found that the money was claimed by a woman who had gone to our home dean crying for help because she had no more money to pay her tuition fees because it had been lost. She was interviewed and asked how much she had lost. "Two thousand pesos."

Sometimes trials and temptations lurk, and if Jesus is not in our heart, we will yield to the temptation and fail to honor the Lord.

Months went by, semester break came, and I went home. As I planned for the new school year I found that my trials were not over. I planned to work in a faculty home as a villager, but that did not work out. I did get to work as a villager, but after a month I got sick; I was hospitalized for hyperacidity, typhoid fever, and gastroenteritis. Oh, how miserable I was! When I got better, although my physical condition was weak I stayed in the dormitory and in school.

Then in March I received a letter telling me that I had received a scholarship I had applied for. There is no place for anything but joy in my heart. *Thank You, Lord. I really believe that You are just a prayer away! I have cast many cares on You, and You have cared for me each difficult step of the way.*

DARLENE D. SIMYUNN

Worth the Cost

In my Father's house are many rooms; if it were not so, I would have told you. I am going there to prepare a place for you. And if I go and prepare a place for you, I will come back and take you to be with me that you also may be where I am. John 14:2, 3, NIV.

MY NOSE PRESSED AGAINST the glass as I strained to catch my first glimpse of the coastline. Within minutes my dream would become reality. I would be in Australia!

One of my good friends had moved "down under" and teased me to come visit. Besides, hadn't I always wanted to visit Australia? Our discussion went back and forth; she thought I should come while I was still single; I insisted that I didn't have the vacation time or money. She reminded me that I had only myself to support, and sent me long, enticing discourses via e-mail of all the breathtaking places she'd visited, the beauty of the landscape, the wonderful people she'd met. I wanted to go. But the ticket was so expensive and the flight was so long; and I'd be by myself, 10 days away from my fiancé, Ron. And it would be a double-digit time change.

But then again, she was right. This was the best opportunity I'd probably ever have. And I could see Lynelle. And maybe a kangaroo or two. So I made the reservations. My boss was gracious and allowed me the few extra days, and that was that. I was going to Australia.

The trip was even better than I had imagined. Everything she had told me was true—and more. To experience it firsthand was so much better than just reading about it. We drove part of the Great Ocean Road, visited a wildlife park, wandered beaches, explored caves, watched penguins, toured Sydney, spotted kookaburras, wombats, koalas, and kangaroos. We talked for hours, often late into the night; we sang along with the radio and giggled about jokes we'd laughed at in high school. I even forgot how much the plane ticket had cost. It was worth every penny to experience this new place with my friend.

Christ promised us that He has gone to prepare a place for us so that we can be with Him and that the place will far exceed our wildest imaginations. Although the trip sometimes seems long, once we are there, actually experiencing it with our Friend, it will be so much more amazing than reading about it or hearing secondhand. It will be worth the cost—any cost—to spend forever with my Jesus. VICKI MACOMBER REDDEN

Whom Do You Look Like?

As for me, I will behold thy face in righteousness: I shall be satisfied, when I awake, with thy likeness. Ps. 17:15.

ONE DAY WHEN I WAS in my first year of college I went to a store near the university to make some photocopies of some texts. As soon as I walked in the door the clerk smiled at me and asked without hesitation, "Are you Guilherme's sister?"

"Well, yes," I replied, surprised and perplexed at the same time by her direct approach and the certainty in her voice. "And how do you know who I am? And how do you know Guilherme?" I asked.

She explained to me then that she had gone to my church several times at the invitation of some casual friends. During one of these visits my brother had been participating in the program. She had thought that he was very nice because of the friendly greeting he had given her at the end of the program.

After their first meeting they had seen each other at church one or two times more, but it was enough for her to remember what he looked like. Not only did she remember what he looked like, but she recognized me as his sister, without ever having seen me before! Their brief meeting, and the friendly reception she had received, had truly impressed her.

This experience made me think of another very important identification for us as Christians; we are brothers and sisters of Jesus. Would someone recognize Jesus after meeting you just a few times? This also makes me reflect on the importance of daily communion with Him and the contemplation of His love and immutable character. A casual encounter or even a weekly meeting is not enough. We need to meet every day with our dear Older Brother so that we can become more like Him—so even strangers will recognize that we are related.

Father, help me once more today to seek the presence of Your Son, Jesus, my Brother, in my life. You understand me and know how difficult this is at times, but You do not let me perish. As I leave my home, Father, I want people to recognize me as Your daughter and see in my smile and in my eyes the love of my Brother, Jesus, for me and for them. — INGRID RIBEIRO WOLFF

Flying Thoughts

I can do everything through him who gives me strength. Phil. 4:13, NIV.

I NOTICED THE SMALL GIRL, or rather her little outfit, and thought it was really a cute outfit, all in coordinated purple. But it wasn't until I saw her mother carry her up the aisle of the plane to the lavatory that I noticed how tiny her body was compared to how old she looked. I also noticed her very strong glasses and that she was unable to hold her head up.

After the two returned to their seats, I noticed that the mother and grandmother were feeding the child with a tube, and my heart went out to all three of them in compassion and gratefulness. Why gratefulness? Because it wasn't I who was facing the challenge of a physically challenged child. I know I'd never have the patience and fortitude to meet such a task. I'm sure God knew that and didn't give me more than I can bear.

I also know that through God's help we can all rise to overcome obstacles that we never dreamed we'd have to face. Maybe I could have handled a developmentally and physically challenged child, but God didn't ask me to do so, and I am grateful. But I want to give my respect to those who do, day after long day.

I think of other women and the challenges they face. How many women have done things above and beyond anything they ever thought they could because they had to? I think of the millions of women in the world who are raising children alone. Many are desperately poor—they don't know where the next meal is coming from. God never asked me to face anything like that. I am grateful, but I also want to do what I can to help make a difference for them.

My thoughts turn to those who are abused, who have escaped from their homes because of violence of any form. Or those who have been divorced and have had to handle situations they never dreamed of. And there are surviving spouses, young and old, facing each day by themselves, when they thought they would always have a partner. So many have found they can do things they never expected to, even feeling good about themselves and what they have accomplished.

My flight is almost over. I have challenges to meet at my destination too. I never thought I could do what I am doing, but I too can "do everything through him who gives me strength." For this I am so grateful.

Ardis Dick Stenbakken

Preparations

Eye hath not seen, nor ear heard, neither have entered into the heart of man, the things which God hath prepared for them that love him. 1 Cor. 2:9.

FINALLY, A TRIP TO the mountains! This long-awaited jaunt seemed overdue. Together with friends Zlata and Helen, I began to eagerly explore towns, shops, and all the interesting tourist areas around Asheville, North Carolina. There was so much to see. A visit to the Biltmore Estate was on our "must" list.

"Oh, just look at this!" one of us would say.

"I know. Take a look at this—isn't it impressive?"

"Did you ever see anything like this?" we would ask in wonder.

Each space and room in the house seemed grander than the previous one. The rich brocades, velvets, satins, and leathers are far more luxurious than any in our own homes. The wood carvings are something to behold. Such opulence!

After hours of admiring the house, we proceeded to the nursery and gardens. Not only were they beautiful; many plants were new to us, and we reveled in their beauty. The variety and beauty were almost overwhelming.

All this made us think of what our heavenly home will be like. We know the plantings and things of this earth are but faint reflections of what is being prepared for us. Nothing could compare to the preparations being made there. When we contemplate this, we know we can't even begin to imagine the glorious home Christ is arranging for us. Temporal things become insignificant, no longer desirable.

There are many beautiful things in this world—both those made by people and things in nature. But even the magnificent flowers and wonderful vegetation that we so delight in now will pale to nothingness when we reach heaven. The delightful scenery that so enthralls us here will not compare to what is being prepared for us. Can't you just imagine us calling to each other, "You have to come see this! It is just incredibly beautiful!"

How meaningful to remember the words "Eye hath not seen, nor ear heard, neither have entered into the heart of man, the things which God hath prepared for them that love him." DOROTHY WAINWRIGHT CAREY

Opening Our Hearts and Homes

And above all things have fervent love for one another, for "love will cover a multitude of sins." Be hospitable to one another without grumbling. 1 Peter 4:8, 9, NKJV.

DURING THE SUMMER MY husband and I would frequently hire boys to help on our farm. They were teenagers, growing and always hungry. I loved cooking for them because they were appreciative and happy. My husband appreciated this because when the boys were happy they worked willingly. Lifting hundreds of 80- to 90-pound bales of hay required many calories each day to maintain a man's strength. At the end of the summer they had physiques to be proud of. No amount of going to a gym and lifting weights could have equaled the healthy exercise they had experienced while working in the fresh air doing useful labor.

Years later we visited in the home of one of "our" boys—Glenn—and his wife, Linda, and their daughters. I remembered Glenn as a young man who loved to play the guitar and make music. He also loved being a part of our family for the three months he was there. When we arrived at their home, his wife surprised me by telling me that Glenn was concerned about whether she had fixed enough food. I chuckled as I remembered his healthy appetite and Glenn making sandwiches of mashed potatoes and gravy and various other items of food.

When Glenn arrived home and we sat down to a delicious meal, he began to reminisce about the summer at our house. He commented, "Every day was Christmas dinner at the Glass house." We smiled, and I felt a sense of relief knowing I had cooked to please his tastes after all. He explained that he loved the bread I made and enjoyed sandwiches, so everything worked as sandwich filling for him.

The hospitality that is extended when we offer good food and the comforts of home show our guests they are loved. Years may go by, but the memories of good food, interesting conversation, and the warmth of friendship remain with us.

Sharing our home with friends and strangers has given us hours of joy. As we reminisce about our guests, our hearts are filled with contentment. We have been blessed by so many special people who have entered the doors of our home and, thereby, the doors to our hearts.

EVELYN GLASS

Of Bicycles and Fathers

Surely God is my salvation; I will trust and not be afraid. The Lord, the Lord, is my strength and my song; he has become my salvation. Isa. 12:2, NIV.

THAT WARM SEPTEMBER DAY I woke up early with sun rays dancing on the walls of my bedroom. I dashed down the stairs. Yes, there it was—a bright-red bicycle leaning on its kickstand in the middle of the living room. A "Happy Birthday" card dangled from the handlebars.

A few months before, I had pleaded for a two-wheeler. I had seen the glance my mother had flashed to Dad. He had shifted uneasily in his chair. I sensed from their grown-up conversations that the Great Depression burdened my daddy.

But any worry about not getting a bike for my sixth birthday was completely erased that morning. Dad carried my very own bike out to the sidewalk. It didn't have fancy handle grips with streamers flying, or silver spokes with tiny flashing lights, as modern bicycles do. Nevertheless, its beauty dazzled me. As Dad lifted me up on the seat, he gave me some basic instructions: "Pedal forward to go; pedal backward to stop."

Very patiently he pushed me up and down the sidewalk for the next three days. "I'm gonna fall! Don't let go, Daddy!" I begged. He always assured me he wouldn't. I learned that I could trust Dad to keep his word. If I hit a bump and wavered, he caught me. He had sacrificed and deprived himself to purchase that two-wheeler. It was his gift to me. I felt so loved.

Dad, a stable force in my life, died when I was 29 years old. A year before that he was introduced to the Savior. Though the grief of losing him was unbearable, Bible studies revealed that I had another Dad. This Father comforted me in my sorrow. He would never fail me either.

"I'm gonna fall! Father, Father, don't let go!"

My heavenly Father's love buoys me up. He is patient with me. If I hit a bump and begin to waver, He catches me. I always trust Him. This Father, like my dad, also gave me some basic instructions: "If you love Me, keep My commandments" (John 14:15, NKJV). Yes, my Father God also sacrificed Himself, but for a greater gift—to purchase my salvation, His gift to me. I feel so loved.

I don't wish for bicycles anymore. I pray to spend eternity with both fathers, my earthly dad and my Father God. And I'll thank them both for never letting go.

MARIANNE TOTH BAYLESS

Bologna

Unless you change and become like little children, you will never enter the kingdom of heaven. Matt. 18:3, NIV.

LITTLE JOHNNY INSISTED ON staying with me for the day while the rest of the family took care of family business. Later, when we were alone, I asked him why he wanted to stay with me. He said he'd made several friends the few times he had visited us before and that he enjoyed my home-cooked meals. I took that as a compliment and went about doing my household chores while he went to round up his friends for play. For a while I didn't hear anything from him. Since we lived in a student apartment complex, the boys were aware that they had to keep the noise down so they wouldn't disturb the neighbors.

I was busy going about my business when I heard the door bang and quickly lock. I tiptoed in to see what was the matter. There was Johnny on the sofa, looking out the window, and his friend was outside pleading. Johnny was "preaching" to the boy about what God said about eating unclean foods and how they weren't good for him. The little boy stood there trying to explain that it was his mother's fault—she had made the sandwich. I remember Johnny replying, "I can't play with you anymore because you eat unclean foods. You are being disobedient to God." His little friend had to promise that he would throw the sandwich away and never eat more bologna so they could remain friends. Believe me, by this time I was laughing, though the boys didn't realize I was watching them. Soon after the small incident the two boys were playing as if nothing had happened.

I learned a lesson that day: always stand for what you believe, and forgive and forget just like a little child. Like Johnny's friend, most of the time I'm quick to blame somebody for my foolishness. If I would just spend time on my knees and in Bible study, it would be a lot easier to do His will. Many times I have shied away from standing for the Lord because of fear of what my peers might think. The boys had another lesson for me, too: use every opportunity that comes your way to enlighten someone about the kingdom to come.

Please, Lord, help me to walk in Your footsteps day by day. It won't be easy, but with You by my side, I'm sure I will make it to that beautiful home.

Sibusisiwe Ncube-Ndhlovu

One Lonely Flower

Therefore, my brethren dearly beloved and longed for, . . . so stand fast in the Lord. Phil. 4:1.

FOR THE PAST FIVE years my husband and I have spent Mother's Day planting red, white, and purple impatiens on either side of our front porch. One of the reasons we like them is that they stay in bloom from May through October or November. For some reason, however, this year they didn't thrive very well. Perhaps it was because of the scorching heat of an unusually hot summer. In fact, our impatiens did so poorly that my husband decided to dig the ground again and plant pansies—white, pink, red, and purple—on the left side of the porch, leaving a small evergreen bush we had planted a few years before on the other side. The pansies seemed to be doing very well, especially with the abundance of rain we had.

Several days ago as I was coming in from work I noticed something unusual. There it was on the right side, next to the bush—one lonely, pink impatiens growing almost hidden beneath the bush's shadow but bright as it could be there at the corner of the house. Its little face was turned upward as if to say, "I'm still here." *It must be lonely,* I thought, *but it's thriving nevertheless.*

It reminded me of how lonely and sad the Christian walk can be at times in a world so full of sin and corruption. I thought of the adversities that beat down on us, causing us to become discouraged at times. The times when the enemy blasts us with an unexpected trial from left field are the moments I've asked the Lord in despair, "What's it all for—what's the use?" Then I think, *By God's grace, I'm still here.* Despite the torrential storms and the heat of trial, our Father seems to hide me in the cleft of His hand, as the bush did for the little pink impatiens, until the storm passes by.

Yes, we'll experience trial and tribulation, discouragement and seeming defeat. But if we remain faithful, and if we look up and recognize again the source of our help, then we'll be able to say, "I'm still here, by God's grace, brightening the corner where I stand."

Lord, please continue to give me strength to stand in the midst of trial and adversity; and when I'm tempted to look down, help me to look up and acknowledge that it's by Your love and mercy alone that I continue to stand.

GLORIA J. STELLA FELDER

The One Hundredth Day

If you have faith as small as a mustard seed, you can say to this mountain, "Move from here to there" and it will move. Nothing will be impossible for you. Matt. 17:20, NIV.

IT WAS A NOVEL IDEA. The teachers wanted to celebrate the one hundredth day of the school year as a way to help it seem to be passing more quickly. They decided to do this by asking each student to bring to school that Friday 100 of any item that could fit in a backpack. The children came up with great ideas: a chain made with 100 links, 100 drops of water, a 100-piece puzzle, a castle made of 100 marshmallows and toothpicks, 100 M & M's, 100 pieces of spaghetti, 100 stickers on a shirt, 100 hot-pad loops, and so on.

My son wanted to bring 100 mustard seeds. I had received a beautiful basket of spices from my sister-in-law the previous Christmas, and, sure enough, there were mustard seeds in it. We proceeded to count them out. It was a difficult task, since they are so very, very tiny. We counted 10 at a time and placed them in a Ziploc bag. But when we finished, we were so surprised! It looked as if there were only about 20 seeds in the bag. We took them out and recounted. Yes, our count had been correct, but the quantity in the bag looked unbelievably small.

I remembered Jesus telling the parable of the mustard seed. He said, "Though it is the smallest of all your seeds, yet when it grows, it is the largest of garden plants and becomes a tree" (Matt. 13:32, NIV). Our faith may be as small as a tiny seed, but we can move mountains with it. With faith in Jesus nothing is impossible for us. Through faith we can access God's strength to help us through the tough times. David understood this source of strength. When he faced Goliath, even though he was a young man, the power of God enabled him to topple the giant.

I need to apply the strength of a mustard seed to my day. When the tasks of being a wife, mother, employee, friend, student, and all my other obligations become almost impossible, I'll remember that I may be a small seed, but with the power of Jesus in my life God will give me the ability to do His will.

If you have the faith of even a tiny mustard seed, nothing will be impossible for you. What a promise! KAREN PHILLIPS

A Basket of Memories

Inasmuch as ye have done it unto one of the least of these my brethren, ye have done it unto me. Matt. 25:40.

HER NAME WAS CAROLYN White, and she holds a special place in my basket of memories. She was my first-grade teacher, back when I wore black stockings and had a Buster Brown haircut. Not only did Miss White teach the six children in her first-grade class, but she had many other responsibilities as well. The school was a red brick building in the small town of Salzburg, Michigan. My sister and I walked dirt roads or over plowed fields to get to school. There were no yellow school buses to take us there.

When I was 9 years old, my father's work required us to transfer to Grand Rapids. It was time to say goodbye to friends and classmates. Living in a strange city was a new experience to a family from the country. Now my sister and I walked to school on concrete sidewalks bordering busy streets, and there were many children in my fourth-grade class.

When we left Salzburg, Miss White presented me with a book that I covet to this day. On the flyleaf she had written in her perfect cursive handwriting, "To a dear little girl I love."

The years flew by, and college was behind me. My sister Vivien, who still lives near Salzburg, wrote to say she had run into Miss White in town. My former teacher still remembered me and expressed a desire to renew our acquaintance next time I was in the area. She still lived in the same house on the same street in the same small town. I recalled the front porch that stretched across the front of her house. It was a nondescript house for a busy woman. What a treat it would be to reminisce about the many years that had come and gone. My travels took me into the area several times to see my relatives, but I never took time to stop to see Miss White.

And then my sister sent me Miss White's obituary. I realized I had never stopped to see her or to renew our acquaintance as she had requested.

Do we live at such a fast pace in today's society that we don't take time to think of others? How often do we put things aside for no reason other than the inconvenience? This was one meeting that didn't materialize, and I will forever regret it. There would have been happy memories for both of us—the little girl with the Buster Brown haircut, and her first-grade teacher.

LAURIE DIXON-MCCLANAHAN

God Answered the Praying

Ask and it will be given to you; seek and you will find; knock and the door will be opened to you. Matt. 7:7, NIV.

THE PROMISES OF GOD will be realized only if claimed. Today's verse reminds me of a very interesting experience that illustrates this text. My husband and I had married, and we'd had our firstborn, a baby girl. The first and second years had gone by, and the third was advancing. We decided that we needed another baby—a boy.

I began to become distressed because, regardless of our attempts, no pregnancy occurred. One day I asked my husband if he felt the same way.

"Yes," he said, "but we must remember to ask God, and He will provide."

We immediately knelt down beside our bed and prayed earnestly for the child we wanted. God answered our prayer, and I conceived. One day—I can't remember the exact day—I dreamed of giving birth to a baby boy. Indeed, I was happy that God had sent us an assurance of our answered prayer in a dream. When God says, "Ask and it will be given to you," He means it. God answers prayers. He's been answering my prayers in many, many ways, and I will never stop seeking the blessings that come from seeking and claiming His promises.

In the stores of heaven are many blessings and gifts. Yet we haven't asked to receive them. The psalmist who had experienced the promises of God said, "Taste and see that the Lord is good" (Ps. 34:8).

Maybe you are in need of a baby, or you have health problems; it could be that you have financial difficulties, or maybe you cannot manage your family well. The answer to all our problems can be obtained through prayer. People may pray for many needs, but seldom do people pray for the gift of children. Perhaps some will pray because they have never had a child at all; but we should pray for all our needs—great or small, first or second.

I don't hesitate to urge all to engage in prayer, for prayer is a source unlimited. I know God has answered my prayers. PAULINE OKEMWA

Unconditional Love

And God made the beast of the earth . . . and God saw that it was good. Gen. 1:25.

AFTER OUR TWO CHILDREN married and left the nest, my husband, Harold, and I decided we needed some four-legged critters to help occupy some of our time and space. First we got Rusty, a feisty Pomeranian that thought he was human. He loved to go blackberry picking with Harold and would follow him through the patch and catch each berry as it was tossed to him.

Then, quite by accident, we acquired two kittens, Midnight and Arf Arf. The three animals became best of friends; they would sleep in each other's arms, or, in this case, in each other's paws.

One day Harold came home from work, opened the back door, and gently laid at my feet the cutest little critter I had ever seen—a baby goat. We knew nothing about raising goats, but Harold had brought her home to join our family. It was love at first sight, and we named her Baby. She accepted us from the start and followed us around the house and yard like a puppy.

One day Harold mentioned that he thought Baby's abdomen seemed a bit disturbed. We watched her for a few days and finally decided there definitely was a problem, so we made plans to take her to the veterinarian. That day we'd had a bad storm that had left the roads like sheets of ice. Harold had to drive carefully, and the 10-mile trip seemed to take forever. I was holding Baby on my lap, and with each bump or jerk of the car she would cry out in pain.

The doctor examined her and told us he would try to relieve some of the pressure by inserting a long needle. When that didn't work, he said he'd have to operate. Even though it was close to midnight, he called his nurse to come and assist him. But before she arrived, our sweet little Baby died. The doctor explained that baby goats need their mother's milk to prevent this very thing from happening. No one had told us anything about feeding little kids, so we had just fed her what we heard was goat food.

Our pets become like members of our family. Even though there may be sad times, they bring us so much joy. I agree with Genesis 1:25: God saw the animals He had made and saw that it was good.

Yes, God, it was very good. Thank You. CLAREEN COLCLESSER

Choosing the Good Part

Mary has chosen the good part. Luke 10:42, NASB.

ON SEPTEMBER 11, AFTER the initial World Trade Center terrorist attack, WTC employees had to decide quickly what was most important in their lives at that moment.

A secretary later told reporters how, immediately after the first plane crashed into one tower, she had urged her two bosses to descend in the elevator with her and flee to safety. Instead, one boss headed toward the coffeepot, while the other visited a restroom. The secretary escaped, but her bosses perished when the tower collapsed.

Later that week a longtime newspaper gossip columnist publicly confessed, "I see now that what I've been doing for years has no importance." In a post-September 11 TV interview, a movie star admitted, "I'm going to change professions. I want my life to count for something important."

We're all familiar with the sisterly squabble at Mary and Martha's house that day Jesus came to visit. We recall that Martha was so overwhelmed by her hosting responsibilities that she wanted her sister, Mary, who had dropped at the feet of Jesus, to help her share the kitchen burdens. Christ gently pointed out to Martha that Mary had chosen the "good part," the important opportunity to spend time in His presence, one-on-one.

Christ knew something Martha didn't. Within three years she would undergo the two greatest faith challenges of her life: the deaths of both her brother and her Savior. Christ knew that Martha needed to understand what was most important and then act on it. Only a clear understanding of who Christ was would fortify Martha to survive, spiritually and emotionally.

Are you clear about what "the good part" should be in your life? The decision to spend a regular time with Jesus in prayer, Bible study, and Scripture memorization is the most important choice you can make in every 24-hour period.

If you're not taking ample time to really know your Savior, ask yourself right now, "How can I rearrange my daily schedule in order to spend consistent time at the feet of Jesus?" Then, in His strength, do what you need to do. Because they knew who Jesus was, Martha and Mary survived the tragic personal—and national—events they soon experienced. Choosing "the good part" today will fortify us for the traumatic events in our immediate futures as well.

CAROLYN SUTTON

Fires

As the fire burneth a wood. Ps. 83:14.

ON THE MORNING OF September 12, 2001, I flew with my husband to New Zealand to spend some time with aged parents. Although I've always asked God for traveling mercies, no matter how long or how short a journey, I will never board an aircraft again with the carefree attitude of the past. Something most of us took for granted—safe air travel—has gone.

But go back a few hours to the evening of September 11—Australia time. I had finished packing our suitcases; my husband was at a meeting. It was getting so late that I went to bed.

"Wake up! Wake up! Look at this. A plane has just flown into a building in New York!" I drowsily stirred, then was instantly riveted to the late news my husband was watching. All through those long night hours we watched those terrible events unfolding. The utter devastation caused by the ensuing fires was almost unbelievable. I, like countless others, was in tears as I watched the World Trade Center buildings collapse. I will never forget the words of one New York firefighter: "We run in while everybody else is running out. It's our job."

It was only a few months later that terrible bushfires blazed around the city of Sydney, Australia. They started Christmas Eve and continued for several weeks as the summer temperatures soared, setting new records. The ferocity of those flames (up to 150 feet high) as they were driven by strong winds, day and night, was frightening to see. Sheer walls of flame devoured everything in their path. As the days ticked by, more and more firefighters were called in from other states to help in the emergency. As I watched the news, again I was in tears as brave firefighters battled the flames, heat, and smoke. Altogether 160 homes were lost, thousands of animals—beautiful Australian wildlife—died, and tens of thousands of acres of bushland were destroyed.

Fires can be destructive, but they can also be instructive. "Is not my word like as a fire? saith the Lord" (Jer. 23:29). May this be the fire that we run to. May this be the fire that burns brightly in our lives. LEONIE DONALD

Be Not Afraid

For God has not given us a spirit of fear, but of power and of love and of a sound mind. 2 Tim. 1:7, NKJV.

THE SUN, BARELY ON the horizon, signaled the start of another day as we were awakened by the melodious voice of my mother singing, "The sun is on the land and sea, the day begun." However, the warmth and comfort of my bed seemed to have this gravitational pull on me, and instead of springing to life, I wanted to snuggle down and sleep for a little longer. Of course, when I heard the familiar footsteps approaching my room, I knew I had to get up. If I didn't, I knew it would not be a gentle prodding to get me out of bed to meet in the living room for worship. Amazingly, though, once I got there I was rejuvenated with the hymns and the Bible texts we had to commit to memory.

We were often reminded that there will come a day when we will have to reach within and use those texts to help us through difficult times. As a child I took the challenge and learned as much as I possibly could, even though I felt that my mother was just sounding that warning to get us to learn the Bible texts. I'm now grown and must admit that she was absolutely correct. I've had to lean on the promises of God many times to get me through difficult situations.

The days following the terrorists' attacks on the World Trade Center and the Pentagon were one such situation. Like millions of people, I was afraid, depressed, worried, anxious, and nervous. I had difficulty falling asleep. When I eventually did, my sleep was always interrupted with images of a burning and collapsing building. One night as I lay in bed watching television to counter my inability to drop asleep, the text for today came to mind. I recalled having learned it years before as a child. As I repeated the text, my fears subsided and I felt at peace. I recalled other Bible verses that provided me with the strength and courage I needed to face another day at work. I turned off the television. I listened to and sang uplifting music. It brought peace and comfort to my soul, and I was able to sleep.

Lord, I want to thank You for today. I know that there are difficult times ahead, but help me to remember that You have the whole world in Your hands. Help me not to worry but to place my trust in You. Thank You for the perfect antidotes.

ANDREA A. BUSSUE

A Willing Mind

And you, my son Solomon, . . . serve him . . . with a willing mind. 1 Chron. 28:9, NIV.

WE HAD MINISTERED IN the two coastal towns of the state for several very happy years. As the minister's wife, I had accepted all the duties that the church invited me to shoulder. I was young, I was eager, and I was full of ideas. As a teacher, I knew that my training would more than equip me for the appointment to the kindergarten children's class, and I loved every minute of sharing my talents in welfare work, as well.

Then came the inevitable transfer to a new district, where we served for three years.

Then a new conference president stunned us by saying, "We want you to go to the two coastal towns and minister there."

It was then that I suddenly felt rebellion in my heart. I told my husband that for six years we had spent our talents in that district. The members there didn't need to have a repeat performance by the family they must view as stale by now. I felt I had nothing new to offer.

Camp meeting time was approaching, and I wondered how my friends in the coastal towns would relate to this appointment. I insisted to my husband that I was not going, and I would tell the president how I felt. My husband, being an obedient servant, was not disturbed as was I, and was mildly amused at my touch of rebellion.

One night at the campground I realized that I couldn't continue indefinitely in rebellion. So after wrestling most of the night, I finally said, "Lord, I guess I'll have to give in if this call is Your will. I'll go where You are calling, and I'll go happily, not grudgingly. Just help me."

I walked then with a lighter step, and friends from the coastal towns greeted us with pleasure that we were coming back to them. Then an announcement over the public-address system called for Pastor Heise. When the interview was over, my husband called me out of the tent to report that we had received a call to another state. I was speechless. But reason told me that the good Lord was saying, "I didn't want you to go back to the coastal towns, either, but I wanted you to be willing to go."

Thank You, Lord, for reminding us that Your greatest joy is seeing Your servants willing to do Your will.

EDNA HEISE

Exactly What I Needed

And if we know that he hears us, whatsoever we ask, we know we have the petitions that we desired of him. 1 John 5:15.

DURING MY MOTHER-IN-LAW'S illnesses I'd been taking college classes. After her death, I continued my studies and did more cleaning, papering, and painting, and kept on with my music job. Three attacks of bursitis in each shoulder greatly curtailed some of those activities. So I became a certified nursing assistant for a health-care agency and nursed patients in their homes.

After lifting too many patients from beds and chairs to their wheelchairs and back again, I developed Morton's neuroma in a nerve in my left foot and had to have surgery. It was time, I knew, to change to an occupation that was less physically demanding. But what could I do? Although I was now the musician at two Methodist churches, I still needed a way to replace the nursing income I had lost.

I talked to God about my need, and the thought came almost right away: I could take in laundry! *Thank You, Jesus! I'll put the ad in the paper tomorrow.* But before I could do that, I saw, under Help Wanted: "Laundry assistant needed part-time to do washing and ironing at local bed-and-breakfast." I called the owners and was interviewed that same day. Dorie Distefano offered me the job, and two days later I started working.

My duties at the charming antebellum bed-and-breakfast include stain removal, washing, and ironing. I've also branched out, mending or restoring quilts, scarves, bedspreads, and tablecloths, including some crocheted items. I like my work. Dorie is kind and patient. Her husband, Vince, is nice too. The pay is good—far better than what I'd earned nursing.

I meet many interesting people in the course of my work. I love the peaceful atmosphere and also enjoy the rest of the Ashton Country House menagerie, which includes rabbits and chickens. From time to time, when Dorie and Vince are away, the housekeeper, Jeanie, and I take turns caring for the animals. There is never a dull moment at the bed-and-breakfast!

Yes, God knew exactly what I needed and helped me find it quickly. When you have special needs, ask for His guidance, and He'll help you, too.

BONNIE MOYERS

Eternal Smile

And God shall wipe away all tears from their eyes; and there shall be no more death, neither sorrow, nor crying, . . . for the former things are passed away. Rev. 21:4.

MANY TIMES I'VE FOUND myself trying to imagine the last minutes of the life of Maxima, also known as Nelly, who died on September 11, 2001, in the World Trade Center disaster. Maxima Jean-Pierre worked in the executive kitchen of the Cantor Fitzgerald offices on the 103rd floor, exactly where the first plane crashed. Did she die instantly? Was she hurt during the impact? Nobody will know—until we get to heaven.

I remember the first time I met Nelly. We were having a series of evangelistic meetings in the area of Far Rockaway. She entered the hall and lit it up with her smile. You had to work very hard to not be attracted to this petite, lively young woman. That night she made fun of my inability to understand and spell her last name correctly on the registration card. And she kept on smiling during the years in which we worked together in the new church.

Nelly enjoyed children very much. After caring for her own four during the week, she still had energy and patience to deal with a bunch more during church Bible classes and during the church service. Every Sabbath she picked up a half dozen from her neighborhood to bring to church. One of the very few times that I saw her upset was when a member suggested that it would be better not to bring so many unruly kids to church. And every week the basement of her house was full of kids for lunch and more Bible stories.

Nelly Jean-Pierre was a blessing to many, including me. Our long telephone conversations, her Christian example, and her love for her family, for children, and for people who suffered made an impact on my life. She decided to initiate a food pantry at the church, and with very little help she did it. She'll always be fondly remembered. It's ironic that she was about to change jobs. She was tired of the long commute and wanted to work closer to home.

There's one thing I regret very much. She invited me many times to visit her new house, and I never went. I said, "Tomorrow." "Soon." "For Thanksgiving." It would have made her happy, but I never did it. It's too late now. But I hope our houses in heaven will be close enough so we can see each other often. I plan to make it there, and I'm sure she'll be there with her beautiful smile. ALICIA MARQUEZ

My Little Sister Is a Brat

I press on toward the goal to win the prize for which God has called me heavenward in Christ Jesus. Phil. 3:14, NIV.

MY LITTLE SISTER IS A BRAT. Anyone who knows her will tell you that's so. Being the youngest of 10 natural children and many others my folks helped raise, Maggie couldn't help being spoiled. She learned to fight back fast. She's sassy, and quick of wit and tongue. Rarely do people leave her speechless. She often leaves them wondering what just happened and pondering whatever she said. That's why, without even knowing it, Maggie is such a good leader.

Her goals were always high standards and hard work. She played in the high school band, and her goal was to play with Doc Severinsen and to meet Tony Orlando and Dawn. When Doc Severinsen decided to tour in Omaha, Nebraska, and play at the Ak-Sar-Ben Coliseum, he chose to have some area musicians join him. Maggie was one of the chosen. He then asked her to join his band, playing her French horn or clarinet. But because of her dedication to Mom and Dad, who were then in their 60s, she chose to stay in Omaha.

Later, after she married and her husband transferred to another city, Doc came through town. Maggie wanted her three boys and husband to meet him. She was impressed and surprised that tickets and backstage passes were only a phone call away. The family all met Doc and got photographs taken with him. Her children were pleasantly surprised that "Mom's stories" were not exaggerations.

Maggie had wanted to get married and raise her own kids without having to leave them with babysitters or day-care providers. And she has accomplished many of her goals. She has a wonderful man she's still married to almost 30 years later, three great kids and three stepchildren, and a wonderful grandson who thrills her heart.

Goals and determination are what make the race of life worth running. We want to run toward our goal of dashing into the loving arms of God and praising our Savior forever. As Christians, our goals include not only ourselves but everyone around us. We can accomplish this, not by being pushy or offensive, but in letting the love of Jesus shine through our eyes and into others' hearts daily. No one has to question where Maggie stands. It's my prayer that others will see Jesus as clearly in you and me as well.

Sally J. Aken-Linke

Words of Life

That I may publish with the voice of thanksgiving, and tell of all thy wondrous works. Ps. 26:7.

IN A FEW DAYS I'll be teaching another writing class. My students' ages range broadly, with some as young as 12; others inch up to 80. I always get excited about teaching because I wonder how many will catch the vision, will not remain wannabes.

I love to write; however, writing is not some easy, magical experience. Writing equals hard work. A good writer doesn't randomly link words together like a daisy chain—he or she chooses the best words to convey a thought clearly and succinctly. As a result, the reader understands easily—and wants to read more.

Though there are many help books for writers, I recommend the Bible as the writer's key textbook. First of all, look at the first words in Genesis: "In the beginning God created the heaven and the earth" (Gen. 1:1). Then skip to the Bible's end in Revelation 22:21: "The grace of our Lord Jesus Christ be with you all. Amen." I can hear an editor saying, "Great beginning, great ending." Between those two succinct verses are inspired words of life, hope, and salvation. Although many authors from varied walks of life wrote those words during a 1,600-year span of time, there is a cohesiveness that grips the reader.

I gear my classes for freelancers who want to write for publication. (By the way, to publish can mean either verbal or written communication. Maybe that's why many writers are also fascinating verbal storytellers.) For most writers, freelancing means consistent publishing for the reading public. This requires commitment and responsibility. It's pleasurable for me to establish that in my students.

At the beginning of the course I teach my students to say with me, "I am a writer." To be that writer, they are told, "You must employ action (worker) words and fire the lazy (slacker) words."

With the *Words of Life* as a textbook, we can apply writing techniques to all other areas of life as well. As we set worthwhile goals, we'll discover how rewarding it is to get action into living, to fire those lazy habits and effectively witness for the Lord. Thus, I teach another writers' class to encourage someone to catch the vision—and get beyond being a wannabe.

Betty Kossick

Just a Box of Juice Bars

I will instruct you and teach you in the way you should go; I will guide you with My eye. Ps. 32:8, NKJV.

WITH A HEAVY HEART I keep thinking of my friend Melanie. She's been sick in bed for weeks. At times I feel so helpless for not knowing what I can do for her. I've taken her food, cards, and flowers and have run errands for her. Each day I've visited with her by phone or at her bedside.

One day I was driving through my small town on some errands and was planning to stop by and visit my friend. I thought, *I don't want to go empty-handed.* I hadn't brought anything along, so I tried to think of something I could buy for her along the way and continued driving toward her home.

The thought came to me to go to the grocery store and buy a box of juice bars. So I took the next turn and drove into the parking lot of the closest grocery store. I went in quickly and headed directly to the frozen food section, where I picked out a box of strawberry juice bars. Then I drove toward her home with my gift in hand.

After giving my friend a hug, I handed her my gift. "What did you bring me?" she asked as she looked in the grocery bag.

She let out a squeal of delight! "Juice bars!" She then told me that she had sent her teenage children to the grocery store with juice bars on the list, but they had inadvertently forgotten them.

It was obvious that God hadn't forgotten, and He sent me to get them! Now it was my turn to get excited. I felt humble as well, thinking about how God used me to bring delight to my friend, knowing that it brought Him delight to see her happy.

Lord, as I go through each step of this day I want You to instruct me through Your Word and the experiences that come my way. I ask You to teach me what I need to know. Help me to be willing to follow Your instructions. Guide my thoughts and actions so they will be pleasing to You. SHARON FOLLETT

Wireless Communications

And God heard them, for their prayer reached heaven, his holy dwelling place. 2 Chron. 30:27, NIV.

HI, MOM. WHATCHA DOING?" My daughter's voice came over the cell phone, loud and clear. For a moment I visualized her still in the house just three miles away, but then reality hit. No, several thousand miles and the massive Pacific Ocean separated us. "I just called to tell you and Dad good night."

As I listened I began hearing a loud rushing sound. "I think we have a bad connection," I commented.

"No," she said, "you're just hearing the pounding of the surf on the beach. I'm sitting by the ocean." Now things really came into a new perspective.

I was suddenly reminded of what marvels of communication we have. A resident at the retirement facility where I am director had recently told me of receiving an e-mail message from a family member in Pakistan. Another told of receiving a call from a grandchild in Indonesia. Many at the retirement facility can still remember the first telephone systems. Now we are equipped with all sorts of communication devices. We have not only telephones but pagers, cell phones, fax machines, voice mail, and e-mail. Distance no longer separates relatives in our world.

I'm also reminded of something my son said when I voiced concern about his moving so far away to southern California. He said, "Mom, you won't really know the difference between whether I'm calling you from California or Atlanta." And that's true. On the telephone it's impossible to judge distances.

The same all-powerful God who gave humans the knowledge to invent the telephone and all other communication devices also provided an even greater means of communication that's available to every one of us. No telephones, electricity, or computers are needed for this miraculous, wireless communication system that has access straight to the very throne of heaven—on the wings of a simple, whispered prayer. All you have to do is use it!

Lord, I need to pick up the prayer line to stay in touch. You seem so close when I can talk to You—You are always there to listen. Barbara Smith Morris

The Baptism

Repent, and be baptized every one of you in the name of Jesus Christ. Acts 2:38.

THE OCEAN WAVES ROLLED on unceasingly in their eternal order. The wide stretch of sand was scarred by the many footprints of people enjoying one more day at the beach on this early day of autumn. Abandoned sand castles and other sand builders' projects stretched down the length of the beach. The sun shone brightly in the blue sky and reflected on the water. It made one wish for summer to continue on and on. Groups of people up and down the long beach tried to absorb the sun as they faced another Maine winter. The more ambitious ones were walking in the waves now that the Atlantic had at last become a little warm.

It was September 21, and a momentous event was to occur. A group of about 30 people had gathered in one spot. Some had brought chairs, some were still dressed in their church clothes, and others had changed into casual clothes more suitable for the place. Little children, excited to see the marvels of sea and sand, were soon wet and dirty. But this was of no consequence to the group. And the regular beach patrons had no idea what was to transpire as they watched curiously from up and down the beach.

Soon the pastor called for attention. He expressed thanks to God for the three baptismal candidates. The three gave their testimonies, then the group pressed closer together. But the voices mixed with the roaring of the waves were often unheard.

It was low tide, and the pastor and the candidates had to walk farther and farther into the water for enough depth for immersion. The rest of the group kept trying to get nearer and were splashed by waves roaring onto shore, snatches of their singing wafting out to sea.

There were embraces and words of cheer as the whole group reassembled on the sand: "I'm so happy for you"; "I am glad you are here with us"; and "I love you." But the words that remained in my mind as I left this beautiful scene came from Barbara, one of the newly baptized: "I have come home."

Jesus has a home prepared for us in heaven, and we know He is coming back for us soon. Will we be there to say, "I have come home, Jesus"?

DESSA WEISZ HARDIN

The Autumn of Our Lives

And pray that your flight may not be in winter or on the Sabbath. Matt. 24:20, NKJV.

SEASON OF MISTS AND mellow fruitfulness, close bosom-friend of the maturing sun." Rarely do I contemplate the beauty of autumn (fall, as we commonly call it in North America) without recalling John Keats's poem "To Autumn." The imagery of warmth and beauty that his words conjure up in my mind has contributed to my love for the beauty of autumn.

Autumn in southern Ontario, Canada, brings crisp, cool nights that are followed by frosty mornings and warm, sunny days. The feel of warm woolen sweaters and blankets, the smell of wood burning in the fireplace, the delicious aroma of home baking, and the taste of hearty, homemade soup all add to the unique and distinct charm of the autumn season.

Now that I'm somewhat older, I've come to realize that autumn is also a season of sadness. Reference to the autumn of one's life indicates declining health, stamina, and vitality for some people. The vivid beauty of nature, painted in varying hues of red, gold, orange, brown, yellow, and green, belies the fact that autumn signals the end of summer and the coming of winter. The beautiful display of autumn colors precedes the falling of the leaves, which are blown away with the wind to rot and nourish next year's vegetation.

Autumn is also a time of reaping. In some places autumn is referred to as harvesttime. We celebrate by giving thanks for a bountiful harvest. Most significant, autumn is the preparation season. Grains and other harvested foods are stored for the long winter months to come. We prepare and secure our homes against the anticipated cold weather. Some of us temporarily migrate to warmer climates. We plan for our survival.

I've learned many lessons from my observation of this annual ritual. In order to survive the attacks of the evil one, we must be prepared. We do so through daily study of God's Word and through constant communion with Him. End-time events might prove to be far more difficult for many of us than the harshest winter we have experienced. The deception of the evil one will be compelling. Our best plan is to use the lessons of autumn to ensure a winter survival.

Dear God, please help me in autumn—or whatever season of life—to be ready to walk with You all the way. AVIS MAE RODNEY

Lightning

My voice shalt thou hear in the morning, O Lord; in the morning will I direct my prayer unto thee, and will look up. Ps. 5:3.

Z*ZZ-CRACKLE-BANG!* LIGHTNING zigzagged through the house. It was 3:30 Sabbath afternoon, and our daughter, Heidi, her husband, and our two grandchildren were sitting in their living room only two inches away from the lightning's path. Stunned, they realized what a close call they'd had. A walk to the back room proved that the computer was working, but the phone was dead. As they looked around, everything seemed OK.

Seconds later a neighbor pounded loudly on the door, shouting, "Get out! Your roof is on fire!" Shocked, because no smoke alarms had sounded, they ran outside in a pouring rain while watching their house burn. They were so thankful to God that they were safe.

"Since the roof burned first, alarms didn't beep right away," a firefighter later explained.

That same morning, as my husband and I had sat in church, I'd felt an overwhelming need to pray for our daughter and her family. They had recently had several difficult situations to deal with, and we knew they needed God's special help. Tears had run down my face as I'd prayed. *Silly,* I told myself. *We came to church to listen, not just to pray during the sermon. I can pray later.* "No," a voice had seemed to say. "Pray now; don't wait!" So I had, all through the worship hour.

That afternoon Heidi called to say their house had burned, but they were all OK. We had prayers of thanksgiving that they hadn't all been napping or that it hadn't happened in the middle of the night. And how grateful we were for an observant and caring neighbor. Then it struck me. I'd sat in church all morning with tears and prayers for them; I knew that was at least part of the reason they were unharmed.

How many times are we impressed to pray for someone or some situation and put away the thought, saying "I'll do it later," when later may be too late? Satan is out there waiting to cause trouble on every hand, and our prayers can rescue. How important it is to listen when the Spirit speaks.

Please, Lord, help us keep our hearts open to Your voice.

Darlene Ytredal Burgeson

Standing in Line

Be still before the Lord and wait patiently for him; do not fret when men succeed in their ways, when they carry out their wicked schemes. Ps. 37:7, NIV.

I WALKED THROUGH THE crowded mall and passed several long queues of people, lines to the cashiers, lines of people trying to cash in for fast-food purchases. Some people tapped their feet as they waited; others were obviously preoccupied. Some seemed annoyed that the person at the head of the line was taking too long to transact business, and emotions flared when a customer tried to break the line.

Parents chased after playing toddlers, who wanted more excitement—anything besides standing in a boring line. Some searched for a shorter line or moved to the line that seemed to be moving faster. Many couples separated, each standing in a different line, hoping that they would reach the cashier first. Cunning grins flashed in victory as the winner invited the loser to join him or her, and they cashed together. An elderly man fumbled as arthritic hands prevented him from separating the bills in his pocket, while an elderly woman tried to retrieve coins that were hiding in the crevasses of her purse.

As I waited my turn to pay for my own purchases, my heart was full of praise. I smiled contentedly and would have shouted out a song of praise if I had thought that it wouldn't be perceived as a bout of madness. The thought caused me to constrain my feelings openly, but inwardly I was singing at the top of my voice: "Thank You, God, for the opportunity that I had to boldly come to You in prayer." I didn't have to wait in a crowded line, nor did I have to depend on my spouse or anyone else to petition God on my behalf. I didn't even have to hurry through my petition so others could have time with God.

Thank You, gracious Lord, that I do not have to join a queue to thank You for loving me, for granting forgiveness, for extending to me a second chance when I make a mess of things. Today I can come boldly to Your throne. There is no one waiting ahead of me. There is no one waiting behind me, so I have no need to hurry my time with You. I can take my time and talk with You, knowing that our intimate moments are sacred. I can—and am—enjoying my private time with You.

GLORIA GREGORY

The Demanding Geese

Trust in the Lord with all your heart, and do not rely on your own insight. In all your ways acknowledge him, and he will make straight your paths. Prov. 3:5, 6, RSV.

I'M WRITING THIS STORY FROM F. D. Roosevelt State Park just outside of Columbus, Georgia, where my husband and I are on a 10-day vacation, camping in our motor home. We're parked by the lakefront and have a perfect view of the geese swimming in the water. Some people are canoeing on the lake, while others are fishing from the pier and at the water's edge. Some children are riding their bikes, and others are playing ball.

It's a beautiful Sabbath day with a gentle breeze blowing, light fluffy clouds drifting across the sky, and the temperature a balmy 76 degrees Fahrenheit. The scene is perfect. To the casual observer, life seems calm and peaceful out here. You'd never know that every day the animals of the park have to be on guard and must outsmart their predators just to stay alive.

While on a walk today we saw several large, fat geese being fed bread by kids and their parents. All summer long the geese are fed by people and become accustomed to getting their food the easy way. When the bread was gone, the geese turned their attention to a little boy of about 5 who was walking nearby. They started following him, honking to get his attention. He turned and saw them, panicked, and ran. The faster he ran, the faster they ran after him, honking and flapping their wings, demanding to be fed. The poor child was terrified and ran into his mother's arms, screaming and crying. My heart went out to him. I remembered when one of my sons was chased by geese at a petting zoo in Tennessee when he was 5 and how scared he had been.

This scene of the demanding geese reminds me of how we humans act so often with God. When we don't get things our way, or get the answers we want from God, we complain, rebel, and pitch a fit. Some even reject God completely when they don't get their way or don't understand why things happen as they do.

Lord, help us not to act like the demanding geese, insisting on our own way. Help us to trust You, to yield to You, and to allow You to be in charge of our lives.

CELIA MEJIA CRUZ

Channeling Love

When you pass through the waters, I will be with you. . . . . You are precious and honored in my sight, and . . . I love you. Isa. 43:2-4, NIV.

AS A CHAPLAIN IN TRAINING, I was about to step into a patient's room when a woman huffed past me, suitcase in tow. Seeing nurses sprint down the hall after her, I realized that this woman must be trying to leave AMA (against medical advice).

A short while later, as I was visiting with her roommate, Alice* wheeled her suitcase in and plopped on the bed by the window. I was glad they had persuaded her to stay, but wow! What could I say to connect with her? I thought, *She's hurting, Lord. Help me to be Your channel of love.*

"Hello," I began. "My name is Heide, and I'm the chaplain on this unit. I'm sorry things are not going very well for you today." That was all the opener Alice needed; soon we were thick in conversation. Out spilled her fears and anxieties about treatment.

Eventually she confided in me that God had forsaken her. She used to be very active in church and had felt God close. But then the burden of caring for her elderly mother, as well as managing her own diabetes and multiple personalities, caused her to drift away from church. "I left Him, and then He left me," she said.

Gently I spoke to her. "Alice, God loves you so much. Even when you slip away from Him, He still loves you. He understands what you've been struggling with. He knows it's hard, and He's by your side, giving you encouragement, ready to help. He's proud of your decision to keep going when you've wanted to give up on life so many times. It may feel as if He's left you, but He hasn't. He loves you way too much to leave you alone."

As joy began to slowly seep into her soul Alice said, "God must love me, because He sent you." I leaned over and put my arm around her shoulders as I prayed aloud for her. She rested her head on my arm and whispered, "No one has hugged me in such a long time."

Afterward, my heart was just bursting in praise to God for allowing me to be His channel of love in such a tangible way. How He wants to use all of us to wrap people in His incredible love! HEIDE FORD

---

* Not her real name.

Cooking by the Book

And the eye cannot say unto the hand, I have no need of thee: nor again the head to the feet, I have no need of you. 1 Cor. 12:21.

FOR MORE THAN 13 years it has been my desire—and an adventure—to collect vegan cookbooks and search out new vegan recipes. Unfortunately for my family, I was not born with an abundance of culinary skills. So I classify myself as "domestically challenged."

At a cooking school I tasted a recipe they had developed called Cheesy Cheeseless Hash Browns. It seemed simple enough; I planned to re-create this for my family someday. When that day came, I searched for my food processor, which hadn't been seen since our last move. Twelve cups of shredded potatoes was daunting, but determination prevailed. I shredded, and then I shredded some more. Finally I could add the rest of the ingredients.

The dish smelled great as it cooked. I couldn't wait to share it with my family, and I was even more eager to eat it myself. Eventually dinner was served. The family began to eat. My oldest child spoke first. "Yuck! I don't like it! It tastes funny!" My husband added, "This is pretty bad; what is it?" I could hear a strange noise as he spoke and turned toward my youngest child. She was spitting it out and gagging. Since I hadn't tasted the hash browns yet, I decided to see what the fuss was about. It took only one bite. It was horrible, and I had no idea why.

As I made a quick replacement meal I kept going over the recipe in my head. Then I realized that I hadn't put in salt. It was amazing how a little thing could make a big difference.

Since I hate to waste anything, I ate those hash browns anyway. The cheesy cheeseless creation filled an 11" x 13" pan, so I had enough to eat by myself daily for more than a week. And every single day I was reminded of how important each of us is in God's church. Even with all the work we put into church as individuals, we need other people to be complete. First Corinthians 12:21, 22 says, "And the eye cannot say unto the hand, I have no need of thee: nor again the head to the feet, I have no need of you. Nay, much more those members of the body, which seem to be more feeble, are necessary."

Lord, I pray that I see people and their spiritual gifts as You do. My judgment can be skewed by my own feelings and agenda. Help me to see people in a way that is beyond what the world sees. Thank You for seeing me in that way.

MARY J. WAGONER ANGELIN

I Know Who Holds My Hand

You will keep [her] in perfect peace, whose mind is stayed on You, because [she] trusts in You. Isa. 26:3, NKJV.

RECENTLY I UNDERWENT SOME elective eye surgery. Even though I had chosen to have it done, I was still shaking inside as I entered the surgery center. A pleasant woman, who introduced herself as Jennifer, greeted me and took me to the surgery prep area. She bustled about getting me ready while I watched other surgical candidates go, one by one, into the operating room.

Suddenly it was my turn, and on unsteady legs I followed the nurse into the next room. It was quite cold in there, so when I lay down on the operating table a blanket was spread over me. That helped to warm me, but in spite of the medication they had given to relax me, I was still apprehensive.

Just after the operation began, I felt the blanket lifted on one side and a hand slipped into mine. Immediately I began to feel more relaxed. Just the feel of that unseen hand took some of the fear away. I was not alone, even though I couldn't see anyone.

The operation went quickly and smoothly, and soon I was back in the recovery room. It wasn't until I was on the way home that I remembered the hand holding mine in the operating room. I still don't know whose it was, but I do know that it made the operation much more tolerable.

Every day I face things, seen and unseen, things that are frightening. This sinful world has become one that's filled with events that can paralyze us with fear. If we were to read the newspapers and listen to the news media each day and hear all the horrible things that happen to innocent people, we would never want to take a step outside of our front doors. But most of us have to venture into the world each day. Fortunately, I know who's holding my hand. I may not be able to see Him, but I know He's there, always with me, always guiding me, always protecting me. I can't be afraid, because I know He's there.

Thank You, heavenly Father, for holding my hand. Thank You for Your loving protection and care over my family. I know that nothing can happen to me today that is not in Your plan.

FAUNA RANKIN DEAN

September 29

Threefold Compassion

He shall cover thee with his feathers, and under his wings shalt thou trust. Ps. 91:4.

THE DEAFENING SOUND OF aircraft roared into our consciousness on that late September morning. My husband, our two small daughters, and I had stepped outside to enjoy the clean fresh air when three planes in close formation thundered low over our heads. At that moment the wing of one plane tilted the wing of the plane beside it, and we watched in disbelief as this suddenly out-of-balance plane began to fall from the sky. It shimmered like a shining silver cross, turning and plunging in the bright morning sun.

Moments later a thick black column of smoke billowed upward from a field just beyond our home. We scrambled into our car and raced to the scene and were the first to arrive at the cornfield, now sheared smooth by the impact. A lone body lay lifeless on the ground. The tail fin of a plane lay in the distance, and wreckage and debris were scattered everywhere. A folded white handkerchief lay at our feet.

We watched as one of the planes turned back, presumably to the airport to report the tragedy it had witnessed. The other continued to circle and hover over the downed plane and its victim. Never had we felt so utterly helpless.

The evening paper carried the story that seemed somehow to be our story as well. It was still our story when, three months later on New Year's morning, the downed pilot's son was born to his surviving spouse. I know this firsthand, because my daughter was born just a few doors down the hall in that hospital the same morning.

As I pondered this incident my thoughts turned to our heavenly triune God. Unlike the pilot who lost his life because of pilot error, our Savior, who knew no sin, came to earth and died because of our sin. The Father's love for us is as deep and overwhelming as was His grief as He watched His dying Son. The Holy Spirit hovers over us in compassion and assurance. As I think of this incredible threefold love that refused to give us up, it has forever banished my doubts. If human beings can express their compassion as did these other pilots for one of their own, how much more does our trinity God care for us, His children! Gratefully I rest in the assurance of His promise: "I will never leave thee, nor forsake thee" (Heb. 13:5).

LORRAINE HUDGINS-HIRSCH

The Three H's

But when he asks, he must believe and not doubt, because he who doubts is like a wave of the sea, blown and tossed by the wind. James 1:6, NIV.

SEPTEMBER IN FLORIDA CAN be dangerous. I have survived 24 Septembers in southeast Florida, so I feel that I can take a little liberty in referring to this month as the three H's—heat, humidity, and hurricanes. Seeking a safe, cool haven is paramount for all should a hurricane come our way. The local newspaper publishes instructions on boarding up windows, locations of shelters, and evacuation maps for available highways. The city leaders are determined that not any should perish.

I, however, have more of a problem with September's heat and humidity. When these two H's press in, my usually easygoing temperament flies out the window. Disappointments, spiritual and otherwise, overwhelm me. I feel a desperate need for a safe haven. The Jupiter Inlet with its famous lighthouse provides that perfect retreat for me. At sundown I escape to sit on its shores. As I look out over the vast Atlantic, I marvel at the large cargo ships slowly sailing to faraway ports. They soon become dots on the horizon. Small commercial fishing boats now catch my attention. They are coming home filled with a successful day's catch. I silently cheer them on as they approach the entrance to the inlet.

The seasoned sailors, both on cargo ships and fishing boats, trust the lighthouse. Its beacon stretches out and slowly sweeps the water. Ships in the shipping lanes see the light from afar and know they are on course. Small boats follow the light to safe harbors. I contemplate the relief that fishers must feel as they step out on dry land with their day's labor intact.

I'm drawn to the squealing sounds of children playing in the surf. Lashing waves lick at little legs. The lighthouse beacon grows brighter as the setting sun dips lower and lower in the west. Mothers call out. Tiny feet run, kicking sand all the way, carrying the children right into loving arms.

In my reverie I am now, more than ever, aware that my Creator and Savior never ceases extending His beacon to me. I ask Him for peace. I look up and fix my course. His saving light leads me. The heat, humidity, and my doubts are forgotten. Even with its reputation, September has been good to me. It takes me to that safe haven I love the best—my Father God.

MARIANNE TOTH BAYLESS

October 1

Ants in My Towel

Let all bitterness, and wrath, and anger, and clamour, and evil speaking, be put away from you, with all malice. Eph. 4:31.

RITA SAT ACROSS THE desk from me, tears rolling down her cheeks. "She's done it again," she said. "She just makes me so mad!" One by one Rita listed the many little things her neighbor had done. Each time she repeated one of these grievances new tears flowed. As I listened I thought about the day I found ants in my towel.

I'd just had my morning shower and was feeling refreshed. I reached for the towel and began to dry myself vigorously to get the blood circulating. Suddenly I felt tiny pricks of pain all over my body. I looked down and found tiny red ants crawling all over me.

I'd been having a battle with these small insects for some time. During the rainy season they move into my house. I'd already chased them out of three cupboards, my clothes closet, and even my bed. Now, overnight, they had found a lovely new place for their nest. When disturbed by my rubbing, they fought back, and it hurt. You can be sure I didn't play host to those ants for very long. I sprayed the bathroom and got a new towel.

How stupid it would have been for me to let the ants stay on my body, biting me whenever they wished, and allowing myself to hurt each time they did. Yet this was exactly what Rita was doing with the little annoyances of her neighbor. Rita held close each thing her neighbor had said, each thoughtless thing her neighbor had done. She kept stirring them up, and each time she recalled these many grudges she had against her neighbor, it hurt all over again. I know, for I've done the same thing, nursing my hurts, refusing to give them up, refusing to forgive, until I realized that by harboring these little "ants" of bitterness I was only hurting myself.

I shared with Rita how I, in a similar situation, had decided to get rid of all the hurts by giving them to Jesus. I suggested that forgiveness is like a bug spray that will rid our hearts of the hurts that come our way. By choosing to forgive and treat the offender as though they had never hurt me, I was choosing to do as Jesus has done for me so many times—treating me with love and compassion I do not deserve. DOROTHY EATON WATTS

The Path That Leads to Paradise

You have shown me the pathway to life. In your presence is fullness of joy, and at your right hand are pleasures forever. Ps. 16:11, Clear Word.

A BUSY HIGHWAY SEPARATES ME from my desired destination. When the traffic clears momentarily, I quickly cross over and proceed until I turn right onto the path I wish to take. A gentle breeze, a cloudless sky, and the warm temperature create a delightful evening for walking. *What a perfect evening to be in the Florida Keys,* I think. *All is well in my world.*

From a distance the aquamarine water of the Gulf of Mexico beckons me to drink in its beauty. Palatial homes line one side of the path. A wrought-iron fence with a locked gate surrounds one of them. A low brick wall shows off another one. Beautiful blooming foliage flanks the opposite side of the walkway. A washout in the path causes a slight detour.

I walk for some distance before returning the way I had come. When I reach the place where I had entered the path, it amazes me to see it continue in the opposite direction. The other times when I had walked this path I'd always thought I had entered at its beginning.

Each of us faces the pathway of life. It really didn't matter which direction I chose for my walk, but the choices we make on the walk of life make a tremendous difference. Each direction yields its own consequences. Our choices reflect where our loyalty belongs. Along life's path are many sights and sounds that either delight or repel the senses. Experiences of life give us precious memories or leave us full of guilt and shame. Obstacles often line the way, serving both as protectors and challengers. Preconceived ideas may lead to a closed mind, hindering progress along our spiritual walk.

I took my evening walk alone. The Christian walk, however, always offers a companion. When invited, He walks by our side every step of the way. When we choose to include Him, the walk takes on a whole new dimension—the joys are greater, the pleasures are deeper. Furthermore, the path leads to Paradise.

MARIAN M. HART

Broken

In sudden fear I had cried out, "I have been cut off from the Lord!" But you heard my cry for mercy and answered my call for help. Ps. 31:22, NLT.

MY COMPUTER WAS SICK, very sick. I am no technocrat, but even I could sense something was wrong. I even wondered if writing by hand would be faster. Some of my friends, experts in the field, came to check out the situation. They suggested deleting unnecessary programs, leaving the CPU on, getting rid of cookies, and many other possible solutions, but nothing helped.

We tried to call for telephone support, but my warranty had expired two months earlier. The troubleshooters were willing to help, but there was a price. I waffled. And then the screen went black. It had frozen. Suddenly $49.95 was a very good price if I could get help quickly.

"You probably have a virus," the technician offered when Dorett and I took the machine into the shop. "We'll check it out and call you in a few days."

The week that it took for my computer to be fixed I was at a loss. The giving and receiving of early-morning greetings from transatlantic friends was gone. So was the reminder of appointments I had made and bills that had to be paid. The scraps of paper on which I scribbled "inspirational brain waves" were a poor substitute for my computer files. Worst of all, the ready-reference guide to research all sorts of phenomena was no longer available.

But our God is infinitely creative. He used that week to bring me closer to Him. As I read the contemporary New Living Translation version of the book of Psalms, my Father showed me some startling similarities between my use of the computer and the joy of relying on Him.

I use today's text when my screen freezes up. When I become as distracted as my computer, He shows me Psalm 101:3: "I refuse to look at anything vile and vulgar." If I forget my spiritual password, I am reminded: "With all my heart I will praise you, O Lord my God. I will give glory to your name forever" (Ps. 86:12). When I fear attack by viruses, "I trust in the Lord for protection" (Ps. 11:1). Psalm 102:27 reminds me to leave my spiritual computer on because "You are always the same; your years never end." But the most comforting thought comes from my Maker's lifetime warranty: "You will show me the way of life, granting me the joy of your presence and the pleasures of living with you forever" (Ps. 16:11).

GLENDA-MAE GREENE

God Is Almighty

You are the God who performs miracles; you display your power among the peoples. Ps. 77:14, NIV.

MY FIANCÉ AND I were on a biking trip through Austria with a tandem. It was our third day, the weather was beautiful, and by lunchtime we had covered more than half the distance to reach our next destination. So far, everything had gone well. We'd had no problems with the bike; however, when we returned from the restaurant, we noticed that our back tire had lost air. The next 20 miles (30 kilometers) were extremely hard to ride, and we reached the youth hostel completely exhausted. Fortunately, we easily found a place to buy a new tire and inner tube, and my fiancé was able to repair the bike quickly.

I was so happy to finally be in the youth hostel room and to get to sleep. There were two other persons staying in the same room, but they went out because there was a party going on in the village. I slept until they returned at midnight. Five minutes later they were snoring in a duet. I'd never heard somebody snoring as loudly as they did and prayed that God would help them to stop and grant me a healthy sleep. But nothing happened. I couldn't fall asleep, and after two more hours I was really desperate. I was so tired—I needed to rest in order to be able to continue our tour the next day. I finally got up, thought about sleeping outside, gave up that idea, and went into the bathroom and prayed with all my heart: *Lord, You know my situation. Please do something! Please help me! Either make them stop snoring or close my ears. I don't know what to do, but You are able to help. Thank You for caring for me.* Then I returned to my room.

When I opened the door to the bedroom, the noise stopped immediately. I was really amazed. In spite of trust in God, after two sleepless hours and the prayer I had said earlier, I didn't expect something like this to happen. I don't know which solution God chose, but what He did for me during that night impressed me a lot. God is almighty; He is ready to help His children at any time. I had never experienced God in such a way before.

I praise You, the God who performs miracles. I ask that You do miracles in our lives today so that Your power may continue to be displayed among the people near and dear to each of us.

HEIKE EULITZ

October 5

The Money Miracle

But seek first his kingdom and his righteousness, and all these things will be given to you as well. Matt. 6:33, NIV.

I WAS EXHAUSTED. I WAS trying to hold down two part-time jobs and needed to do some study as well. I was going to have to give up one of my jobs. I had an enjoyable job in the local church conference office and a very stressful job (which paid twice as much) as the head occupational therapist in a rehabilitation center.

Then my study arrangements suddenly changed, and the stressful job became impossible to maintain. When I asked God how we were ever going to manage financially, He seemed to whisper to me that I needn't worry, that He would find new ways for me to write for Him, something I've always loved doing. So I decided not to work full-time in the conference office but to take the risk of spending one day at home writing.

Over the few months since I gave up my well-paying job we have seen God work many miracles. Within a few days I had a big writing contract. Then the month before that contract finished, I was asked to write a book. Then another book offer came! But when you write a book, it can be years before you see any money, and I wondered how God would provide for us while we waited. Then we discovered that we'd been paying too much tax for the previous two years! The Inland Revenue sent us several big checks that we hadn't been expecting.

More money came from another unexpected source when the water in a spa pool I had visited was found to be contaminated with bacteria. I was ill for a few days and thought I might have gotten only a free visit as compensation, but instead I was sent another large check. It seemed as though God was having fun with thinking of new ways to surprise us with His amazing provision. We'd been praying for a car for years, and suddenly we were able to buy the one we needed.

Sometimes things look so impossible to us, but they're not for God. When we take a step of faith, He's always right there, doing something amazing. We've never missed the money from my occupational therapy job. And, come to think of it, wherever we've worked, however much we've earned, we've always had just enough to make ends meet. What more could we want?

KAREN HOLFORD

Mushrooms for Ray

Instead of the thorn shall come up the fir tree, and instead of the brier shall come up the myrtle tree: and it shall be to the Lord for a name, for an everlasting sign that shall not be cut off. Isa. 55:13.

MY GREAT-NIECE RAY HAS been going through a lot lately. She had been rejected by her mother, as well as other people in her life. This has brought on depression and paranoia. She and her 5-year-old son now live with her grandmother in Georgia. About a year ago she gave her life to the Lord and was baptized. Satan has not let up on her since that time.

Ray is a very talented and smart young woman, and her passion is doing hair. She'd been unemployed for a long time and was becoming discouraged. She decided to put the Lord to a test and prove Him. She asked the Lord one night to protect and bless her grandmother's home.

The next morning there were mushrooms in the front yard. Her grandmother's front yard was the only one in the whole complex that had mushrooms growing. She concluded that those mushrooms were an answer to her prayers and proceeded to count them—33 mushrooms on the lawn in front of the living room window.

Not knowing what her granddaughter had prayed for, the grandmother plucked up the mushrooms because she didn't want her great-grandson to get hold of them. That day Ray received three offers to work in a beauty salon. When she returned home from one of the interviews, she saw that the mushrooms were gone, so she asked her grandmother about them. When her grandmother told Ray what had happened, Ray was upset and explained to her grandmother that those mushrooms were a sign that God had answered her prayer.

Her grandmother told her that if those mushrooms were for blessings and protection of the house, then the next morning there would be more mushrooms popping up. And the very next morning there were again mushrooms on her front lawn; they are still there. If they disappear, it is because God wants them to and He thinks that Ray doesn't need reassurance any longer that He hears and answers prayers.

God answers prayers in a number of ways: through His Word, or through an individual, or through nature. He answers prayers in ways that someone like my niece can understand.

OLIVE LEWIS

A Child's Faith

Before they call, I will answer; and while they are yet speaking, I will hear. Isa. 65:24.

IT WAS 1980 WHEN we moved to Moradabad, a well-known city in India recognized as the City of Brass Wares. My husband was asked to take leadership responsibility for a church-related school. It was nice to be with the students, and I liked teaching. We have two boys who at that time were too small to go to school, but in the coming year the older one started classes.

One day about a year later he came home complaining of a stomachache. We gave him some medicine, but by the evening he was burning with fever. We took him to our family doctor, who diagnosed him and prescribed some medicines. The treatment was for five days. Two days passed, and the fever remained the same. In the evening we again took him to the doctor, who changed the medicine. When we came home, we all knelt and prayed. After prayer we gave our son the new medicine. A half hour later he started crying, "Dad, I'm dying; please hold me tight." My husband held him tightly to his chest, but our son kept murmuring that he was going to die. All of a sudden he asked us to pray to Jesus. We immediately pleaded that God would spare his life.

Sometime during the night he suddenly wanted milk. Too weak to say anything, he just pointed in the direction of it. That very moment we thanked God for restoring the life of our son. I recalled the verse "But my God shall supply all your need according to his riches in glory by Christ Jesus" (Phil. 4:19). Surely the Lord did take care of our need and the need of our dear son. He gave him strength and granted him mercy.

Today our son has completed college and is preparing for further studies. God has always been merciful to my family. Whenever we cried for help, He hearkened to our voice and blessed us according to our needs.

Thank You for being our living God, for guiding us in Your path like a beacon in the dark night. Thank You for giving us wisdom, strength, and knowledge to do our best in all endeavors. Thank You, Lord, for Your love and concern shown to our family. Grant us Your mercy so that we may ever remain faithful till the end. TARAMANI NOREEN SINGH

More Than I Asked

Now unto him that is able to do exceeding abundantly above all that we ask or think, according to the power that worketh in us. Eph. 3:20.

I'VE BEEN MONITORED FOR my low platelet count for about 15 years. The doctors know of no reason for the low count and have no recommendations for improving it. As long as I don't bruise myself or hemorrhage, no prescription will be necessary.

I'm getting used to the regular platelet report being "around 50." Anything below that makes me nervous because I know I will have to go on prednisone, which is a strong drug with serious, unwanted side effects. Within 24 hours of giving a blood sample, I usually get a call from my doctor, telling me the "low stable" news. Instead, one afternoon the dreaded report arrived from my doctor's office. My platelet count was down to eight, and I needed to check in immediately to the outpatient ward of the hospital for another blood sample and a prescription.

"Oh, no!" I said. "I don't like that."

"I know," the nurse soothed. "But this is serious. You have no choice. The doctor on call will give you a prescription."

As I donned my coat and grabbed the car keys I prayed that the prescription would be a low dosage for a short time. I prayed that my body would respond quickly to the medication and that I could go on with a normal life.

Since I wasn't an emergency patient, no one was rushing around to take care of me. That gave me time to do more praying and try to keep calm. I told myself that my problem could be fixed in a few short weeks with medication. This wasn't like a terminal illness, after all.

I waited a long afternoon at the hospital until the blood count was done. Finally the doctor called me in. I held my breath, anticipating his verdict.

"I don't think we have a problem here," he began. "Your count is 52. Either yesterday's count was an error, or this is a better sample."

I released the trapped air in my lungs and sent a prompt prayer to heaven. I never thought of asking God to make this blood count higher. Surely He is a great God, capable of doing "exceeding abundantly above all that we ask or think."

EDITH FITCH

Marie

May the Lord repay you for what you have done. May you be richly rewarded by the Lord, the God of Israel, under whose wings you have come to take refuge. Ruth 2:12, NIV.

IT WAS AN UNLIKELY SCENARIO that our paths would have ever crossed. But God is like that, isn't He? She was an elderly woman who had grown up on a farm near Hutchinson, Kansas. Marie came to Nebraska to study nursing, becoming the first clinical specialist in the state. She outlived three husbands and spent much of her life as a single mother raising three children. At 71, she lived in low-income housing, had arthritis, and was confined to a wheelchair.

At the time I was a woman in her 40s, a city-raised, stay-at-home mom of four for 14 years.

It was just a simple request: "Could someone read the Bible to me?" I had no way of knowing that at that moment Marie lay in a hospital bed with little chance of life. She had fallen, breaking the femur bone above the knee that had just been replaced one month before. With a bleeding disorder, she had had 17 pints of blood pumped into her; yet her life still hung by a thread.

In church that Sabbath I heard her simple request. God was tugging at my heart. "Yes," I said to myself, "I can do that." I had little knowledge of who she was; however, driving to the hospital and reading the Bible to her was something I could do.

She told me precisely what she wanted to hear. I read out of the book of Ephesians. We spent only a few quiet moments together before her daughter arrived. There was something in those sacred moments of sharing God's Word that bonded us together. The power of the Holy Spirit created a kindred spirit, similar to the way Ruth and Naomi were connected.

By God's grace, Marie lived. "God kept you alive for me," I told her. During the next five years I was blessed with her friendship. She was a powerhouse for the Lord, announcing God's power everywhere she went.

In May, after much pain and many hospital stays, she was laid to rest. I will always remember her simple request. For if I had chosen not to respond to the Holy Spirit's nudging, I would have never experienced the many, many blessings God intended for me through Marie. KAREN PHILLIPS

God Is Here to Stay

I am the Lord, your God. . . . I am with you. Isa. 43:3-5, NIV.

SO, DO YOU KNOW Neetjee?" Melissa slipped in through the open patio door.

"Do you mean Nietzsche?" I asked. "How old do you think I am, anyway?"

"Do you know him?" she persisted, ignoring my attempt at humor.

"I know of him, but no, I don't know him personally!"

"Dirk's uncle said that according to Neetjee, God is dead." Melissa pronounced the last three words very deliberately. "What do you suppose he meant?"

"I don't know for sure," I replied, "although I'd guess it was his way of questioning whether God had ever really lived at all."

Once again our dinner conversation was cut out for us. There was a lot to discuss, including our inability to see God physically in the same way we see each other. "For me, it all boils down to experiential faith," I said finally. "That, and the way in which the brain functions."

"How so?" Melissa's eyes looked at me very steadily.

Groaning inwardly, I wondered why I always had to explain every statement I made. Groping for a suitable metaphor, I asked, "How do you know that when you take a deep breath your lungs will fill with air? You can't see it."

"Experience!" Melissa replied instantly. "Because I've done it for years and years."

"Same thing," I said. "I've had a personal connection with God for years and years. No other friendship gives me the same results."

"So I guess God is here to stay—at least in our lives," Melissa said matter-of-factly.

"Actually," I remarked, "that's what a couple scientists who've been researching neurobiology have concluded. They wrote about it in their book *Why God Won't Go Away.*"

"Great! Next time I see him I'll ask Dirk to tell his uncle," Melissa announced as she disappeared to the patio.

"Thank You for being here to stay," I said aloud.

"You talking to me?" Melissa asked, breezing back into the room.

I shook my head. "Just chatting with God."

ARLENE TAYLOR

October 11

Life Was Good

And the cares of this world, and the deceitfulness of riches, and the lusts of other things entering in, choke the word, and it becometh unfruitful. Mark 4:19.

SOME YEARS AGO I was often depressed without knowing why. But I had all the "goodies" in my life—dancing, gambling, parties, laughter, and fun. I collected and read all the series of the juiciest science fiction, whose characters lived phony lives just like mine. I had a good job, I was not in debt, and I had a car to go wherever I wanted and enough clothing and jewelry to get me through. I was in reasonable health, my husband was good to me, and life was good.

One day I realized I hadn't been feeling as chipper and optimistic as usual. I managed to put on a phony cheerfulness when anyone was near. Even my garden and flowers began to hold no meaning. And I went through the motions of entertaining, partying, and living. *What is all this?* I often thought.

One morning I awoke feeling as though the world was going to end—literally. *Perhaps a walk will make me feel better,* I thought to myself.

As I turned down the little dirt lane by my house an overwhelming depression came upon me. I looked at a little wildflower—never would there be any more beauty. Then I looked up at the trees with their lovely shades of green leaves, and I crumpled by the roadside, tears flowing like a waterfall as I said goodbye to them all.

Struggling to regain my composure, I tried to look through my tears at the road ahead, but there was no road beyond five feet in front of me. It was all closed in with scraggly brush, fog, and darkness. This frightened me, and, jumping to my feet, I turned around and hurried home.

The next year was much the same. Then in 1995 I went to camp meeting—and my whole life changed. The Lord reached deep inside of my heart and healed me in an instant. Since then my life has had meaning and purpose.

Following the vices of the world and satisfying the lusts and desires of the flesh do not bring lasting satisfaction. If you are suffering from depression, anxiety, or sadness, perhaps you are missing God. You may laugh and think that this will not happen to you. God has made a tremendous difference in my life. I pray that He is making a difference in your life as well.

VIDELLA MCCLELLAN

Somra

Inasmuch as you did it to one of the least of these My brethren, you did it to Me. Matt 25:40, NKJV.

DURING OFFICE WORSHIP ONE morning at Karmatar someone mentioned that a man was lying in the gutter near the gate of the mission compound. As soon as worship was over we rushed out to see him. We looked at him closely, but no one dared touch him. From his waist down he was swollen. He was caked with mud, and ticks were crawling under his arm. To our nonmedical eyes his case was hopeless!

Two other women and I decided we couldn't just forget him—we weren't going to stand helplessly by. We decided to do what we could to relieve his suffering. We asked the gardener and the guard to help carry him into a room and bathe him. The poor man almost died of exhaustion. His heart was racing. When it slowed down, we placed him on a bed as we took the ticks off his body. We then asked the guard to call the doctor. We learned that the man's name was Somra. Because he was ill and not able to work, his relatives had driven him out of the house.

While waiting for the doctor, we fed him a soft-boiled egg. When the doctor arrived, he said that this was the worst food we could have given him, for it was obvious the man had nephritis, and the albumin in the white of the egg would probably kill him. He gave Somra an injection and prescribed some pills.

The three of us stood by his bed and asked God to heal Somra. We took turns caring for him and feeding him during the day and asked the guard to check on him during the night. In spite of our continued prayers, we felt that Somra was going to die. But God surprised us and the physician by a miraculous healing. Somra was thankful and happy, but he was lonely. He asked us to get him a wife. His relatives found a young woman who was willing to marry him, the village authorities restored his property, and we built him a small hut. Somra continued to work for the mission as a gardener.

In spite of our best efforts, Somra simply couldn't comprehend the simple story of Jesus and His love, even though he attended church services faithfully. Our loving God who healed his body will one day heal his mind. Pray today for those like Somra, who need to know a loving Savior.

BIROL CHARLOTTE CHRISTO

Comfort in Time of Distress

Blessed are those who mourn, for they will be comforted. Matt. 5:4, NIV.

ONE SUNDAY MORNING I was busy doing my chores when I heard a rap on the front door. It was a friend's son bearing a message from his mother, who was not feeling well and desperately wanted to see me.

I walked the short distance to her house to see the reason for this unusual request. To my surprise, I found her in agony. For a moment I thought that death was about to take a loved one. She then related her story. I was shocked to learn how her dreams had been shattered just a few weeks before fulfillment. She was devastated.

I tried to encourage and comfort her, but to no avail. I helplessly watched her writhe in pain as I pondered how to relieve her trauma.

After a while I decided to pray for her. We closed our eyes, and I began praying. Although I've forgotten most of the prayer, I remember saying, "Lord, please put her to sleep." When I was through, I noticed that she was really sleeping. I got frightened, not knowing exactly if she was just sleeping or if something else was happening. I decided that despite my fears I would not awaken her. Soon I noticed that her behavior didn't seem life-threatening. So I waited as she slept for about 20 minutes. When she awakened, she opened her eyes and said, "I heard when you said, 'Lord, put her to sleep,' and then I didn't hear anything else." After that peaceful rest, she was calmer and more able to cope for the rest of the day.

My mind turned to a favorite hymn. I had just seen that God does care about us, and He is the only one who can meet our deepest needs. Sometimes He answers instantly, and sometimes His answers take longer, but He hears and He cares.

"Does Jesus care when my heart is pained too deeply for
mirth and song;
As the burdens press, and the cares distress, and the
way grows weary and long?
O yes, He cares—I know He cares! His heart is
touched with my grief;
When the days are weary, the long nights dreary, I
know my Savior cares."—Frank E. Graeff.

Bula Rose Haughton Thompson

Happy as a Kitten

Again, if two lie down together, they will keep warm; but how can one be warm alone? Eccl. 4:11, NKJV.

THE GROUND WAS WHITE with the first frost of the season. Entering the barn, I saw four little kittens cuddled into their nest. Each was drawing warmth from the others, and with their soft coats of fur they were very comfortable. Upon awakening they began to play and enjoy the activity of kittens. Their mother sat to the side quietly watching their antics.

When my daughter-in-law poured a little milk into their dish and filled other dishes with commercial cat food, they quickly lapped up the milk. The delicious warm liquid coursed through their digestive system. Little teeth made crunching noises as they chewed the dry food. Appetites satisfied, they again turned to play for a while, then went back to their nest to curl up and snooze. I thought of the phrase "happy as a kitten."

We humans need the warmth we gain from close association with friends and family. We may not always be physically close, but emotionally we can draw comfort and peace from our relationships. The knowledge that we have a treasured friend with whom we can share goals and ideas gives us an inward warm glow. Knowing they will always be ready to support and love us means so very much.

I'm thankful for family members who, like the kittens, have chosen to cuddle close and create a warm nest. The blessings have continued through the years. Our children have loved to return through their growing-up years to the place where they drew warmth and love. The laughter and joy that is present as we play together brings smiles and an inner joy.

Loneliness leaves us feeling sad and cold. Gathering together and sharing our joys, sorrows, and love causes loneliness to vanish. Like the cute little kittens cuddled in their nest, we gain warmth when we choose to remain close with those we love.

Dear God, today help me to remember that You are the true source of the warmth I need. You keep me warm in spite of the chill of the frost that Satan sends my way. Staying close to You makes me "happy as a kitten." Thank You for Your assurance. EVELYN GLASS

What Is a Christian?

For I think that God hath set forth us the apostles last, as it were appointed to death: for we are made a spectacle unto the world, and to angels, and to men. 1 Cor. 4:9.

THE STRANGER BEGAN HER long-distance business call by telling me about rivals who had almost ruined her company. "I'm a Christian, but those ——— people cheated, lied, and stole. They ruined me. The ——— wretches drove me almost to bankruptcy."

Her foul language shocked me, but as she claimed to be a Christian, I tried to calm her and switch the conversation to forgiveness. "The Bible says . . . " I ventured.

She'd never read it.

"Do you pray?" I asked.

"Not since childhood," she replied.

"What church do you attend?" I tried again.

"If I go anywhere, it's the community church. I don't hold with this New Age stuff or those people who go from door to door."

The conversation continued as I tried to point her to Christ, who loved her and could solve all her problems. She seemed unmoved. After I replaced the receiver, I wondered how this woman could call herself a Christian when her tongue, lifestyle, and vindictive attitude belied her claim.

Christianity is a responsibility. It's not something that can be put on and off like a coat or left behind when we go places where no one knows us or when we speak on the phone to a stranger.

In 1 Corinthians 4:9 Paul tells us that as an apostle he was a "spectacle," on display before people and angels. How much greater spectacle are we who live in this permissive society immediately before the second coming of Jesus.

People expect so much of those who claim the name of Christ. They might not worry what kind of language they hear from others, but they are quick to notice if a Christian swears. They see a colleague pilfer from the boss and acknowledge it with a knowing wink, but if that person claimed to be a Christian, they would brand him or her as a hypocrite. Most people don't keep God's commandments themselves, but they notice if a professing Christian does wrong.

Dear Lord, help us never to disgrace the precious name we bear by acting or speaking in an un-Christlike manner. Amen. GOLDIE DOWN

Blessed Amnesia

Blessed be the Lord, who hath not given us as a prey to their teeth. Our soul is escaped as a bird out of the snare of the fowlers: the snare is broken, and we are escaped. Our help is in the name of the Lord, who made heaven and earth. Ps. 124:6-8.

THESE ARE NOT OUR trees! Where are we? Have we missed our road?" These words interrupted our pleasant conversation as we made our way home from a fact-finding excursion to plan for an upcoming retreat. A U-turn revealed we had been on the wrong road for about three miles (five kilometers). We joked for a while about the driver's "senior moment" but soon regained the pace of our conversation. It wasn't long before we again noticed that there was something strange about our road. Were we heading in another wrong direction? Someone insisted we were on the right road this time because the sea was to our right. But was it?

About three miles later we identified a landmark that removed all doubt—we were going the wrong direction. The sea was definitely on our left. With that discovery we made our second U-turn, this time in silence. Joan, our driver, was now close to tears. This was a road she had traveled many times and had never become lost. There had been only three roads at the roundabout. How could this have happened? Was she losing it? Fear was turning into panic as she wondered out loud what was happening to her.

In the darkness of the night I was prompted to allay her fears by suggesting that God was trying desperately to save us from danger. In desperation Joan retorted, "Couldn't He find another way than to tamper with my sanity?"

To this I responded, "If God had spoken audibly to you, you may have jumped out of the car, leaving us in greater danger." We all chuckled at the thought. Then, as if by inspiration, I shouted, "There is our accident! Here is what God has saved us from." As we passed the flashing lights of a police car our emotions were too great for a single word.

The Spirit spoke to each of us about our timely deliverance. It soon became clear to all of us that God had struck not one but four university lecturers with amnesia to detour us from the snare of the devil. Rounds of "Hallelujah! Praise the Lord!" filled the car at the realization of God's care and tender mercies toward four women—and the safe return from blessed amnesia.

PATRICE E. WILLIAMS-GORDON

The Roots

Therefore put on the full armor of God, so that when the day of evil comes, you may be able to stand your ground, and after you have done everything, to stand. Stand firm then. Eph. 6:13, 14, NIV.

I HAD JUST FINISHED PLANTING 250 tulip bulbs and felt tired but happy. This time I was sure I did it the right way—deep, and even deeper for the bigger bulbs. The previous year I hadn't planted my bulbs deeply enough, and a little downpour of rain had washed away most of the dirt, causing a disaster. The bulbs had stuck out of the ground, and the flowers weren't that great at all. This year I had also sorted out the colors: two rows of pure yellow, a row of red, one with orange, another of white, and another with yellow and white.

One Sunday morning I was busy clearing a flower bed that had been damaged by a tornado; I wanted to prepare for another flower bed. That little area of land took me a long time to clear and caused me many aching muscles. Why? It was hard to remove all the deep roots of the bushes and perennial plants there, especially those that had intertwined with the roots of the tree. Everything in the bed had been damaged when a huge tree fell, cutting the bushes and ruining the flowers. What I did not realize, though, is that when the roots of these bushes and perennial plants are anchored deep and intertwined together, they can survive any disaster. If I hadn't pulled the roots, I could have enjoyed the beauty of the flowers and bushes the following spring.

In our Christian experience we need to have deeper roots. If our Christian experience is a shallow one, we'll be in danger of being washed away in life's storms. We need to be anchored to the stronger hands of Jesus Christ. Prayer, Bible study, and love for others are the good soil that will strengthen our roots. With our faith firmly rooted in Christ, no storm of life can break us. A tornado may come to dampen our spirit, or maybe the storm of losing a loved one or a job may disturb our peace, but with our roots intertwined with Christ we will survive. With our hands clasping Jesus' hands, no winds of strife can move us.

Lord, thank You for anchoring me through the storms of life. Please hold my hands today, and help me not to let go of Yours. JEMIMA D. ORILLOSA

Shame on Me!

And we know that all things work together for good to them that love God, to them who are the called according to his purpose. Rom. 8:28.

DEALING WITH AN ELDERLY parent can be rewarding, amusing, and challenging. My mother-in-law has an Alzheimer's-type dementia. She may ask the same question 10 times in one hour. Since she gets up very early, it can be a long day for her. Other times the day is too short. She also has "twilight syndrome." On cloudy, gloomy days her mind becomes very confused, and she is ready to go to bed by 2:00 in the afternoon.

Mother is almost 98 years old, and we're trying to keep her in our home for as long as we can; we can do this as long as she is mobile. I have osteoporosis, and she's much larger than I. If she were bedridden, I would be unable to care for her. We encourage her to walk down our long hall with her walker, and on warm spring, summer, and fall days she walks out to the carport, where she sits and watches the dogs play in the dog yard and listens to the birds sing. She's legally blind but still has some peripheral vision.

I debated what to do to keep her from going to bed so early and finally decided to hide her nightgown on dark days and encourage her to stay up "just a little longer." I often feel guilty for doing this since I don't like to be deceptive, but she needs to stay as active as possible or she'll lose bone density and muscle strength.

I wonder how the Lord feels when He lets us go through trials and tribulations, knowing that it's "for our own good." It's hard to understand how He could let His Son die that we might live, but He chose to do just that. If He hid His face when Christ died on the cross, He must cringe when we weep or complain about our trials. There's no problem or difficulty we face that can compare to what the Father and Son endured for us. We can know that both of Them are suffering right beside us in any pain we may bear. Many have said that until we have also suffered, we cannot really understand what Jesus did for us. My prayer for you is that you will think daily about the sacrifice made for you on the cross and accept whatever the Lord permits for you today.

LORAINE F. SWEETLAND

Living Today, Planning a Future

His sister stood at a distance to see what would happen to him. Ex. 2:4, NIV.

MY HEART POUNDS IN my chest so hard that I can even feel it in my head. I awaken from another terrible dream about losing a loved one—my son, my daughter, my mother, my husband. I'm told this is common when someone loses someone very dear to them when they are young.

My oldest sister was a great friend when I was little. Helen was 16 years older than I—we had a lot of kids in our family. She took me to church every week and made sure my hair was just so. Her goals included making sure I could read before she married and left home. She was afraid the others might not teach me, so she did.

She helped me memorize the Lord's Prayer and the Beatitudes. She taught me to read *Peter Pan* before I even started kindergarten. After she married and left home, I sometimes stayed overnight with her, and she would encourage me to read a book of children's prayers. And then within a year and a half she died. A drunk driver killed her and her unborn child, leaving us all to grieve and miss her greatly.

Helen didn't know her time was short, but she prepared for eternity, as I hope we all do. She sang songs of praise as well as modern-day tunes. My husband says I burst out in song in a similar way to what I've described my sister doing. We must prepare daily for the final day and yet live our lives with hope and joy despite all the pain and grief. When she died, the sun went out for a while inside us all. It leaked back in, little by little, but left a gash that was slow to heal. Scars remain.

My joy is that one day we'll be reunited and that the same Lord she loved and trusted for eternal life is the One I also love and trust. That is a hope—to meet again with the dear sister who taught me to read and sing and live life to the fullest. She gave me a foundation for my faith, preparing me to meet Jesus in the clouds at His soon return.

Lord, You have said that someday "the dead in Christ will rise first. After that, we who are still alive and are left will be caught up together with them in the clouds to meet the Lord in the air. And so we will be with the Lord forever. Therefore encourage each other with these words" (1 Thess. 4:16-18, NIV). We claim that promise today.

SALLY J. AKEN-LINKE

Don't Miss Your Flight

As you look forward to the day of God and speed its coming. That day will bring about the destruction of the heavens by fire, and the elements will melt in the heat. But in keeping with his promise we are looking forward to a new heaven and a new earth, the home of righteousness. 2 Peter 3:12, 13, NIV.

FINALLY MY SEVEN DAYS of women's ministries seminars in Nairobi, Kenya, were over. I was tired and eager to get home. I packed my suitcase that night before retiring to bed. I was excited just thinking that early in the morning I would catch my flight to Harare, Zimbabwe. I was scheduled for the 8:00 a.m. flight, so I needed to get to sleep early, as I would leave the hotel for the airport at 5:30 a.m.

I called my husband before I slept and told him what time to meet me at the airport. His response was "Please don't miss your flight." He was looking forward to seeing me, just as I was looking forward to seeing him. I always miss my home when I am itinerating. There is no better environment than home. East, west, south, and north, home is the best.

I awakened with the alarm at 4:30. I could have stayed in bed for a little longer, but I was afraid that I might oversleep and miss my flight. The words of my husband kept on ringing in my mind: "Don't miss your flight." I was looking forward to meeting my husband at the airport and finally going to my home environment.

This reminded me that just as my husband was looking forward to seeing me and driving me home, Jesus is speaking to each one of us and wants to take us home. One day Jesus will take us on a flight to heaven, and He is pleading with each one of us not to miss that flight. He is looking forward to taking us to our heavenly home.

If I had missed my flight that day, I would have had to wait for two more days to catch another flight. We must not miss our heavenly flight, because we'll not have an opportunity to catch another flight. We all have the opportunity, through the grace of God, to prepare ourselves now for the heavenly flight.

PRISCILLA BEN

Termite Attack

Do not lay up for yourselves treasures on earth, where moth and rust consume and where thieves break in and steal. Matt. 6:19, RSV.

SEPTEMBER 11, 2001, IS a day that most Americans—and many people around the world—would rather forget than remember. That day America declared war against terrorism. I remembered that a few days earlier my husband and I were patting each other on the back. We had passed the one-year mark of living and serving the church in Pakistan. Then the attack on the Twin Towers in New York happened. A string of events followed that made it dangerous for foreigners to stay in Pakistan. We didn't want to leave, but our church headquarters and our embassy said we must. We had two days to pack a few belongings and do all the necessary preparations for our departure.

I didn't think much about leaving our few belongings. However, my vast collection of photo albums was a great concern. I packed them all in storage boxes so they wouldn't be lying around gathering dust while we were gone. Dust storms in Pakistan are common as well as unpredictable. I considered these albums my treasures. They chronicled our lives, travel, and work over a span of at least 30 years on three continents.

Our evacuation leave stretched from one month to four months. Finally we were allowed to return. My husband, who returned first, gave me the bad news as soon as I entered our home. Termites had gotten into the boxes and ruined the albums. I was too tired that night to look into them, but morning revealed a dismal sight. I couldn't believe what I saw. Most covers were eaten up, their edges ragged and the inside pages tattered. I racked my brain on what to do. Could they be saved? Were our memories gone forever?

It took me a week to clean up the mess. Fortunately, only a few pictures were badly damaged, and most were saved. I was tempted to throw some away, but after carefully wiping each one I decided they were worth keeping again.

My earthly treasures are fragile and temporary. Now I heed my Father's counsel: "But lay up for yourselves treasures in heaven, where neither moth [nor termites] nor rust consumes and where thieves do not break in and steal" (Matt. 6:20, RSV).

MERCY M. FERRER

Simplicity

And he said: "I tell you the truth, unless you change and become like little children, you will never enter the kingdom of heaven." Matt. 18:3, NIV.

I AM SIMPLY AMAZED AT the innocence of children. They speak what's on their hearts without wondering whether or not it will make them seem silly. We adults, on the other hand, are a little more hesitant.

Every week at church we have what we call praise and petition time. The prayer leader usually asks for praises first, and I admit that the adults are frequently all too silent. But the children aren't. While I sit and wonder if I'll be thought strange if I raise my hand to say I'm thankful for the sunshine, the children share their praises: for ponies and kittens and chickens, for the creek to swim in, for the fun they had on a caving expedition. The list is long and varied, but usually simple. Of course I'm thankful for small things, but they almost seem too trivial to mention at prayertime in church. Only big miracles seem appropriate there. But the children don't know that. They're thankful to their friend Jesus, and they want to share their joy.

After the praises come the prayer requests. The adults generally have more of those. We ask for healing for loved ones, for comfort from grief, for God's help in difficult situations. But the little ones aren't silent here, either. They also have needs to bring to God in prayer. Again, the list is varied—and simple: please pray for my daddy; our kitty is missing; I mashed my finger with a hammer this week and would you please pray that it gets better? The last request came from my own young son just this past Sabbath, and as he started to say it, I almost told him to be quiet. It was too trivial to take up time at church—a story of a mashed finger. Yet, thankfully, at the last moment I closed my mouth and didn't say those words.

The fact that the God of the universe cares so much about us is almost incomprehensible to me. The same God who takes care of the stars and planets wants me to bring my sorrows and my joys to Him. He's glad when I appreciate the beauty in the sunrise, and He feels my pain over the death of a pet. He doesn't want me to wait until something major happens to bring my requests and praises to Him. I like to imagine that there's a smile on His face as He listens to the children at our prayertime. Didn't Jesus Himself instruct us to become like little children? RACHEL ATWOOD

God, Where Are You?

"We have suffered terror and pitfalls, ruin and destruction." Streams of tears flow from my eyes because my people are destroyed. Lam. 3:47, 48, NIV.

IT WAS A BEAUTIFUL, sunny Tuesday morning. I was on vacation in California. Just an ordinary day. But September 11 will no longer be an ordinary day. Mention of 9/11 will bring to mind images forever seared in memory. As I sat mesmerized in front of the TV set, I thought, *Is what is happening true?* I found it hard to believe that some people could hurt thousands of innocent kindred human beings in the name of their God. I was confused, hurt, and angry.

Two months later a work assignment brought me to Cambodia—and face to face with the atrocities of the killing fields. The attack on America pales in significance as we consider that an estimated one third of the total population of Cambodia was tortured, killed, or died of starvation and disease during Pol Pot's reign of terror. Those who survived that era will never forget the day their trust was betrayed. *God, where were You during the Pol Pot regime?*

In Luke 24 we read of a story of another time. Cleopas, a disciple of Jesus, was feeling devastated, depressed, angry, and disappointed because Jesus had just been crucified. His high hopes for an earthly kingdom had been utterly shattered. Only a week before, enthusiasm had run high as Jesus rode into Jerusalem with everyone shouting, "Hosanna! Blessed is He who comes in the name of the Lord!" (Mark 11:9, NKJV). The hosannas were still ringing in his ears, and Cleopas couldn't believe that the King who had talked so confidently about His coming kingdom had been arrested, tried, and crucified all within such a short time. As Jesus walked with them, they didn't realize that their Master and Lord was close by. Luke 24:31 tells us that their eyes were opened when Jesus repeated a tradition they had shared in the breaking of bread.

Yes, when by His Spirit our eyes are opened, we will see where God has been working all the time. First Corinthians 13:12 reminds us that in our sinfulness we can see only dimly, but when we have the privilege of coming face to face with our Savior we will understand fully.

We now have proof that God was busy on September 11 saving many who could have died on that day. In Cambodia many were protected by God, and others found safety in refugee camps. God was there; He has always been there; we're just not always aware of His presence.

Sally Lam-Phoon

My Caring Heavenly Father

Delight thyself also in the Lord; and he shall give thee the desires of thine heart. Ps. 37:4.

MY BROTHER-IN-LAW PETE, his wife, Ruthe, and I were visiting my family in Michigan. We had planned to make some trips to visit areas of interest over a three-week period.

One day Ruthe and I thought of another place we wanted to visit. It was the site of a favorite Christian TV production center. We thought how great it would be to tour this facility and meet some of the people we'd seen only via the TV. After calling their main office and being assured they conducted tours, we began the trip.

From time to time as we traveled I prayed silently that this would be a truly inspiring visit and, if possible, we'd meet the couple who were the founders of this dream come true.

We arrived and were warmly received at each building we toured. The tour guides were gracious and informative. Everyone we met was so happy with the work they were doing for the Lord. We were impressed that the Lord was blessing there.

After spending a few hours touring, we asked if they could recommend a place to eat before we started back to Michigan. We were directed to a lovely restaurant in a nearby country town. We left the TV production facility a little disappointed at not having met the founders of this ministry.

We found the delightful country restaurant and, as we entered, who should be just finishing their lunch but this couple. We visited with them for a few minutes before they had to leave.

As my brother-in-law later said: "The Lord provided the icing on the cake for us," completing the blessing of our visit. We left that little corner of God's country with thanksgiving and a blessing. We had made some new friends and came away enriched. The Lord had even provided perfect weather for traveling and sightseeing.

How our heavenly Father delights in giving us "the desires of our hearts," just as we delight in giving our children "the desires of their hearts."

PATRICIA MULRANEY KOVALSKI

Praying for a Baby

Wait for the Lord; be strong and take heart and wait for the Lord. Ps. 27:14, NIV.

MOMMY, I'M NOT praying anymore!" my 3-year-old exclaimed.

I glanced at my mother before I responded. "Why, sweetheart? Why aren't you going to pray?"

Lillian looked at me with a scowl. Then she exclaimed, "I'm not praying because God doesn't listen to me. I asked God for a baby sister, and He hasn't been listening to me!"

Lillian had started praying for a baby sister the previous summer. She'd been quite happy being my only child until she went to Florida for the summer to visit my parents. While she was there Lillian found out that her best friend, Amanda, had a new baby brother. Once she saw the baby, the sibling-envy bug bit Lillian. Whenever I called to see how she was doing, Lillian would tell me about her day, and then she'd end every conversation with "Did you know Amanda's mommy had another baby? She had a baby boy!" Lillian started asking Jesus for a baby sister almost immediately. A year had now passed, and Lillian still didn't have a baby sister; she was beginning to doubt. How do you explain to a 3-year-old—even my mature 3-year-old—that sometimes God answers our prayers in a way we cannot always understand? How do you explain that God's timing is not necessarily our timing? How do you explain that "No" or "Not now" is sometimes an answer? It took a little persuading, but eventually Lillian said she understood and would continue praying.

More than two years passed after that conversation. The day Cassandra, Lillian's much-prayed-for baby sister, was born, Lillian squealed with delight and said, "A sister, a sister! I have a baby sister!" Then she added, "I knew God would answer my prayer; I just had to wait a bit!"

What faith! Lillian had prayed the same prayer every night for more than two years. Yet she believed that God would send her sister. Do I have that much faith? Do I pray and then wait patiently on the Lord?

Lord, please give me but a fraction of a child's faith. Give me faith the size of a mustard seed so I too can move mountains. Tamara Marquez de Smith

Memories of a Mockingbird

Though I walk in the midst of trouble, thou wilt revive me: thou shalt stretch forth thine hand against the wrath of mine enemies, and thy right hand shall save me. Ps. 138:7.

MY 3-YEAR-OLD TABBY CAT, Tinkerbell, was pregnant with her first litter and a few weeks from delivery. She enjoyed going out into the yard and basking in the sun. One day a mockingbird began swooping down on Tinkerbell every time she went outside. Strangely, the bird never came near Midnight, my 10-year-old cat, who also lay in the yard. The bird would peck Tinkerbell relentlessly as she lay in the grass trying to snooze.

Several times Tinkerbell tried to catch the bird, but her pregnant state made it difficult to move quickly. Other times she tried to ignore the bird. My children, annoyed at the bird's persistence, took turns trying to squirt it with water or shoo it away with the broom. They even threw lightweight objects near the bird to get it to leave Tinkerbell alone. My husband, tired of the aggravating bird, suggested using his BB gun. "Absolutely not!" I protested, but off he went to buy BBs anyway. Once home, he didn't remember where he had put the gun. I was relieved! The relentless bird attacks continued. Eventually, out of pity, we began to make Tinkerbell stay inside the house where she was safe.

Finally the bird disappeared. No one knows where it went, but we were all happy that it was gone. Cautiously I started letting Tinkerbell outside again. She was able to enjoy a week or two of savoring the warmth of the sun before her three kitties were born. Some days I'd hear a mockingbird off in the distance and think, *Oh no, it's taunting someone else's pet!*

We are often assailed by the "enemy." He swoops down and mocks and attacks us from all sides. He makes life miserable for us; he injures, maims, and kills our spirit. Whatever it takes to hurt, humiliate, or discourage, he's willing to do. Even the tactics of well-meaning family or friends can't help. God is our only safety. He knows and cares what we go through and is able to rescue us from the wiles of the devil.

Thank You, Lord, for loving me so much that You revive me when the enemy wears me down. Help me to trust in You completely and be safe in Your hands today.

Iris L. Stovall

Outward Appearances

The Lord does not look at the things man looks at. Man looks at the outward appearance, but the Lord looks at the heart. 1 Sam. 16:7, NIV.

I WAS VISITING MY FRIEND Rockella. Her 5-year old sister, Francine, was in the room. Music was playing on the stereo, and Francine and I were talking about her day at school. Francine turned the discussion toward the music being played. "These people are not Christians," she said of the singers. Curious, I asked her to explain. She told me she had looked at the tape jacket and that the singers were not smiling. "God's people are happy people," she said, "so these people can't be God's people, because they don't look happy at all."

Seizing the opportunity to plant spiritual truth in her young mind, I told Francine that we must be careful about how we form impressions based on appearances. "God looks at the heart," I told her. I smiled as she remained quiet while thinking this over. The lesson was sinking in.

A few moments later Francine spoke again. "Yes," she said thoughtfully, "*God* looks at our hearts, but *we* can see only the outside."

I chuckled quietly at her logic and agreed, but her observation has remained with me. While we should not judge others, our outward appearances are usually what others focus on. It is true that our appearance is often—though not always—a reflection of what is going on inside us.

My heart overflows with joy when someone I just met comments, "You must be a Christian." At those times I know that Christ's love can be seen shining through me. These instances are not as often as I would like. Many times I'm sure people look at my attitude and say, as Francine did, "She can't be a Christian."

Instead of attempting to change what others see, I would do better to get to the root of the matter. Even as God sees my heart and knows my intent, He can help to change any wrong attitude I may have. When I have the right attitude, others can see from the outside.

Francine was right after all. We can see only the outside, even if God does see the heart. But when God has made the heart right, others will know. Our outside will become as beautiful as our inside.

Lord, please make my heart a reflection of You. ABIGAIL BLAKE PARCHMENT

Perfect Obedience

When thou art in tribulation, and all these things are come upon thee, even in the latter days, if thou turn to the Lord thy God, and shalt be obedient unto his voice; . . . he will not forsake thee. Deut. 4:30, 31.

WHEN I WAS VERY young, my family moved from Michigan to California. My sister and I lived with our aunt and uncle near Fresno for a few years while our parents were working about 100 miles away. Since my sister was in school during the day, I had my aunt's full attention. She did so many nice things for me and with me—reading stories, playing games, and singing to me. These were precious times I'll always remember.

After a couple years my aunt became pregnant, and in October, two days after my birthday, she had a baby boy they named Gordon. My uncle wanted to go to see his wife and son at the hospital; but what should he do with me? In those days they didn't allow children in the hospital. So we drove to the hospital, and he parked the car. He put all the windows up, but left about two inches on each for air. He locked me in the car with strict instructions not to open the door or roll down the window. Even at 5 years of age I would never think of disobeying my uncle Glenn.

It can get very hot in Fresno at times. It was about 110° F, and as I sat there I got hotter and hotter. After a while my mom and dad came to the hospital to visit my aunt and saw me in the car. My dad told me to unlock the car door or roll down the window, but I wouldn't do that because Uncle Glenn had told me not to for any reason. Finally, since they could see I was getting redder and redder in the face, my dad broke the small side window to get in and lift me out.

Are we as determined to obey God as I was to obey my uncle? Do we obey, even though it's a hardship and no matter how much heat is put on us to disobey? no matter how uncomfortable or inconvenient it is? Think about it: are we as committed to God as I was to Uncle Glenn?

Lord, help me today to always obey Your words and never let others deter me. Amen.

ANNE ELAINE NELSON

Appetite for Sin

And David sent and inquired after the woman. And one said, Is not this Bathsheba, the daughter of Eliam, the wife of Uriah the Hittite? 2 Sam. 11:3.

KING DAVID DIDN'T KNOW her name or who she was; he just noticed that she was a beautiful woman who was taking a bath. He wasn't spying through the keyhole, nor did he knock down the door to her bathroom. He simply took a late-night walk on his roof. Perhaps he was motivated by the idleness of the palace or simply attracted by the beautiful woman. We don't know what she did, or did not do, to attract him. However, none of these excuses could decrease David's guilt or his appetite for sin.

David discovered that the woman was Bathsheba, wife of Uriah, a faithful man in the king's army. David, with uncontrolled thoughts of lust in his head, ordered that she be brought to him, and soon he slept with her. I don't know if she was passive, permissive, or without choices; the fact is that the Bible mentions only the attitude of David. The adultery was consummated, and the appetite for sin was satisfied for the moment.

The consequences were great. David lost his peace of mind when he learned that Bathsheba was expecting a child. Uriah, her husband, was away in combat. David worried about how to hide what had happened. He tried to hide his sin by making it look as though the baby was Uriah's child, but when that didn't work, he ended up ordering Uriah's assassination, then married his widow.

How about us? How do we think and react when we're tempted? I consider the appeals of seductive TV series, soap operas, captivating TV commercials, billboards, magazines, and other entertainment. All of these can cost a lot if we give our attention, our strength, and, yes, even our life by yielding to these appeals. It is so much better to give our life to the Lord and let Him live in us, controlling our sinful desires. The price of sin is high and causes extreme suffering. The story of David's family is certainly an example of this.

Our prayer for today should be *Lord, how difficult it is to control our carnal desires! Help us so that we can be faithful and firm in service to Your kingdom and to our family. Amen.*

CASSANDRA MARTINS

Knowledge of Good and Evil

I will set no wicked thing before mine eyes. Ps. 101:3.

MY FIRST YEAR AS A missionary to Guam was one of the happiest years of my life. One main reason was that I didn't own a television set. Having grown up on way too much TV, I greatly missed it at first. But without it I had much more free time to read more, write more, and witness more. As my mind became clearer and more pure, I became convinced that "TV-free" was the life for me.

Then I went through what I call "news withdrawal." Because I was living nearly halfway around the world, I rationalized that I needed to keep up on current events. So I'd catch a glimpse of world news while visiting in homes. But a glimpse here and there only left me wanting more.

While shopping at the local mall that fall I strolled past an electronics store displaying a big-screen TV at its entrance. CNN's *Headline News* was on. *Maybe just five minutes,* I told myself. *Perhaps there's something I need to know.*

My "need to know" was the lure that made the trap successful. I stood, half-dazed, as I gazed into the huge screen, filling my mind with the corruption of the world. Within moments of starting my news fix, I realized I had the "knowledge of evil." Not only was I aware of the evil that was happening in the world, but I was also suddenly aware that I was standing in the midst of dreadfully horrific Halloween decorations. The funny thing was, I hadn't noticed the decorations a few minutes before. While I was TV-free, God protected me from seeing evil. But when I went against my convictions and chose knowledge of the world over peace and purity, it was as if my protective blinders disappeared.

I was reminded of Eve in the Garden of Eden. Her desire to know everything, her dissatisfaction with the information bestowed upon her, helped Satan to deceive her. Thousands of years later the devil continues to tempt God's children in very similar ways, albeit with different bait. And for each of us it may be different temptations. Let's pray for wisdom to spot Satan's traps before we're caught in them. Let's turn from evil to live.

Thank You, Lord, for protecting us from evil. Please help us keep our minds focused solely on You so that the world has no hold on us and evil has no power over us. CLARISSA MARSHALL

Expect the Unexpected

The Lord's lovingkindnesses indeed never cease, for His compassions never fail. They are new every morning; great is Thy faithfulness. Lam. 3:22, 23, NASB.

SABBATH AFTERNOON STARTED OUT beautifully with clear skies and a slight breeze. As teen leader at our church, I'd arranged what I thought would be a relaxing nature adventure for our lively teen group. Fourteen canoes filled with energetic teens were launched into the Econolahatchee River for a winding nine-mile, downstream ride. Before we'd completed the first mile, two canoes had swamped, one paddle was lost, four kids were soaking wet, and one "dinner-plate-size" spider was pummeled with canoe paddles to the accompaniment of high-pitched screams and frantic tree-hugging.

With all of the canoes once again carrying their passengers in the upright position, we made it almost two more miles before the clouds rolled in and it started to rain. Then we heard the thunder, and before we were halfway down our stretch of river, the lightning started striking frighteningly close. More canoes flipped. Shoes, drinks, and life jackets were rescued as they floated downstream. Then a tree fell into the river after we had all passed under it.

There are many twists and turns on the Econolahatchee River, but one particularly sharp bend was too much for a pair of stressed-out teens. In the rain and thunder they not only swamped their canoe, but they managed to totally sink it in six feet of water and get it stuck under a submerged tree. For the next hour a group of very wet teens stood on the bank shouting encouraging words to a group of even wetter teens in the water as they tried to rescue that canoe. A rope was finally secured around it, and the canoe was pulled out.

Finally we all resumed canoeing. The thunder began to lessen, the rain slacked off, and the canoes stayed upright. As we paddled the last mile of that endless stretch of river, we talked about how we all just might make it safely home. Then as our very damp crew rounded the last bend in the river, we were struck by an amazing sight. There, directly over the canoe-launching area, was the beautiful arch of a perfect rainbow!

God is not only our faithful protector; He delights in thrilling us with unexpected beauty just when we need it the most! SUSAN WOOLEY

The Bittersweet Season

To every thing there is a season, and a time to every purpose under the heaven. Eccl. 3:1.

He hath made every thing beautiful in his time. Eccl. 3:11.

THE QUIET LAKE WATER in front of our cabin is now finger-numbing cold, and there is a rim of ice along the shore. As the brisk west wind skims across the lake, I can hear the pleasing sound of nature's wind chimes: the tinkle of the ice as it breaks against the sand and the reeds.

Each tree is ablaze with color today. The red and orange maples, the yellow birch, and the golden aspen are beautiful to behold. It's as if each tree has its own inner lightbulb and God has plugged them in simultaneously, lighting the world with His reflected glory. Everywhere the forest trees are busily scattering their leaves profusely as they patiently design the colorful patchwork quilt in which the earth and the animals will snuggle cozily during the long winter months.

There is a pungent smell of burning wood from fireplaces, and I see that many of our neighbors have already winterized their cabins and taken in their boat piers for the season. At twilight yesterday I saw two flocks of Canada geese overhead, their V formation arrowing southward. Their plaintive honking signaled everyone to follow.

As I walked along our lane to our mailbox, I found a few wild berries clinging to the bushes, and some blue wildflowers still bloomed on the hillside. When I neared the top of our driveway, a doe and her two fawns stood silently among the tall pine trees, watching me, and three large partridge flew up from the grass. Occasionally I glimpse a white snowshoe rabbit or a hawk as I take my daily walk; it is comforting to know that a few of our wildlife friends are still with us.

The days are shorter now. The mornings are frosty and the evenings have a chill, but I savor each one as a precious jewel in my golden string of cherished memories. I find myself yearning to hold onto October with both hands, pleading with it to linger just a little longer.

It is a sad time, this bittersweet season. It is an all-too-short breathing space between the busy, hot days of summer and the many cold days of winter. But I have the hope that spring will return, green and gentle and generous, as a result of God's ageless and unchanging promise to each of us, and once again, the cycle of life will begin.

ROSEMARY BAKER

True Love

Love is patient, love is kind. 1 Cor. 13:4, NIV.

I READ AN ARTICLE THE other day about a single woman and her 13-year-old cat. When she brought a new puppy into her home, the elderly cat was so upset that it stopped using the litter box and started using the floor. The woman ignored the situation until the cat wet the woman's bed. Then she had her cat euthanized.

That story upset me so much. The very next morning my 15-year-old cat wet on my foot. "Bad cat!" I yelled, and put him in the bedroom for a time-out. Then I washed up and went about my day. Because I love my cat, I'm willing to clean up after him. Getting rid of him never entered my mind.

If you want to have a house that's perfect and always company-clean, don't get a pet. Puppies chew on things. Cats scratch up the furniture. Don't have children. They break things and color on the walls. And don't even think about what could happen when they become teenagers. You'd better not get married, either. Hubby will drink out of the milk carton and leave the toilet seat up.

Love is patient. It means putting up with things that you probably wouldn't put up with from strangers. Sometimes it involves little things, such as listening to Uncle Paul's description of his gallbladder surgery for the tenth time or staying up until midnight sewing your daughter's costume for the school play. Sometimes love requires more of us: sticking by a friend who's in prison, checking your son into a drug rehab center, holding your father's hand when he's dying.

Loving means making sacrifices and compromises. When you love someone, your time isn't all your own. It means making allowances for people when they don't always live up to your expectations. Loving is part of being human—perhaps the best part.

True love knows no limits. True love was Jesus sacrificing Himself so that we might know eternal life. True love accepts the fact that people, like pets, sometimes make a mess of things. True love is always waiting patiently to clean things up.

Gina Lee

Teakettle Tea

Blessed are the dead who die in the Lord. . . . "Yes," says the Spirit, "they will rest from their labor, for their deeds will follow them." Rev. 14:13, NIV.

I CAN STILL SEE DADDY sitting at the Formica table eating his breakfast: a big bowl of cornflakes with sliced banana and a steaming cup of teakettle tea. Newspaper in his left hand, he'd eat quickly, drain the cup, and go out into the winter darkness. This "tea" was a winter treat. Daddy poured boiling water into a cup half filled with milk, stirred in a little sugar, and there you had it—teakettle tea.

I'd beg for a sip—and always get one, or else a cup of my own. Today I know it was poor folks' tea, but back then I thought he was awfully smart to know how to make something that good.

Parents are one-dimensional to kids. Kids don't conceive of parents having lives beyond what impacts them. Even when I was a teen and Daddy mentioned that he'd bought a dime bag of peanuts and walked to the zoo on his lunch hour, it never occurred to me that it was because he didn't have lunch money. When we were in high school, he added a part-time job. It was mostly night shift and was hot, dirty work—nothing like the pencil-pushing accounting he did by day.

Once we took a trip to Europe together, Daddy and I. We saw the *Mona Lisa* in Paris, ate Indian food in Amsterdam, and walked between the walls of the Ishtar Gate (from Daniel's Babylon) in the Pergamum Museum in East Berlin. Unforgettable. Except for his wandering off and getting "lost," I always thought that Daddy was the best travel companion one could have.

Eventually he moved to Maryland to be near my family and me and became famous among us for his peanut-butter-and-jelly sandwiches. My son said he added a special ingredient—love. Time flows on. Years meld into one another. Age creeps up gradually, and, looking at him, I think of a line from a country song: "Why's he all dressed up like some old man?" Still, I count myself and our family blessed.

What are these sunny ties of experience that bind a family together if not a glimmer of eternal light to come? *Thank You, God, for the blessing Daddy was in our lives for so many years. And thank You for the promise of heaven, where we'll travel the universe and return to tag along on a tour led by Christ Himself.*

PENNY ESTES WHEELER

November 4

Just Keep Laughing

The One enthroned in heaven laughs. Ps. 2:4, NIV.

WHO SAYS GETTING OLD isn't fun? My absentmindedness, forgetfulness, and clumsiness have given me lots of belly laughs. When something unusual happens, I don't take it seriously but chalk it up to experience. No one is ever too old to learn, you know.

One day as I was making bread, I reached down under the kitchen sink and pulled out a spray can of cooking oil. I sprayed the first pan, but instead of smelling like butter it smelled more like lemon. Furniture polish! I stood there trying to figure out why I had gone under the sink instead of to the upper cabinet. Looking at the correct can, I realized that both had a yellow cap. My subconscious mind knew yellow was the color. I'm still smiling over that one.

One of my funniest experiences was also in the kitchen. I was making a homemade pancake concoction in the blender, using a spatula to push the liquid down the sides. All of a sudden the blades grabbed the rubber, and like a tornado, the spatula spun up into the air, carrying the mixture with it all the way to the ceiling. What goes up must come down, and when it did, I was dripping with the sticky stuff. So were the cabinets and floor. After the shock was over, I laughed till I hurt.

Another time I went into the bathroom to brush my teeth and grabbed the wrong tube. It wasn't until I started scrubbing my front teeth that I realized I had squeezed Desitin on my toothbrush. Have you ever tried getting Desitin out of your toothbrush—not to mention your mouth? Then there was the time I reached into my purse in the dark for lip balm, only to smear concealer all over my mouth. Beware of what you do in the dark.

Eventually we all forget important appointments, special days, and where we put something. We trip, drop valuables, and put things where they don't belong. But there are many worse things that can happen—and that probably will—in a person's lifetime.

Lord, I know You must have a sense of humor as You watch some of our antics. It also must give You great pleasure to see us put the experiences of life in their proper perspective instead of getting mad or sad. Please continue to laugh with us as we grow old.

DONNA MEYER VOTH

The Dream

Cast all your anxiety on him because he cares for you. 1 Peter 5:7, NIV.

WE WERE MISSIONARIES IN GHANA, West Africa. In the space of three months our lives had been struck by one blow after another. Our daughter had been very ill; our little son had two serious illnesses and later had a strangulated hernia that his father had to operate on; and, finally, I was ill and our baby girl was born prematurely. She lived only two days.

A few months later I woke up one night from a horrible dream. In my dream our servant, Peter, had arrived as usual to do the first job of the day—boil all our drinking water. Our toddler son had wandered into the kitchen to "help," as he often did. When Peter struck a match to light the gas stove to boil the water, there was a tremendous explosion, and the kitchen and those in it were destroyed. I was trembling from the horror of that dream. I turned over and tried to go back to sleep, but sleep wouldn't come.

I thought that perhaps if I went all the way out to the kitchen and assured myself that there was no leaking gas to cause such an explosion, I could go back to sleep. So I got up, walked past the sleeping children's rooms, through the door into the dining room, and through another door into the kitchen. It wasn't until I opened the kitchen door that I smelled it. Gas! I rushed in to check the burners. But no burner was on. So I went into the pantry and turned off the gas at the tank. It was propane gas, and the tank in the pantry was connected to the stove by a pipe through the wall.

I went back to bed and went straight back to sleep. When we got up the next morning, we found the cause of the leak. That small pipe through the wall had rubbed on the rough wall, and a hole had been made in it. Had I not gotten up in the night and turned off the gas, the kitchen would have been full of gas when Peter came. He wouldn't have recognized the smell or the danger, and my dream might have been reality.

There was no reason I should have dreamed about a gas leak. I believe that God was saying, "I do care about you. I care enough to send you a dream, to make you get up in the night to prevent a catastrophe." This experience settles for me the question of whether God is interested in our lives. He is, and He doesn't allow us to suffer more than we can bear.

RUTH LENNOX

Grace

From the fullness of his grace we have all received one blessing after another. John 1:16, NIV.

IF YOU ARE MORE THAN 13 years old, you can probably remember a time in your life, as I can in mine, when you were anything but the queen of grace. It got so bad for a while that my family actually called me Grace. I'm sure they'd deny it, but they may remember a few of the incidents when I was less than graceful. It seems I was very clumsy, or at least I felt that way. I still don't feel all that confident in some circumstances and am afraid that I'll spill the punch at a formal reception, or fall down the stairs in front of everyone, or do something else to embarrass myself.

I remember one incident as if it were yesterday. I was making a cake—a chocolate cake—for some special occasion. The smell of chocolate wafted through the kitchen, and I could hardly wait for the finished product. Finally it was baked, and it looked beautiful. It had even risen evenly. It would be perfect right from the oven, but when covered with fudge frosting—it makes my mouth water just writing about it. I took it out of the oven ever so carefully, turned to place it on the cooling rack—and flipped it upside down on the kitchen floor. Don't ask me how I did it. That is the thing with gracelessness—there is no reason.

When it comes to our spiritual lives, there is no reprieve from gracelessness either. We can all have grace—as much as needed, all the time, anywhere, as often as necessary. And that grace comes free of charge or effort. It is offered to each of us liberally.

Grace is a hard thing to understand, but it exemplifies Jesus. And Jesus exemplifies grace. John 1:14 says, "The Word became flesh and made his dwelling among us. We have seen his glory, the glory of the One and Only, who came from the Father, full of grace and truth" (NIV). Verse 17 says that "grace and truth came through Jesus Christ" (NIV).

We believe by grace (Acts 18:27); grace builds us up, and grace gives us an inheritance among all those who are sanctified (Acts 20:32). Best of all, we are justified by grace (Rom. 3:24) and receive redemption and forgiveness of sin by His grace (Eph. 1:7). Further, it isn't static: "But grow in the grace and knowledge of our Lord and Savior Jesus Christ." And as the rest of that verse says, we too say, "To him be glory both now and forever! Amen" (2 Peter 3:18, NIV).

Ardis Dick Stenbakken

Listening?

I will instruct you (says the Lord) and guide you along the best pathway for your life; I will advise you and watch your progress. Ps. 32:8, TLB.

AT FIRST I HAD HAD a great deal of enthusiasm and a good bit of confidence that something would come up. I'd gone on several job interviews before the official end date of my current employment. I was sure that I'd have another job even before this one was over with. "After all, I'm smart, and I've developed a wide set of skills that are quite marketable," I reasoned.

The end date came and went. Days turned into weeks; weeks soon became months. I thought of one venture, then another. I joined different organizations in order to "network." I scoured the paper and various Internet sites. I applied for a wider range of positions, bought teach-yourself books and software packages to learn some new things, and volunteered my services in order to keep my skills up. The result? Nothing.

The techniques that I'd used so successfully in the past just weren't working. What was I doing wrong? Was I a little too cocky on that recent interview? Did I overdress on the other? Question after unrelenting question swirled in my head as I left yet another unsuccessful interview.

Frustration came to visit, and discouragement threatened to move in. The goals on my neatly planned time line that I'd set for myself began to unravel as success eluded me. "Time is a gift; use it wisely," my husband advised in his effort to encourage.

"You've been placed in this situation for a reason," another friend observed. "Have you asked the Lord why and what?" she questioned.

And so, after months and months of trying, after going full speed ahead and simply asking and expecting a blessing on my plans and endeavors, I stopped. I asked. And I found that the Lord had been talking to me all along. I just wasn't listening—again.

Lord, thank You for loving me enough to use whatever means necessary to get my attention so that we can talk, and I can learn to hear, listen, and obey. Speak, Lord, for Your servant is listening. Maxine Williams Allen

November 8

Unwanted Interruption

For God has not given us a spirit of fear, but of power and of love and of a sound mind. 2 Tim. 1:7, NKJV.

GLANCING AT MY WATCH, I saw it was almost time to leave for our weekly prayer group session. Knowing that my friend who hosted the circle had just moved into a new house, I had bought her two rosebushes in our favorite colors, red and pink. I would give them to her after the group left, I decided. Picking up the potted plants, I walked out to my car and placed them in the back seat.

As I put the first plant in the car, to my horror a tiny brown lizard dropped off. I froze. It doesn't matter that I was born in Jamaica, where the greenest and largest varieties of these reptiles abound. Nor does it matter that I live in Florida, where they also live. The thought of being in the same enclosed space with a lizard is something that makes my skin crawl. I knew from past experience that trying to talk myself out of this fear was as useless as shooing the now-hidden lizard away.

I drove off. I would not be late for the prayer circle. "Please, Lord, don't let that lizard crawl on me. Help me not to get in an accident if it does. Please take me there safely," I prayed earnestly.

The radio was on. The well-known evangelist Billy Graham was speaking, telling a story about a gambler. I got so involved in the well-told tale that the miles sped by, and I was at my friend's house without once thinking of the little reptile. And I never saw the lizard again.

Talking about the incident with my friends, I saw how much my heavenly Father cared for me by creating a distraction, and He kept me safe.

"It is not the will of God that His people should be weighed down with care. But our Lord does not deceive us. He does not say to us, 'Do not fear; there are no dangers in your path.' He knows there are trials and dangers, and He deals with us plainly" (Ellen G. White, *Steps to Christ*, p. 122).

I thank the Lord for answered prayers and for His protection of His daughter. I also pray that one day my fear of God's little creatures will be taken away—maybe in the world made new, maybe before that day.

GLORIA HUTCHINSON

Fifteen Beans

For I was hungry and you gave me something to eat, I was thirsty and you gave me something to drink, I was a stranger and you invited me in. Matt. 25:35, NIV.

IF YOU COULD ONLY SEE, you wouldn't be able to swallow your sandwich." So ends a luncheon conversation between two missionaries, described by Dr. David C. Thompson in his book *On Call.* This quote has stuck with me through the years, daring me to really look at what lies around us.

Recently those words were hammered home with a vengeance. Eight adults and two children gathered in our apartment in Toamasina, Madagascar, for a lovely after-church meal. Animated conversations bounced between French and English, suffused with the universal language of laughter. The food was tasty and abundant—two casseroles, three salads, rice, garlic bread, and a decadent dessert.

Several hours later my husband and the others went to a choir concert in a poor suburb. Walking down a sandy lane, he stopped to talk to a Malagasy family we know well; the children often accompany us to church. Eight of them sleep in a rickety bamboo and thatched hut that rivals the size of our bathroom. One of the young girls was making supper over a charcoal brazier. She showed Colin what was boiling in her pot: 15 small, dried, white beans. Fifteen beans to split among two adults and 10 brothers, sisters, and visiting cousins.

As Colin related this tale, my still-digesting lunch suddenly felt like lead. We knew that our Malagasy friends lived in poverty, but really seeing it is a lot different from simply knowing. James 2:15, 16 haunted me: "Suppose a brother or sister is without clothes and daily food. If one of you says to him, 'Go, I wish you well; keep warm and well fed,' but does nothing about his physical needs, what good is it?" (NIV). None at all.

If you could only see, what would you see? Hurting parents, afraid to talk about their gay son? The frustrations of a single mom, who's reeling from the aftermath of a messy divorce? A runaway teen? A friend with an eating disorder? The ache of clinical depression, the scars of sexual abuse, the loneliness of a surviving spouse?

You might even see 15 beans.

Kimberly Baldwin Radford

The Fruit of Prayer

O Lord my God, I cried out to You, and You healed me. Ps. 30:2, NKJV.

FOR SEVEN LONG YEARS of married life Esther and Henry had been praying to God for a child, hoping that someday God would surely hear their prayer. Friends and well-wishers had also prayed on their behalf for a child. I too had been pleading with God to grant their plea.

At last I heard that God was answering—Esther was expecting a baby! Then I heard that Esther was admitted to the hospital for her delivery. I rushed to the hospital and found that an emergency surgery was needed. Her friend Percy and Esther's mother-in-law were helping to get her into the operating theater.

Soon the nurses arrived to take her. Just before they wheeled her away, Percy reminded me that I should pray for her. We prayed. And then we sat anxiously waiting. Finally delightful news came that a healthy female child was born, and Esther was doing well too. We all were very excited.

Soon after that the anesthetist came out of the operating room. When he went to change from his scrubs, he found, to his surprise, a dead six-inch snake in one of his shoes. Each one of us present gave a different opinion as to how it got there, but one thing was evident: a dead snake cannot enter a shoe. So we concluded that it must have been in the shoe and gotten killed by the foot of the anesthetist without his even knowing it when he had hurriedly come for the emergency.

We were greatly moved by such a miraculous saving of three lives that day. If the anesthetist had delayed in coming or had sensed the snake, the lives of the mother and the child might have been in danger. The child, named Annette, was an answer to many prayers, and she is part of a miraculous blessing.

Thank You, God, for Your shower of grace. Sometimes You are answering prayers when we don't even know it. Help me today to remember to put my faith in You at all times, regardless of the circumstances or outward evidences.

BALKIS RAJAN

Sharing the Fish With Mary

I have shown you in every way, by laboring like this, that you must support the weak. And remember the words of the Lord Jesus, that He said, "It is more blessed to give than to receive." Acts 20:35, NKJV.

MANY YEARS AGO IN my native Trinidad I bought a huge fish. About to store it in the refrigerator, I was startled by a strong impression. "Give half of this fish to Mary." I tried to ignore the voice, but it insisted that I obey. I took the fish to Mary's house.

At the sound of my call, Mary came to the window in tears. When I asked what was the matter, she said between sobs, "There isn't anything in the house for my children to eat."

"Just this piece of fish?" she asked sadly when I handed her the bag.

I knew I had to do more. "Send one of the older girls home with me," I instructed.

"It'll have to be the youngest," the mother explained. "I've just done the wash, and only my youngest has clothes dry enough to wear."

When the little girl arrived, I stocked a basket with just about everything I had in my pantry and sent her home. A few minutes later she was back. "Mommy wants matches to light the stove." After she left, I buried my head in my pillow and wept bitterly at their dire need.

Later the mother's gratitude was overwhelming. But I couldn't stop there. I went to my friend's home down the road. "I've just discovered a dire need for clothing. Three young women have nothing to wear. How soon can you make three dresses for them?"

"As soon as I finish cooking we will go to the store," she said.

"No, dear," her husband interrupted gently, "go right away. I'll finish the cooking."

We bought the material that morning. She took the girls' measurements, and by sundown she was back with three lovely dresses.

One day Mary asked that I take the two older girls to church on Sabbath. I was overcome with joy. After many months they willingly joined the baptismal class and then requested baptism. Years later I reconnected with one of the older girls. A flow of communication came my way. Then she brought her husband and son to meet me. Such a reunion!

Yes, our wonderful God used half a fish to save souls for His kingdom.

EILEEN FURLONGE

A Lesson for Al

For the Lord does not see as man sees; for man looks at the outward appearance, but the Lord looks at the heart. 1 Sam. 16:7, NKJV.

HIS NAME WAS AL, and every morning he stood on the corner of a busy intersection lined with Federal buildings in downtown Washington, D.C. Armed with a smile and an outstretched hand, he limped from car to car speaking to all the drivers, asking for donations. Some responded by dropping coins, others passed on dollars, and the rest, like me, stared straight ahead, wishing for the light to turn green.

One day as I was driving toward this intersection I felt a pull on my steering wheel. As the car labored forward I knew all too well that it was a flat tire. *Now what do I do?* I mused. Caught at the light, I opened the door and walked toward the passenger side to confirm my suspicion. Amid honking horns, glaring looks, and muffled profanities, I heard a tenor voice say, "Need some help?"

There stood Al. With no other assistance in sight, I sheepishly accepted his offer.

While he changed my tire, I learned that Al had been a mechanic. Then he lost his job and couldn't find another, and had been forced to the streets. "Miss, when you don't have a phone and a permanent address, it's hard for employers to reach you about a job. How are they gonna call you if they decide to hire you? People who come through here every morning and look at me probably think that I can do better. But I'm trying, miss. I am really trying."

When Al completed the job, I handed him $15. And for months, as I drove up to this busy intersection, I slowed enough to hand him my lunch and scraps of paper with job leads. Some weeks later Al announced that he'd found a job and would be moving on. Of course, my heart rejoiced, and I saw him no more.

But I was never the same after this encounter. Sometimes God puts people in our path to open our eyes and heart. While Al apparently improved his life, I also grew through this acquaintance and improved mine.

Thank You, Father, for loving me enough to place a person like Al in my path.

YVONNE LEONARD CURRY

A Spectacular Show

Our soul has escaped as a bird from the snare of the fowlers; the snare is broken, and we have escaped. Our help is in the name of the Lord, who made heaven and earth. Ps. 124:7, 8, NKJV.

THE SABBATH HOURS ARE drawing to a close, and as I look out into my backyard I watch a spectacular show. It is lively, colorful, and accompanied by beautiful music. The Baltimore and orchard orioles, blue jays, hummingbirds, rose-breasted grosbeaks, goldfinches, redheaded woodpecker, and their many friends are the actors. It is a show rivaled by no other.

I watch the grosbeaks as they drive other birds away from the feeder. Even those of the same species aren't welcome to dine with them. The orioles fuss at each other and think they should be the only ones to enjoy their repast. The goldfinches are more sociable and will allow their friends to join them as they have a little supper. Little ruby-throated hummingbirds are the most intriguing to watch. Two males and two females gather at the feeder and eat in harmony, drinking the nectar provided. Blue jays, with their crest positioned so jauntily upon their heads, fly in to grab a few seeds, then fly to the nearby oak tree. The Harris sparrows and their friends gather at the base of the feeders to glean the spilled seeds.

All at once the birds disappear, and I see a cat or two on the prowl, lurking in the grass. They sit quietly, ready to pounce on any unsuspecting bird that may be near. The calico cat climbs a tree, hoping to have a better chance to nab a tasty treat. But they are unsuccessful, and I rejoice for the birds. Soon the felines tire of their fruitless hunting efforts and go back to the barn. The birds return, and the show goes on.

Are we as wise as the birds and know enough to hide when Satan is on the prowl? He may not always be so visible, and he will come at us in various ways. He will use people to discourage us and cause us to feel worthless. Feelings will be hurt, and we may say or do something in retaliation that will be our downfall. Like the birds, we need to be wise and flee Satan's temptations.

Evelyn Glass

November 14

My New Home

Let not your hearts be troubled. . . . In my Father's house are many rooms. . . . And when I go and prepare a place for you, I will come again and will take you to myself, that where I am you may be also. John 14:1-3, RSV.

AS I WALK ALONG the road I see many unfortunate beings lying around. Some sleep on old coats or newspaper; some have an old carton flattened to use as a mattress; others lie on the cold ground.

There are those, however, who live in a shack in an informal settlement or in a room somewhere. They have a bit of shelter over their heads. There are those who are a bit better off and live in council-owned cottages with one or two rooms. Still others own their homes. Jesus said, "For you always have the poor with you" (Matt. 26:11, RSV).

It was never my privilege to live in a big house. I grew up in a very humble home. I would browse through magazines with pictures of beautiful homes and would daydream of having my own beautiful home someday. I'm now in my sunset years and still live in a small, humble dwelling.

Not too long ago we were invited to someone's home. It was situated on a few acres of land with a beautiful view. There was a huge garage that could house more than two vehicles, and a large swimming pool shimmered in the sunshine. A large glass-enclosed deck overlooked the pool and was perfect to lounge around in. They had an ultramodern kitchen, with no shortage of food. Living near the sea, they also owned a boat. Wow! With so many rooms in the house, I could not even count. To me it was like a maze—I didn't know which way to turn to find my way out. How many people would even dream of setting foot in a house like that?

Sometimes we get dissatisfied with our condition, especially when in circumstances beyond our control. We long for something bigger and better. I'm encouraged by today's text: "Let not your hearts be troubled. . . . In my Father's house are many rooms. . . . And when I go and prepare a place for you, I will come again and will take you to myself, that where I am you may be also."

I am longing to move into my brand-new house; in fact, it's better described as a mansion. It's all paid for—no financial headaches. Will you be my neighbor?

PRISCILLA ADONIS

Women's Work

Likewise, teach the older women. . . . Then they can train the younger women . . . so that no one will malign the word of God. Titus 2:3-5, NIV.

FEW OF US APPRECIATE the implication that certain tasks are "women's work." But if we look closely at Scripture, we find there is work for each of us to do. There are four W's.

First, we have to be willing. First Peter 5:2 says, "Take care of God's flock. . . . Watch over it because you want to, not because you are forced to do it. . . . Do it because you are happy to serve, not because you want money" (ICB). This hits a little too close to home! As a part-time assistant pastor on a stipend, I often wish for more adequate compensation. But Peter reminds me that I should do this work not for money but because I am happy to serve willingly.

Second, we women need to be worthy. First Timothy 5:17 says, "The elders who rule well are to be considered worthy of double honor, especially those who work hard at preaching and teaching" (NASB). Truly, none of us are worthy in ourselves. In fact, I often feel totally unworthy of the privilege of ministry. It's only Christ who can make us worthy, or upright and holy, as another translation puts it.

Third, we need to be wise. Titus 2:3-5 says: "Instruct the older women to behave as women should who live a holy life. . . . They must teach what is good, in order to train the younger women to love their husbands and children, to be self-controlled and pure, and to be good housewives who submit themselves to their husbands, so that no one will speak evil of the message that comes from God" (TEV). God even promises to give us this wisdom: "If any of you lacks wisdom, let him ask of God, . . . and it will be given to him" (James 1:5, NKJV).

Last, we women need to be worry-free, as outlined by Jesus in Matthew 6:25-34: "Don't worry about the food or drink you need to live, or about the clothes you need for your body. . . . The thing you should want most is God's kingdom and doing what God wants. Then all these other things you need will be given to you" (NCV). How much of our precious hoarded energy do we expend on needless and actually counterproductive worry? Don't worry, it says.

None of these four W's is something we're able to muster up ourselves or in our own strength. All four come from Christ who alone fits us for our women's work.

BECKI KNOBLOCH

Salted, Sugarcoated, Watered-down Sin

He that covereth his sins shall not prosper: but whoso confesseth and forsaketh them shall have mercy. Prov. 28:13.

THERE ARE NUMEROUS USES for the mineral known to us all as salt—some good, some not so good. Most of us are aware that too much salt causes hypertension and can lead to kidney failure and other serious illnesses. That's why it's imperative that we limit our sodium intake.

Unless we read labels on everything we eat, we'll never be able to approximate the amount of sodium we consume in our daily food intake. Canned, boxed—even frozen—foods are preserved in salt. Smoked meat and fish contain moderately large amounts of salt, even after soaking and cooking.

When we focus on the sugar content in breads, cakes, and pastries, a considerable amount of sodium that's hidden in these products sometimes goes unnoticed. After eating foods high in sodium or pastry-filled treats covered with various kinds of sugars, we have a tendency to drink a lot of water.

This phenomenon reminds me of sin. Sin is notorious for hiding behind righteousness and misrepresenting the truth. It has a way of slipping into our lives like hidden sodium and sugarcoated goodies. Sometimes it's watered down so quickly and smoothly we don't realize that we've been engulfed by sin until we're already suffering from its results.

All of us are guilty of sin, it's true (Rom. 3:23), but there is still hope. We have an Advocate who doesn't want any to perish but desires that all be saved.

God loves us so much that He sent His Son to give His life in order to save ours. Jesus waits for us to ask for forgiveness so that He can intervene on our behalf. No matter how big the sin we may have committed, we are privileged to take it directly to the Lord. Jesus Himself made that possible. "I am the way, the truth, and the life: no man cometh unto the Father, but by me" (John 14:6). God promises to have mercy on those who confess and forsake their sins. I am claiming that promise today.

Jesus, I thank You for dying on the cross for my sins. Please help me to recognize my sins and confess them to You so that I may live eternally. I thank You and praise You.

CORA A. WALKER

What a Week!

This is the sign of the covenant I am making . . . : I have set my rainbow in the clouds. Gen. 9:12, 13, NIV.

WHAT A WEEK! How often do you say that? Quite a bit, I'd wager. One Friday afternoon I was definitely saying it. It had been a really rough week, and the Colorado weather wasn't helping with its cold, drizzly rain. I was in a hurry, of course, to get all the shopping done and then get to my in-laws in time for dinner.

By rushing through the store I was able to finish in record time, but I was tense and stressed. I was walking—or, should I say, almost running—to my car when I looked up and saw the most beautiful double rainbow I had ever seen. Both bows were brilliant and rich with color. I'd never seen anything like it, and I love looking for rainbows.

I started to sing as I put my groceries in the car and started for home. I was just praising God for the beauty of the rainbows and making up the words as I drove. I felt so blessed! It was amazing how the cares and stresses of the week faded from my mind.

I'm not a true songwriter, but the joy of the Lord would not be contained that day. I can't really remember the tune or the words of the song now, but I do remember the chorus and the awesome feeling that filled my heart as I praised God that afternoon. The chorus went something like this: "Thank You, Lord, for letting the light of Your love make rainbows in my dark and dreary world." It was a true worship experience, and I know that God was there with me in my car.

Rainbows always remind me of the promise that God gave Noah and the earth after the Flood. He promised to never again destroy the earth with water, but that wasn't His only promise. When I saw the rainbows that Friday, I was reminded of all His promises: "He will never leave you nor forsake you" (Deut. 31:6, NIV); "'I will strengthen them in the Lord and in his name they will walk,' declares the Lord" (Zech. 10:12, NIV). Philippians 4:13 is also a promise that I take comfort in. But one of my favorite promises is found in John 14:1-3. Jesus promises to come back and take me home with Him. So no matter how bad life might seem today, remember that because of Jesus all of God's promises will be kept, and, therefore, someday all of this will be only a memory that grows dim in the direct light of God's love.

JULI BLOOD

Teach Them to Your Children

Summon the people before me and I will instruct them, . . . so that they can teach my laws to their children. Deut. 4:10, TLB.

ONE OF THE LESSONS we most enjoyed in following the counsel of God was teaching our children to pray. They quite enjoyed echoing the words that we spoke, but soon they felt they could "fly" on their own. Some moments were comical as they put in baby words their thoughts. Our daughter declared her antipathy to old Satan when she prayed, "Please, Jesus, come and live in my heart; I don't want Satan to live in my heart; he can go and live in his own heart."

Our eldest was quite imaginative and wove the daily happenings into his brief prayers. For example, Mrs. Hanbury had brought him a gift when invited to our home for supper. He didn't forget the kindly gesture, and his prayer seemed to involve a double-edged concept of conversation with the Lord. He prayed, "Please bless Mrs. Hanbury for bringing me a present, and help her to bring me a bigger one next time."

Gradually the children learned to limit the requests for material things and search rather for the thanksgiving mode of prayer, finding blessings for which to be truly thankful. Growing further, they learned the joy of reaching out in prayer for those they loved and for those who needed special help from the good Lord. But there came a time when my son's spontaneous prayer brought enormous joy.

I was involved with the Women's World Day of Prayer, and since it was to be conducted in our church, I was to be the preacher. My husband was absent at conference meetings, so the children would be left alone. Our house was right next to the church, so there was no real need for concern, but I was somewhat stressed at the thought of leaving them, together with the responsibility of preaching. Seven-year-old Lyell sensed my tension and, sitting up in his bed, said solemnly, "Don't be nervous, Mommy, because I will say a 'Dear Lord' for you."

That darling child could never know, apart from the lingering hug we shared, what calm that childish assurance brought to me. I said in my own heart, *Thank You, Lord, for the privilege of teaching these little ones the precious blessings of prayer. Let them always know the blessing both received and given in praying for others.*

EDNA HEISE

Lord, I Want to Go Home

You number my wanderings; put my tears into Your bottle; are they not in Your book? Ps. 56:8, NKJV.

AS I RAISED MY knuckles to rap on the door I could hear sobbing within the room. I'd come to the dorm room of a friend to ask her to go to a program in the gym with me. After hesitating for a moment, I gently knocked. Through the sobbing a voice said, "Come in."

Ilene lay on her bed, holding an envelope and a letter. "Ilene, what's wrong?" I asked. Her sobs increased.

"Is your mother OK?"

She nodded but sobbed on. When she could speak, she told me the letter was from her mother, telling her that her older brother and sister, who had been away from home working their way through college, had managed to get home for the weekend. Only Ilene was absent from the family.

I could only say, "Oh, Ilene!" I nearly shed tears myself. Ilene had stayed at the school all summer, working to help pay her own tuition. There had been no money for a trip home. Home was three states away, and her farm family was struggling to keep things going.

At one time or other I had felt the strong yearning in my heart to go home. It can be overwhelming—the desire to see mother and father and feel the joy of going home to those so dear to my heart.

We look forward to a wonderful homecoming soon. Ilene's parents, as well as mine, have been asleep in Jesus during much of the past 50 years. As the years went by we became adults. Our education was finished. We had a career, and then we had our own families. As our children became adults they scattered to the four winds and gave us grandchildren. Many fond memories live in our hearts and minds that can still fill our eyes with tears as we think of them. But we know that the time of reunion is just ahead of us. What a joyful time that will be when God wipes away every tear, and we can once again embrace those we loved so much and we can say joyfully, "Praise God; we have come home at last!" VERA NELSON

Bread, and Much More

Lo, children are an heritage of the Lord. Ps. 127:3.

SHE DIDN'T SPEAK ENGLISH. She had four small children. Her husband's company had "folded." There was no income. And there was no food.

It was a school holiday, and she had brought her third-grade son to the service center to translate for her. With his help I secured the required information and prepared a food coupon for them. Then I turned to the little boy, asking him what he wanted to be when he grew up. He shrugged his shoulders (a common response). "Really," I persisted, "if you could be anything you wanted to be, what would that be?" He leaned toward me and quietly responded, "A doctor."

"You can be a doctor!" I exclaimed. "You certainly can be a doctor! Just say to yourself every single day, 'I'm going to be a doctor.'" Then we talked about the prerequisites for becoming a doctor—going to school every day, studying hard, getting good grades—that sort of thing. Quite spontaneously I humorously asked, "When I get to be an old woman—hey, I'm already an old lady!—and you are a doctor, if I get sick, will you take care of me?" His big brown eyes twinkled, and he grinned broadly. "I sure will. I sure will take care of you."

Twice during that brief conversation his mother had interrupted us. Probably she was trying to make sense of the concerned conversation I was having with her young son and my accompanying enthusiastic gestures. His interpretations, though, seemed to satisfy her, and with food coupon in hand and broad smiles all around, mother and son went to secure the needed assistance.

I continued thinking of this intelligent little boy and the many other children everywhere just like him. Each of them is a "heritage of the Lord." All of them need to become aware of their individual potentials and opportunities. All of them need mentoring and encouragement as they struggle to attain their dreams. I was happy to be a conduit in arranging food for four hungry children, a distraught mother, and an unemployed father. But the real satisfaction came in the opportunity to begin instilling a vision in a young mind that perhaps could result eventually in breaking the crippling cycle of poverty in which they live.

Bread for the hungry? Indeed. But more than physical bread for the "heritage of the Lord."

LOIS E. JOHANNES

House for the Master

The King shall answer and say unto them, Verily I say unto you, Inasmuch as ye have done it unto one of the least of these my brethren, ye have done it unto me. Matt. 25:40.

RIDING DOWN THE HIGHWAYS and lanes of Cambodia, I felt as though I was inside a machine that tossed me around and up and down. The driver of our van was careful, but I almost had to close my eyes as I watched ahead—sinkholes, ruts, and roadbeds had been washed out in the frequent floods. The former Communist government had left the country in shambles, from the transportation to the poverty to the illiteracy of the victims of its oppression. Most people still live in extreme poverty.

The people were deeply grateful for help given by the mission relief organization with which I was traveling; it included small stipends for pastors, bicycles for Bible workers, rice for people left starving as a result of the floods, as well as Bibles, songbooks, and thatched-roof chapels for their worship.

As we drove down one of the narrow, rutted byways to meet with a group of believers, I noticed a row of tiny shelters beside the road. They were perhaps 8 feet by 10 feet, with thatched walls and roof. I wondered if they could be chicken houses or some kind of animal shelters. They were certainly too small for people to live in.

We climbed the pole ladder into the church and sat on the floor for the worship service. After the meeting, when we had started our return trip, our translator asked, "Do you remember that certain woman?" And he described her as best he could. "I learned that this believer has no home. A woman who lives in one of those tiny shelters beside the road allows her to share that crowded 8' x 10' space with her. Our member so much wants to have a little space of her own. I gave her enough money to build a similar home for herself."

"How much will it cost to build her a new home?" we asked.

"Eighteen dollars (U.S.), which is enough to buy the thatch and poles to build her own hut. The church members will help her put it up. She was so grateful for the opportunity to have a place of her own."

I could close my eyes and almost hear Jesus' voice: "Thank you for My home. You have done it unto Me." RUTH WATSON

A Stranger, and You Took Me In

For I was hungry and you gave Me food; I was thirsty and you gave Me drink; I was a stranger and you took Me in; I was naked and you clothed Me; I was sick and you visited Me; I was in prison and you came to Me. Matt. 25:35, 36, NKJV.

IT WAS A VERY COLD morning sometime toward the end of November. My husband and I were having our early-morning three-mile walk. After about two miles, my husband said he had to hurry home; I chose to finish my walk. As I was about to go around the corner of the block, I met a young boy who was wearing a scanty T-shirt that cold day. He must have been about 10 or 11 years of age. I had walked around that particular street for years, but I'd never met that boy before. Could it be that he had just moved into this neighborhood?

I greeted him with a smile and a "Good morning!" I was surprised he returned my greeting, because boys and girls usually don't care to answer.

When I had rounded the bend, I thought, *I should have offered him my jacket. And I could have invited him to come eat breakfast with us.* I hurriedly tried to go back, but he was nowhere to be found. I ran toward the main road and looked to the left and to the right, but there was no trace of him.

I felt so bad, because I knew I had missed doing something good for someone that morning. I reasoned that perhaps the next day I would see him again. But I never saw him again.

As I was finishing my walk, I asked God to forgive me of my sin of omission. The words of Jesus reverberated in my inmost soul: "For I was hungry and you gave Me no food; I was thirsty and you gave Me no drink; I was a stranger and you did not take Me in, naked and you did not clothe Me, sick and in prison and you did not visit Me" (Matt. 25:42, 43, NKJV).

Would God forgive me for my insensitivity, especially toward the needs of that young boy? Perhaps he was an angel in disguise. Oh, how I wished I'd been quick enough to recognize the need that cold morning. My prayer, that day and every day, was for God to give me another opportunity to be the Master's hands or Jesus' feet or lips. As one popular quote says: "Only one life, 'twill soon be past; only what's done for Christ will last."

OFELIA A. PANGAN

Lost: My Joy

Restore unto me the joy of thy salvation. Ps. 51:12.

HAVE YOU EVER HAD your joy stolen? Oh, I know you may be saying, "How can you steal something that's intangible?" But the enemy of our souls, Satan himself, has a master plan in mind—and that is to steal our joy. Why is joy such a precious commodity to Satan? Because once he steals our joy in Jesus, his next target is our soul.

The sad thing is that many people don't realize that their joy is linked to their relationship with Jesus. We feel that joy comes from a good church service that must include good music, good preaching, and good feelings. More often than not, we blame the pastor and the church leaders for stealing our joy when we feel that the church service didn't leave us feeling joy-filled.

Well, it's time to face the truth. As long as we don't make our daily time with God the first priority in our lives, then our joy will be short-lived. As a matter of fact, it may even be nonexistent. How can I face the unexpected challenges of each new day when the Source of my strength is gone? How can I have peace of mind and joy untold when the One who supplies that joy and peace is not given first place in my life?

One of the greatest joys I experience is that every time I talk about joy and the joy-stealer in our lives, I see people's lives change. It's as though a light goes on in their life as they realize that joy is not a feeling but a state of mind. It's not affected by external situations and events but by our internal relationship with Jesus.

I thank God for the message of joy He has given me to share with women and men I meet in my travels. The message came with a price—through trials and tribulations God has taught me the message of joy, but I can't say I would have had it any other way. Learning the true source of my joy and that I can hold on to it despite the challenges I face each day has made all the difference in my life.

I don't know what challenges you face this day, but I do know that you're not alone. Your joy may be stolen, but it's not lost. The source is Jesus. Why not spend some time with Him today and have your joy cup filled? Our God is in the restoration business—restoring joy.

HEATHER-DAWN SMALL

A Showcase of Grace

And God is able to make all grace abound to you, so that in all things at all times, having all that you need, you will abound in every good work. 2 Cor. 9:8, NIV.

GRACE. THAT ONE-SYLLABLE WORD has retained its simplicity and beauty in the midst of a corrupt world. Philip Yancey, in his book *What's So Amazing About Grace?* calls it the best word.

Perhaps nothing can help us understand this profound theological concept better than to see it in practice in the life of a person who is overwhelmed by grace. Much like the Holy Spirit, symbolized by the invisible wind, this potent power is best expressed in a life rather than described in limited human language.

God arranged for me to better catch a glimpse of grace through a chance meeting with Kate, a surviving spouse in her 70s. From looking at her, in her old and worn-out garb, no one would ever have guessed that she had donated more than a half million dollars toward the cause of God.

She has experienced the wondrous grace of God of which she feels so unworthy. She doesn't ask God for blessings; instead, her philosophy in life is to keep every penny so she can use it to help others. Her daily prayer is to ask God to send her those who need help. She doesn't feel the need to buy new clothes, or even indulge in some exotic expensive fruit she enjoys. Her entire focus in life is on how she can assist in making others less fortunate more comfortable.

Kate has strength flowing through her 75-year-old fingers that would put many a 45-year-old to shame. Her gift of massage has blessed many a soul suffering from pain. Those who stop by from time to time to seek relief from pain also benefit often from the bountiful harvest of her little garden. She truly believes that the God she serves will abundantly provide for her all that she will ever need.

What a showcase of grace! She was so full to overflowing with the glorious gifts that God had showered upon her that she felt she could never repay God for what He has done for her. Her only response to this amazing grace is to represent God in helping others on earth.

SALLY LAM-PHOON

My Grateful Prayer

And him that cometh to me I will in no wise cast out. John 6:37.

EACH MORNING I BEGIN my day with this prayer:

Father God, thank You for granting me another day of life, for Your merciful protection over us during these days of terrorism. Thank You for Your unfathomable love in giving us Your only begotten Son, Jesus, "that whosoever believeth in him should not perish, but have everlasting life" (John 3:16). I'm a "whosoever," Father. I believe in Your Son, Jesus. Please help my unbelief!

Thank You, dear Jesus, for being willing to leave Your glorious, heavenly home to come to earth as a baby, a child, and a young man who faced unending temptations! Yet You overcame each temptation hurled at You! My thank-You is so inadequate for the loneliness, hunger, rejection, mockery, spitting, and cruelty You suffered during Your life here on earth. Thank You for the scourging You endured until Your back was raw and bleeding. Thank You for attempting to carry that sliver-filled cross, fainting beneath its load! Thank You for enduring the piercing, thorny crown. Above all, thank You for enduring those awful square nails in Your hands and feet. Thank You for remaining on that cross in painful shame and nakedness—thirsty, hungry, and in painful agony—feeling utterly forsaken by Your Father. In one second You could have chosen to jump off of that cross and forget about dying to save us sinners. But You didn't—You endured it all because of Your great love! I cannot begin to fathom Your great love and sacrifice, Jesus!

You said in John 6:37: "Him that cometh to me I will in no wise cast out." Thank You for that promise and the many other promises of love and hope You have given us in Your Holy Word, the Bible!

Until I can thank You face to face on that heavenly shore, please accept my sincere thank-You now for Your inconceivable love and sacrifice on the cross to save even me. Eagerly I look forward to thanking You throughout all eternity and falling at Your nail-scarred feet to thank You for giving Yourself so unselfishly to save me. Help me give myself to You just as unselfishly, today and always. Amen.

NATHALIE LADNER-BISCHOFF

Macaroni Miracle

Cast all your anxiety on him because he cares for you. 1 Peter 5:7, NIV.

AT FIRST I DIDN'T think of it as a miracle. Actually, I thought it was a horrible mistake. My grandson, whose parents lived nearby, was home for Thanksgiving vacation and had brought three friends with him who lived too far away to go home. Since these boys were eager to earn some spending money and we had some odd jobs that needed to be done, they were soon working in our yard.

"You better fix them something to eat at noon," said our older daughter, who was also visiting. "The boys will probably still be here then, and they'll be hungry." Her suggestion was to fix some macaroni. "Boys always like macaroni," she said.

"Do you think three packages would be enough?" I asked.

"I'm sure it will be," she said, although her only experience in feeding young people was cooking for her nephews and nieces.

By the time I had cooked three packages of macaroni I had two big kettlesful. Then the boys went back to our son's house to eat lunch without saying anything to us. *My husband and I will be eating macaroni for a week,* I thought.

That afternoon I decided to take the cooked macaroni down to our daughter-in-law so that she could feed it to the boys later. When we arrived we found that company had come in and the young folks, now including two teenage girls, had decided to go on a hike along the river. Our grandson was used to this sort of thing, but we quickly realized that they were on a challenging hike that would take longer than they had planned.

Our daughter-in-law, busy with extra guests and caring for her disabled husband, had just planned a light supper, but we knew the young folks would return tired and with ravenous appetites. Extra macaroni to the rescue! Our daughter soon had two macaroni casseroles in the oven, and several hours later when the weary hikers returned, the casseroles were eaten with gusto. What I thought had been a disaster had turned into a welcome meal for hungry hikers.

Thank You, Father, for Your promise to care even about such humble things as macaroni. BETTY J. ADAMS

Reverse Shopping

You do not realize that you are . . . poor. . . . Buy from me gold refined in the fire, so you can become rich." Rev. 3:17, 18, NIV.

I *KNOW THERE'S A LESSON in this somewhere,* I told God, *but what?* I was in the middle of one of my most embarrassing moments, looking for God to calm me.

Have you ever experienced reverse shopping? It is really quite the rush!

You see, I had just purchased some special delicacies at my favorite health food store, making sure to stock up on those refrigerated and frozen food items. That was when the sky fell.

"Your credit card has been denied. You don't have enough credit," the woman at the cash register said. She looked sorry but firm.

I was celebrating finishing the first week at my new job after being out of work for a month and a half. Things had been rather lean, but a real paycheck was in sight, and I felt sure I had enough cushion in my account for some special treats. Not so. Upon calling my bank, I was told about a policy that played a part in this lower-than-expected balance. On principle, I don't carry cash or my checkbook, so I was definitely in a bind. I was poor, but didn't know it till then. I'd been shopping with gusto, with no knowledge concerning my true state of affairs.

"Oh, I'm so sorry," I offered, trying to save face. "I'll be glad to return the items to the shelf."

And so here I was, returning each item from a full basket of goodies. It took a lot less time to "shop" in reverse, and I found it to be a lot less expensive! Somehow I managed to wear a smile on my face as I reshelved. Aisle by aisle, I prayed, *This had better be a good one.*

I felt humiliated—and humbled. I hit a new low. In that moment I saw myself with striking reality. I was poor (and felt miserable and wretched besides). The veil of superficial contentment had been stripped away. Though God allowed me to absorb that feeling for a long time, He didn't abandon me there. He brought me home, and I ate lunch from the tasty options He had earlier provided for me. I found it profitable to let God purchase my humility rather than to buy whatever I wanted. JANEL RAELENE PALMER

A Sack of Rice

God shall supply all your need. Phil. 4:19.

THIS FAMILY EXPERIENCE RELATED by my older sibling began when the Japanese declared war, now called World War II. We lived in Artacho, in the Philippines. Father and my oldest brother, David, joined the National Guard and learned that the military would guard the safety of the community. Preparing for any eventuality, Father gave each of us children who were old enough a backpack, ready to pick up when it came time to leave.

Entrusting our lives to God, everyone felt secure until the infantry began marching on the road a few yards from our house. Mother, who was nursing our 3-month-old sister, became fearful, even more so when the cavalry came on the heels of the infantry. When they heard enemy planes overhead, soldiers on horseback sought refuge behind and under the eaves of our house. The commotion made Mother shake with fear. When the baby began crying nonstop, mother begged to seek safety in the hills where Josefina, whom my parents had adopted years earlier, lived with her husband. Father hesitated, then relented and asked David to escort the family.

We stayed with Josefina only a short time before Father called us back. Buses took about 60 of us to a place where we camped in the woods for months. The company broke up after the Allied Forces surrendered. Father led his family on foot to where he had once pastored, to the property he had bought near the church he planted. Before long, a congregation met every Sabbath. After the service he invited members who lived farther away to lunch at our home.

One Friday Mother announced, "We have no rice." But at the setting of the sun, as usual, Father began singing—his call for worship—and the family joined him in "Day Is Dying in the West." In his sermon the next day, he told of Mother's no-rice warning, then added, "This morning, early, I found a sack of rice on the front porch. The Lord provided."

A man stood up. "Pastor," he began, "I was passing by your house, carrying a sack of rice. When I heard you singing, I didn't want to break the Sabbath, so I dropped the sack on your porch, knowing it would be safe there."

Father replied: "The Lord supplied. Brother, come with your family to lunch."

CONSUELO JACKSON

Spiritual Pioneers

In My Father's house are many mansions; if it were not so, I would have told you. I go to prepare a place for you. And if I go and prepare a place for you, I will come again and receive you to Myself; that where I am, there you may be also. John 14:2, 3, NKJV.

SHORTLY AFTER MY FAMILY moved to Nebraska, there was a reenactment of the wagon trains moving west on the Oregon Trail. One of the covered wagons started rolling down a steep embankment. The tongue of the wagon broke, leaving the frightened occupants careening down with no way to stop. That very scenario had been a very real danger to the pioneers.

At various sites along the trail there are markers telling about the harsh conditions the pioneers faced. I began to think more about these people, especially the women. They were making decisions to leave their homes, their families, and everything familiar to join their husbands in an unfamiliar, untamed land—the Western frontier. Some of these women were "mail-order brides" with no real knowledge of the men to whom they were about to pledge their lives. But they went because of a promise, the promise of a better life. Some of the women were simply following their husband's desire for a new and different life. But none really had a clear picture of what lay ahead. They were journeying by faith, placing their trust in a man, sometimes in an unseen man. Some of these women were sorely disappointed in what they found. Others held their heads high and made the best of it. But most found that the hard journey there had been just the beginning.

Like the mail-order brides of old, we too are on a journey toward a Husband we have never seen. But we have His love letters filled with promises of good things to come. We too have to leave the familiar surroundings of this earth to be with Him in His wonderful home. Now is the time to step forward in faith, trusting the unseen, because we can be sure that it far exceeds what we have now. Nor do we really have a clear picture of where we're going. "Eye has not seen, nor ear heard, nor have entered into the heart of man the things which God has prepared for those who love Him" (1 Cor. 2:9, NKJV).

One thing we can be sure of, though. Unlike those pioneer women, we will have no cause for disappointment when we arrive at our Promised Land. And we will discover that the wonders of our new home will surely be more than worth the hard journey.

RACHEL ATWOOD

Be Content With What You Have

Be content with such things as ye have. Heb. 13:5.

SOME FRIENDS OF OURS invited us and a whole houseful of other people to their home for dinner one Sabbath. My friend had been a professional cook, and she loves to entertain.

I went into the kitchen to ask if there was anything I could do, but she told me she had everything under control. She went to the refrigerator and pulled out a huge white oval porcelain serving dish with a beautiful arrangement of lettuce, sliced tomatoes, onions, beets, green beans, and cucumbers—something you might see at an elegant restaurant. Then she took out a large, red bowl filled with cold, tempting potato salad. A couple lovely casserole dishes were last to come out of the refrigerator, and she promptly popped them into the oven. I was impressed!

The food was set out on a nicely decorated table, and we served ourselves. There was so much food that I couldn't fit everything onto my plate. But even though the food was delicious, what impressed me most was how it was served. I loved her beautiful platters and decorative bowls.

I began to think of my own china set. It was a wedding gift—38 years ago. It's still a nice set, but let's face it—it's old. And it's for only eight people; I usually entertain at least 10 at a time. I thought, *I really could use some new serving bowls and platters. The rustic Mexican serving dishes I use are more than 20 years old.*

A few weeks later Hecht's department store was having a 50 percent off sale in their china department. So guess what? I ordered new china and serving bowls, and invited my friend and her family over. Unfortunately, my new china didn't arrive before my guests did, so I ended up serving them on my old set of dishes. I was disappointed until my friend asked me, "Where did you get your lovely Mexican bowls? I've been looking all over for something like this." When I told her I had bought them in Mexico, she said, "Well, I might just have to go to Mexico to get some."

I almost laughed. Here I'd been wanting what she had, and she was wanting what I had. How funny we human beings are. I need to remember that experience whenever I become discontented with what I already have.

NANCY CACHERO VÁSQUEZ

Pressing Through the Crowd

She had heard the reports about Jesus, and came up behind him in the crowd and touched his garment. For she said, "If I touch even his garments, I shall be made well." Mark 5:27, 28, RSV.

THERE IS A BIBLE story I especially relate to because it's about a woman who suffered with "female" problems. In Jewish society this made her unclean, untouchable. So besides being sick, weak, and in constant pain, she was very lonely. Looking for healing, she had spent a lot of money on doctors, and they had only made her worse. She had tried everything the world had to offer, but had found no relief. Then she heard about the miracles of Jesus, and hope surged through her, giving her the strength to go find Jesus.

When she arrived, there was a throng of people following Jesus from place to place. I'm sure she began to despair of ever speaking to Him, but her faith took over, and she believed that if she could just touch His garment she would be healed. She reached out and barely touched the border of Jesus' robe, and instantly the flow of blood stopped. She was healed!

Jesus felt the healing power leave His body; He turned and asked, "Who touched Me?" The disciples were incredulous. With all the people pressing around, how would Jesus even notice? But this was a different touch, a touch of faith that had resulted in healing. When He heard her story, Jesus said, "Daughter, your faith has made you well; go in peace, and be healed of your disease" (Mark 5:34, RSV).

Our problems may not be physical; perhaps they are mental, emotional, or relational. It doesn't matter what label you give them. How many times do we try all that the world offers? We go to doctors or therapists. We buy self-help books. We talk to friends and anyone else who will listen. We do Internet searches. We contact church prayer chains. All these things are good. The problem is that so many times we try what the world offers before we give our problems to Jesus.

The only way to true healing and peace is to reach out in faith and place our needs in the hands of Jesus. We must press through the crowd of the world and touch Jesus.

Lord, help me to remember to turn to You first and put my faith in You, putting aside all the distractions of our modern times. For I want to be healed and to live in Your peace.

JUDY MUSGRAVE SHEWMAKE

An Intimate Moment With God

Come, let us bow down in worship, let us kneel before the Lord our Maker. Ps. 95:6, NIV.

WITH EACH TEARDROP THAT fell from her almond-shaped eyes, she washed the specks of grime from His feet. With her long, thick, black hair, she dabbed them dry. With tenderness she cradled His feet in her hands and with gentleness removed the top from her white alabaster jar. She poured the perfumed oil slowly until all of it had trickled over His feet.

She looked into His eyes, eyes that reflected so much love she could hardly bear to look at them. Yet to tell the truth, she could hardly bear to look away.

It was an intimate moment—a moment shared between the Creator and the created, the Savior-to-be and the daughter in need, the One to be worshipped and the one to give worship. It was a moment when the heart of God and the heart of His child were as they were always meant to be—together.

In Luke 7 we see a picture of plain, unadulterated worship. It is the story of how a woman saved a whole year's wages to buy perfume to say thank You to her Savior by anointing His feet. She did it simply because she adored Jesus. She worshipped Him for who He was and what He had done for her. He had given her freedom from the consequences of her sins. She took sheer delight in worshipping God and kneeling at His feet.

The picture is a pleasurable one but possibly far removed from our experiences of today.

When was the last time you wanted to break open a bottle of perfume in honor of God? When was the last time you wanted to kneel by His feet? When was the last time you felt joy just in worshipping God?

In the midst of our desire to achieve, accomplish, seek acknowledgment, and find acceptance, the picture of the woman and her alabaster jar can seem very distant to what is going on in our lives. Yet real heartfelt worship of God can provide what each of us is seeking—fulfillment within our hearts.

Want a challenge for today? Then break open a perfume jar, worship God, and share an intimate moment with your Creator. Your heart will truly be satisfied.

MARY BARRETT

Caught in the Storm

Master, carest thou not that we perish? And he arose, and rebuked the wind. Mark 4:38, 39.

IT WAS IN DECEMBER, a hot summer's day in South Africa, when I attended the wedding of a friend's daughter. I'd decided that I wouldn't attend the reception, so immediately after the service I left for home.

My way home goes through town, so I decided to stop by a furniture store to look for a washing machine that I badly needed. I couldn't wring out my washing properly because of painful finger joints. I came across one at a reasonable price, and the sales associate and I had started talking business when it suddenly became dark, and a strong wind began to blow. It blew off rooftops and uprooted trees and stripped iron from roofs. And then came a heavy rain.

I wondered, *What next?* Soon the streets were flooded and cars swerved in all directions, some crushed under the heavy tree branches. Water streamed through several parts of the shop ceiling. The sales associate and a few other workers immediately placed buckets in those places to catch the water.

Then a big piece of roofing zinc hit the huge front window, missing one customer by inches. Fear gripped me. I silently prayed, *Lord, help me,* fearing that water would gush into the shop, where I had thought I was safe. A cold wind blew into the shop, and lightning reflected in all the mirrors.

In that moment I knew how the disciples must have felt when they were caught in the storm at sea and cried out, "Master, carest thou not that we perish?"

Suddenly all calmed down, and I knew that Christ had rebuked the storm, as He had done on the sea.

As I walked out into the stillness of the town I saw that the pavement was strewn with leaves and pieces of glass. I made my way home by walking over debris until I finally found a taxi.

I wondered if I still had a home. My heart rate increased, and my steps slowed. Thankfully, I saw no damage to the house and thanked God for His deliverance.

Help me, Lord, to remember that in the raging storms of life, You care.

ETHEL DORIS MSUSENI

December 4

A Valuable Lesson Learned

Honour the Lord with thy substance, and with the firstfruits of all thine increase. Prov. 3:9.

MY MOTHER HAD TWO children, both girls. My sister was 10 years older than I. When she got married and moved to another area, our relationship became somewhat fractured, but my mother allowed me to make frequent visits to her house. As time passed, my sister had six children, all very close in age. At her husband's suggestion, she never worked outside the home. But even though her husband was employed, the family began experiencing financial difficulty. Eventually the time came when she had used up all her credit and was having a problem getting family necessities.

I had already relocated to New York City, where I was employed as a registered nurse, when my sister asked for my assistance. This I readily gave by sending her my tithe money. I rationalized that since I was giving it for a worthy cause, the Lord would understand. I was soon to learn how wrong I was.

In my desire to help others, I had begun tutoring a young woman whom I had encouraged to attend nursing school. She came to my house three times a week, and after our sessions I would drive her home. One rainy night I was making a turn to park my year-old car at the back of my house, something I had done safely many times before. That night, however, I scratched the entire left side of the vehicle. This accident upset me, because I knew how expensive it would be to repair. The next day I took the car to the repair shop."

"How much is this going to cost?" I asked.

I was shocked when I was told that the job would cost me the same amount of money as the tithe I had sent to my sister. It was then that I realized what a terrible mistake I had made. Of course I paid the bill and asked the Lord for His forgiveness, promising Him that I would never do that again.

More important, the experience taught me a valuable lesson I won't forget as long as I live. I want to honor God's requests of me. God always blesses when we're faithful, because He is faithful. DOLORES SMITH

Better Not Forget Your Friends

I will never leave you nor forsake you. Joshua 1:5, NIV.

I FOUND ALEX TO BE unusually quiet one afternoon as I was driving the school bus. "I'm sure going to miss you!" he said, breaking the silence. After a pause he continued, "You better not forget your friends!"

Six-year-old Alex, the youngest of three children, rode my bus every day. How could I forget this curly-haired comedian? One morning as he boarded the bus his first words were "You better not be late!" At first I didn't remember that his class was in charge of the Week of Prayer and that Alex was to offer the prayer. I suddenly realized that this was important to him. His teacher had printed a short prayer on a piece of paper that he tried desperately to memorize: "Dear Jesus, help us to learn more about You, and please bless Pastor . . . " His mind drew a blank. He tried again and again. Finally he got it after the third time and finished with a hearty "Amen! Bravo!"

I suggested it may not be a good idea to add the "bravo." He agreed. "Will you come in for worship?" he asked as we got closer to the school. I said I would.

Then came Alex's birthday, and for weeks he reminded me. "Are you going to get me something?" My standard answer was "I'm too poor." My answer seemed lame, so I decided to get something small, for less than a dollar. I waited until it was almost time for him to get off the bus before I gave him the package. Eagerly he tore off the wrapping and shouted, "Just what I always wanted!" It was a package of cherry-flavored gum. He was thrilled. He took one piece for himself and shared the rest with his brother, sister, and other friends.

My husband had accepted a transfer to another conference. That meant I had to leave my job in the middle of the year. On the afternoon of my next-to-last day Alex was seated behind me—but this time it was his choice. "I know what you're going to do tomorrow. You're going to drive back to school after you drop us off. You'll go to your car and, as you drive away, you're going to cry. You'll wish you were with us."

That happened six years ago, and so far I haven't forgotten my friends, especially Alex.

Thank You, my forever Friend, for never forgetting us either. VERA WIEBE

Content Whatever the Circumstances

I have learned to be content whatever the circumstances. Phil. 4:11, NIV.

A BROCHURE FOR A WILDLIFE reserve caught my eye, and I picked it up. While the protection of bats, bettongs, and giant freshwater lobsters is very laudable, I'm sure, what really interested me was the platypus pictured on the front. This unique Australian resident is, as the brochure explained, a semiaquatic, egg-laying mammal with webbed feet and a leathery snout that resembles a duck's bill. (The first specimens to be seen by European scientists 200 years ago were thought to be fakes.) Now, I had seen platypuses behind glass at the zoo, in an environment carefully prepared to simulate their natural habitat; but I had never seen one "in the wild."

This apparently wouldn't be easy to achieve. Besides being endangered by things associated with human habitation—domestic dogs and polluted waterways—the platypus, the brochure warned, is instinctively shy. It is usually active only at dawn or dusk, but has excellent eyesight in low light and is good at detecting any changes or movement in its environment. One would need to dress from top to toe in dark clothing, try to stay hidden behind trees or bushes, avoid using flashlights or flash cameras—and be prepared for disappointment.

As it turned out, I achieved my wish with surprising ease. I simply went for a late-afternoon walk with my sister as guide and, as the light faded, suddenly there it was! This platypus obviously hadn't read the textbooks—or the brochure from the wildlife reserve. It was living, not in some remote bushland stream, but in the creek running through a public park in a small seaside town with children's play equipment, houses, and traffic only yards away! We stood on the little bridge over the creek and watched in delight as it went about foraging for food just beneath our feet, swimming and diving effortlessly. We marveled at the Creator's expertise, His love of variety, and His sense of humor! And something about this small creature that ignored the conventional wisdom and the odds against it and simply got on with its life really appealed to me.

Lord, let me learn a lesson from an unconventional platypus—the secret of being content whatever the circumstances. Even when my environment seems hostile, let me not merely survive but thrive in Your care. And let me be a source of delight to all those who come my way. JENNIFER M. BALDWIN

The Repaired Dryer

Is anything too hard for the Lord? Gen. 18:14, TEV.

I WAS AT HOME ONE Sunday evening when suddenly I heard my sister, Daicy, say, "Lanny, our dryer is not working!"

"Oh, no, please, not this time!" I murmured. I looked at the dryer, but apparently there was nothing I could do—it just couldn't be started. So as we had our evening worship that night I decided to bring this problem to the Lord. "Lord, please help us," I prayed. "I don't know what is going on with this dryer. It worked well before, and now suddenly it's not working. You know that we do need this dryer, Lord. Help us so that, according to Your will, we can have our dryer work again." After I closed my prayer I went to see if the dryer would work as usual, but it still didn't.

The next morning I checked again. Nothing. So I decided to check the Web site to find out more information from the manufacturer regarding the repair cost. Unfortunately, the dryer was no longer under warranty.

I felt sad as I realized that buying a new dryer would cost a lot, but repairing the present dryer would also be expensive. Plus, winter was coming, and driving back and forth to the public Laundromat would be very difficult during winter.

The next Sunday evening, exactly a week after my dryer quit, I tried it again—and this time it worked! I was so happy that I called my mom and my sister to come see what was happening. And there we were, in front of the dryer, watching while it ran smoothly as though there had never been anything wrong.

All of us said, "Praise the Lord!" Our hearts were filled with joy and thankfulness. We agreed that we have an awesome God. I still don't understand how my dryer works well again without any repair being made, but one thing I know for sure: God is in control.

Thank You, Lord, for showing Your unfailing love and help to me. My heart overflows in praise each time I use my dryer. Thank You for these reminders—there's nothing impossible with You. LANNY LYDIA PONGILATAN

The Long-awaited Snow

Come now, and let us reason together, saith the Lord: though your sins be as scarlet, they shall be as white as snow; though they be red like crimson, they shall be as wool. Isa. 1:18.

I FOUND MYSELF WISHING for snow. After I had heard on the radio and seen on the TV that it was snowing, my thoughts went back to my childhood days, and I began reflecting on my reasons for wanting it to snow. Oh, how I had loved playing in the snow! Throwing snowballs, making our famous snowman using my dad's old straw hat, old red tie, and whatever we found for eyes, nose, and mouth . . . My sister, brother, and I had enjoyed eating snow ice cream my mother would make using sugar, milk, and flavoring. I thought of my mother's reason for wanting snow. She would say, "A big snow will kill the germs." My grandson Trevor's wish was for "No school tomorrow!" During my years of working I too enjoyed snow days.

During my adult years the reasons for wishing for snow changed. I no longer wanted to play in it or eat it. I didn't even want to walk in it—I just wanted to look out the window and watch the falling snowflakes.

I remembered that no matter how much I wished for snow, it would come only when God was ready to send it. As the famous saying goes: "He may not come when I want Him to, but He's always on time."

Surprisingly, in January 2001, as predicted by the weather forecaster, snow began falling, spreading a white blanket over the lawns, housetops, and trees. As I sat by the window, watching the snowflakes, I thought of our Creator, the maker of all things, who has made each snowflake in its own design.

I thank Jesus for the lovely white snowflakes He sends and for the provisions He has made for my sins. Although I sin, He's willing to forgive me through Him and by Him. I pray, "Whiter than snow, Lord, whiter than snow. Lord, wash me, and I shall be whiter than snow."*

I long to be ready for Your return. I know not the hour nor day, but You said it, and I believe Your Word, for Your Word is truth and does not change.

ANNIE B. BEST

---

* Modified from the song "Whiter Than Snow," no. 318 in *The Seventh-day Adventist Hymnal.* Published by Review and Herald Publishing Association.

Computers!

Search me, O God, and know my heart; test me and know my anxious thoughts. Ps. 139:23, NIV.

I HAD SUCCESSFULLY PRINTED one side of our church directory and put it back in the printer to print the other side. Then I started typing on another project. I was making good progress and had thoughts of doing some fun things in the afternoon. When the printer stopped, I glanced at the finished product. *Oh, no, it can't be!* I thought. I had put the paper in wrong, and the back side was printed upside down. "What a waste of paper, ink, and time," I groaned. It had to be done over.

When the directory was finally done, I tried to print a copy using colored ink, but the printer kept sending me messages I didn't like, then finally froze up. I couldn't "escape," so I had to shut down the computer. When I tried to turn it back on, the switch wouldn't work. *Now what?* I decided to call a computer-literate friend for advice. After all was said and done, it was decided the cause might be dust. My frustration level was really rising.

I unhooked all the plugs connected to the back and hauled the computer out to the garage where my husband keeps an air compressor. I was going to do this job well. Sure enough, the computer was layered with dust, and I was choking by the time I finished cleaning it out. Back in the house, I vacuumed the rug where the computer rested and damp-wiped all the plugs and cords thoroughly.

After reconnecting everything, I turned on the computer and was pleased to hear the normal sounds it makes warming up. I was beginning to feel some internal stress begin to release—until I noticed that the monitor was blank. It was now midafternoon. So much for having any fun. I called my husband to the rescue because I couldn't remember how to get the cover off the surge box. He couldn't either, but he finally did, and everything was OK inside. Then I noticed that one of the auxiliary switches was off. Turning it on revealed the start-up screen. Relief.

I'm sorry to admit it, but during this whole process I never once thought to ask the Lord for help solving these problems, nor for patience to deal with them. I guess it's no surprise that neither did I thank Him when all was resolved. I can't help wondering how this scenario might have been different had I remembered my true Helper.

DONNA MEYER VOTH

December 10

The Noncompliant Heart

There is a way which seemeth right unto a man, but the end thereof are the ways of death. Prov. 14:12.

COME QUICKLY; COME QUICKLY!" she said, running to me. "Come and see Mr. S."

"What's the problem?" I asked, running behind and trying to catch up with her so that I could see what was happening to my patient.

Turning the corner, I stopped in my tracks. There near the vending machine was Mr. S, chomping down a chocolate bar. A candy wrapper and two more unopened candy bars were in his hand. The problem with this scene was that Mr. S, a "brittle" insulin-dependent diabetic, was overloading on sugar.

As we talked he continued to eat. Opening a wrapper, he began eating another candy bar. No amount of reasoning would sway this man. Nothing that was said to him by any of us (a small crowd had gathered by the break room to watch) made any difference. He just kept on eating. "I've had diabetes for a very long time," he said, "and I know this candy won't hurt me." Then he took the uneaten candy and walked to his room. This is the kind of noncompliant patient who is just so—so noncompliant (for lack of a better word). Unfortunately for him, he really did do some damage to his system that day.

Are we like this patient, sometimes attracted to people and things we know will hurt us? Despite counseling and good advice, do we continue to play with danger?

Sometimes we're attracted to the very things we know will hurt us the most. Yet feeling powerless to resist, we continue telling ourselves, "This is OK." Today God wants you to know that if what you are doing is hurting you, then it's not OK. He wants you to know that you are not powerless—the strength you need is available. God is our protector, and He will give us the strength and power we need to resist all harmful situations. We must do our part, however, and take it to Him in prayer. Only by tapping into Jesus, the power source, will we be set free. When we call upon the power of God, He will come and fight our battles.

Dear Jesus, please change my heart and help me to be compliant. Take control of my life and my problems and give me strength to overcome. Amen.

WENDY WONGK

God's Timepiece

Let us lay aside every weight, and the sin which doth so easily beset us, and let us run with patience the race that is set before us. Heb. 12:1.

ONE OF MY HUSBAND'S hobbies is to repair clocks and watches. Anywhere he sees a clock sitting idle, he will check to see if he can get it working again. Because of this hobby, we've accumulated more clocks and watches than we need—15 of them. All are working.

One day I noticed that our open-faced clock was dead. I discovered that it had been more than 20 minutes since the clock had stopped. My husband immediately took the clock down to check it and was surprised to find that the second hand was firmly bound to the side of the clock by a strand of silk, which made it impossible for it to move. He cleaned the spider's web off; then the clock was again running nicely.

"Come look at this again," I called to my husband not long after. There was the same clock, dead again. This time the spider had reinforced its attack by binding all three hands with its silky thread. So my husband cleaned the web away once more, and soon the hands were free to resume their duty of keeping perfect time.

Sin is so much like that spider. It may attack us first in a small way, but whether the sin is big or small, sin is sin. Sin will always cripple us so that we'll not be able to run the race. Sin will also reinforce its effort to keep us crippled.

Our clocks that have glass covers have no problem with any spider. We also need to protect ourselves with the shield of faith so that sin won't enter our lives. It's only by faith that we shall be overcomers. John says, "This is the victory that overcometh the world, even our faith" (1 John 5:4).

We need not be tied down by the weight of sin, for Jesus has freed us. With His help we can run the race and be overcomers. We are God's timepiece to help others know that time is drawing close to Jesus' return. Let's keep ticking on God's perfect time and plan till Jesus comes.

Birdie Poddar

His Angels Keep Thee

For he shall give his angels charge over thee, to keep thee in all thy ways. Ps. 91:11.

THE YEARS HAD SLIPPED by since college, and Rahn, a close friend with whom my son Jack had kept in touch, was now getting married. Jack and Rahn lived at opposite ends of the country, but the girl Rahn was marrying lived at the opposite end of the world—Russia! Jack flew to Moscow to attend the wedding and planned to do some sightseeing, never dreaming what lay ahead.

At the end of a great day of sightseeing and photography there was one more building to photograph—the KGB building. Jack left the car, crossed the street, and shot his photos. Suddenly two armed guards appeared, shouted to the driver to leave, and grabbed Jack, taking him into the KGB building. Jack soon found himself in a thick-walled cell with no way out, not knowing what his fate would be. He spent what seemed like an eternity praying to his heavenly Father to help him.

Finally the cell door opened, and a man in civilian clothes entered and asked in a soft-spoken voice for Jack's passport and visa. While the man studied these documents, Jack explained again and again his ignorance of a law forbidding photos to be taken of the KGB building. This man harshly reprimanded the two guards and released Jack with his camera and film intact.

Jack was out of the KGB jail cell but now found himself alone in Moscow, not knowing which direction to take. He needed to meet someone who spoke English and who also had a cell phone. He had his host's apartment address and cell phone number. He saw a young man coming up the street toward him, and to his relief this young Russian spoke perfect English and had a cell phone. Within just a few minutes he connected Jack with his host and hailed a car, and Jack was soon back at the apartment.

Jack is certain this young man was his guardian angel in disguise. After hearing Jack's story, I realized what a dangerous situation my son had been in that day. How thankful I was that while growing up in a Christian home he had learned to trust and pray to his God.

Though my children have homes of their own, not a day goes by that I don't pray for them and place them in God's care. All of us need His constant presence and sustaining. PATRICIA MULRANEY KOVALSKI

God's Children

"I know the plans I have for you," declares the Lord, "plans to prosper you and not to harm you, plans to give you hope and a future. Jer. 29:11, NIV.

I'VE LEARNED SOMETHING ABOUT myself these past few years, and that is that I'm more likely to cry for other people than for myself. Maybe it's because I have so many blessings that I feel "rich" with the things that really count—relationships in my family, with my friends, and especially with my God.

A very few years ago my heart ached for a dear young friend of mine who had a darling little boy with expressive brown eyes and an infectious laugh. Then she lost three babies, one after another. I took flowers and a card when I visited her after the third precious little person had passed away. My friend and I hugged for a while and talked. Later she said to me, "You know, Ursula, I think about when we go to heaven and three little children will come running to me—or maybe they'll still be babies, and I'll have all these wonderful children to get to know. Won't that be wonderful?" What a great trust and hope she has in Jesus!

Then one evening I had a sense that she was pregnant again (although there was no outward evidence of her pregnancy), but I didn't say a word. We kept looking at each other; then she said, "You're right, you know." I was so startled that she had read my thoughts. "I don't think I can take it again. I don't feel at all positive about this," she continued.

And then I heard cautious me saying something I wasn't aware of processing through my brain. "It's going to be fine this time," I assured her as I gave her a hug. "There is a wonderful text we can claim. I'll write it on a card and let you have it tomorrow." I was numb, wondering how I could have said such a thing.

I prayed. How I prayed! And God reminded me that each morning I ask Him to use me to bless others in any way that fits His plan. He assured me that this was His plan.

Seven and a half months later my dear friend delivered a beautiful baby girl. How we praised God! How we still praise God. She is a special child, His gift to a brokenhearted mother—and to a hesitantly trusting friend.

Ursula M. Hedges

My Answered Prayer

He can do great wonders; His steadfast love endures forever. Ps. 136:4, Clear Word.

AS AN ARMY RESERVIST, I was called to active duty after the September 11 terrorist attack, to serve with my unit in Hawaii for a period of one year. One particularly rough day I was on the verge of tears as I sat in the dining facility alone, eating supper. Throughout the day I'd been asking God to give me the strength to make it through; I didn't understand why He had allowed me to have such a hard day. I thought about the day's events and felt sorry for myself. I was trying to learn a new job. I had to use a computer program that I'd never even heard of before, and I just couldn't grasp it. The workday had seemed unusually long, and I felt tired and missed my family, friends, church, and whole other life I had left behind three months earlier. When I finished eating, I just sat there and told God that I couldn't possibly handle anything else and that I felt I'd had more than my share of trials for the day.

I got up and walked outside. There were a number of birds on the sidewalk, completely ignoring people as they walked by. But one bird in particular got my attention. For some reason I turned around, walked back, and knelt down by the bird. I expected it to fly away, but it didn't. If it wouldn't fly, I figured it was unable to. I thought it was hurt and couldn't fly, so I began asking God why He was giving me this experience. I love animals, and my heart especially goes out to ones that are hurt. I put my hand down in front of the bird, and it jumped up on my finger. I petted it and talked to it, at the same time asking God what to do, because I couldn't just leave it there, knowing it was hurt. After a few minutes the bird jumped off my finger and suddenly flew away. It wasn't hurt after all!

While I'd been wondering why God had allowed yet one more bad thing to happen to me, He was giving me pleasure from one of His lovely creatures. When I realized that, I thanked God for a perfect ending to a day that I'd thought was all bad. He knew what I'd been through and how I felt, and He knew exactly what to do to bring me out of the depression.

"He listens whenever I call, so I will depend on Him as long as I live" (Ps. 116:2, Clear Word).

KAREN BARNES SWAN

Making Memories

Trust in the Lord with all thine heart; and lean not unto thine own understanding. In all thy ways acknowledge him, and he shall direct thy paths. Prov. 3:5, 6.

I HAVE QUITE A FEW memories of my life in North Dakota. (I'd just turned 4 when we moved to Indiana in March 1927.) Fortunately, all these memories are happy ones.

Even though I recall very little about our house, the picture of my birthday cake on the cupboard shelf is still vivid in my mind. I remember the small neighborhood store and the school where my brother started first grade. We used to scramble up and down the large tube fire escape on the side of the building.

My memory bank yields up more dramatic scenes of my later childhood—my first year in school and the hunger pangs I experienced at recess on the days I had eaten no breakfast. Those were Depression years, and times were hard. A hobo came to our back door one day, asking for food, so my mother made him two egg sandwiches. He tolerated our inquisitive stares as we watched him eat the sandwiches.

Early memories always include flickering oil lamps and unheated upstairs bedrooms with never enough warm covers on cold winter nights, when sleeping three in a bed wasn't unusual. I recall the teenage years of bobby sox and penny loafers, of a quickly stolen kiss from the neighbor boy while sitting on the porch swing on a warm summer day.

In 1939 I met my husband-to-be. We married 15 months later and eventually had two children. Through the years we were blessed with six grandchildren and six great-grandchildren.

I cherish all those memories and am happy for the stacks of photo albums in the bookcase, because the scenes in my mind tend to become foggy with the passing of time. As I get older, some of the past events seem more like a dream than reality. There are times I can recall only bits and pieces—those almost-forgotten names and places and fading images where distinct faces used to be.

I can't control my destiny, so I need continual guidance from my heavenly Father that I will make daily decisions that will help determine memories I'll be making from now on. And whether those memories are happy or sad, I'll be content.

"A [woman's] heart deviseth [her] way: but the Lord directeth [her] steps" (Prov. 16:9).

Clareen Colclesser

May I Pray With You?

O God, listen to my cry! Hear my prayer! . . . For my heart is overwhelmed. Ps. 61:1, 2, NLT.

IT WAS 3:00 IN THE morning, and I was wide awake. In the stillness of the night I heard muffled voices and the sound of a radio. I crept from bed. The house was quiet; everyone was sleeping. Puzzled, I returned to bed and lay quietly. How I wished I could sleep. I heard sounds again, rose a second time, and glanced out my window. No lights on in neighboring houses, and no one on the street. I got back in bed. A few minutes later I heard louder voices. I threw on my bathrobe, ran downstairs, and flung open the front door. At first I saw nothing. Then a woman emerged from a car near the corner intersection. Sobbing uncontrollably as she walked, she flopped onto the pavement across the street from my home.

I ran toward her, my bare feet pounding the cold pavement. "Are you OK? Is there something I can do for you?" I asked. She said nothing and continued crying. I reached out, touched her shoulder, then began to rub her back gently. "Can I help you?" I again asked. Still no response. My stomach knotted, and my feet felt frozen. I felt foolish. I didn't know what to do, but I couldn't just leave. I asked once again, and in the early-morning light I saw her head move. I hesitated, then asked, "May I pray with you?"

Through several sniffles I heard her softly say yes, and as I began to pray I heard the car coming toward us. My heart leaped. Suppose this person was angry or crazy or jealous or—

"Lord, I don't know what's troubling this young woman," I prayed, "but You do. Please, Father, comfort and protect her and give her peace of mind. In Jesus' name, amen."

I patted her shoulder, wished her well, and made an immediate dash for home. Moments later she got her jacket from the car and slowly walked up the street. My heart was heavy as I watched. I whispered another prayer for her safety and her peace. It was now 5:15 a.m., and I knew that God had allowed me to be awake in the middle of the night to minister to this young woman, to share His love. Perhaps my intervention gave her strength, courage, or hope. Maybe it made a difference for her. It surely made a difference, a big difference, for me.

Heavenly Father, help us to be aware of the people around us who are hurting and to be willing to share You and make a difference in their lives. Amen.

Iris L. Stovall

The Star of Bethlehem

The Spirit is God's guarantee that he will give us everything he promised and that he has purchased us to be his own people. This is just one more reason for us to praise our glorious God. Eph. 1:14, NLT.

IT TOOK MONTHS TO LOCATE just the right star to adorn the top of our Christmas tree. That star was all gold, was the right length and breadth, and, above all, fit my limited budget. When I got home, I tied it to the little pointed branch right at the crown of our six-foot tree. The star covered the little branch, and to secure it I wound lots of twine around until the branch was hidden. That tree was now perfect, a most beautiful sight—a symbol of the season of giving and goodwill.

Christmas trees, be they fir or spruce, are always pointed at the top. Why is this? Because in the forest, where Christmas trees abound, too many trees exist together, each fighting for survival. In order to be healthy, each has to reach for the sky and strive to keep its topmost branches in the sunlight, its source of life. Every spring a new shoot forms at the top. This shoot holds the potential for growth and survival. This new shoot is made up of five points; the middle point assumes a leadership position as "king," having the responsibility to draw nutrients from its roots deep in the ground and to reach for the life-giving properties of the sun. This leader, or king pointer, has only one focus—to ensure that the whole tree survives.

What a vital lesson in Christian leadership! In all its simplicity this dual function of the king pointer reminds Christian leaders of the significance of digging deep into the study of the Word of God and reaching daily for the Sun of righteousness, knowing full well that we draw life and light for our souls through Him.

That pointer at the top came in useful as an anchor for my tree-topper, my shining star. It held the star firmly in place. The king pointer, almost hidden from sight by twine, gave all its glory to the star. Likewise, as Christian leaders, all that we do is to the praise of His glory. It's not position that calls us to do God's work; it's not for our own self-realization or self-fulfillment. It is a call to do His bidding and to show forth His glory. What a privilege that the Star of Bethlehem has chosen us as His vessels from which He can shine, eclipsing our own feeble inadequate efforts as a channel of His love and grace.

SALLY LAM-PHOON

A Cheerful Beggar

It is more blessed to give than to receive. Acts 20:35.

I DON'T KNOW HIS NAME. It never occurred to me to ask, and yet I know him by his smiling face. Even now I see his face when I think of him. He's a beggar.

Walking along Main Street in Poona, India, I was often stopped by a certain cheerful beggar. He can't walk because his legs are deformed. So he sits on a piece of wooden board that has four wheels and propels himself by putting both his palms down on the road. He can move quite fast, especially when he sees someone he recognizes, and I was one of those. I found this beggar different from the rest. He was cheerful, and while others acted as though the contributors owed them something, he appreciated whatever was given. It reminds me of the 10 lepers whom Jesus cleansed—only one of them returned to thank Jesus.

Meeting and giving to this beggar created some kind of bond between us so that whenever I saw him I was prompted to give him something. I never gave him a lot, not even enough for a meal, but whatever I gave he accepted gratefully. He inspired me to give more and to give happily. Because of him, I collected coins during the week and handed them to him whenever I went out shopping.

We were transferred from Poona to Hosur. In time I forgot all about this beggar. After a year or so, we made a trip to Poona. One day, while walking along crowded Main Street, I was surprised to see my friendly beggar wheeling fast toward me and giving me a broad smile. I was happy to see him too, and even more so when he asked, "Where were you all this time? I have not seen you for so long!" Imagine being missed and remembered by a beggar! I was touched, and I appreciated his remembering me.

This poor beggar taught me a few lessons. Be cheerful in spite of disabilities. Be content and appreciate whatever is given. Be friendly if you want friends. If you want to be truly happy, you have to form a habit of giving, and giving cheerfully, for God loves a cheerful giver. I've also learned not to give just for the sake of giving or to get rid of someone, but to stop, look at a person, and give enough to prompt a smile from them. God emptied heaven in giving His Son to die for us.

BIROL CHARLOTTE CHRISTO

Pretty Gifts

Remember the words of the Lord Jesus, how he said, It is more blessed to give than to receive. Acts 20:35.

I HAD A DEAR FRIEND who used to phone me, ask me how I was doing, then pray for me over the phone. This meant so much to me. We sometimes gave each other gifts.

One day her daughter, Linda, told me that when she visited her mother, her mother served tea in very pretty teacups. When Linda asked where those pretty teacups came from, her mother replied, "Priscilla gave them to me." Not too long after that, her mother passed away. Linda told me, "She always treasured those teacups."

I will also treasure the gifts I received from my dear praying friend and the prayers that ascended on my behalf when I needed them most. Isn't it wonderful to have friends like that?

I have another Friend who intercedes for me. He also bestows so many gifts and blessings on me. I'm so unworthy of His wonderful love to me—much more than I deserve! He gives me gifts that I'll always remember Him by. Most of the gifts He gives are very unique and beautiful—the sunrise each morning, the sunset each evening. He never uses the same colors to paint the sky!

Occasionally He sends me a rainbow to cheer me after a "rainy" day of tears. He sends the stars at night that are like tinsel glittering in the dark sky. He has given me planets to behold—strategically placed—and the moon with its various phases. He gives the sun that warms me in the day, and rain that falls to cool the earth and water the dry ground and gardens. He has given so many animals—and even some for us to care for as pets at home. He has given the birds (what a great variety of beautiful birds!), making the air vocal with their sweet songs. The trees and shrubs give us shade with leaves in many shapes and sizes. There are the flowers I admire too. Some are delicately fragrant, others enjoyed for their beauty. The butterflies that flit around—what iridescent colors they display! And there's the gift of honey from the bees, too.

Thank You, dear God, for the wonderful gifts You send each day. May we not complain about what comes our way but appreciate more Your love shown to us in such special ways. PRISCILLA ADONIS

Teasing Someone

My little children, let us not love in word, neither in tongue; but in deed and in truth. 1 John 3:18.

EVERY YEAR AT CHRISTMASTIME as I was growing up in California, my favorite aunt and uncle and their two children would get together with us. Sometimes we'd go up to their place near Fresno, and some years they'd come down to our place in Glendale.

One Christmas when their son, Gordon, was about 6 years old and his little sister, Maureen, was about a year old, they came to our place. We looked forward to their coming with great expectations. We always had so much fun playing with them.

Well, Christmas morning came, and we got to open all the gifts. Auntie and Uncle Glenn always gave such neat gifts; I still have many of those special things they gave to me. Among the presents Gordon received was a pair of slippers. Oh, how he loved those slippers! He carried them around all the time, hardly putting them down for a minute. When he did put them down, my sister, Priscilla, who was 16, thought it would be fun to tease him. So she grabbed them and started taunting Gordon. Every time she'd get close and he'd try to get them, she'd hold them up so high that he couldn't reach them. At first Gordon got real upset, but after a while he began to get madder and madder. I tried to tell her she should give the slippers back, but she didn't listen. She was having too much fun at his expense. Then all of a sudden it happened, just when Priscilla wasn't expecting it. Gordon hauled off and gave her a real good kick in the side of her neck. It just about laid her out cold.

Gordon grabbed his slippers about the same time my mom and aunt came rushing in and found Priscilla on the floor. A nice mark on her neck verified the story Priscilla told them. Auntie was about to reprimand Gordon when I jumped in with the whole story!

I'll just say that Priscilla learned a lesson that day about carrying teasing too far. She also learned what the Bible meant by the statement that the one who causes the other person's anger is just as guilty as the one who gets angry (see Matt. 5:22). The golden rule would fit well too. "Do unto others as you would have others do unto you" (see Matt. 7:12).

Lord, help me today never to be mean to another, but to show only Your love.

ANNE ELAINE NELSON

Gospel According to You

Let us not become weary in doing good, for at the proper time we will reap a harvest if we do not give up. Therefore, as we have opportunity, let us do good to all people, especially to those who belong to the family of believers. Gal. 6:9, 10, NIV.

GIVING AND LIVING AND sharing the gospel isn't that hard. Here are a few sketches . . .

Stephanie observed that the waiter, who doubled as cashier, was trying to satisfy the customers in the crowded restaurant. They all wanted their order now! As Stephanie paid her bill she said, "You're so stressed out. You must be terribly tired at the end of the day. Here's a relaxing story for you to read when you get home." As Stephanie laid down a little leaflet, the rushed waitress smiled, appreciating the kindness.

* * *

Marge took a little Christmas basket to a neighbor, Kirstin, and noticed her wearing a hat.

"What a cute little hat!"

"Well, thank you. It helps, after my chemo, to cover my head."

"You've had cancer?"

"Had surgery, and just finished my third round of chemo."

"I'm so sorry! I had no idea. Let's pray about it." And Marge prayed with her neighbor, as she had some months before when Kirstin's father passed away. Kirstin was deeply grateful.

* * *

Marie offered to send Christmas cards to all the members of the class at church. The teacher signed the cards and wrote personal messages, enclosing an inspirational message with each. Unfortunately, several of the cards were returned because of wrong addresses, including one to Terry. When Marie saw Terry at a church potluck, she said, "Terry, we're so glad we found you! Your Christmas card came back. Could we update our record on you?"

"Surely," Terry responded. She then tore open the card, and her face mellowed and softened. She seemed on the verge of tears. "This is the only Christmas card I've gotten."

A little leaflet, a little prayer, a little card—all of them can share the gospel.

Ruth Watson

Mary's Ride

So Joseph also went up from the town of Nazareth in Galilee to Judea, to Bethlehem the town of David, because he belonged to the house and line of David. He went there to register with Mary, who was pledged to be married to him and was expecting a child. Luke 2:4, 5, NIV.

I LOOKED AT THE BEAUTIFUL scene on the Christmas card—an idyllic scene of a quiet starlit night. Nothing is moving except the little donkey led by the man. On the small animal's back sits a very pregnant woman.

Yeah, I bet, I thought. I've been in the lands of the Middle East, and I've seen people riding donkeys, but never have I seen a *woman* riding a donkey, much less with the man walking as she rode. It was always the other way around.

When we lived in Wyoming, I was asked to do an interview for a newspaper feature of a woman who was soon to celebrate her 100th birthday. She told me about how she and her husband had been among the early pioneers in the Big Horn Basin. They'd come out from eastern South Dakota by covered wagon. She said she had been pregnant with her ninth child at the time.

"Wasn't that hard, riding in the wagon?" I asked.

"Oh, my dear," she said with a look that indicated she felt sorry for me, who had not yet had a baby. "I walked. It was much too rough in the wagon."

The text doesn't give us nearly enough information. All it says is they "went there." We know they were poor people, so it's likely they walked the 80-some miles (130 kilometers). I did a lot of walking just before the birth of my second child, and it helped make it an easier birth. I'm hoping that Mary's long walk made it easier for her. With every weary footstep she must have pondered the wonders of God for us. How willingly she had said, "I am the Lord's servant. May it be to me as you have said" (Luke 1:38, NIV). There was no hospital, no pain relievers. Was there a midwife? Were there other women there to help Joseph? So many questions, and so few answers!

Yes, I think Mary walked. But whether she walked or rode, at this Christmas season the challenge for me is to value and appreciate what God worked out for my salvation. It wasn't easy for Mary, for Joseph, for the Son of God. Praise the Lord, they were willing to be used.

ARDIS DICK STENBAKKEN

Our Great God

And my God will meet all your needs according to his glorious riches in Christ Jesus. Phil. 4:19, NIV.

THE PHONE CALL BROUGHT those dreaded words, "Mom, I've been in an accident!" My youngest daughter, who lived on the other side of the United States, had been driving home late at night from a meeting. She was only 20 minutes from home when she rounded a slight curve on the two-lane highway and found a power pole and wires blocking the way. A man who'd been drinking had hit the pole, bringing it down across the roadway. It was impossible for her to stop, and in an instant her large Suburban was totaled. Even though all the windows had been broken out by the impact, my daughter suffered only a small cut on her thumb—which was a miracle in itself.

With a family that included four children, she knew that their second car, a small Volkswagen, would not be adequate to meet their needs. Fortunately, the insurance company paid for the rental of a minivan for six weeks while they searched for a replacement for the wrecked Suburban. In California, where I live, they are available on almost every lot; but in the Northeast they seemed to be scarce. Her husband spent hours scanning the Internet, while she spent hours on the phone. And all the relatives on both coasts spent hours praying.

The time came to turn in the rental car, and they still hadn't found another Suburban. A few days later they got a call about a car, then discovered that they had missed out because of a broken fax machine. They decided to drive to the city and take the first one on the lot, even thought it wasn't what they wanted.

As they rounded the corner to the lot, there it was: their car, almost exactly what they wanted, and it had just arrived on the lot the day before! So they drove home with their special Christmas gift. Since it wouldn't fit under the Christmas tree, they put the tree inside it. Now they finally had a Suburban, a Christmas tree, and a big answer to prayer. They realized, however, that cars, trees, and things don't bring happiness. It's the peace that comes from knowing that God is in control and that He will take care of us. And that indeed He will take care of us as He sees best, even though it's hard to wait and wonder. BETTY J. ADAMS

King of Light

Proclaim the excellencies of Him who has called you out of darkness into His marvelous light. 1 Peter 2:9, NASB.

IT WAS THE KIND OF dark night you see only way out in the country, the kind that allows large creatures to sneak up on unsuspecting children and breathe on the backs of their necks. It was on this night that Uncle Richard told Jeannie and me to get him something out of the barn. I was 9 years old, and I hated the dark. I didn't know of one good thing that had ever happened in the dark. The barn was at least two miles from the house—OK, maybe 200 feet—but I knew I'd never make it back alive. I was beginning to think that it might not have been a good idea to spend the night with my cousin. Jeannie, who also wasn't excited about darkness, and I tried lots of excuses, but Uncle Richard wouldn't relent. He finally pushed us out the door, telling us to "just hurry up!" As the last ray of comforting lamplight snapped off behind us, he yelled, "And don't worry about the bears!"

We survived our frantic scramble to and from the barn, and Uncle Richard still gets entirely too much joy out of teasing unsuspecting relatives.

I'm still not thrilled about being alone in the dark, but now I know that God doesn't like the darkness either. And God cares so much about us that He wants to give us our own special light. "In the beginning" the first thing He did was to create light. A warm, beautiful light, perfect for a brand-new world. Centuries later God knew the darkness would be scary for those thousands of newly freed Israelite slaves, and He gave them a huge, comforting night-light. And then, 2,000 years ago, the darkness was forced to evaporate before the majestic light emanating from thousands of beaming angels proclaiming the birth of the King of light.

"Then spake Jesus again unto them, saying, 'I am the light of the world: he that followeth me shall not walk in darkness, but shall have the light of life'" (John 8:12). During this wonderful holiday season may you forget all about the darkness and contentedly rest in the spectacular light Jesus has reserved just for you! And don't worry about the bears! SUSAN WOOLEY

A Gift of the Heart!

Thanks be to God for his indescribable gift! 2 Cor. 9:15, NIV.

ONE OF MY YOUNGEST nieces is 8-year-old Alina Julianna Heinanen. She is the third daughter of my sister, Amy, and my Finnish brother-in-law, Markku. Alina speaks three languages fluently: Finnish, English, and the language of love! In 2000 we enjoyed having the Heinanen family spend Christmas with us. One of the highlights of that holiday came when Alina presented her gift to me.

When we began the gift exchange, Alina went quickly to the tree to secure a small package that she'd wrapped. It was light, and rattled when I shook it. I didn't have a clue what was inside, but I began to unwrap the small package, punctuating the process with words and expressions that demonstrated my eagerness to discover the nature of Alina's special gift. She stood at my elbow while I struggled to remove an abundance of tape. When I'd peeled back the wrapping paper, I discovered a small, plastic, heart-shaped box. Inside the box were two tightly folded dollar bills and a shiny quarter. Alina's eyes continued to search mine for every ounce of joy and surprise I exhibited in response to the cost of her gift. "I saved my whole month's allowance just for you!" she said with childlike pride.

Then, bending her knees in order to make eye contact with me, she spoke the truth. "I wanted to spend it, but I wanted to give it to you more!"

It's been a year and a half, and I've discovered that I just can't spend Alina's gift. It cost too much. Her sacrifice was too great. I've designated a special place for her gift on my desk, and it provides a daily reminder of what a true gift really is. It's one that requires planning, sacrifice, self-control, and a spirit of generosity—and she had exhibited them all. It's true that hers wasn't the largest box under the tree that year, nor was it the most expensive. But it was the most precious.

Let's give a gift to our Lord today that matches Alina's gift, a gift that demonstrates commitment, sacrifice, and a determination to give our best to the One who gave His all. A "heart gift," such as the heart that held Alina's gift of $2.25. Remember, Jesus cherishes cheerfully given "heart gifts."

Rose Otis

God Watches Over Me

God was in Christ reconciling the world to Himself. 2 Cor. 5:19, NKJV.

BY THE TIME I WAS 7 years old I had attended a variety of churches sporadically. I knew about the baby Jesus but very little about the grown-up Jesus. Several people had told me that God's eyes were watching over me every moment. I liked God, and as I sat under a tree in our orchard I was thinking about Him. I felt sure He could see me at that moment and decided to put Him to the test.

I tried going into the various farm buildings on our place and was satisfied that He was aware of where I was and was watching over me. But there was one place I dreaded to try: the huge, earth-covered potato cellar that I feared because it was so very big and dark and earthy smelling. I was afraid of its vastness and darkness, even with adults along. But I thought that if there were any place where God could no longer see me, it would be in the "spud" cellar, which was empty in the summer.

I went to the huge door on the south end and pulled it open wide enough for me to slip in. I stepped forward a few steps and let the door close behind me and waited in the eerie darkness. Even there I knew that God's eyes were upon me. I was so pleased! I ran back into the sunlight, rejoicing that God would always know where I am. When my little sister got up from her nap, I took her to our favorite place in the orchard and told her what I had discovered about God.

When I was 10 years old, while we children practiced for a Christmas program at a small community church, another girl and I looked at pictures in a Bible storybook. I saw a painting of three crosses with a man nailed to each. I asked her, "What are those people doing?"

She replied, "Oh, that's the way they treated each other in those days." I didn't have a clue.

When I was 13, a wonderful person came to our home one day a week for several months and studied the Bible with us. Then I understood why the baby Jesus came to this world and that He grew up to be nailed to a cross to bring salvation to all people. Then I learned much more fully to love and trust Jesus, the Son of God, who came that Christmas to reconcile the world unto Himself. And He truly is always with us! Vera Nelson

The Special Assistance Pass

I am the light of the world. He who follows Me shall not walk in darkness, but have the light of life. John 8:12, NKJV.

WHEN SOMETHING GOOD HAPPENS, I like to share the experience in hopes that others may likewise be blessed. I want to share with you a special blessing that came to our family. For years my sister, Jan, and her husband, Jess, talked about it and hoped to do it someday—take our son, Sonny, to Disneyland. They'd been there several times, and they felt that Sonny would enjoy a certain playground. The hope became reality two days after Christmas.

On their previous visits they'd noticed that people with various disabilities had been escorted to the front of the waiting lines. Sonny, who's 15, is severely mentally challenged, and waiting in long lines could cause undesirable behavior. Uncle Jess phoned Disneyland in advance to inquire about the special service extended to those with disabilities. He was told to go to the city hall office inside the Disneyland gates and obtain a special assistance pass for Sonny.

Sonny had a wonderful day—13 exciting and fun-filled hours at Disneyland. His party of six all were escorted to the front of the lines. In all, we enjoyed 14 attractions, each with waiting lines of 90 to 120 minutes each. I personally had never encountered such huge crowds of people. I was amazed! There seemed to be an atmosphere of total contentment. People were there to enjoy themselves, and no one seemed to mind that those with disabilities were granted special consideration.

For several days, including Christmas Day, Sonny's dad had taken pictures with no film in his camera. He only discovered this fact after a couple hours at Disneyland. Those "senior moments" are priceless. *Thank You, Lord! We still have some great pictures of our Disneyland adventure. And more thanksgiving—Aunt Jan and Uncle Jess have our holidays on videotape.*

It's my hope that others can see the Light of life, Jesus, in my family and me. I dream of the new earth, where we shall dwell in contentment for eternity. All will be perfect there—no more disabilities, pain, or sorrow. When we pray for opportunities to tell others about Jesus, He will grant us the desires of our hearts as we work and play in hopes of expanding His kingdom.

DEBORAH SANDERS

Homeward Bound

In my Father's house are many mansions: if it were not so, I would have told you. I go to prepare a place for you. John 14:2.

GOING HOME! WHAT INEXPLICABLE joy the thought of home gives. Just thinking of home brings images of laughter and happiness, a chance to spend precious time with loved ones, and a time to catch up on the latest news within the family and to reminisce on old times. Sadly, home is not a happy place for everyone.

Because of the destructive nature of sin, home can be a place of sadness, a place where evil lurks and misery rules supreme.

As my husband and I prepared for our annual trip to our island home, I had a sense of elated anticipation. This trip was in celebration of my mother-in-law's eighty-sixth birthday. Hers has been a life of sacrificing for her family. It was fitting that the family say thank you in this tangible way. Family and friends would gather from England, Canada, the United States, and other parts of the island to join in the celebration.

Although I've spent more than three quarters of my life away from the home island, each visit is a special occasion for me. The people, sights, sounds, music, food, and blue Caribbean Sea invoke a special feeling of belonging. After a week or two in paradise, though, I'm ready to return to my other home—the place I've called home for more than half of my life. It's where my mother, siblings, children, grandchildren, and friends are. No wonder it is said that home is where the heart is.

There is yet another home I yearn for. The Lord has promised that He has gone to prepare this home for me. My heavenly home is beautifully described in Revelation 21 and 22. In this home, I am assured, there will be no sorrow, pain, tears, or parting. What a wonderful homecoming it will be to be reunited with our loved ones!

Like David, I too can say that "my soul longs, indeed it faints for the courts of the Lord; my heart and my flesh sing for joy to the living God" (Ps. 84:2, NRSV). I want to go to that heavenly home, don't you? Please join me today in asking God to keep our feet from straying as we journey to our heavenly home.

AVIS MAE RODNEY

The Class of '59

A friend loveth at all times. Prov. 17:17.

I WENT TO A WONDERFUL class reunion toward the end of 2001. It was for our form 2 class of 1959. (Form 2 is the equivalent of grade 7 in America). The reunion was held in the little country town of Waiuku, New Zealand. It was so good to go back to where I'd lived as a child and where I'd received my early schooling. I'd seen only two of my former classmates (twice) over the years, so the day was looked forward to with great anticipation. Three "girls" had spent many hours tracking down former pupils. Even though many still live at Waiuku and the surrounding district, a number lived in other parts of the country, and some of us had emigrated overseas.

What a fun time it was that afternoon! There was so much laughter and so much talking. Some people were easily recognizable, such as Veia. I remembered her as the girl who had the most beautiful red hair. She has a beautiful nature to match. Another delightful catch-up time was with Bette. Her hair was always an unruly mop of curls, and she had hated it. The passing of the years has tamed those curls. "That's one good thing about getting older," she laughed. Then there was the "Isn't it a small world?" as Jenny and I discovered she had worked for a very good friend of ours for 17 years in another town in New Zealand.

There were others I couldn't place. I'd look at someone's face, then to their name badge, then back to the face. After all, 42 years is a long time. The room rang with laughter all afternoon, and everyone was sad when it was time to go home. Promises were made to keep in touch; addresses and phone numbers were exchanged. We had another class photo taken, and since receiving it in the mail I've spent a lot of time looking at face after face, remembering those childhood days.

The best reunion of all will be soon when Jesus comes to take us home to heaven. There we will catch up with friends. Friends of recent years and friends of years ago. Friends who lived too far away to see frequently. And our very best friend, Jesus, will be there at the reunion that will never end.

LEONIE DONALD

What's Your Idol?

Neither have I gone back from the commandment of his lips; I have esteemed the words of his mouth more than my necessary food. Job 23:12.

THE DEAREST IDOL I have known, whate'er that idol be, help me to tear it from Thy throne, and worship only Thee."

These lines from my mother's favorite hymn sang themselves in my brain as I prayed one morning. I wasn't satisfied with my Christian experience. I had an uneasy feeling that there was something coming between my God and me. But what could it be?

I knew that inordinate love for family, food, fashion, a car, a house, a boat, a garden—anything that we love too much—can become an idol to separate us from God. I mentally searched my heart and lifestyle. I couldn't find any idols that I needed to tear from my heart. There was no addiction, no possession, no obsession that came between God and me. Then why did I feel so far from Him?

Suddenly a word flashed into my mind—workaholic. Ah, was that it? I've always been a Martha. Was work coming before God?

Of course not. Private prayer was the first item each day, followed by Bible reading. I was meticulous about putting God first, as Job did. "I have treasured the words of His mouth more than my necessary food" (Job 23:12, NKJV).

It didn't take much heart searching to realize that my kind of "putting God first" was hollow. Even though I read my Bible, I wasn't concentrating; the words weren't getting through to my heart. I tried reading aloud, and that helped a little. But more often, even while I was reading Scripture aloud, another part of my mind was busily assembling the tasks I had planned.

Work—being busy—was my idol. I was never happier than when I was doing two, preferably three, things at the same time.

"Dear Lord," I prayed, "forgive me. Right now I have a dozen tasks screaming to be done. Please help me to put them out of my mind and concentrate on worshipping You. Thank You."

Next I asked Him to help me with all the work waiting to be done—and He did. Now that I've turned my idol over to God, my life is so much easier. Why don't you try it?

GOLDIE DOWN

The Collector

Do not lay up for yourselves treasures on earth, where moth and rust consume and where thieves break in and steal, but lay up for yourselves treasures in heaven. Matt. 6:19, 20, RSV.

ARE YOU A COLLECTOR? I am. I seem to find a reason to keep all sorts of stuff. My husband has been a minister for 28 years, and we've moved a lot of times. I've gotten used to the idea of packing and unpacking. Several years ago we moved from a 2,800-square-foot house to an 1,800-square-foot house and had to give away or throw away lots of "good stuff." Some had been in the attic for years. I found fabric I had bought 16 years earlier when my daughter was a baby.

Then, just a few years later, we moved again and had to go through the process all over again. Just two weeks ago we finished going through the boxes still piled in the garage. Some of those boxes had gone through two moves and had been packed for the past six years. I found all sorts of things I had completely forgotten about. Some things had holes created by silverfish and moths.

Now we're moving again. I'm going through closets, drawers, and boxes in the attic and wondering why in the world I've saved some of that "good stuff." I probably won't look at it again until the next move, so why keep it?

I think the reason I keep it is an inner need for some constancy in my life. When I was a child, my family moved between New York City and Miami, Florida, at least once every two years. The year I was 10 and in the fifth grade we moved five times during the school year. When we moved, I wasn't allowed to keep my toys or anything else except for my clothes. I have no keepsakes passed down from my grandmother. All I have for childhood memories are a few photos that all fit into one shoe box. The longest I've ever lived in one house was six years. Some people live in the same house all their lives. I can't even imagine what they would have to go through the day they have to start packing to move.

As I was going through piles of "good stuff" last Sunday, I thought about the time of trouble and the coming of Jesus. We won't be able to take all this "good stuff" with us on that move. I'm tired of packing and moving and can't wait for that day when we can go home with Jesus and won't need to pack for the trip or worry about keepsakes.

Come quickly, Lord Jesus. CELIA MEJIA CRUZ

AUTHOR BIOGRAPHIES

Betty J. Adams is a retired schoolteacher, wife, mother of three, and grandmother of five. She's written for *Guide* and her church newsletter. She's involved with community service in her church and enjoys her grandchildren, quilting, and traveling, especially on mission trips. **Feb. 20, Apr. 28, Nov. 26, Dec. 23.**

Priscilla Adonis is women's ministries coordinator at her local church and enjoys writing and sending notes of encouragement. Her daughters live in New Zealand and California, so she writes often and longs to see them again. She has one grandson, who's 5. Women's retreats are the highlight in her life, and she enjoys making and working Bible quizzes. **Apr. 4, June 24, July 7, Aug. 14, Nov. 14, Dec. 19**

Sally j. Aken-Linke resides in Norfolk, Nebraska, with her husband, John. Her strong Christian faith and her experiences as a single mother raising two children provide a basis for her poetry and short stories. Sally and her husband are active in air medical transport and are near completion of an airplane. She enjoys reading, music, and working with young people. **Feb. 24, June 20, Sept. 17, Oct. 19.**

Maxine Williams Allen resides in Orlando, Florida, with her husband and two small sons. She owns her own computer and business consulting company, Tecnocentric. She loves to travel, meet people, and experience different cultures. Her hobbies include writing, reading, and computers. She has a special interest in family, children's, and women's ministries. **June 30, Nov. 7.**

Mary Wagoner Angelin lives in Ooltewah, Tennessee, and is editor of the newsletter at her church in Cohutta, Georgia. She's a social worker at an inpatient psychiatric facility. Mary and her husband, Randy, have two children, Barbara, 5, and Rachel, 3. Her hobbies are therapeutic humor, exercising, hiking, writing, vegan cooking, and volunteering. **May 17, Sept. 27.**

Joelle Ashley graduated from Andrews University in 1994 with a Bachelor of Arts in English and taught high school English for six rewarding years. In 1998 she married Daniel Ashley, and God entrusted them with two amazing little people, Hannah Elise and Joshua Reece. Currently she squeezes in a little work as a curriculum developer/instructional designer for a Web-based training development company. **May 3.**

Rachel Atwood writes from central Kentucky. She is a homeschooling mom who likes helping out at church and collecting out-of-print Adventist books. She is the sister of Asenath Blake, who has also contributed to this devotional book series. **Apr. 7, Oct. 22, Nov. 29.**

Rosemary Baker, a freelance writer living in Iowa, is author of the children's book *What Am I?* and has had contributions in *Shining Star, Kids' Stuff,* and other magazines. She is a member of the Iowa Poetry Association and the Quint City Poetry Guild. She's active in church, does volunteer work, and enjoys working with children. Arts, crafts, poetry, music, and painting are her hobbies. **May 6, Nov. 1.**

Jennifer M. Baldwin writes from Australia, where she is clinical risk management coordinator at Sydney Adventist Hospital. She enjoys church involvement, travel, and writing, and has contributed to a number of church publications. **Aug. 12, Dec. 6.**

Mary Barrett, who works in pastoral ministry with her husband, is also a writer and a speaker. They have two daughters. For relaxation she loves to be with family and friends. **Dec. 2.**

Marianne Toth Bayless is a secretary-clerk in a local high school in Palm Beach County, Florida. Writing family memories for her four children began as a hobby but has blossomed into much more. She's traveled to Hungary twice to trace her heritage. She has been active in her local church and now serves as women's ministries leader. **June 15, Sept. 4, Sept. 30.**

Dawna Beausoleil lives with her husband in rural northern Ontario, Canada. Though her active lifestyle has been curbed sharply by chronic fatigue syndrome, she still loves to sing and write, and play with her cat and dog. The long winters are great for jigsaw puzzles, and the glorious summers perfect for flower gardening. **Jan. 21.**

Priscilla Ben, formerly women's ministries director, Eastern Africa Division, is publishing director for the Africa-Indian Ocean Division of Seventh-day Adventists. She taught for 12 years before becoming a full-time literature evangelist in Zambia. Married to Pastor Strike Ben of Botswana, she's the mother of one daughter. Her hobbies include reading, cake decorating, traveling, and jogging. **Oct. 20.**

Annie B. Best is a retired teacher and the mother of two grown children. She enjoys being with her three grandchildren, reading, and listening to music. She's worked as leader in the beginner and kindergarten departments of her church, which she enjoys and finds rewarding. Her husband of 53 years passed away in 2001. **Apr. 16, Aug. 10, Dec. 8.**

Dinorah Blackman lives in Panama with her husband and baby, Imani. **Apr. 22.**

Juli Blood, a first-time contributor, has been happily married to Gary since 1994. They were missionaries in Korea for a year. Juli fills her days with reading and writing. She has a cat, Sandy, that didn't enjoy Korea as much as she and her husband did. **Nov. 17.**

Rhonda Bolton has a burden for both personal and public worship and feels that the crucible of ordinary life is where the greatest opportunity for true worship and personal growth presents itself. She and her husband, Bob, live in the beautiful Pacific Northwest, where God sends the rain on the just and the unjust alike. **Mar. 25.**

Wendy Bradley is a deaconess who keeps busy visiting and keeping in touch with present and past church members. She loves writing for pleasure, and keeping in touch with friends. She's recently taken up cross-stitch. She loves going for strolls with her husband, David, and hopes to spend more time with him visiting the many beautiful spots of England when he retires soon. **Jan. 7.**

Darlene Ytredal Burgeson is a retired sales manager. Her hobbies include sending notes and seasonal cards to shut-ins and people who live alone. She enjoys writing, gardening, and photography. **May 19, Aug. 3, Sept. 23.**

Andrea A. Bussue was born on the Caribbean island of Nevis. She holds a master's degree in education and currently works as an administrator in Washington, D.C.

At church in Hyattsville, Maryland, she started a children's choir and has been a Sabbath school superintendent for years. She loves children and enjoys reading, traveling, sewing, and meeting people. **Feb. 10, Aug. 21, Sept. 13.**

Dorothy Wainwright Carey is a happy wife, mother, and grandmother. When she retired from the federal government several years ago, she was privileged to become involved in all levels of church committees. Her interests include church activities, nature, animals, people, and reading. **Mar. 6, July 16, Aug. 26, Sept. 2.**

Birol Charlotte Christo is a retired schoolteacher. During her active service she also worked as an office secretary and a statistician. She lives with her husband in Hosur, India. The mother of five married children, she enjoys gardening, sewing, and making craft items to finance her project for homeless children. **Mar. 19, July 24, Oct. 12, Dec. 18.**

Clareen Colclesser, a retired L.P.N. and a surviving spouse since 1994, has two children, seven grandchildren, and six great-grandchildren. She enjoys her family, quiet times with a good book, and her summer retreat near Lake Huron, Michigan. Clareen stays active in her church and with her hobbies, which include writing letters and short stories, and reading her collection of interior-decorating magazines. **Mar. 2, May 20, July 18, Sept. 10, Dec. 15.**

Lalnunmawii Colney, the women's ministries director for northeastern India, was in the process of editing the August 28 devotional when she unexpectedly died in June 2002. Doctors were unable to diagnose the cause of her fever. The devotional was submitted by her husband. She had a great burden to help and uplift the women of her union. **Aug. 28.**

Donna Cook lives in Colcord, Oklahoma, but attends the Gentry, Arkansas, Seventh-day Adventist Church, where she is active in prayer ministries. She does in-home care for the elderly and is a hospice volunteer. She likes to crochet, garden, help those in need, sew for her granddaughter, spend time with her husband and mother, and spend June with her grandchildren, telling them about Jesus. **Mar. 23, July 14.**

Celia Mejia Cruz is a pastor's wife, mother of five adult children, and grandmother of five. A church elder and women's ministries leader, Celia is pastoral assistant and church secretary at the church where Mario, her husband, pastors. Celia enjoys entertaining, reading, playing with her dog, and collecting Siamese cats. **July 28, Sept. 25, Dec. 31.**

Yvonne Leonard Curry is a scientist who works as a director for diversity programs in science for underserved populations. A single mom of two teenagers, she enjoys running, crocheting, reading, and writing. **Mar. 14, Nov. 12.**

Becky Dada is the principal of a secondary school in Ibadan, Nigeria. She and her pastor-husband have four children. She's been involved with women and development programs and publishing Bible games and youth magazines. She is now writing the history of Adventist women in west Nigeria. Her hobbies are conducting Revelation seminars, giving talks, reading, and writing. **Jan. 12, Apr. 9.**

Phyllis Dalgleish writes from South Africa. A surviving spouse, mother of three, and grandmother, she has had 45 articles and stories published and has also worked as an editor at the Karachi Adventist Hospital in Pakistan. Her hobbies are writing, crocheting, and traveling. Physically healthy and active, she won a gold medal as the oldest grandmother to complete a school 7K walk. **July 23.**

Wanda Davis is a chaplain at Florida Hospital East Orlando, Orlando, Florida. She is a commissioned minister with the Florida Conference of Seventh-day Adventists. Wanda is married and the mother of three teenagers. She enjoys preaching, teaching, facilitating small groups, and gardening. **Feb. 2.**

Fauna Rankin Dean, a published freelance writer-photographer and seminar presenter, lives in northeast Kansas with her husband on a "golden retriever ranch." They have two sons and a daughter who light up their lives. In her spare time she enjoys reading, gardening, sewing, and traveling. **Apr. 24, Sept. 28.**

Bernadine Delafield lives in Maryland, where she works as project coordinator and assistant director of Adventist Communication Network at the North American Division office. She enjoys several creative hobbies, such as gardening, writing, interior design, music, and, most of all, her grandchildren. She sings with the National Christian Choir. **Jan. 1.**

Winifred Devaraj was a teacher for more than 25 years. Now she is a women's ministries director in India. She's a pastor's wife and has one son who is a medical director at the Ottapalam Seventh-day Adventist Hospital in Kerala, India. **Feb. 5.**

Laurie Dixon-McClanahan, now retired, was a Bible instructor for the Michigan Conference of Seventh-day Adventists. She keeps busy with gardening, quilting, reading, genealogical research, letter writing, culinary arts, and e-mail. **Jan. 26, Apr. 13, Sept. 8.**

Leonie Donald has lived in Brisbane, Australia, since 1987 and enjoys the warm climate. Her hobbies are reading, exercise, and spending hours in her garden, which tells her of God's love. She has held many church positions over the years, but really enjoys being with and teaching the little ones. **Apr. 10, June 25, Aug. 13, Sept. 12, Dec. 29.**

Goldie Down passed away in 2003. She was a retired minister's wife, writer, teacher, and mother of six children, and a missionary in India for 20 years. She has 25 nonfiction books to her credit, as well as numerous stories and articles in magazines and newspapers. She helped her husband, David, produce two archaeological magazines that uphold the Bible. **Jan. 3, Apr. 2, May 29, Oct. 15, Dec. 30.**

Louise Driver lives in Beltsville, Maryland, with her pastor-husband, Don. They have three grown sons and four grandchildren. At church she is involved with music and women's ministries. She is children's coordinator in the Potomac Adventist Book Center. Her hobbies are singing and music, skiing, reading, crafts, gardening, and traveling to historical places. **June 16.**

Joy Dustow is a retired teacher who enjoys taking an active part in the social and spiritual activities of the retirement village in Australia where she resides with her husband. They read the devotional book each day and receive pleasure in knowing that from the sale of the book many have an opportunity to receive an education in a Christian environment. **July 10.**

Heike Eulitz, originally from Germany, left when she was 19 and has been working for more than seven years as office secretary in the Euro-Africa Division of the Seventh-day Adventist Church in Bern, Switzerland. Recently elected as an elder in her local church, she is active in prayer ministry. Her hobbies include crafts, baking, nature, and swimming. **Oct. 4.**

Gloria J. Stella Felder works as an administrative assistant in Queens, New York. She and her pastor-husband are the parents of four adult children and have five grandchildren. Gloria enjoys music (listening and singing), writing, spending time at home, and spending time with her grandchildren. She has published one book and is working on another. **Mar. 13, June 8, Sept. 6.**

Mercy M. Ferrer writes from Pakistan, where her husband worked as treasurer of the Pakistan Union. They have been missionaries to Egypt, Cyprus, and Russia, and have a daughter and son in college. Mercy enjoys traveling, cooking, entertaining, word games, photography, and gardening. She loves e-mailing family and friends. **Feb. 16, Oct. 21.**

Valerie Fidelia is a missionary in the Middle East, ministering to families, children, and women. She has a special interest in health issues. In her local church she is music and worship coordinator and children's ministries leader. Married for 40 years, Valerie is a mother and grandmother. Her hobbies include music, embroidery, puzzles, and reading. **Mar. 15.**

Edith Fitch is a retired teacher living in Lacombe, Alberta, Canada. She volunteers in the archives at Canadian University College and is a member of the Lacombe Historical Society. She enjoys doing research for schools and churches, as well as individual histories. Her hobbies include writing, traveling, needlework, and cryptograms. **Jan. 14, Apr. 17, June 14, Aug. 9, Oct. 8.**

Sharon Follett writes from Dunlap, Tennessee, a small town in the beautiful Sequatchie Valley, where she teaches music and works alongside her husband, Ron, as he pastors. They have two grown daughters and are looking forward to the birth of their first grandchild. **June 10, Sept. 19.**

Heide Ford was the associate editor of *Women of Spirit* at the time of this writing. Heide lives in Maryland with her husband, Zell. She holds a master's degree in counseling and loves reading, watercoloring, and whale watching. **Sept. 26.**

Suzanne French lives in Florida with her husband and enjoys attending church in Palmetto, where she is active in women's ministries. She is currently working but looks forward to retirement within the next year. **Jan. 15.**

Eileen Furlonge grew up in Trinidad. She is a retired nurse who writes from Palm Bay, Florida, where she is Sabbath school secretary and a Sabbath school teacher in her church. She enjoys travel, singing, cooking, baking, reading, and helping others. **Nov. 11.**

Edna Maye Gallington is part of the communication team in the Southeastern California Conference of Seventh-day Adventists and is a graduate of La Sierra University. She's a member of Toastmasters International and the Loma Linda Writing Guild. She enjoys freelance writing, music, gourmet cooking, entertaining, hiking, and racquetball. **Feb. 9, Apr. 5, June 21.**

Evelyn Glass enjoys her family and loves having her grandchildren live next door. She and her husband, Darrell, live in northern Minnesota on the farm where Darrell was born. Evelyn is active in her local church and community and writes a weekly column for her local paper. She has served as women's and family ministries director for the Mid-America Union Conference of Seventh-day Adventists. **Apr. 20, June 19, Sept. 3, Oct. 14, Nov. 13.**

Carrol Grady is a minister's wife who is enjoying retirement in the beautiful Pacific Northwest. She is the mother of three and grandmother of six, whose spare-time delights include quilts, music, writing, and reading. Much of her time is devoted to her ministry for families of gays and lesbians. **May 5.**

Mary Jane Graves retired in North Carolina after working at many jobs, from society editor of her hometown newspaper to years spent as a school librarian and registrar. She and her husband have two adult sons and two granddaughters. Gardening takes up much of her time during the spring and summer months. **Aug. 6.**

Carol J. Greene, a grandmother of four, lives in Florida. A valiant prayer warrior, she is involved with two prayer circles in her church. She often acts as a volunteer Sabbath school teacher. **June 1, July 20.**

Glenda-mae Greene recently retired to Palm Bay, Florida. A devoted Sabbath school teacher and inspirational speaker, she revels in the joy of being the honored aunt of three nieces and a nephew. **Feb. 15, May 16, Oct. 3.**

Janet M. Greene is a cardiac rehabilitation nurse, wife, and mother of two girls. Her major objective is that her daughters see Jesus in everything every day. She is active as an associate Pathfinder director with the expanded goal of having 25 other young people also see Jesus in everything. And yes, she is still a shopaholic. **Apr. 26.**

Gloria Gregory is a minister's wife, mother of two, and motivator who encourages others to unearth their hidden potential. **Mar. 30, May 8, Sept. 24.**

Dessa Weisz Hardin lives in Maine with her husband. She enjoys traveling, writing, reading, and teaching children. An added dimension is grandparenting. **Feb. 18, Sept. 21.**

Marian M. Hart, a retired elementary school teacher and nursing home administrator, works with her husband doing property management. As a member of the historic Battle Creek Tabernacle for 28 years, she has served as a volunteer in many different capacities. Six grandchildren make her a proud grandmother. **June 9, Oct. 2.**

Ursula M. Hedges is a retired secondary school teacher-administrator who holds a master's degree. She was born of missionary parents in India, and she and her Australian principal-husband have given 10 years in mission service in the South Pacific. Ursula is a church elder, a published writer, and a qualified interior designer. She is women's ministries director for the North New South Wales Conference of Seventh-day Adventists in Australia. **Feb. 8, May 18, Aug. 24, Dec. 13.**

Edna Heise is a minister's wife who retired with her husband to Cooranbong, New South Wales, Australia. She is a chaplain of a retirement lodge and enjoys visiting, writing, public speaking, and gardening—especially when the frosts haven't "bitten" her lovely flowers. Her eight grandchildren are her special delight. **June 18, Sept. 14, Nov. 18.**

Denise Dick Herr teaches English at Canadian University College in Alberta, Canada. She enjoys books, words, and the exciting possibilities of a blank sheet of paper. **Jan. 27, June 27.**

Marguerite Hilts, mother of six adult children, lives in Oakland, California. A widow, she is retured from the Social Security Administration, where she worked for 22 years. She is active at her church, and delights in spending time with her children, all in California; 12 grandchildren; and seven great-grandchildren. She also enjoys association with the Federated Kings Daughters, Inc. **Apr. 12.**

Karen Holford was working with her husband in family ministries when she wrote these devotionals. She has authored several books, including one with 100 different creative ways to pray. She enjoys meaningful contemporary worship, quilting, writing, and walking in the Lake District with her husband, Bernie, and their three children. She is also studying family therapy. **Jan. 17, Feb. 13, Apr. 21, July 5, Oct. 5.**

Jackie Hope HoShing-Clarke, an educator, has served as a teacher, assistant principal, and principal. She is the director of the precollege department at Northern Caribbean University, Jamaica, and is currently studying for a Ph.D. in education. Jackie is married to Pastor Blyton Clarke; they have two children. **Mar. 4.**

Lorraine Hudgins-Hirsch is retired in Loma Linda, California. She has worked at the Voice of Prophecy, Faith for Today, and the General Conference of Seventh-day Adventists. Her articles and poems appear frequently in various publications. She has also written two books of poems. **Mar. 16, Sept. 29.**

Cheryl Hurt is a retired registered nurse who lives with her husband, Brett, in California. She is a full-time volunteer, doing the Lord's work with great joy. **Mar. 26.**

Gloria Hutchinson is a registered nurse and single mother of an "adopted" son, who is also her nephew. She works for an elder-care facility as an assessment nurse coordinator. She recently completed an Associate of Science degree. She is Sabbath school secretary and assistant health ministry coordinator at her church. Her hobbies are sewing, reading, and working on a computer. **July 25, Nov. 8.**

Shirley C. Iheanacho, originally from Barbados, resides in Huntsville, Alabama, with her husband, Morris, of 34-plus years. She has had the unique privilege of working in the office of the president of Oakwood College for 20 years, assisting four college presidents. She enjoys her two grandsons, playing in the handbell choir, singing in the church choir, and encouraging people. **Apr. 30, June 23, July 6.**

Aleah Iqbal is a freelance writer who lives with her family in Willimantic, Connecticut, and has homeschooled her children for 10 years. Her publishing credits include a book of poetry, original recipes for community cookbooks, and health store newsletters. She has hosted her own local cable television show and is currently writing a children's book. **Mar. 18.**

Consuelo Jackson, Ph.D., is now retired. She enjoys her husband, son, daughter-in-law, and grandson. She taught at a community college and a university and worked in medical records and quality assurance. A greeter and a worker in health and temperance at her local church, she enjoys music, bird-watching, and writing. **July 27, Nov. 28.**

Monica Jackson passed away in August 2003. She was married and had two growing sons, one of whom she was homeschooling. She was very active in the children's department of her Palm Bay, Florida, church. **Mar. 1.**

Judy Haupt Jagitsch writes from central Illinois, where she and her husband live in retirement. They have five children and four grandchildren. Judy has worked in all the levels of children's ministries in her local church and is presently the church clerk. Her grandchildren are her greatest pleasure, followed by beautiful colors and vegetarian cooking. **May 13.**

Lois E. Johannes is retired from overseas service in southern and eastern Asia and lives near a daughter in Portland, Oregon. She enjoys knitting, community service work, patio gardening, and her four grandchildren and two great-grandchildren. **Feb. 25, Nov. 20.**

Elaine J. Johnson is a preschool teacher who's been married for 36 years to her best friend. She has four children and a baker's dozen of grandchildren. She enjoys working with children, drawing, writing, meeting people, and using her computer. She is a Sabbath school superintendent at her local church. **July 22.**

Pauletta Cox Johnson and her husband, Mike, live in a small town in southwest Michigan, where she grew up. She is an interior designer and a freelance writer (mostly children's books). She enjoys gardening, sewing, and crafts. Active in her home church, she is the proud mother of three grown sons, two daughters-in-law, and two young grandsons. **May 12.**

Emily Felts Jones is a musician and recording artist who writes from Goodlettsville, Tennessee. **Jan. 25.**

Sonja Kalmbach, at the time of this writing, was studying German, American studies, and Scandinavian studies at the University of Tubingen, Germany. She works as an English and German teacher at a Swedish school and is about to receive her teacher's degree for English and German. **July 26.**

Becki Knobloch, a first-time contributor, writes from Oregon. **May 9, Nov. 15.**

Toya Marie Koch is a freelance writer and designer living in Hagerstown, Maryland. She is the director of the Chesapeake Conference worship team and the junior/earliteen leader at the Highland View Academy church. Toya, who is married, has no children but has two cocker spaniels and two cats. She is an amateur musician and photographer. **Mar. 8.**

Betty Kossick continues to work as an independent journalist. During her more than 30 years as a writer, she's had the opportunity to give honor to the Giver of talents: "I'm a very ordinary woman who has been allowed some very unordinary opportunities to praise Him through writing." **Apr. 19, Sept. 18.**

Patricia Mulraney Kovalski is a retired church school teacher, surviving spouse, mother, and grandmother. She loves being with her family, traveling, swimming, teaching a woman's Bible class, and doing crafts. She lives in southwest Florida. **Feb. 14, Oct. 24, Dec. 12.**

Annie M. Kujur is a wife, mother of two grown children, and grandmother of two boys. She was the fourth of seven sisters. Birol Christo and Birdie Poddar, sisters number two and three, respectively, are also contributors to these devotional books. **May 4, Aug. 11.**

Mabel Kwei, the wife of the president of the Seventh-day Adventist Gambia Mission Station in West Africa, is the director of education at West African Union Mission. She is also director of women's ministries and a lecturer at the University of the Gambia and the Gambia College. She works with her husband in pastoral work and likes reading. **Aug. 17.**

Nathalie Ladner-Bischoff, a retired nurse, lives with her husband in Walla Walla, Washington. Besides homemaking, gardening, and volunteering at the Walla Walla General Hospital gift shop, she reads, writes, knits, and crochets. Her stories have been published in several magazines, and she has written a book, *An Angel's Touch.* **Feb. 26, Nov. 25.**

Sally Lam-Phoon is the director for education and women's ministries and Shepherdess coordinator for the Southeast Asia Union Mission in Singapore. Her passion is to work with women to discover their potential and help them to achieve peace and happiness in the Lord. She is married to Chek Yat Phoon, and they have two daughters, Michelle and Rachel. **Mar. 12, Oct. 23, Nov. 24, Dec. 17.**

Margaret B. Lawrence is a nationally recognized educator and the first female elder at the Berean Seventh-day Adventist Church in Baton Rouge, Louisiana. She is a local newspaper columnist who enjoys writing, sewing, and public speaking. **Mar. 22.**

Gina Lee is the author of more than 650 published stories, articles, and poems. In addition to writing, she works at a library. She shares her home with four cats. **Feb. 21, Apr. 15, June 7, Aug. 25, Nov. 2.**

Ruth Lennox, a retired family physician, likes to write and produce monologues of first-person stories of Bible women. She and her husband have three married children and four young granddaughters. Ruth enjoys playing with them and reading to them. **Mar. 17, Nov. 5.**

Cecelia Lewis writes from Huntsville, Alabama. She is a Bible instructor and teaches baptismal classes for adults, youth, and children at the Oakwood College church. She enjoys tutoring at the elementary school, reading, writing, gardening, and being a member of the bell choir. **Feb. 23.**

Olive Lewis is a medical technologist who attends church in Atlanta, Georgia, where she is a youth teacher and director. She's written poems, plays, and a book and is working on two more books. She's been nominated numerous times for poetry awards. She is an advocate for youth, and the works that she has written have been with them in mind. **Oct. 6.**

Bessie Siemens Lobsien, a retired missionary librarian and great-grandmother, enjoys visiting with family, helping in church work, writing newsletters and advertisements, and sewing for Seventh-day Adventist orphanages. She is a grateful recipient of many of God's wondrous blessings of healing in her lengthening life. **Jan. 22, Feb. 27, May 24, Aug. 1.**

Sharon Long (Brown) is from Trinidad but lives in Alberta, Canada. A social worker and manager of two child welfare offices in metro Edmonton, she resides with her husband and three of her children. (Her eldest daughter and two grandchildren live nearby.) Sharon enjoys writing, baking, reading, and sewing (when she gets a chance). She is active in her church. **Jan. 19, Mar. 28, May 31.**

Alicia Marquez was born in Montevideo, Uruguay, and has lived in New York for more than 30 years. She is a senior accountant and has worked previously with the Spanish television program *Ayer, Hoy y Mañana.* She collaborates with the family and women's ministries in presenting seminars, preaching, or doing anything else needed. **Sept. 16.**

Clarissa Marshall, formerly an overseas missionary, is now involved in short-term ministry work in the Southern states. She longs to reach the multitudes for Christ by means of radio, the written word, music, and health evangelism. **July 30, Oct. 30.**

Cassandra Martins is an educator, journalist, and marketing operator in the publishing house Hoje Maringá. She is a member of a church in Paraná, Brazil, and the mother of three children. **Oct. 29.**

Vidella McClellan is a respite care worker, home care provider, and homemaker. She is active in church and is interested in public speaking. A wife and a grandmother of seven, she enjoys her children and grandchildren, the country life, travel, and cats. Her hobbies include gardening, crafts, writing, reading, scrapbooking, and writing stories for enjoyment and inspiration. **Jan. 18, Mar. 9, Apr. 14, May 27, Oct. 11.**

Marge McNeilus comes from Dodge Center, Minnesota. She is a homemaker who also works in the family business. She's been church clerk for many years and is women's ministries leader in her church. She has four adult children and seven grandchildren. Her hobbies include traveling, writing, photography, crafts, and music. **Feb. 4.**

Patsy Murdoch Meeker lives with her cat, Tibby, in Virginia. Patsy is a mom, stepmom, and stepgrandma. Reading, writing, and instrumental music are among her interests. **July 21.**

Nadege Michel was born on the island of Mauritius, but she's made Australia her home for the past 32 years. In addition to her work with transplant and pacemaker support groups, she also enjoys cooking, reading, and traveling. Nadege has three adult children and seven grandchildren. **July 9.**

Quilvie G. Mills is a retired community college professor who is now actively engaged with her pastor-husband, H. A. Mills, in the operation of their church. She loves people, makes friends easily, and does all she can to assist young people in achieving their educational aspirations. Her hobbies include music, reading, traveling, and gardening. **July 8.**

Marcia Mollenkopf, a retired schoolteacher, lives in Klamath Falls, Oregon. She is active in local church activities and has served in both adult and children's departments. She enjoys reading, crafts, hiking, and bird-watching. **Jan. 9, Jan. 31.**

Esperanza Aquino Mopera is the mother of four adult children, a grandmother of five, and a charge nurse at the Lake Taylor Transitional Care Hospital. Her hobbies are gardening and watching birds. **Mar. 31, May 14.**

Barbara Smith Morris is executive director of a nonprofit retirement center and presents a devotional over the speaker system daily. For seven years she served as a Tennessee delegate, representing housing and service needs of low-income elderly. Barbara is a presenter of seminars on elder life issues. She has four grown children and is the grandmother of six. **June 6, Sept. 20.**

Bonnie Moyers lives with her husband and four cats in Staunton, Virginia. She is a musician for a Methodist church, works as a laundry assistant for a nearby bed-and-breakfast, and does freelance writing whenever she can fit it in. She is the mother of two adult children and has one granddaughter to enjoy. Her writings have been published in many magazines and books. **Mar. 24, Sept. 15.**

Ethel Doris Msuseni is a retired professional nurse and teacher living in Umtata, Eastern Cape, South Africa. She likes cooking, listening to music, and sewing. **Dec. 3.**

Lillian Musgrave and her family have made northern California their home for more than 40 years. She enjoys family and grandchildren—and now has a great-grandchild, too. Other interests include music, writing (poetry and songs), and church responsibilities. **June 13.**

Sibusisiwe Ncube-Ndhlovu, a native of Zimbabwe, Africa, is currently in the United States for further study. Her hobbies are cooking, watching soccer with her husband, reading, and visiting with friends. **May 15, July 11, Sept. 5.**

Judy Neal, a registered nurse, is currently a student at Andrews University in the Master of Divinity program. She is a mother and grandmother and enjoys reading, music, sewing, and camping (when there is time from all the reading and paper writing that graduate school demands). Currently living in Berrien Springs, Michigan, she calls herself a gypsy. **Jan. 6.**

Joan Minchin Neall was born in Australia, lived in England, and now makes her home in Tennessee. She is a registered nurse, and she and her retired pastor-husband have four adult children and nine grandchildren. She is the women's ministries leader for her church. She enjoys journaling, young women's Bible study groups, and spending time with her family. **Aug. 4.**

Anne Elaine Nelson, a retired elementary school teacher, is still tutoring. She has written a book, *Puzzled Parents,* and has four children who have blessed her with 11 grandchildren. Her husband passed away in 2001. Active in church work and women's ministries, she lives in Michigan and enjoys sewing, music, photography, and creating memories with her grandchildren. **Aug. 18, Oct. 28, Dec. 20.**

Vera Nelson is a retired secretary who lives in Hayden, Idaho. She serves in her church Community Services center and the church library. She enjoys reading, writing, helping with an occasional Maranatha project, and trying to learn how her new computer works. **Nov. 19, Dec. 26.**

Beth Versteegh Odiyar lives in Kelowna, British Columbia, Canada. She has managed the family chimney sweep business since 1985 and has twin sons and a daughter at college. Beth enjoys mission trips and road trips to visit family. She loves creativity and hopes to be a writer. At church she is in leadership roles and has spent years as Vacation Bible School and children's Sabbath school department leader. **July 29.**

Pauline Okemwa writes from Eldoret, Kenya, Africa. She is a first-time contributor this year. **Sept. 9.**

Alanna O'Malley writes from Virginia and is a first-time contributor. **July 12.**

Cristine Jeda Orillosa is a student at Pacific Union College in Angwin, California. At the time of this writing she was a student missionary at Chuuk in the Federated States of Micronesia. She loves Jesus very much and loves writing, singing, snorkeling, and swimming. She enjoyed teaching kindergarten and primary pupils in Chuuk and now misses her little angels. **June 22.**

Jemima D. Orillosa works in the Secretariat Department at the Seventh-day Adventist Church world headquarters. She lives in Maryland with her husband and two teenage daughters and is active in her local church. She enjoys gardening and making friends. **Mar. 10, May 25, Aug. 16, Oct. 17.**

Rose Otis was the first director of women's ministries for the General Conference of Seventh-day Adventists. Next she became vice president for ministries for the North American Division and then vice president of the Texas Conference. She began this women's devotional book project and edited the first six books. She enjoys water sports with her family, writing, and being home. **Apr. 11, July 1, Dec. 25.**

Hannele Ottschofski lives in southern Germany and is an elder in her local church. She has four daughters and one grandson. A pastor's wife, she is the editor of the conference Shepherdess journal. She gives piano lessons, directs a choir, and loves to prepare PowerPoint presentations for her seminars. **Jan. 23, Mar. 29, July 19.**

Ivone Feldkircher Paiva is a minister's wife, mother of two children, and grandmother of two granddaughters. After working 23 years as director of schools, she now works in education administration for her church in North Paraná, Brazil, and has a daily radio program. She likes to read, embroider, write, travel, and present seminars on education and family. **June 5.**

Janel Raelene Palmer lives in Lincoln, Nebraska. She graduated from Union College in 2001 with a social work degree. Her spiritual gifts include evangelism, intercessory prayer, and creative communication. She enjoys giving Bible studies and quilting, and is part of Joshua Ministries, a lay ministry. **Apr. 23, Nov. 27.**

Ofelia A. Pangan serves God with her minister-husband in the big paradise island of Hawaii. She loves reading, gardening, traveling, and playing Scrabble. Even more, she loves visiting her three grown-up children and their spouses and her grandchildren. **Jan. 20, Apr. 8, May 26, Nov. 22.**

Revel Papaioannou is an almost-retired English teacher, mother of four adult sons, and grandmother of nine. She keeps busy as a pastor's wife and enjoys mountain hiking, reading, and collecting stamps, coins, and phone cards. **Mar. 21.**

Nicole Paradis-Sydenham has served as women's ministries director in Canada for 12 years, working in three conferences: Quebec, Manitoba, and, currently, Alberta. Born in Montreal, Quebec, she is fluently bilingual (French and English). She makes her home in Lacombe, Alberta, with her pastor-husband and four children. **June 11.**

Abigail Blake Parchment has enjoyed a love affair with her Savior, Jesus Christ, for many years now. She is married to Sean, and they make their home in the Cayman Islands, where they were both born. She enjoys reading, singing for the Lord, spending time with friends, and traveling. She looks forward to spending eternity with Jesus and the readers of this devotional book. **Oct. 27.**

Betty G. Perry resides in Fayetteville, North Carolina, with her retired pastor-husband. They have two adult children and four grandchildren. An anesthetist for 27 years, she is now semiretired. Her hobbies are playing the piano and organ, doing arts and crafts, trying new recipes, and, most recently, quilting. **Aug. 20.**

Karen Phillips and her husband, John, have four children. For the past 15 years she's been a stay-at-home mom. She has directed Adventurer and Eager Beaver groups, sings in the church choir, and is lunch mom at the church school in Omaha. Some of her writing has been published in the Kansas-Nebraska Conference women's ministries publication *Heartbeat From the Heartland.* **Jan. 28, Mar. 11, May 21, Sept. 7, Oct. 9.**

Birdie Poddar lives in northeastern India. She and her husband enjoy retirement but keep busy. She enjoys gardening, cooking, baking, sewing, reading, writing, and handcrafts. They have a daughter, a son, and four grandsons. **Aug. 22, Dec. 11.**

Lanny Lydia Pongilatan, from Jakarta, Indonesia, works as a professional secretary. She was an English instructor for Indonesian Professions in the Indonesian-American Foundation. She enjoys playing the piano, listening to Christian gospel songs, reading religious books, playing tennis, and swimming. **Dec. 7.**

Maria Baldão Quadrado is a minister's wife and mother of two children. She taught in two high schools for 23 years. Currently she's women's ministries and Shepherdess director in Brazil and has a program on the local radio station. She lives in Maringá, Paraná, Brazil, where she enjoys preaching, working with women, and traveling with her family. **June 28.**

Kimberly Baldwin Radford moved to Madagascar in 1999 and has fallen in love with the land of lemurs and lizards. Kim and three Malagasy women organized sewing, embroidery, and health classes for the poor in her neighborhood. The Radfords have recently started a sponsorship program, funded by a United States church, and plan to begin literacy classes for the students' parents. **May 1, Nov. 9.**

Balkis Rajan is director of women's, family, and children's ministries of the Upper Ganges Section in Hapur, Uttar Pradesh, India. She has worked for 22 years as a teacher. Balkis is the mother of two children. **Nov. 10.**

Vicki Macomber Redden is a secretary in the book division at the Review and Herald Publishing Association in Hagerstown, Maryland. She enjoys traveling, photography, scrapbooking, and spending time with those she loves, especially her new husband, Ron. **Aug. 30.**

Barbara J. Reinholtz is semiretired but works as registrar for the North American Division Evangelism Institute extension school. The mother of three married children and grandmother of two, she has held several church offices. A published author of short stories and children's poetry, she enjoys people, music, and crocheting. Best of all, she enjoys being wife and best friend to her husband, Laun. **Aug. 8.**

Darlenejoan McKibbin Rhine was born in Omaha, Nebraska, raised in California, and schooled in Madison, Tennessee. A surviving spouse with one adult son, she holds a Bachelor of Arts in journalism and was public relations secretary at her church in Los Angeles, California. Now retired, she writes books, poetry, and magazine articles. **May 22.**

Avis Mae Rodney, a justice of the peace for the province of Ontario, is possibly the first and only Black female justice of the peace in Canada, and also the first ombudsperson appointed by the Seventh-day Adventist Church in Canada. A wife and the mother of two adult children, Avis enjoys long walks, gardening, reading, crocheting, and spending time with her five beautiful grandchildren. **Jan. 13, Mar. 20, May 10, Sept. 22, Dec. 28.**

Deborah Sanders shares from her personal journal, *Dimensions of Love,* which has become a writing-prayer ministry. She lives in Canada with Ron, her husband of 36 years. They've been blessed with two children, Andrea and Sonny. Sonny is mentally challenged with psychomotor retardation and autism. Deborah thanks those who care about caregivers. **Feb. 11, Apr. 6, May 11, Aug. 15, Dec. 27.**

Sônia Rigoli Santos has a degree in theology and was the first Brazilian woman to obtain a master's degree in this area. A minister's wife and mother, she worked for nearly 20 years as a teacher. Currently she is a leader of women's ministries in Ijuí, Rio Grande do Sul, Brazil. She likes to produce and present radio programs, and she enjoys writing. **Jan. 10, June 26.**

Marie H. Seard assists in the Ministerial Association of the world headquarters of the Seventh-day Adventist Church. She was reelected chaplain in the Washington Inter-Alumni chapter of UNCF and continues her service in the Oakwood College Alumni Association. She enjoys her ladies club, Les Charmes, and the Say It Now With Flowers committee. **Mar. 7.**

Donna Lee Sharp is pianist, organist, parish ministry director, and Sabbath school teacher for her church. She uses her musical skills on the keyboard in both her church and community. Gardening, bird-watching, reading, traveling, and reaching out to her far-flung family make her life fulfilled. **Mar. 27.**

Carrol Johnson Shewmake, a retired pastor's wife, is active in prayer ministry in her local church and conference. She has written five books on prayer and coauthored a book on witnessing. She often speaks at retreats, camp meetings, prayer breakfasts, and church prayer weekends. She has four adult children and eight grandchildren. **Jan. 24, June 3.**

Judy Musgrave Shewmake and her husband, Tom, live in northern California. They have a married daughter, a son studying for the ministry, and a son and daughter whom she teaches at home. Judy is editor of *The Adventist Home Educator,* a newsletter for homeschoolers. Her favorite hobby is writing, and she also enjoys reading and making memory scrapbooks. **Dec. 1.**

Rose Neff Sikora and her husband, Norman, live in the beautiful mountains of western North Carolina. A retired registered nurse, Rose enjoys camping in the travel trailer, writing, spending time with her three grandchildren, and helping others. She has had articles and stories published in several magazines and in this devotional book series. **Jan. 30.**

Sandra Simanton is a family therapist in Grand Forks, North Dakota. She lives in nearby Buxton with her husband and two children. She enjoys sewing and rubber stamping. **June 4, Aug. 27.**

Darleen E. Simmonds writes from Hempstead, New York. She is the Sabbath school superintendent for her church, as well as the Bronx-Manhattan district leader for women's ministries. For relaxation Darleen enjoys singing and playing the piano. In her spare time she ministers to senior citizens. **Mar. 5, July 13.**

Darlene D. Simyunn is a student at Mountain View College in the Philippines. She enjoys playing the piano and guitar and singing. **Aug. 29.**

Taramani Noreen Singh serves as an office secretary in the Adventist church administrative offices in Vārānasi, Uttar Pradesh, India, where her husband is the regional director. They have two college-age sons, who are studying and preparing to serve the Master in the future. **Jan. 2, Oct. 7.**

Heather-Dawn Small is the associate director for women's ministries at her church's world headquarters in Silver Spring, Maryland. A native of Trinidad and Tobago, she is the mother of a college-age daughter and an elementary school son. She says she loves travel, reading, embroidery, and stamp collecting. And "joy" is her favorite word. **Feb. 7, Nov. 23.**

Dolores Smith is a retired registered nurse and a certified midwife. She worked as a nurse practitioner for many years in a large metropolitan hospital, and she holds a master's degree in education. For outstanding and dedicated service, she received the Woman of the Year Award in 1996 from women's ministries. She enjoys traveling. **July 31, Dec. 4.**

Tamara Marquez de Smith writes from Bay Shore, New York, where she lives with her husband, Steven, and their two daughters, Lillian and Cassandra. Tamara is currently the youth leader, a deaconess, and the music coordinator at her church. **Oct. 25.**

Ardis Dick Stenbakken edits the submissions to this book as she travels the world leading out in women's ministries for her church. She and her husband, Dick, a retired Army chaplain, have two married adult children and one granddaughter. Ardis especially enjoys helping women discover their full potential in the Lord. **Jan. 4, Apr. 29, July 3, Sept. 1, Nov. 6, Dec. 22.**

Iris L. Stovall, a certified CLASS (Christian Leaders Authors and Speakers Services) communicator, praises God for opportunities to share her life's experiences with other women. Her children and grandchildren bring sunshine to her life. **Aug. 5, Oct. 26, Dec. 16.**

Rubye Sue is a retired secretary who works at a self-supporting school, where she enjoys interaction with the students. Rubye, 80, and her husband, 87, still travel and look forward to visits with their children, grandchildren, and great-grandchildren. **Jan. 16, Jan. 29.**

Carolyn Sutton, a freelance writer and speaker, lives in Grants Pass, Oregon, with her husband, Jim. They enjoy camping, gardening, and sharing Jesus in practical ways. **May 7, Sept. 11.**

Karen Barnes Swan now lives in Hagerstown, Maryland, with her husband, David, and son, Josh. At the time she wrote this devotional she was stationed with the Army at Camp H. M. Smith in Hawaii. Her e-mail address is kswan831@yahoo.com. This is her first contribution to the devotional books. **Dec. 14.**

Loraine F. Sweetland is retired in Tennessee with her husband, three dogs, and 98-year-old mother-in-law. She chairs the church school board and the Family Life Center building committee, as well as volunteering as treasurer for her local food co-op. In her spare time she works on genealogy. **Jan. 5, Apr. 3, Aug. 7, Oct. 18.**

Frieda Tanner, a retired registered nurse, keeps busy by sending Bible school materials all over the world. She now lives in Eugene, Oregon, to be near her two grandchildren. **June 2.**

Arlene Taylor is director of infection control and risk manager at St. Helena Hospital in California. As founder-president of her own corporation, she promotes brain-function research. She is a professional member of the National Speaker's Association and received American Biographical Institute's American Medal of Honor for Brain-Function Education in 2002. **Feb. 22, May 23, July 17, Oct. 10.**

Tammy Barnes Taylor runs her own day-care. Married 17 years, she has three boys and one girl. She enjoys Creative Memories scrapbooking and loves to read and write stories. **Feb. 3.**

Sharon M. Thomas is an elementary school teacher. She and her husband, Don, a social worker, have two sons who are graduates of Oakwood College. She enjoys reading, walking, biking, and shopping. Feb. 17.

Stella Thomas works as a secretary in her church's Global Mission office. She is grateful to God for giving her the opportunity to work for Him in spreading the gospel to many unentered areas of the world. **Feb. 28.**

Bula Rose Haughton Thompson is a dental assistant who works at the Cross Keys and Pratville health centers in South Manchester, Jamaica. She is a couturier par excellence whose other hobbies are singing, reading, and meeting people. **May 30, Oct. 13.**

Nancy Ann (Neuharth) Troyer and her husband, Don, pastor two churches in Georgia. They have one daughter, Stephanie. Nancy spent 24 years traveling around the world with her husband, a United States Army chaplain. To keep awake in church, "Nancy, the Notetaker" takes sermon notes in calligraphy with line drawing illustrations. **July 4.**

Nancy L. Van Pelt is a certified family life educator, best-selling author of more than 20 books, and internationally known speaker. For the past 20 years Nancy has taught families how to really love each other. Her hobbies are getting organized, entertaining, having fun, and quilting. Nancy and her husband live in California and are the parents of three adult children. **Feb. 1.**

Nancy Cachero Vasquez is coauthor with her husband of *God's 800-Number: P-R-A-Y-E-R,* and she is editor of *Paginas del Alma,* the 2003 Spanish women's devotional book. She loves to travel, read, write, and try out new recipes. She and her husband, who were missionaries in Ecuador, have three adult children and two grandsons. **Nov. 30.**

Tammy Vice is a wife and the mother of two beautiful girls. She is currently serving on the board of the Autism Society of Middle Tennessee. Her ministry, Know the Hope, focuses on strengthening families with special needs by building support and understanding in churches and communities through awareness and education. **Apr. 18.**

Donna Meyer Voth is a substitute teacher and volunteer for the American Cancer Society. She enjoys giving Bible studies, watercolor painting, traveling, and camping. She and her husband live in Vicksburg, Michigan, and have a daughter in college. **June 29, Nov. 4, Dec. 9.**

Cindy Walikonis is a mother, pastor's wife, and registered dietitian residing in Walla Walla, Washington. Her hobbies include hiking, creative writing, creative vegetarian cooking, teaching health and nutrition classes in the community, and working with the women's ministries committee at her church. **Apr. 1.**

Cora A. Walker lives in Queens, New York. She is a retired nurse and an active member in her local church. She enjoys reading, writing, sewing, classical music, singing, and traveling. She has one son. **May 28, Nov. 16.**

Anna May Radke Waters is a retired administrative secretary. She is an ordained elder in her church and has served as a greeter. At the top of her hobby list are her seven grandchildren and her husband, with whom she likes to travel and make memories. She enjoys doing Bible studies on the Internet and answering prayer requests for Bibleinfo.com. **Feb. 12, Mar. 3, June 17.**

Ruth Watson served in Thailand with her physician-husband for 13 years. Though now retired, she has served briefly in the Dominican Republic, Fiji, Thailand, Laos, and Cambodia. She loves helping her grandchildren and her primary class in Bible school and is also a deaconess at her church. **Jan. 8, Nov. 21, Dec. 21.**

Dorothy Eaton Watts is an administrator for her church headquarters in India. Dorothy is also a freelance writer, editor, and speaker. She has served in India for 24 years, founded an orphanage, taught elementary school, and written more than 20 books. Her hobbies include gardening, hiking, and birding (with more than 1,400 in her world total). **Feb. 19, Apr. 27, Aug. 2, Oct. 1.**

Lyn Welk works as a bereavement counselor at a hospital in South Australia. She also aids children from disadvantaged families in family and youth services. She has a full-time position as pipe organist at a church in Adelaide and enjoys choir work and Christian fellowship. She loves caravanning, outdoor photography, and spending time with the family. **Aug. 23.**

Penny Estes Wheeler, a wife, mother, and grandmother, cherishes her Texas childhood and still feels at home in wide-open, barren places. She enjoys reading and rubber stamping, and recently established a book reading club in her community. The founding editor of *Women of Spirit,* Penny is a freelance author and speaker at retreats and other events. **Nov. 3.**

Vera Wiebe has been in team ministry with her husband for 30 years. She's been involved with women's ministries in three conferences and is presently the leader. She enjoys music, especially playing the piano. Her hobbies include sewing, knitting, reading, and classical music. Becoming a grandmother has brought her a lot of joy. **Apr. 25, June 12, Dec. 5.**

Mildred C. Williams lives in southern California and works 13 hours a week as an almost-retired physical therapist. The rest of the time she enjoys studying and teaching the Bible, writing, gardening, public speaking, sewing, and babysitting her granddaughter. **Jan. 11, May 2, July 15, Aug. 19.**

Patrice E. Williams-Gordon lectures in the College of Natural and Applied Science at Northern Caribbean University in Mandeville, Jamaica. An active minister's wife, she enjoys team ministry with her husband, Danhugh. She delights in her two daughters, Ashli and Rhoni, while trying to keep up her hobbies of reading, speaking engagements, and planning special events. **Oct. 16.**

Ingrid Ribeiro Wolff is married and is the daughter of missionaries, having spent three years of her childhood in Angola. She is an educator and an elementary school teacher who loves children. She also makes handicrafts and likes to write children's poetry and programs. She dreams of the opportunity of one day writing a children's book. **Aug. 31.**

Wendy Wongk is a registered nurse who homeschools her two sons, Colin, 12, and David, 14. She loves talking to people and loves her husband and her God (not necessarily in that order). Currently she and her husband are volunteering in south Georgia, working to make a difference in the lives of the poor. **Dec. 10.**

Susan Wooley works as a home health nurse and lives with her husband, Steve, in Florida. They enjoy the beach, their boys, and each other. **Feb. 6, Oct. 31, Dec. 24.**

Aileen L. Young, a resident of Honolulu, Hawaii, is married to Thomas. She is a retired elementary and secondary educator and a published author. Her interests include the Bible, writing, reading, watercolors, walking, tennis, swimming, music, traveling, and working in her church, including women's ministries. She is the mother of two sons and has two grandchildren. **July 2.**

Prayer Requests

While I live will I praise the Lord:
I will sing praises . . . while I have any being.
—Psalm 146:2

Prayer Requests

Thou hast said it. I take Thee at Thy word.
—Ellen G. White, in Signs of the Times, *Dec. 25, 1893*

Prayer Requests

The Lord is nigh unto all them that call upon him.
—Psalm 145:18

Prayer Requests

Let the words and example of my Redeemer
be the light and strength of my heart.
—Ellen G. White, in Review and Herald, *Aug. 10, 1886*

Prayer Requests

He shall give thee the desires of thine heart.
—Psalm 37:4

Prayer Requests

Here am I, Lord, and all that I am is Thine.
—Ellen G. White, in Review and Herald, *Jan. 4, 1887*

Prayer Requests

Evening, and morning, and at noon, will I pray.
—Psalm 55:17

Prayer Requests

Take me, O Lord, as wholly Thine. . . .
Use me today in Thy service.
—Ellen G. White, Steps to Christ, *p. 70*

Prayer Requests

Trust in him at all times; . . .
pour out your heart before him.
—Psalm 62:8